THE NEW Europe

into the 21st century

W

G N Minshull

Revised and updated by M J Dawson

Hodder & Stoughton

A MEMBER OF THE HODDER HEADLINE GROUP

ACKNOWLEDGEMENTS

The author and publishers thank the following for permission to reproduce copyright material in this book:

Allen and Unwin, *Regional Problems and Policies in Italy and France*, Allen and McLennan Fig 17.4; ADP Association of Airports, Fig 5.7; The European Commission, Fig 1.7; Eurostat, various publications, Figs 1.4, 1.5, 1.6, 3.10, 8.8, 8.9a, 8.10, 9.3, 9.4, 10.3, 17.2, 18.2, 20.4, 20.6, 21.1; The Times, Fig 10.5a; Wiley, *The City in Western Europe*, D Burtenshaw Fig 19.8.

The author and publishers thank the following for permission to reproduce copyright photographs in this book:

Adam Opel A G, p. 70; Aerofilms, pp. 69, 118; J Allan Cash, pp. 34, 56, 69, 109, 192, 205; Articapress, p. 180; Belgian Institute of Information and Documentation, pp. 12, 71, 142, 231, 280; Belgian National Tourist Office, p. 63; British Steel Corporation, p. 137; The Danish Tourist Board, pp. 305, 309; The Embassy of the Federal Government of West Germany, p. 40; The French Government Tourist Office, pp. 95, 366; The German National Tourist Office, pp. 157, 267; Robert Harding, pp. 93, 98, 109, 116, 152, 260, 359, 368, 381; Bart Hofmeester, pp. 44, 125; Horizono Holidays Ltd, p. 378; The Italian Institute, pp. 145, 322, 327, 328; The Italian State Tourist Office, p. 321; The National Tourist Organisation of Greece, pp. 350, 352, 355; Portuguese National Tourist Office, pp. 377, 389; The Royal Netherlands Embassy, pp. 123, 289; Schiphol Airport Authority, p. 283; The Shannon Free Airport Development Authority, p. 348; ZEFA, pp. 53, 225, 247, 256, 285, 288.

Every effort has been made to contact the holders of copyright material but if any have been inadvertently overlooked, the publisher will be pleased to make the necessary alterations at the first opportunity.

Cataloguing in Publication Data is available from the British Library

ISBN 0 340 64318 8

First published 1978
Second edition 1980
Third edition 1985
Fourth edition 1990
Fifth edition 1996

Impression number	10	9	8	7	6	5	4	3	2	1
Year				1999	1998	1997	1996			

Copyright © 1996 G. N. Minshull and M. J. Dawson

Typeset by Wearset, Boldon, Tyne and Wear.
Printed in Great Britain for Hodder & Stoughton Educational, a division of Hodder Headline Plc, 338 Euston Road, London NW1 3BH by Redwood Books, Trowbridge, Wiltshire.

CONTENTS

PREFACE TO THE FIFTH EDITION

One of the most significant developments in Western Europe since 1945 has been the growth of integration. This book deals with the emergence of the European Union (EU), incorporating the EEC or Common Market, as a geographically significant, economically powerful and politically durable unit. The book gives an overview of the origins and evolution of the EU since 1951, integration policies, the dramatic growth in material wealth during the 1960s, the resource base and patterns of economic and regional geography. Since the first oil price shock of 1973, the industrialised world has experienced major changes in its terms of trade. Conditions of rapid inflation have been followed by the recessions of 1979–82 and the early 1990s, industrial decline, unemployment, and severe regional problems. Nevertheless, the EU is a very important economic unit and a major trading bloc. Its institutions have become more democratic, and its external relationships, particularly with the developing world, have become much more significant.

The difficult economic period of the late 1970s and early 1980s was accompanied by a slowing down of the pace of integration. This has been referred to as 'Eurosclerosis'. However, the accession to the EU of Greece, Spain and Portugal and the unification of Germany, added a new geographical dimension and assisted in a 'great leap forward in integration. The Single European Act of 1987 was accompanied by the removal of all remaining barriers to trade and economic harmonisation culminated in the Single European Market in January 1993. Moves towards economic and monetary union (EMU) were initiated at the Madrid summit in 1989. In 1992 the Treaty on European Union (the Maastricht Treaty) was signed and came into force in November 1993 setting the timetable for a three-stage transition to full EMU and a single currency by 1999. In a global context, as the relative decline of the superpowers takes place with the break-up of the former Soviet Union and the creation of new states in Eastern Europe, the EU is experiencing a major enhancement of its economic strength and political status despite the recession of the early 1990s. The accession of Austria, Finland and Sweden to the EU in 1995 is part of this strengthening process.

The fifth edition of this book deals with all 15 Members of the EU. The economic geography of the book stresses the key concept of core and periphery and is organised around a balance between systematic and regional geography. Major revisions to all chapters have been made, with statistics updated to the early 1990s.

This experiment in European integration is of interest to geographers in demonstrating the indivisibility of knowledge. It is a case study of the developed world which illustrates the physical character and resource-base of Western Europe, the historical and cultural diversity of nation states, regional contrasts between core and periphery, the shrinkage of distance, and the restructuring of economic and social space by political cooperation.

G N Minshull & M J Dawson

1

THE DEVELOPMENT OF WESTERN EUROPE: THE EUROPEAN UNION

INTRODUCTION

The theme of this book is the economic geography of Western Europe and the internal and external pressures which are altering its whole economic and political structure. Essentially it relates to the growth and enlargement of the European Union (fig. 1.1).

The principal characteristics of Western Europe may be summarised thus: countries with a relatively small land area and great physical diversity; many nation states separated by historical precedent and language barriers; wealthy countries with relatively dense populations; an industrialised and urbanised way of life; a well-watered environment with adequate fertile land and a temperate climate which supports a commercial system of agriculture.

PHYSICAL CONFIGURATION

Western Europe is a triangular-shaped sub-continent with its base to the east merging into the Eurasian land-mass. It is a rim land tapering towards the west and having the Atlantic Ocean on its north-western side and the Mediterranean Basin on the south. The overriding characteristics are a relatively small land-area and an irregular configuration consisting of diverse peninsulas, islands and shallow continental seas.

There are four broad physiographic regions (fig. 1.2) and these underline the diversity and emphasise an east–west alignment. On the north-western rim lie the Atlantic uplands and Scandinavian mountains. The single most significant physical region is the north-west European Plain, an extensive

ALB.	ALBANIA
BEL.	BELGIUM
LUX.	LUXEMBOURG
MAC.	MACEDONIA
NETH.	NETHERLANDS
RU.	RUSSIA, Part of
SWITZ.	SWITZERLAND
Gib.	Gibraltar
Li.	Liechtenstein
Mo.	Monaco
S.M.	San Marino
V.C.	Vatican City

FIGURE 1.1   *The European Union (source – Drake)*

lowland stretching from the Bay of Biscay across France into the Rhinelands. A complex central region of mountains, valleys and plateaux (Hercynian) lies from the Massif Central across into the Rhine Uplands. This is succeeded to the south by the Alpine system, the highest in Western Europe with peaks exceeding 4000 m, which stretches across the Mediterranean coastlands from Spain to Italy and Greece. Contained within

FIGURE 1.2   *Physical regions of the EU*

the Alpine system are further examples of Hercynian plateaux such as the Spanish Meseta, basins of tertiary deposits such as the Ebro valley in Spain and the Plain of Lombardy in Northern Italy, and the fringing lowlands and islands of the Mediterranean Basin.

There are *three* significant implications for the human and economic geography of Western Europe:

(a) The most extensive areas of fertile productive lowlands lie in the north and west, whilst the Mediterranean regions are mountainous, with small, discontinuous lowlands, and generally adverse for development. The agricultural productivity, mineral resources and population density of north-west Europe have enabled it to become the 'core' region, whilst the Mediterranean regions have in many ways become the 'peripheral' zones.

(b) There is a contrast to be found between largely continental states like France and Germany, and traditionally maritime states such as the United Kingdom and the Netherlands. The configuration of the coastline has helped to create a basic diversity of interests.

(c) The east–west trend of the major physical features is pierced by several very important north–south routeways based on river valleys. The two most important of these are the rivers Rhine and Rhône and their tributaries, and their economic effect has been immense. They form major core areas, particularly in the case of the Rhine valley, and they have been instrumental since ancient times in creating routeways and links between the Mediterranean and the North Sea. With the additional element of Alpine passes such as the St. Gotthard and Mt. Cenis, the mountain systems have never been the barrier they might have been. Trading links and interdependence between north and south have been considerable since Roman times.

POLITICAL FRAGMENTATION

Western Europe is politically most diverse with many different groups of race, culture, language and religion. It was here that the nation state originated. During the Roman Empire, and later under Charlemagne, considerable parts of the sub-continent lay under one rule, but this has never been the normal pattern. It has only occurred for short periods since then, during war, and imposed by force, as in 1939–45.

The earliest nation states included France and England. France is a relatively compact nation state based around its core area, the Paris Basin. It is a key country forming a 'bridgeland' and having a nodal position between the Atlantic Ocean, Mediterranean Sea, English Channel and Rhinelands. In England's case, the expansion to become the United Kingdom was assisted by the unifying and protective effects of the sea. The sea has also had a stimulating effect upon England's outward-looking maritime character and was a major factor in the establishment of the empire.

Other nation states illustrate the changing patterns of territory and the strains of nationalism. The Netherlands originated in the sixteenth century after a war of independence from Spain, and Belgium. Created as a buffer state in 1830 it is an uneasy coalition of Flemings and Walloons. Small territories such as Luxembourg are a reminder of the medieval importance of the Grand Duchy as a fortified city-state. Italy and Germany were both merely 'geographical expressions' until 1866 and 1871 respectively. Since then, particularly in Germany's case, the impact of nationalism and militarism has been responsible for many territorial upheavals. The Rhineland economic centre of Western Europe was an area of political instability and divided between five countries. Alsace, Lorraine and the Saarland have changed hands between France and Germany on several occasions.

Wealth from trade

Western Europe produced great trading nations from very early times. Rome was a great trading empire as well as a military one, and the city states of Venice and Genoa were founded upon trade with the Mediterranean and the East. As early as the eleventh and twelfth centuries the Netherlands and Belgium were the centres for the trading activities of the Hanseatic League, and Bruges, Ghent and Amsterdam were famous trading ports. From 1492 Spain and Portugal led the European thrust into the 'New World' and built up great empires in South and Central America, Africa and the Indies. They were followed by France, the Netherlands and in particular by Great Britain whose overseas trade and empire was based upon sea power. The accrued wealth from commerce helped build up capital and laid the foundations for the Industrial Revolution. The supply of raw materials from overseas has thus become an essential part of life in Western Europe, and the area's dependence upon world trade has become a dominant characteristic.

Western Europe: the site of the 'Industrial Revolution'

Industrial growth began in Western Europe from the late eighteenth century onwards. The use of coal and steam power together with iron and steel products forged the basic industrial sinews which enabled these countries to act as world powers. In the UK the canals and railways enhanced the movement of raw materials and industrial products. A powerful navy provided maritime supremacy and the consolidation of imperial possessions over a quarter of the world's surface. Raw materials from the colonies and the demands of their market served industries and increased the export trade. The UK in particular, but also France, the Netherlands and eventually Germany, became world powers, with large colonial empires. The phrase 'workshop of the world' was used to describe the UK in the mid-nineteenth century. This was no myth: the UK was the first in the field and had little or no competition. In 1870 the country produced 70 per cent of the world's ships and exported coal, steel and textiles to all parts of the world. Many of the world's railway systems such as those of Argentina and India were built with British capital, skill and manufactured products. At the end of the nineteenth century Western Europe as a whole accounted for approximately 90 per cent of world industrial production.

The diversity was now compounded. Industrial growth was centred on the UK, Belgium and Germany, those countries which had major resources of coal and iron ore. Industry and dense populations developed in the heavy industrial triangle and along the Rhinelands. The UK at this time was more concerned with imperial possessions than with Europe. This was Britain's period of 'splendid isolation'. Germany from 1871 onwards was powerful, nationalistic, industrial and urbanised. By contrast, France, once the most powerful nation in Western Europe, had few coal resources, remained under-industrialised, and went into a long period of decline. Italy and the Mediterranean states remained largely backward with peasant-based economies. Spain and Portugal, losing most of their colonial empires during the nineteenth century, and lacking in mineral resources, failed to industrialise and became economically peripheral to Western Europe. They entered a period of political instability and eventually dictatorship. The diversity of interests and the different stages of development were the basis of

	USA	UK	Japan	EU (12)
Area (1000 km^2)	9373	244	378	2363
Population (millions)	255	58	124	347
Persons per car	1.8	3.0	3.4	2.8
Steel production (million tonnes)	93	16	110	132
Energy consumption (kg per head)	7850	3680	3530	3450
Grain production (million tonnes)	316	22	14	169
Meat production (million tonnes)	30	4	4	34
Motor-vehicle production (millions)	5.7	1.3	9.4	13
Exports (ECU million)	344 716	144 522	261 755	1 136 487
Crude-oil refining capacity (million tonnes)	761	92	237	621
Coal production (million tonnes)	801	84	8	185
GDP (ECU 1000 million)	4586	806	2834	5421

ECU = European Currency Unit

FIGURE 1.3 *Comparative economic resources, 1992*

the growing French fear of German domination. This developed into war on three occasions, 1870, 1914 and 1939, and the major scene of contention was the Rhineland, now a key economic area in Western Europe.

The loss of world-power status: elements of weakness

By the mid-twentieth century, however, it was apparent that the economic supremacy of Western Europe could not last. The small nation states of Europe were caught up in the exhaustive process of fighting two world wars, as a result of which their infrastructure of housing, railways, port facilities and industries was badly damaged. The cost of fighting the Second World War left the UK in debt to the USA, and Western Europe had to accept Marshall Aid from the USA. The French railway system had to be completely rebuilt. The German Ruhr was devastated. Production of basic industries throughout Europe was dislocated until 1948, after which the flow of economic aid through the Organisation for European Economic Co-operation (OEEC) began a slow recovery. The wartime disruption of trade had forced the primary producing countries to look elsewhere for their imports of manufactured goods, and after the war these markets were no longer assured to the Western European nations. The change in attitudes and political awareness throughout the world forced the rapid dissolution of the colonial empires so that from 1945 to the mid-1960s practically all the former European colonies became independent. This meant that the sources of raw materials and the colonial markets were no longer under the political control of Europe. The UK and France were reduced effectively to nations of approximately 50 million people. Germany was reduced in size and partitioned. The new state of West Germany, though larger and more powerful than East Germany, was in no position to exert control over central Europe (Mitteleuropa) as it had done previously. The UK and West Germany were industrial and urbanised, and depended heavily upon imports of food and raw materials. Many raw materials were exhausted. Coal was now more expensive to mine in Western Europe than in other parts of the world. This reduction of economic, imperial and political influence in the world after 1945 has been called 'the dwarfing of Europe'. It marked a geographical, economic and political watershed.

The emergence of the 'super powers'

The declining advantage of Western Europe contrasted strongly with the growth of the 'super powers', the USA and USSR. By the twentieth century the land powers based upon huge continental interiors had overtaken the smaller Western European nation states. These continental powers had certain basic advantages. Their huge size was once a disadvantage, but then they developed efficient internal lines of communication, brought by the transcontinental railway and airlines. They gained from their large land space, huge populations and vast reserves of mineral wealth, which made them less dependent on world trade. In the USA, San Francisco and New York, over 4830 km apart, are in fact only hours distant from each other. The USSR was 90 times as large as the UK and nine times larger than Western Europe. Its vast land extent was referred to by Sir Halford Mackinder in his 'heartland' theory. Apart from their great size and resources the two super powers also dwarfed the individual Western European countries in terms of their industrial production. Reference to the steel industry shows the weakness in size of the individual European countries. In 1992 even Germany's steel output of 40 million tonnes does not bear comparison with that of Japan (110 million tonnes) or the USA (93 million tonnes). Fig. 1.3 (page 6) shows that the contrast is particularly dramatic in the case of the UK which was certainly a world power politically, economically and militarily during the nineteenth and early twentieth centuries. The continental powers of the USA and USSR were practically self-sufficient. Their latitudinal extent and extensive agricultural interiors meant that many of their food supplies could be produced within their own frontiers. The comparisons of food production in fig. 1.3 show why the USA, although the richest country in the world, is not, pro rata, the greatest trading nation. The country does not need to trade as do the Western European nations.

New elements: economies of scale and global competition

By the 1950s, Western Europe was a rapidly shrinking sub-continent in distance terms. Modern communications, including air transport, motorways, the telephone and television, created speed and flexibility and opened up new contacts. Tourism was becoming a major Europeanising force. A rapid increase in intra-European trade took place in the immediate post-war years, by contrast with the tariff barriers which had severely curtailed trade in the 1930s. By 1953 trade was over three times the value of 20 years previously. Food production rose rapidly as recovery got under way, with the large population stimulating demand, so that it was possible to see a potential self-sufficiency level for most foodstuffs.

There is also a very important economic factor. In modern technological civilisation the product of a large economic unit is more efficient than the sum of its parts. In a continental unit such as the USA there is unhindered movement of raw materials, labour, capital and the finished product to all parts of the country, allowing high productivity and specialisation in favourable localities. By contrast the national frontiers of Europe have hitherto hindered the most economical use of resources. A large population provides a basic and substantial home market. Without this assured home market it is very difficult for industry to sustain large-scale production. It is not worth investing huge amounts of money in plant and equipment unless a profit is guaranteed, and this profit comes primarily from the home market. Mass production and assembly line methods work most efficiently under economies of scale, and when they serve a large market. The American car industry is so large that one single company, General Motors, produces more than the entire British car industry. The more that is produced, the less, proportionately, each unit costs. Thus the Americans can sustain superior technology, large-scale production, efficiency and relatively low costs. Also the cost of industrial technology, research and specialised equipment is now so great that smaller countries have difficulty in finding the money needed for research and development. An example here is the space programme and aero-engine production. Rolls Royce in 1971 had developed the RB211 engine. So much research and development money was required before any payment was forthcoming from US aircraft companies. Costs escalated far beyond the estimates, the company could not find the money and went bankrupt. On the other hand, British and French firms combined to make Concorde, one of the most advanced civil aircraft in the world.

A study of the UK during the mid-twentieth century reveals a prolonged fight for export markets against increasing, efficient, and often superior competition. There has been such a low growth rate because of the near static home market, a steady invasion of American industry, and lack of investment in new equipment and industrial technology. Japan, which began to industrialise in the 1930s, and which rapidly recovered after the Second World War, began a sustained, efficient onslaught on European and American markets and by the 1960s had become a world economic power, second only in wealth to the USA. First in heavy industry such as shipbuilding, then in the car industry and electronics, Japan has successfully secured a large segment of world markets and is an economic power of world dimensions. In Western Europe only Germany has successfully competed on a broad front.

The threshold for economies of scale has been raised by new technology and changing raw-material sources. The steel and petroleum industries are now sited at waterside locations dependent upon imports of raw materials in large bulk carriers. Steel works are usually now vertically integrated with all processes carried out in the same plant. The vehicle industry is dominated by a few large companies and is horizontally integrated. High-technology industry requires large-scale financial backing and research capability. The establishment of branch plants outside the national territory for marketing purposes has led to the development of the multinational company.

Conclusions may be drawn from these facts that the consolidation of a single European market in this rapidly changing scene appeared logical and economically justifiable. In countries like France and the UK, 55 million people is not a sufficiently large economic base in the rigorous conditions of modern international competition. Reference to fig. 1.3 illustrates how, when Western Europe is taken as a whole, its productive capacity bears comparison with that of the super powers. The integration of production in a highly developed sub-continent such as Western Europe compares favourably with the American model. The replanning of economic operations from national scales to a European scale was the justifiable basis upon which the ideas of a Common Market in Western Europe germinated in the post-1945 period.

POST–WAR INTEGRATION IN EUROPE: THE INITIAL STAGES

A change of the greatest significance has been taking place in Western Europe since 1945. In its economic context it is a reflection of the relative decline in status of these nation states since the nineteenth century. The replacement of the nations of Western Europe by a unified state has never really been an accomplished fact since the days of the Roman Empire, or Charlemagne in the ninth century. All attempts since then by individual nations to impose unity upon Europe have resulted in wars. The revolution in political cooperation which has occurred stems from the desire for creating unity, maintaining peace and increasing security. The radical difference is that the movement towards unity is now accomplished by agreement between the nations concerned.

A large number of attempts at increased cooperation emerged out of the economic chaos of 1945. Recovery required a joint programme of economic aid and monetary cooperation which was given form and direction by OEEC, the Organisation for European Economic Co-operation. This involved very substantial American aid which was received by 18 nations in all. In the defence sphere, the Western European Union, comprising the United Kingdom, France and the Benelux countries, was supplanted in April 1949 by the North Atlantic Treaty Organisation (NATO). Aimed at the collective defence of North America, the North Atlantic and Western Europe, this has been one of the most significant and successful steps towards continental security. Political cooperation began in May 1949 with the Council of Europe. This is a consultative assembly in Strasbourg, now consisting of representatives of 34 European states, which deals with cultural, administrative, environmental and social matters of general interest. It has no executive powers, but is a useful sphere of cooperation.

Benelux

In 1947 the Benelux Union was formed by Belgium, the Netherlands and Luxembourg. Although these are three of the smaller nations in Western Europe, it was an initial move of the greatest significance. The Union allowed for the free movement of capital, persons, services and goods across frontiers, for the coordination of economic policy, and for a common trade policy towards countries external to the Union. These criteria of economic integration were a pointer to the future.

The European Free Trade Association

The European Free Trade Association (EFTA), formed in November 1959, was a loose association of seven nations with a limited object of 'the abolition of all tariffs on industrial goods between the seven member states'. The member states were the United Kingdom, Norway, Sweden, Denmark, Portugal, Switzerland and Austria. EFTA was not a customs union, but was a means of expanding trade and ensuring that a broad alignment in tariff reductions was kept in line with that of the EEC, which was already in existence. The UK certainly saw it as a 'bridge', or bargaining counter, for the time when it could negotiate full membership of the EEC. Although the free trade area still functions, it is at a reduced level since most of its members are now members of the EU.

THE EUROPEAN ECONOMIC COMMUNITY (THE COMMON MARKET)

The first community 1951–72: 'The Six'

The machinery of economic cooperation was established by six countries initially, all of whom were strongly motivated in different ways. France required a practical means of controlling the powerful German coal and steel industry in a supra-national way. France also saw the great advantages to be gained from expanding agriculture in a European market. West Germany was anxious to be rehabilitated into the European family of nations, and also needed markets for its rapidly expanding industries. The smaller Benelux countries were great trading nations and keen on European unity for both commercial and security reasons. Italy, not part of the trunk of Europe, had always felt isolated and needed the links which would help expand its economy. The Common Market, though primarily economic in its objectives, was also seen as a great reconciliation between France and West Germany in particular.

One market for coal and steel

The European Coal and Steel Community (ECSC) was set up on 18 April 1951 by France, West Germany, Italy and the three Benelux Union countries. A supra-national authority was formed to administer the coal and steel industries of the six countries, and to 'abolish import and export duties,

Brussels: the Berlaymont building, headquarters of the European Commission

subsidies and restrictive practices, and to establish free and unrestricted movement of coal, iron-ore, scrap, pig-iron and steel between the member countries'. As an experiment in cooperation this was a crucial pointer to the future. Six European countries had placed a basic sector of their economy into a common pool administered by a supra-national authority. This psychological success was matched by dramatic practical results. The production of crude steel and rolled products by 'The Six' rose dramatically from 1952 (42 million tonnes) to 1971 (103 million tonnes). The Heavy Industrial Triangle (Chapters 2 and 3) found a new impetus with the cross-frontier integration of its resources. The ECSC also found a successful social and regional role. From 1957 the run-down of the coal industry necessitated plans for the retraining of workers, industrial development loans to overcome unemployment, and the adaptation of the industrial structure of declining areas (Chapter 2).

The Common Market (EEC)

The Treaty of Rome was signed on 25 March 1957. This established the basic tenet of economic integration by means of four progressive harmonisation processes. These were:

---

1 **Internal tariffs:** Barriers to the free flow of trade between 'The Six' were to be dismantled and customs duties on goods bought from each other were to disappear in stages.
2 **Customs union:** All six Member States were to apply to external countries a common external tariff. This created a customs union with the six states progressively becoming one trading unit.
3 **Internal mobility:** There was to be free movement of labour, goods, services and capital between the six member countries.
4 **Economic integration:** Common policies throughout 'The Six' were to be applied to harmonise transport, industry, energy and agriculture.

Euratom

The European Atomic Energy Authority (Euratom) was set up for the coordination of nuclear research and to provide the conditions necessary for the ultimate production of nuclear energy on a large scale.

INTEGRATION POLICIES AND ECONOMIC GROWTH DURING THE 1960s

The customs union and abolition of internal tariffs was completed by 1968, ahead of schedule, and during 1965 the three executives, ECSC, EEC and Euratom, had been merged into a single executive, known as the EEC Commission. Meanwhile the essential policies of economic integration were being created. In 1961 anti-monopoly regulations and steps to create free movement of labour, capital and services were devised. Implementation of the Common Agricultural Policy (CAP) began on 14 January 1962. In 1963 the Yaoundé Convention was signed with 18 African states. This was essentially a preferential trading relationship for the supply of tropical food and raw materials to the EEC in return for aid and a guaranteed market. It marked the emergence of the EEC as a trading unit of world dimensions.

The most startling measure of success during the 1960s was the rate of economic growth of 'The Six'. Comparisons between 'The Six' and the UK (figs. 1.4, 1.5) reveal many disparities in terms of gross domestic product and exports. There are many and complex reasons for this pattern and the stimulus given by the Common Market may be only partially responsible for the rapid growth. West Germany in particular gained a great deal from Marshall Aid, and its industrial structure was completely rebuilt, gaining the benefits of new technology. Its defence costs were much lower and labour troubles much less of a problem than those in the UK. However, the greatest single stimulus on the continent was probably the change which was

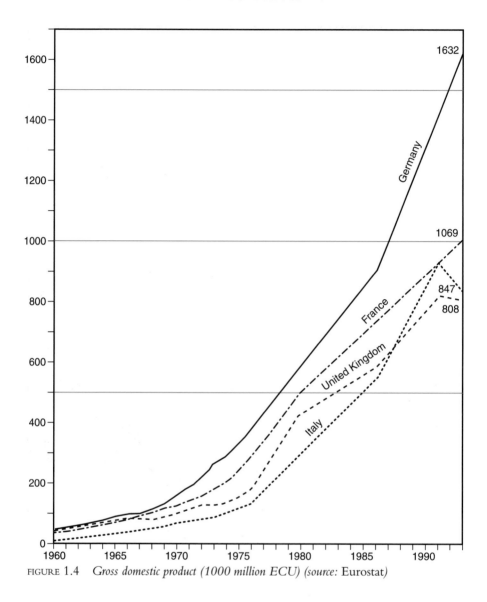

FIGURE 1.4   *Gross domestic product (1000 million ECU) (source:* Eurostat*)*

taking place in the composition of the workforce (fig. 8.10, page 191). The movement off the land caused by agricultural improvements created an enormous reservoir of labour for industry in Italy, West Germany and France. This allowed considerable industrialisation without labour shortages and consequent rises in labour costs, such as those which had occurred in the UK. West Germany had the benefit of large numbers of refugees from the east many of whom were skilled workers, and an influx of migrant workers from Southern European and Mediterranean countries such as Turkey and former Yugoslavia. West Germany rapidly became the largest single industrial power in the EEC.

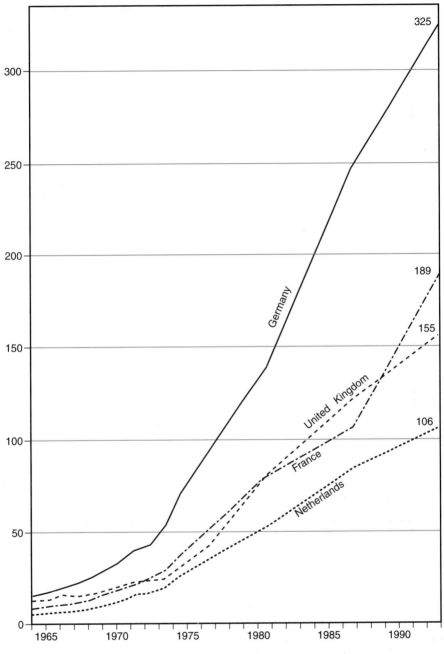

FIGURE 1.5 *Total export trade (1000 million ECU) (source: Eurostat)*

Other notable wealth expansion however was in France and Italy. France now gained the benefits of expanded markets for food production and became the 'granary of Europe'. French and Italian industry rapidly expanded on the basis of favourable terms of trade with the developing world's raw materials producers, new energy sources based on oil and the development of consumer industry based on an expanding industrial–urban labour force. The industrial revolution which had been only partial in France and even less in Italy now completed its development, and these two countries became major industrial powers in a short space of time.

The six Common Market countries as a whole enjoyed remarkable growth and prosperity during the period up to 1973. They developed into a large and powerful economic group, capable of comparison with the major world powers (fig. 1.3). Furthermore, the EU as a whole is potentially self-sufficient in food. Across Western Europe there are large stretches of agriculturally productive lowlands (fig. 1.2). There is a considerable latitudinal extent and a climatic range which gives a wide spectrum of agricultural types, and enables the EU to be a major food producer. The advantages of scale and latitudinal extent are perhaps the two most significant criteria upon which the success of the EU is based.

ENLARGEMENT FROM SIX TO NINE (1973)

During the 1960s there was a realisation in the UK that a significant and momentous change had occurred on the Continent. The UK was a small, highly developed and populated island with a static home market, an economy based upon trade and without the resource base of an empire, and was offshore to a developing continental unit of powerful proportions. The UK exports one-third of its car production, two-fifths of its engineering products and one-third of its chemical manufactures. During the 1960s, the 'Wind of change' speech by Prime Minister Harold Macmillan could be applied not only to the decolonisation process in Africa and elsewhere, but also to the closer real and perceived links (psychological, physical and economic) which the UK now had with its neighbours in Western Europe. On 8 November 1961 the UK, Ireland, Denmark and Norway began negotiations for membership of the EEC. These lasted for nearly a decade, largely because of the intransigence of the French President, Charles de Gaulle, who insisted that the UK was not ready for Community membership. Immediately after the resignation of de Gaulle in April 1969, negotiations were resumed and succeeded very quickly. By this stage the original Six had the will to enlarge and strengthen the Community, and on 1 January 1973 the UK, Ireland, and Denmark acceded to the EEC, now enlarged to nine member countries (fig. 1.6).

THE MEDITERRANEAN ENLARGEMENT, 1981–86

When Greece, Spain and Portugal emerged as democratic states in the 1970s after varying periods of dictatorship, they moved rapidly to seek admission to

		Area (1000 km²)	Population (millions)
SIX 1951	France	544	58.0
	Germany	357	81.6
	Italy	301	57.3
	Netherlands	41	15.4
	Belgium	31	10.1
	Luxembourg	3	0.4
NINE 1973	United Kingdom	244	58.3
	Ireland	70	3.6
	Denmark	43	5.2
TWELVE 1981–6	Greece	132	10.4
	Spain	505	39.2
	Portugal	92	9.9
FIFTEEN 1995	Austria	84	8.0
	Finland	337	5.1
	Sweden	450	8.8
Total		3234	371.3

FIGURE 1.6   *EU area and population figures, January 1995* (*source:* Eurostat)

the EEC. The accession of Greece in 1981 and Spain and Portugal in 1986 involved a whole range of strategic, economic and geographical implications for the EEC.

Greece had had an association agreement with the EEC since 1962. This was the first and most wide-ranging arrangement of this type ever undertaken by the EU. It addressed issues of harmonisation of agricultural policies, competition, free movement of persons and services and coordination of economic policies. Between 1967 and 1974 the monarchy was replaced by a military dictatorship. During this period relations with the EEC were suspended and not resumed until 1975 when Greece, having restored a democratic government, applied to join the EEC as a full member without waiting for the full implementation of the Association Agreement with its transitional provisions. The Commission was concerned over Greece's ability to adapt, and recommended a transitional period of some years. Greece did not accept the conclusions of the Commission and pressed ahead for a quick decision on full membership. In 1976 the foreign ministers of the EEC overruled the Commission and the Accession Treaty was signed in 1979 and entered into force in January 1981.

Having been one of the pillars of Western civilisation in classical times, with a great empire and the home of great philosophers and architects, Greece fell into a long decline, and for several centuries was mis-ruled as part of the Ottoman Empire in the Balkans. Greece emerged in the twentieth century as an under-industrialised, semi-developed country with the bulk of its population working on the land. Greece has a population of

10.4 million, and in area is almost the same size as England and Wales. The environment is extremely difficult, being mountainous and desiccated with a semi-arid Mediterranean climate. Mount Olympus, at 3200 m, is the highest mountain. There are three physical regions, the rugged Pindus mountain chain which covers 80 per cent of the country, and several small areas of lowland, principally around Athens, Thessaloniki and in Thessaly. Finally there are the Greek islands in the Aegean Sea, a complex group which includes Crete and Rhodes and the Cyclades archipelago.

Portugal was one of the first European colonial powers, but since the seventeenth century had suffered a long decline for several reasons. It is almost totally lacking in mineral resources, hydro-electric power had been retarded by irregular river regimes, and industrialisation was limited. The single most significant source of income was the revenue from the tourist industry in Lisbon and the Algarve. The African colonial empire proved a costly drain on scarce resources during the long guerrilla war in the 1960s and the 1970s, after which the last two major colonies, Angola and Mozambique, became independent. There was a long period of dictatorship under which economic development was neglected. During this period Portugal had little prospect of becoming a Member of the EU, but a Special Relations Agreement was reached in 1972. After the 'Red Carnation Revolution' of April 1974, which brought down Caetano's government, there was a turbulent period when little progress was made on Portugal's links with the EU, but after the election of a democratic government in 1976 significantly closer cooperation began with financial assistance for Portugal's economy. However, when Portugal first opted for EU membership in 1977 its economic policies were wholly inconsistent with those of the EU. The many years of prolonged economic difficulty in the late 1970s and early 1980s culminated in a severe economic recession in 1983–4, and when Portugal joined the EU in 1986 the country was Western Europe's poorest and most backward country. Nevertheless, the improvements in the Portuguese economy since accession have been very substantial. An average GDP growth rate of 4.5 per cent was achieved in the period 1986–90 compared to 3 per cent in the preceding decade, and the inflation rate has fallen from more than 22 per cent in 1985 to 5.3 per cent in 1994.

In 1970, after over two years of negotiations, a preferential agreement was reached between Spain and the EEC, but further negotiations were ended in 1975 in protest at the trial and execution in Spain of five men alleged to have killed police officers and civil guards. Later in the same year Franco died and in 1976 the EEC resumed trade negotiations in the light of the changed political situation in Spain. In 1977, after the first Spanish general elections since 1936, Spain formally applied to become a member of the EU, and the treaty of accession was signed in 1985.

Spain, with 39 million people, is by far the largest economy, next to Italy, in the Mediterranean region. It is a country of great potential and with significant resources, but one in which industrialisation started late. On the north coast are coal reserves. Bilbao extracts iron ore from open-cast mines and is the centre of a declining steel-producing area. The Sierra Morena is a substantial producer of copper, lead, silver, zinc, manganese and mercury. Major rivers such as the Guadalquivir, Tagus and Guadiana are being harnessed for hydro-electric power. As well as irrigation control, and increased agricultural productivity, this is significant for industrial development. Spain now closely follows Norway and Italy in total HEP production. Though semi-developed, it is thus experiencing transformation from an agricultural into an industrial country. The change has been relatively rapid during the last three decades, for several reasons. These include the opening up of the country to Western influence from American air bases; the enormous influx of capital from the tourist trade since the 1960s which has given Spain finance for development projects; the end of the dictatorship on General Franco's death and the subsequent change to a constitutional monarchy. The rapid transformation in the economy is reflected in vast differences between underdeveloped regions, and core regions in which development has been concentrated.

Problems stemming from the 1981–1986 enlargement

There were considerable differences in levels of development between the three new Mediterranean members and the rest of the EEC. The convergence of economies is basic to EU policy, but this was made more difficult by the economic recession, and the advent of the three countries added to the problems. Spain had a high growth potential, and in many ways was comparable to Italy. Greece had a per capita income rather lower than Ireland. Portugal had a lower per capita income than any other member of the EEC, and needed considerable aid and investment assistance. The proportion of peripheral regions and problem economic sectors in the EEC increased substantially.

There was a further tilt towards agricultural interests, with an increase of over 50 per cent in the number of people working in agriculture, and a 24 per cent increase in agricultural production. These Mediterranean products added to the imbalances of production already existing in the EEC. Wine, olive oil and certain types of fruit and vegetables were already close to a structural surplus, and this tendency was exacerbated. French wine producers were very concerned about Spanish competition in the area.

Greece, Spain and Portugal depended on imports for over 80 per cent of their energy, compared to 54 per cent for the other EEC countries. With development in prospect, energy consumption was expected to rise steeply, thus placing increased burdens on the energy-supply situtation. Thus a fresh impetus to reduce dependence upon imported energy was vital.

The budgetary cost to the Community was substantial, involving in particular the Regional Development Policy, Social Fund, agricultural support, and the EIB. The Mediterranean states faced severe adjustment problems. Spanish industry in particular had developed behind strong projective barriers, and the removal of these caused pressure, unemployment, and closure for vulnerable industries. As a result, a long transitional period proved necessary as the Spanish economy gradually reduced its tariffs and harmonised its competition rules, integrated its trading patterns, restructured industry and diversified agriculture to face competition in a common market.

Finally there were political and strategic considerations. It was feared that the accession of the three new members may eventually cause a geographical shift in emphasis southwards to the Mediterranean basin, that three new languages may cause a slowing-up of integration and there was always the danger that a community of 12 may have to be organised into a loose confederation of two tiers of developed and semi-developed economies; a core and a periphery. It was to combat that possibility that the European Commission in 1985 produced the Integrated Mediterranean Programmes (IMP) designed to raise income levels and improve employment possibilities in the Mediterranean regions of the EEC.

Geographical and strategic advantages

Geographically, Spain and Portugal have helped to create a coherent European framework. They are physically contiguous with Western Europe, whereas Greece lies in the eastern Mediterranean basin and is physically detached. All three Mediterranean states have helped to complete the natural southern limits of Europe; the EU's role on both sides of the Mediterranean has been strengthened and its strategic links with north Africa extended. Economically, there are nearly 60 million people in the three Mediterranean countries, with Greece as a major force in world shipping, and Spain as a substantial industrial power with rich mineral resources. Already the world's largest trading unit, the EEC's weight in international trade increased still further.

GERMAN UNIFICATION (1990)

During the 1980s, reforms in the former USSR, democratic pressures in most of communist Eastern Europe and eventually reforms in Poland and Hungary led to rising expectations amongst all East Europeans and a tide of optimism. In September 1989 the Hungarian government dismantled the country's fortified border with Austria allowing an exit to the West for East Germans who had gone to Hungary 'on holiday'. The German Democratic Republic (GDR) then banned travel to Hungary but this created a crisis as several thousand East Germans sought refuge at West German embassies in Bucharest, Prague and Warsaw. Demonstrations led to the resignation of Erich Honecker, the Socialist Unity Party General Secretary, the East

German government's resignation and then the opening of the Berlin Wall on 9 November 1989.

Once the Berlin Wall was opened and more crossing points between the two Germanys were created, thousands of East Germans travelled West. Many returned to their homes in the East, but by January 1990 some 344 000 had decided to stay, placing intolerable strains on social services (particularly housing) and adding to the problems of the West German labour market. In February 1990 it was agreed that negotiations over economic and monetary (and subsequently political) union between the two Germanys would begin after the free elections in East Germany the next month. German unification implied integration of the GDR into the EU, and it was agreed that this would be achieved by the GDR becoming part of the Federal Republic of Germany (FRG) and therefore simply enlarging the territory of the FRG. Thus, German unification was very much a special case for the EU as it involved negotiations with the existing Member State and not the new Member.

The treaty establishing a monetary, economic and social union between the two Germanys came into effect in July 1990, and that for political union was signed in October 1990. The five Lander in East Germany were reconstituted, and the 23 boroughs of Berlin were grouped to form the state of Berlin, which became the capital. A trust agency (*Treuhandanstalt* or THA) was charged with the privatisation of the GDR economy, and the East German Mark (*Ostmark*) became convertible to the West German Deutschmark on a 1:1 basis, meaning that overnight East German salaries and wages were now paid in Deutschmarks.

The speed of political events in Germany in 1990 gave the Commission little time in which to investigate the possible consequences of the GDR joining the EU. The unification of Germany took place at a time when the EU was preoccupied with negotiations regarding the completion of the Single Market programme and closer economic, monetary and political union (the so-called 'deepening process'). The Commission had already given its opinion on further enlargement (widening) when Austria applied for membership in 1989. Their view was that enlargement questions would not be addressed at least until after the single market had been completed in 1993. German unification thus occurred at a most inconvenient time for the EU.

There was also concern about German unification in many Member States, particularly France and the UK. The new Germany would be the largest country in the EU not only in terms of population but also in economic terms, accounting for over 25 per cent of the EU's agricultural and industrial output. The German language would also become the most widely spoken language in the EU. However, other Member States saw *advantages* in German unification as it could serve as a vital catalyst in attempts to speed up the process of European integration, and full EU economic, monetary and political union would bind the new Germany to Western European political and economic institutional structures, thereby preventing an enlarged Germany from playing an independent role in Europe.

Unification led to a 30 per cent increase in Germany's population, giving her grounds for additional voting powers in the Community's institutions. The decision-making structure of the EU had been designed so that the smaller countries were not overshadowed by the larger members (France, Italy, the UK and West Germany), and these four had themselves been granted an equal number of Commissioners, MEPs and voting rights. However, the German government did not press its right to another Commissioner and a further 18 MEPs, although more recently the EU *has* agreed to an increase in the number of German MEPs.

The GDR's trading links with the COMECON countries also created a problem for the EU, but the Commission decided to respect the GDR's treaties with the former USSR and the countries of Eastern Europe as it felt that increasing tariffs on East European exports to the former GDR would be contrary to the spirit of cooperation that the EU was hoping to build up with these countries and that it would retard the process of economic reform in Eastern Europe. It was also felt that jeopardising East German markets in the COMECON countries could accelerate the collapse of the East German economy.

The application of the CAP to the former GDR was also problematic. The reform of the farm sector in the East required not only the disbanding of the state collective farms but also the introduction of new pricing structures. Applying the CAP required substantial reductions in agricultural production and labour and a shift to more environmentally friendly farming practices. The application of a set-a-side policy resulted in over 600 000 ha of arable land being taken out of production in 1990–91, and the slaughter of dairy herds in order to meet EU milk quotas led to 120 of the 264 dairies being shut down in the space of a few months in 1990–91.

The technological gap between East and West Germany was even more marked in manufacturing. Antiquated machinery produced poor-quality goods at high cost and with considerable waste. Surplus capacities existed in the steel, chemicals, heavy engineering, shipbuilding and textiles sectors. Infrastructure needed repairing, and there was serious pollution of soil, air and water due to uncontrolled waste disposal and poor maintenance. In 1990 the former GDR's nuclear plants were shut down on the grounds of safety, but state aids to industry, in particular for steel and shipbuilding, were allowed to continue.

The poorer Member States of the EU (Spain, Portugal, Greece and Eire) were most concerned that their aid from the EU would be reduced as a result of East German membership, but in the event their assistance was *maintained* at the same time as new assistance was agreed for the former GDR. The cost of unification has been immense. Privatisation of the East German economy, job-creation schemes, retraining of workers, combating urban and rural deprivation, provision of new infrastructure and environmental improvements have required significant financial transfers from the West to the East. The cost of this has exposed problems in the former FRG: declining competitiveness, rising wage costs and growing regional disequilibria. At the same time the former GDR economy has collapsed, leading to anger and bitterness from East Germans as whole sections of industry have been closed down or where sell-offs to West German investors has led to the redundancy of workers.

German unification, paradoxically, has been a most *divisive* experience so far for the Germans, but the united Germany nonetheless occupies a key geographical position in the Europe that has developed since the fall of the Berlin Wall. The historical links of the former GDR with the COMECON countries re-emphasise Germany's, and the EU's, commitment towards, and responsibility for Eastern Europe. Since 1990 Germany has actively promoted the idea of a widening of the EU to encompass the new nation states of Central and Eastern Europe. Germany has an obvious interest in maintaining the stability and increasing the prosperity of its East European neighbours, either to prevent large flows of migrants into Germany or to secure German investment and trade outlets in Eastern Europe. Germany will play a pivotal role in the EU's relations with Eastern Europe during the latter part of the 1990s and in the twenty-first century.

ENLARGEMENT FROM TWELVE TO FIFTEEN (1995)

On 1 January 1995 Austria, Finland and Sweden joined the EU, bringing the number of Member States to 15. This enlargement does not significantly modify existing EU policies since: the new Member States have similar economic policies to those of the EU, they are net contributors to the EU budget and, as members of the European Economic Area (EEA), they had previously adapted their legislative background to the framework ruling the Single Market. However, they *will* serve to influence some EU policies, for example environment and social policies such as for health and safety, as their own policies are well-developed in these areas.

Austria became a member of the European Free Trade Association (EFTA) in 1958, and during the 1960s the idea of EU membership was first considered by Austria. A Treaty of Association was signed in 1972, and in 1987 a formal application for full EU membership was made. From January 1993 Austria was a member of the EEA – the EU/EFTA free-trade area.

Formal negotiations on EU membership opened on 1 February 1993. A key stumbling block was a 1991 agreement negotiated with the EU limiting trans-Alpine road traffic (such traffic is expected to increase with expanded East European trade). In March 1994 negotiations over EU membership were completed and it was agreed that the transit agreement should last until 2004, although negotiations on lifting the limits are to be held earlier if the improved railway infrastructure under construction reduces exhaust pollution by 60 per cent. A further benefit to Austria was the agreement that Burgenland would qualify for regional assistance.

On 12 June 1994 the Austrian people decided in a referendum to join the EU from January 1995. The 'yes' vote was unexpectedly high (66 per cent in a high turnout of 81 per cent) and represented a defeat for the right-wing Freedom Party (FPO) of Jorg Haider, who at one point had gained nearly 20 per cent of the vote with his anti-immigration stance. Even in Tirol, where the Alpine transit issue was critical, over 56 per cent voted 'yes'.

Traditionally, Finland had adopted a very cautious attitude to the EU, and its policy was almost entirely governed by the legacy of the Cold War. Her geographical position with the Soviet Union on her eastern border meant that she pursued a policy of neutrality. EEC membership was out of the question as the EEC was a Western free trade organisation and was viewed with great suspicion by the Soviets. Finland viewed EEC membership as being too sensitive and directly contravening its credible policy of neutrality.

There were also important economic reasons for Finland remaining outside the EEC. From the mid-1950s to the late 1980s, Soviet share of Finnish foreign trade represented 20 per cent of the total, and trade with the former USSR also secured Finland's substantial energy needs through cheap oil. In 1988 Finland was the former USSR's second largest trading partner. In addition, the Finnish economy is highly concentrated in the economic sectors of forestry, paper and pulp industries and farming, and the main farming- and forestry-interest organisations were opposed to EEC membership.

In 1961 Finland became an associate member of EFTA while still guaranteeing rights to the former USSR, and only after two years of consultation with the Soviets was Finland able to apply for a free trade agreement with the EEC in 1971. This came into force in 1973 but it was balanced by a similar free trade arrangement with the former USSR. However, the continuing growth of the EEC as a major trade bloc led Finland to develop an increasingly European trade policy, and in 1986 Finland formally became a full member of EFTA. Nevertheless, it was only the ending of the Cold War and the eventual collapse of the Berlin Wall that enabled Finland to fully participate in the European Economic Area (EEA) and eventually apply for membership of the EU in March 1992. Negotiations were completed in March 1994, and in October 1994 a referendum in Finland accepted EU membership, with 56.9 per cent voting 'yes' (the inhabitants of the Aaland Islands in the Baltic Sea were able to hold their own ballot in November 1994, with 73.7 per cent in favour).

Although Finland's agricultural policy objectives are similar to those of the CAP, there will be a problem for Finnish agriculture as levels of support given by the Finnish government have been up to twice the level given in the EU due to the need to support low population densities in harsh climatic areas. The government has estimated that there could be a 50 per cent reduction in labour. There is a transition period, and farmers will get some partial EU aid to compensate for the reduction in agricultural prices, although this aid will be reduced over a period of five years.

The Arctic and sub-Arctic regions have problems of long distances and low population density. They do not qualify for 'objective 1' status assistance, so a new 'objective 6' has been agreed for regions with a population density of less than 8 inhabitants per km^2.

Sweden viewed the negotiations on creating the EEC in 1957 with only partial interest and never seriously considered EEC membership as the proposed customs union would have supra-national authority conflicting with Sweden's desire to maintain sovereignty. In fact it was Sweden who first proposed the alternative European Free Trade Area (EFTA) in 1958. This allowed Sweden the greater benefits of free trade without sacrificing political sovereignty in a customs union. However, when the UK and Denmark, in 1960, and Norway, in 1962, applied to join the EEC, Sweden feared isolation and asked for association status.

In 1972 Sweden signed a free trade agreement with the EEC, but the fall of the Berlin Wall in 1989 effectively ended the division of Europe between the super powers that had been so prominent in the Cold War and had led Sweden to adopt a policy of neutrality. The continuation of this policy was now questioned by many Swedes, and in July 1991 Sweden formally applied for EU membership thus abandoning its long-standing policy of neutrality. Negotiations actually began in 1993 and agreement was reached in 1994. The Swedish people then approved EU membership in a referendum in November 1994, with 52.2 per cent in favour. There were clear majorities in favour of membership in Stockholm, Malmö and Göteborg, but majorities *against* in the north. The negotiating process had run relatively smoothly since much of the work had already been done in negotiations for the 1992 EEA Treaty between the EU and the members of EFTA.

Despite manufacturing accounting for 30 per cent of Swedish GDP and 31 per cent of labour, most Swedish industrialists do not fear EU competition as there has been a substantial growth in research-and-development-(R & D)-led companies (such as in chemicals, pharmaceuticals, electronics and telecommunications) which give Swedish firms a competitive edge.

In agriculture Swedish policy has favoured reform since 1990, with price regulations abolished, tariffs lowered on imports and export support abolished. These instruments will have to be reintroduced given the importance of price and market policy to the CAP, but full integration into the CAP has been fully accepted by Sweden from the first day of accession. Any particular problems in the harsher rural environment of the north may be offset by the introduction of the new 'Objective six' regional assistance status (nearly half of Sweden will be entitled to EU assistance).

In Swedish agriculture there has been a reduction in the use of toxic chemicals and pesticides in response to consumer demands, and during negotiations one important Swedish demand was that the country should not have to lower its environmental standards in areas where it has stricter rules than those of the EU. The outcome was that Sweden will be allowed to keep its rules while waiting for the EU to move closer to Swedish standards. In the few areas where there are no current EU plans to move closer to stricter rules, Sweden will keep her rules for four years. During this period the EU will conduct a review of its environmental rules, including those on the regulation of cadmium, arsenic and various chemicals. If Swedish and EU rules still diverge after four years, Sweden intends to retain her standards, citing the 'environmental guarantee' in the 1957 Treaty of Rome.

The accession of the new Member States has strengthened the economy of the EU, raising its total GDP by around 7 per cent so that it is now 10 per cent more than that of the USA. The area of the EU has expanded by more than a third (Japan is only one-ninth of the area of the EU). For the first time the EU shares a border with the former Soviet Union. Finland's 1200 km border with Russia will be an essential geopolitical element in the EU's future Common Foreign and Security Policy.

THE EU INSTITUTIONS

The main distinguishing feature of the EU is its decision-making process (fig. 1.8), page 28.

France Germany Italy UK	10 votes each
Spain	8 votes
Belgium Greece Netherlands Portugal	5 votes each
Austria Sweden	4 votes each
Denmark Eire Finland	3 votes each
Luxembourg	2 votes

FIGURE 1.7 *Allocated votes in the Council of Ministers, January 1995 (source:* European Commission*)*

(a) It is essentially a confederation of national states, each with its own government. The Heads of Government meet periodically at 'Summit Meetings', known as 'The European Council'. Member States can also agree to call an intergovernmental conference (IGC) in order to change existing treaties or agree to new ones. Perhaps the most well-known of these was the one at Maastricht in December 1991.

(b) The governments are represented by one minister each on the 'Council of Ministers'. This body is the effective link between the national governments and the Commission, and it receives policy proposals from the Commission and takes decisions which are then passed to the Commission for implementation. On some issues, such as tax matters, all the ministers must agree, but in many areas new measures can be agreed by a simple majority (eight countries out of 15) or a 'qualified majority' (QMV) based on the addition of the votes allocated to each Member State (fig. 1.7). Out of the possible 87 votes, a QMV is constituted by 62 votes where the Council's deliberations are based on a proposal from the Commission. In other cases of QMV the 62 votes must also include votes in favour by at least ten Member States. A further complication, the amended Ioannina Compromise, permits a minority of Member States to muster a total number of votes of between 23 and 25 to temporarily block a decision taken by QMV. In this case the Council will try to reach a solution that can be adopted by at least 65 votes.

(c) The European Commission is the executive, permanent civil service – the workhorse – of the EU, with its headquarters in the Berlaymont Building in Brussels. It is directed by 20 Members, with France, Germany, Spain, the UK and Italy having two members each, and Austria, the Netherlands, Belgium, Ireland, Luxembourg, Greece, Portugal, Denmark, Finland and Sweden one each. The Commission initiates policies, draft legislation, and administers the day-to-day mechanics of a customs union of almost 372 million people.

(d) A large body of some 9000 people is the working secretariat for the Commission and Council of Ministers.

(e) The Court of Justice, which sits in Luxembourg, administers EU law and arbitrates in disputes involving the EU treaties. The Court of Auditors checks that the EU budget is correctly spent.

(f) The European Parliament at Luxembourg and Strasbourg is the developing political assembly. It works on a consultative basis, with specialised committees which review policy-making and the composition of the budget. The Maastricht Treaty has given the European Parliament, for the first time, the right to initiate legislation. Since June 1979 its Members have been elected directly by the electorates of the Member countries. The European Parliament currently has 626 Members (MEPs) elected for a five-year term of office. The number of MEPs elected by each country varies according to the size of the country. Germany, being the largest, elects 99, France, Italy and the UK elect 87 each, followed by 64 from Spain, 31 from the Netherlands, 25 from each of Belgium, Greece and Portugal, 22 from Sweden, 21 from Austria, 16 from each of Denmark and Finland, 15 from Eire, and finally, 6 from the smallest state, Luxembourg.

(g) ECOSOC (or ESC) represents employers, workers and other categories of citizen in the EU, and it is consulted on most EU legislation. COR, the Committee of the Regions, consists of representatives of regional and local bodies and is an example of the principle of subsidiarity as it seeks to involve those bodies closest to the citizen in Europe.

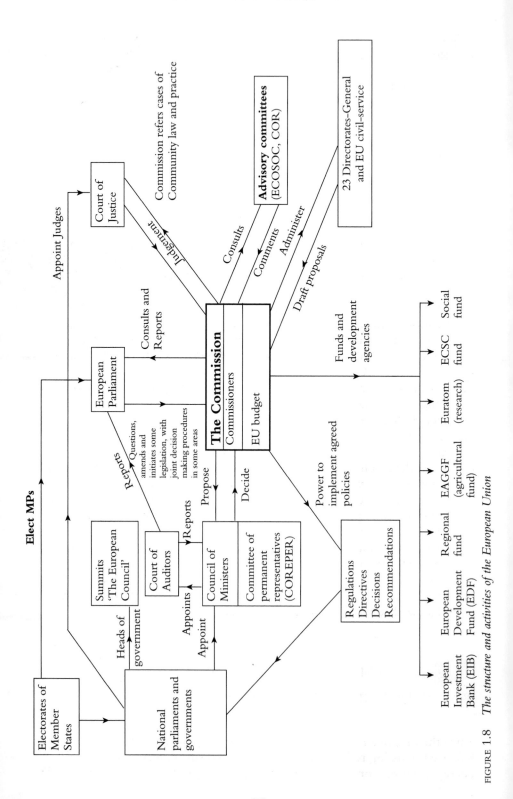

FIGURE 1.8   *The structure and activities of the European Union*

At the present time the EU consists essentially of a confederation of countries which are cumulatively delegating broad areas of economic policy to a common machinery, so that decision-making lies between national governments (represented by the Council of Ministers), the European Commission and the European Parliament, in a tripartite system of control.

THE EU BUDGET, FUNDS AND POLICIES

Since the phasing-out of national contributions, from 1 January 1979, the Commission has had three direct sources of income. These are its 'own resources' based upon agricultural levies and customs duties, plus a percentage of Value Added Tax proceeds. The budget is one of the most important single elements which allows the EU to function as an effective supra-national organisation and to administer policies on a European scale.

The EU's institutions are the practical means by which the policies of economic integration are implemented (fig. 1.8). One of the earliest successes was the ECSC (Chapter 2). The European Social Fund has become the principal agency in the fight against unemployment with industrial retraining and social welfare schemes. The Common Agricultural Policy (Chapter 8) has been concerned primarily with funds to stabilise farmers' incomes by means of the EAGGF (European Agricultural Guidance and Guarantee Fund). The EDF (European Development Fund) finances economic development schemes in countries which have association and trade agreements with the Community. Most significant is the EIB (European Investment Bank) (Chapter 10). This works closely with the Commission and provides loans for development and modernisation projects. Examples are projects like the Val d'Aosta motorway, an essential link in the early integration of Italy and the rest of the EU. A significant development was in 1974 with the inception of the Regional Policy (Chapter 10). The financial aid available under this agency underlines the important principle that economic harmonisation between regions is as important as that between national economies.

THE CONTEMPORARY ECONOMIC SITUATION: TOWARDS THE 21ST CENTURY

Since the oil price rise of 1973 which triggered inflation and recession, there has been a major reduction in economic activity. As an example of this, energy consumption fell by 13 per cent in Western Europe between 1975 and 1985. Unemployment levels rose rapidly and have remained stubbornly high, and there has been a lessening of the pace of economic integration during which the process of convergence in the EU has been slowed considerably. The danger of protectionism has been revived but the peripheral countries of the EU have in the end been worst hit by the effects of the recession.

Other international factors have become more significant. One of the most important is the process of developing-world industrialisation based upon cheap labour and lower costs in which Newly Industrialised Countries (NICs) such as Taiwan, Hong Kong and Brazil have become major industrial competitors against more established older industrial countries. This is the price of the international redistribution of labour which has become very significant. The need for fewer raw materials and the use of replacement materials has led to the decline of many basic industries.

High labour costs in Western Europe and the robotisation of many basic processes have led to the shedding of labour, the so called 'shake-out' or the restructuring of the workforce in traditional industries such as steel, shipbuilding, textiles, and heavy engineering. There is a greater emphasis on skills, services, high-value-added products such as electronics and consumer goods, and tertiary- and quaternary-sector growth which includes tourism, financial and legal services, etc. The mismatch of employment during these major changes from the secondary to the tertiary and quaternary sector has caused severe unemployment. The regional impact has been severe for heavy industrial districts, particularly those inland such as Lorraine, the West Midlands and even the Ruhr. Equally the dispersal of industry, counter-urbanisation and the decline of inner cities with associated unemployment and social tensions have become major problems. Major revival policies have been necessary for many of the older industrial conurbations in the EU. Easier access to the low-wage economies of Eastern Europe could create difficulties for such policies.

A major rural crisis has also developed. The over-production of foodstuffs in the EU reached crisis levels in the 1970s and 1980s and the budgetary cost levels of the CAP became impossible to support. The CAP still takes some 58 per cent of the EU budget and it has been necessary for some redirection of the use of these resources; hence the CAP has been under major political pressure for some time. At the same time as this agricultural crisis is continuing, levels of environmental concern have increased quite dramatically. The farmer needs to be the custodian of the countryside, and a major redirection of land use into forestry, conservation and leisure pursuits is very necessary. The Green or Ecology parties have become a major political force in many West European countries, particularly in Germany and the new entrants in 1995 have more clearly developed environmental policies.

In spite of the slow-down in economic activity during the recession, the absorption of three Mediterranean countries, the unification of Germany and the opening of markets in Eastern Europe, the EU has seen great achievements. Internal trade patterns between the Member States have emerged so that nearly 61 per cent of their total trade is *within* the EU. Even the UK now does 54 per cent of its trade with its partners and this percentage is rising each year.

One of the most significant achievements was the commitment in 1985 to create a frontier-free internal market – the Single European Market (SEM) – across the EU by 1993. The initiative for the Single Market programme came from Jacques Delors when he first became President of the European Commission in January 1985. The aim of the Single Market programme was to eliminate the remaining physical, technical and fiscal obstacles to the free movement of people, goods, services and capital within the EU. This would enable Member State firms to benefit from a home market of truly continental dimensions and take advantage of scale economies thus generated to increase their world-wide competitiveness.

The concept of a large, single market, unhampered by internal frontiers, was at the very core of the objectives set in the Treaty of Rome in 1957. However, despite progress over the years many awkward barriers remained which kept the market fragmented. The Single European Act (SEA) of 1987 (Chapter 22) formalised political and institutional change within the European Community to enable the Single Market to be achieved. The measures that were introduced meant that individual import restrictions that Member States had been allowed to maintain had to disappear by the end of 1992 – e.g., in terms of car imports from Japan, restricted national markets, like that of the UK, are being gradually opened up so that imports will be totally liberalised by the year 2000. Exporters from outside the EU are finding themselves increasingly selling into a single market of almost 372 million consumers with a uniform (or mutually recognised) set of norms, standards and procedures. They no longer have to face 15 different national requirements.

CONTEMPORARY POLITICAL DEVELOPMENTS

The greatest degree of political integration occurred in the EEC during the period from 1951 to the late 1960s, and there was a pause in the rate of integration after that. From the mid-1970s onwards some major political changes took place. Cumulative causation, illustrated by the cooperation, harmonisation and political processes which had worked since the mid-1960s, had become a habit. The change of name from the EEC to the European Community signalled a change from an economic bureaucracy to a political unit. The Community was beginning to cooperate in external affairs, having a single spokesperson for the Member States in major world conferences.

The European Community (EC) is now the European Union (EU). The Treaty on European Union (the Maastricht Treaty), which was signed at Maastricht in February 1992 and came into force in November 1993, has made far-reaching changes. It established the EU, embracing all the forms of cooperation that have been built up in the preceding institutions – foreign and security policy, justice and home affairs, and economic and monetary union (the three 'pillars' of cooperation) – with an agreement that these will be strengthened further. For the Maastricht Treaty to come into force, the parliaments of all Member States (12 at that time) had to approve or ratify it in accordance with the constitution of their country. For some this meant a referendum had to be held. The Treaty was very controversial, with some fearing that it eroded sovereignty and would lead to a 'United States of Europe'. In Denmark the Treaty was narrowly rejected in a referendum in 1992 but then narrowly approved in a second referendum in 1993. All EU countries have ratified the Treaty, but both Denmark and the UK have negotiated a number of opt-out clauses.

In 1979 two major steps forward were taken. The European Monetary System, the EMS, was established on 13 March 1979, with the European Currency Unit, the ECU, and the exchange rate intervention mechanism creating a zone of monetary stability throughout the Union. This was only a partial success since the UK did not fully join the system. The Delors Report of 1989 proposed further economic and monetary integration. The logic behind this was that the economic gains derived from the Single Market could be greatly enhanced by the creation of an economic and monetary union (EMU) and, ultimately, a single currency. Exchange rates would stay the same, and indeed there would be no need to change money from one currency into another.

The Maastricht Treaty set the timetable for a three-stage transition to full EMU and a single currency by 1999. It was recognised that fixed exchange rates and a single monetary policy and currency could lead to serious difficulties unless the economic policies and performances of all those who adopted it were sufficiently similar. The Treaty sets out clear economic tests ('convergence criteria') which countries will have to pass before they can move towards fixed exchange rates, a single monetary policy and a single European currency. At present only France and Luxembourg meet these criteria, but it may be that some countries will make the change before others. The 1999 deadline for full EMU has been called into question by the currency turbulence of 1992 and 1993 and the economic recession following that.

Also in 1979, the first direct elections to the European Parliament in Strasbourg took place. The European Parliament was remarkable for the early establishment of major groups by political tendency rather than nationality so that a normal political spectrum from left to right soon emerged as a major integrating force. The Single European Act and the Maastricht Treaty have substantially enhanced Parliament's powers, although they did not go all the way to meeting the Parliament's demands for it to always have an equal say with the European Council in decisions. However, the establishment of a co-decision procedure and an assent procedure in certain areas and a cooperation procedure in others has made the Parliament into a veritable legislative body.

However, there is no doubt that further changes will need to be made to the institutions of the EU as it 'deepens' (that is, as existing Member States work more closely and effectively together) and 'widens' (that is, continues to enlarge). Switzerland remains a candidate for EU membership, and Turkey, Cyprus, Malta, Hungary, Poland, Romania, Slovakia, Latvia, Estonia, Lithuania, Bulgaria and the Czech Republic have also applied. Relations between the EU and its neighbours in the European Free Trade Area (EFTA) and Central and Eastern Europe represent one of the most dynamic aspects of the EU's external policy. The EU and the EFTA states have maintained special preferential relations since the early 1970s when the EEC concluded free trade agreements with each of them. The progressive creation of the Single European Market led the EFTA countries to review their relationship with the EU, and three of them eventually joined in 1995. In 1989 Delors made an innovative proposal for a 'third way', for EC–EFTA relations, lying between the free trade framework that existed then and full EC membership. This became the European Economic Area (EEA) which was signed in 1992 and took effect in 1994.

The dramatic events in Eastern and Central Europe from 1989 onwards have seen further applications for closer ties with the EU. The first signs of a change of attitude towards the EU on the part of COMECON members came several years before 1989 when Hungary and former Czechoslovakia approached the EC with requests for wider trade links beyond the scope of very limited sectoral agreements that had hitherto been negotiated. Agreements between all the East European countries and the Soviet Union were negotiated between 1988 and 1990. These negotiations were already under way when the revolutions in Eastern Europe took place. Since then the agreements between the EU and Hungary, former Czechoslovakia, Poland, Bulgaria and Romania have been upgraded. The EU has devised a new type of association agreement for these countries – 'Europe' association agreements.

The 'Europe' association agreements provide for free trade but also include economic and technical cooperation, financial assistance and a political-dialogue chapter. The first 'Europe' association agreements were concluded with Hungary, the Czech and Slovak Republics and Poland – the so-called Visegrad countries who were furthest advanced in the reform process. Since then 'Europe' association agreements have also been concluded with Bulgaria, Estonia, Latvia, Lithuania, Romania and Slovenia. The EU also has more limited trade agreements with Albania, and has also negotiated so-called Partnership and Co-operation Agreements with some CIS members – Russia, the Ukraine, Byelarus, Kirgizstan and Moldova.

2

ENERGY: A VARIETY OF SOURCES

The West European economy is based upon manufacturing industry and therefore has a fundamental requirement for large quantities of energy. Furthermore, energy needs to be available on a long-term, substantial and low-cost basis if industry is to plan and compete effectively. This chapter seeks to illustrate the diversity of energy resources which are now available to the EU nations, their changing geographical location, and the political economy of the supply and demand of energy.

There are five main primary sources of energy: coal, oil, natural gas, nuclear energy and water power. These are used for the direct production of heat for industrial purposes although this is frequently converted immediately into electrical energy, which may be regarded as secondary energy. Electricity is perhaps the most significant of all twentieth century forms of energy because of its easily distributable nature and its liberalising effects upon industrial location.

COAL

Coal provided the energy for the Industrial Revolution which began in Western Europe in the eighteenth and nineteenth centuries. It occurred in thick seams at, or relatively near, the earth's surface and many coalfields, such as the Ruhr, or Northumberland and Durham, were by rivers or the sea, facilitating easy movement in the days before railway networks were established. More important in the days of nineteenth century technology was coal's versatility. As a source of direct heat it was used as a home fuel; as coke it could smelt iron ore, and could be used in the manufacture of pottery and glass and in most basic industrial processes. It was the energy source which encouraged the development of steam-driven machinery and the locomotive. Coal powered the railway network of Europe and the navies which maintained British, French, Dutch and German colonies, trade and military supremacy. Its usefulness as an important source of energy has been prolonged into the twentieth century by its availability as a generator of electricity in power stations. In addition to contributing to the early industrialisation of the Continent, coal also dominated the original location of the large-scale European manufacturing industry. Coal was low in value in relation to its bulk, being expensive to transport and inefficiently used, so that factories tended to concentrate close to the pithead. Most nineteenth century industrial regions developed on or near coalfields. The most industrialised nations – Germany, the UK and Belgium – were those with the major coalfields. France, Spain and Italy, in particular, lagged behind the other nations because of their relatively poor endowment of coal. Italy had

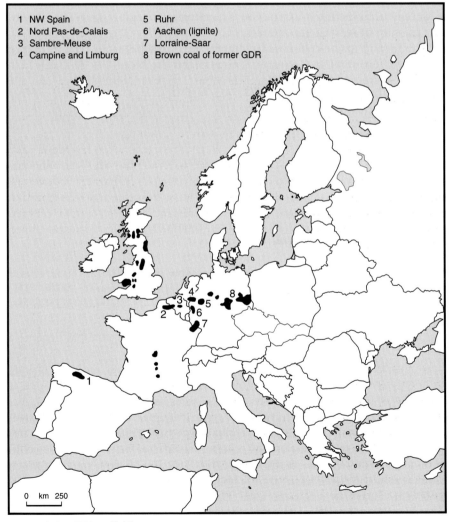

1	NW Spain	5	Ruhr
2	Nord Pas-de-Calais	6	Aachen (lignite)
3	Sambre-Meuse	7	Lorraine-Saar
4	Campine and Limburg	8	Brown coal of former GDR

0   km   250

FIGURE 2.1   *EU coalfields*

scarcely any coal at all, France only one major coalfield, the Nord/Pas de Calais, and Spain the Oveido coalfield on the north coast.

The major coalfields

There are two major coal provinces within Western Europe (fig. 2.1). In the UK the large coalfields are found generally north of a line from Bristol to the Wash, and these gave rise to the concentration of British manufacturing in the Midlands and the North. Each coalfield specialised in a major branch of manufacturing: for example steel and non-ferrous metallurgy in South Wales, shipbuilding on the Clyde, and textiles in Lancashire and West Yorkshire. Such manufacturing zones developed their coal-based industrial activities during the nineteenth century, and these dominated the UK economy until the inter-war period when coal was beginning to give way to the pressure of new energy sources.

The second major coal-based industrial area stretches from Lille in France across to Dortmund in Germany. This contains the Nord/Pas de Calais field of France, stretching to the Sambre/Meuse coalfield of Belgium; and the Kempenland and Limburg fields, extending eastwards to Aachen and the Ruhr in Germany. At the southern apex of the triangle lies the Saarland coal basin and the coal and minette iron ores of Lorraine and Luxembourg. This is the 'Heavy Industrial Triangle' which as late as 1952 was responsible for 95 per cent of the coal and 86 per cent of the steel produced in the six EEC countries. It is still the most significant single area of heavy industry on the Continent.

Falling demand for coal

Technological change and the discovery of new energy sources have caused a dramatic reduction in the role of coal since the early 1950s. The exhaustion of the best and most easily accessible coal seams, the labour-intensive character of coal-mining and the expense of transporting it compared to alternative, competitive fuels has meant that coal has become a very much more expensive source of energy. This process has been accompanied by the demise of the open coal fire, together with the change in energy consumption from coal to oil and electricity by major users such as the railways, the shipping fleets and the steel industry. Air pollution has created a need for cleaner forms of energy. Primary hydrocarbon fuels such as oil and natural gas, the new technology fuel uranium, hydro-electric power, and the secondary energy source, electricity, have all combined to produce a highly varied energy supply (fig. 2.2). In addition, they are much more easily distributed and transferable by pipeline or cable, and are less bulky and heavy to transport. Coal, therefore, has become a high-cost and inconvenient fuel despite research into increasing its efficiency. As late as 1951, at the beginning of the EEC's existence, coal provided two-thirds of its primary energy, and in the UK the proportion was as high as 90 per cent. Since then, however, although total energy requirements have risen, the share of coal has fallen dramatically, both relatively and absolutely. Coal production has fallen from 447 million tonnes in 1962 to 159 million tonnes in 1993.

	EEC (6)		UK			France		EU (12) (including East Germany from 1992)			
	1951	1972	1951	1986	1993	1986	1993	1982	1985	1986	1993
								Commission objectives			
Coal	67	21.5	90	31.9	24.3	10.5	6.5	20.5	16	18.8	14.7
Lignite		2.8					0.3	3.8		3.4	5.0
Oil		59.5		37.1	38.3	42.8	39.6	48.7	40	45.6	43.8
Natural gas	33	11.7	10	23.2	27.0	12.3	13.3	17.8	25	17.9	20.5
Hydro-electric and nuclear energy		4.5		7.8	10.4	32.7	40.3	9.2	19	14.3	16.0
Total energy consumption (mtoe)	247	675	158	193	212	175	219	961		1042	1190

mtoe = million tonnes of oil equivalent

FIGURE 2.2 *Percentages of primary energy consumption*

The smaller, modern coal industry

The coal industries of Western Europe have been considerably contracted and modernised (fig. 2.4). The National Coal Board (which later became the British Coal Corporation) of the UK is an example of this restructuring. Since 1947 nearly 900 of the small and less productive pits have been closed and production concentrated in modern efficient pits. Productivity has been increased considerably by long-wall coal-face machinery, by power loading, and by the construction of power stations for electricity generation adjacent to the pitheads, thus reducing the transport costs of coal.

The workforce of over 1 million in 1914 has thus been dramatically reduced (fig. 2.5). Mechanised coal-cutting and loading has increased from 2 per cent of total production in 1947 to over 90 per cent now. The East Midlands coalfield (Derbyshire, Nottingham, Leicester and Yorkshire) has now emerged as the main coal-producing area. At the end of the miners' strike in 1985 there were 169 pits and 171 000 miners. Within five years over 100 pits had been closed and the workforce had fallen by 90 000. A study was then commissioned by the Conservative government to advise on the commercial viability of British Coal. The study recommended that by 1994 all but 14 pits should be closed and 40 000 jobs ended. Despite considerable opposition most of the study's proposals have been implemented, with only 17 working collieries remaining in 1994. One of the reasons for this dramatic decline has been the so-called 'dash for gas' – the increasing use of gas as a fuel for electricity generation. Prior to 1991 the EU had banned the use of gas for this purpose to reserve gas for other uses and to maintain a strategic reserve in case of crisis. In 1993 British Coal offered 28 collieries for lease/licence to the private sector, and in 1994 the government announced its intention to offer British coal for sale in five regional packages. The pace of contraction has slowed considerably now that British Coal is producing about 67 million tonnes of coal per year and the industry has slimmed to a smaller size. (Some of the closed pits have reopened under private ownership.) In contrast, open-cast coal-mining has increased in recent years because of the high profitability of this form of mining. Open-cast mines employ approximately 15 000 people in the UK.

The other major coal province in the EU has experienced similar problems. Although there has been considerable retrenchment in total production, the pattern varies considerably. Productivity has been constantly low in the small isolated coal basins of the Centre/Midi of France and the South Belgian coalfield. Production in the latter was phased out in 1992 with the closure of the last two mines. The Nord/Pas de Calais has always suffered from thin, disturbed seams and, with reserves practically exhausted and mining increasingly expensive, output ended in 1991 (fig. 2.4). By contrast, the most important single coalfield in Western Europe, the Ruhr, is far more productive. Its output per person is the highest in the EU. Nevertheless, it too has seen rationalisation, with the number of miners falling from 300 000 in 1960 to the current figure of 70 000. Lorraine is another efficient coalfield and has become relatively much more important to France. As in the UK, modernisation and rationalisation in these areas has been undertaken by large-scale authorities. The bulk of French coal production is the responsibility of the nationalised company Charbonnages de France (CdF). Ruhrkole AG now controls production in the Ruhr coal basin.

The Spanish coal industry has followed a significantly different process. Production from the small Oviedo coalfield has been the basis for the heavy industrial districts centred upon Bilbao and the northern coastal region. As the Spanish economy has rapidly developed since the 1960s the production of coal has been raised to about 18 million tonnes. Coal in Spain is produced by more than 200 companies. The leading company, Hunosa, is publicly owned while most of the rest are held privately. The coal is of poor quality, with high ash and sulphur content, and this, coupled with major geological difficulties, makes Spanish coal extremely expensive. The industry is, however, overstaffed and under-capitalised with far too many small collieries, and faces considerable rationalisation (fig. 2.3). Capacity reductions are being implemented in the least competitive mines, involving 12 000 job losses – 6000 in HUNOSA and 6000 in the private-sector mines. At the same time the government has proposed an action plan to tackle the major economic and social problems of the mining regions.

Cooperation in the coal industry

The importance of coal to the economies of Western Europe was recognised by the formation in 1951 of the first agency of cooperation, the ECSC (European Coal and Steel Community). Although this has since been integrated into the EU treaties, it was the first significant landmark of economic cooperation and success in the post-war period. By the Paris Treaty of 1951, the original Six decided to remove internal price barriers and transport discrimination, customs duties and quotas on coal, coke, pig iron, scrap and steel, thereby establishing a single market for these products. For the first time in history the great resource area of the 'Heavy Industrial Triangle' could be considered as one efficient geographical unit. Instead of four groups of national coalfields, separated by national frontiers, there was now a single resource of some 230 million tonnes of coal per annum on the market at a common price. The ECSC played a major role in coordinating coal production and reducing the internal costs of energy. More significantly, this cooperation had a major psychological value in pooling the resources of an area which had been a major bone of contention between France and Germany for over 150 years.

ECSC policy experienced a marked change in emphasis due to the changing role of coal. In 1951 coal played the largest part in energy supplies, providing 67 per cent of the total energy of the original Six. This was a period of rapid post-war industrial growth, and with an acute shortage of fuel, priority was given to the maximum output of coal. The rapid rise of thermal electricity production from coal-fired power stations was a major growth factor. As an example, French production rose to a high point of 59 million tonnes in 1958.

During the 1960s this pattern changed dramatically. The days of energy self-sufficiency based upon coal had gone. The ECSC controlled and guided the decline in coal production caused by competition from oil and natural gas, and cheaper imported non-Community coal. There was a phased reduction of output, and closure and amalgamation of collieries to create fewer but more efficient units. Annual demand for coal in the original Six dropped by over two-thirds up to 1972 (fig. 2.2), and coal now provides just under 15 per cent of total energy consumption. In the UK, the degree of dependence upon coal has also declined, with it providing 24 per cent of total energy requirements. The improvement in the efficiency of the coal industry has been remarkable, with the modernisation and mechanisation of collieries. The EU has recognised that areas suffering from mine closures face special problems, and has created a fund called Rechar. Community grants have been provided for retraining redundant miners, attracting new economic activities to replace mining, housing grants, improved safety

Bergkamen 'A' in the Ruhr: a coal-fired power station

	Coal production by country (million tonnes)					Significant collieries		Underground workers			
	1962	1971	1981	1986	1993	1986	1993	1971	1982	1986	1993
Germany (including E. Germany from 1992)	147.1	117.1	95.5	87.1	64.2	33	19	135 000	122 000	107 000	71 800
France	52.3	33.0	18.6	14.4	8.6	15	5	60 000	28 100	18 500	7000
Netherlands	11.8	3.7	nil	nil	nil	nil	nil	6000	nil	nil	nil
Spain	12.6	10.6	14.6	15.9	18.2	272	134	-	33 200	33 600	24 000
United Kingdom	200	147.1	125.3	104.6	67.2	110	22	221 000	170 000	108 400	21 000
Belgium	21.2	10.9	6.1	5.6	nil	5	nil	24 000	16 000	13 300	300
Total EU (12)		**447.1**	**312.4**	**245.6**	**227.9**	**158.5**					

Luxembourg, Italy, Ireland, Denmark, Greece and Portugal – insignificant production

FIGURE 2.3   *EU (12) coal production 1961–93*

Coalfield	1961	1971	1972	1974	1981	1986	1993	Comment
Belgium								
Campine (Kempenland)	9.6	7.3	7.3	6.3	5.8	5.6	nil	The last mine at Zolder closed in 1992
South Belgium	11.9	3.6	3.1	2.6	0.3	nil	nil	Sambre–Meuse valley. Nil production
Germany								
Ruhr	120.3	96.4	88.9	83.0	76.7	67.7	51.5	1993 production very efficient from 14 large collieries
Ville (Cologne) (lignite field)	–	–	110.0	–	122.9	117.0	106.4	Made into briquettes as fuel
Aachen	8.7	6.8	6.5	6.2	5.2	4.9	1.6	Only one colliery remains open
Saar	16.0	10.6	10.4	8.9	11.5	9.4	9.1	Production from three collieries
Lower Saxony	2.0	2.9	2.6	2.2	2.4	2.4	nil	
Former GDR	–	–	–	–	–	87.7	54.2	Brown coal (lignite) produced from large open-cast mines in Cottbus and Halle-Leipzig regions (now part of Sachsen-Anhalt, Sachsen and Brandenburg Länders). Considerable pollution problems and production being reduced
France								
Nord/Pas de Calais	26.9	14.5	12.6	9.0	3.9	1.9	nil	Production ended in 1991
Lorraine	14.0	11.5	10.9	9.1	10.9	9.4	7.4	The most efficient French coalfield with reserves of 400 million tonnes (4 collieries in 1993)
Centre/Midi	11.2	6.9	6.2	4.8	3.7	2.6	1.2	Small isolated coal basins to be phased out
Netherlands								
Limburg	12.9	3.7	2.9	0.8	nil	nil	nil	Production phased out completely in 1976
Spain								
Central Asturiana, Sur, Bierzo Villablino Narcea, Este Leon-Palencia, Aragon								
Cataluna-Baleares	12.6	10.6	–	14.6	14.6	15.9	18.2	Asturias province – poor-quality coal
United Kingdom								
Derby, Nottinghamshire and Yorkshire	82.7	68.5	55.8	55.0	65.5	60.3	24.0	The largest and most efficient British coalfield. It contains the Selby coalfield and the Vale of Belvoir, with estimated reserves of over 700 million tonnes
Northumberland and Durham	33.7	19.2	15.2	12.9	13.7	10.8	2.8	Considerable rationalisation with only 1 colliery in 1993
West Midlands	16.1	8.6	6.5	5.4	8.6	4.9	⎱ 19.6	Production now confined to Cannock and Warwickshire
Wales	18.2	12.1	9.5	7.6	7.6	6.9	⎰ (combined)	Considerable exhaustion. Only 2 mines open in 1993
North West	12.8	13.5	10.6	9.9	11.4	10.5	nil	
Scottish	17.5	12.5	9.8	8.6	7.4	5.6	1.7	Only one colliery open in Fife
Kent	1.6	1.0	0.7	0.6	0.6	0.4	nil	Low cost, high productivity
Open-cast mines	8.6	10.6	10.4	9.8	14.4	14.0	14.2	
Portugal								
Douro	–	–	–	–	–	–	0.2	One colliery. Production to be phased out

FIGURE 2.4 *EU (12) coalfields production (million tonnes)*

techniques and research into new uses for coal and its by-products. Particularly in the Franco–Belgian coalfield, there has been a wave of development of new industrial estates in the decaying mining areas. Altogether, about half a million workers have been retrained. The basic achievement of the ECSC has been to adapt its policies to periods of expansion and contraction and to have aided the restructuring of an ailing industry.

The coal industry remains problematic. After the actions and control of oil by the OPEC (Organization of Petroleum-Exporting Countries) from 1974 onwards, it was envisaged that the role of coal would grow again, with a particular increase in cheap imports from the USA and Poland. Domestic coal output has continued to decline however since 1973. The Netherlands and Belgium have terminated production. In the UK and Germany, the best endowed countries, there has been closure of uneconomic pits and major investment in new deep mines. There are regional, political and social implications, however, and the 1984 labour unrest in the UK was a symptom of this. The Germans want to negotiate a new system of subsidies for their coal industry as they are heavily dependent on coal for generating electricity. They also have the problem of the former GDR's lignite (brown coal) industry with its open-cast workings (the largest is Laubag which straddles the Lander of Brandenburg and Saxony–Anhalt) and poor environmental legacy. Large tracts of the brown-coal-mining area south of Leipzig are to be restored as a 'European Energy and Environmental Park'. The indigenous production of coal remains subject to internal labour problems, environmental problems, cost and efficiency considerations and external pressures from the fluctuating cost of oil and cheap imports of coal from the USA and Poland. It is caught up in the global political economy. Hard coal imports to the EU have been increasing year by year since 1988, but 1993 saw the first substantial drop from 136.3 million tonnes in 1992 to 115 million tonnes in 1993. The USA is the main supplier, followed by South Africa, Australia, Colombia and Poland.

Oil

The consumption of oil in Western Europe increased enormously during the 1950s and 1960s, at an average rate of 10 per cent per year. This was due partly to the relatively low cost of production of the refined product, and partly to the advantage of oil in servicing large, expanding and non-competitive markets such as aviation fuels. In addition, oil was competitive in the production of electricity in thermal power stations, in home heating, and in the petrochemical industry with products such as artificial fibres and plastics.

Consumption of oil by the enlarged EU was over 520 million tonnes in 1993 (fig. 2.6). This represented approximately one-third of the international

	Number of miners	Collieries	Production (million tonnes)
1947	900 000	908	195
1956	704 700	840	209
1967	409 700	483	184
1971	285 000	292	147
1973	250 000	285	118
1977	240 000	231	121
1982	288 000	176	121
1986	140 000	110	105
1991	62 121	53	91
1993	20 794	22	67

FIGURE 2.5   *Changes in the United Kingdom coal industry*

	Production	Imports
Germany	3.1	99.6
United Kingdom	95.2	61.6
France	2.8	78.9
Italy	4.6	86.9
Netherlands	3.3	55.3
Belgium	nil	30.9
Luxembourg	nil	nil
Denmark	8.3	5.4
Ireland	nil	1.9
Greece	0.6	14.3
Spain	0.9	53.5
Portugal	nil	11.6
Total	118.8	499.9

FIGURE 2.6   *EU (12) consumption of crude oil, 1993 (million tonnes)*

movement of oil, with most imports coming from the Middle East. The dependence on imported oil is one of the most vulnerable areas of the European economy from both a strategic and a financial point of view.

In spite of this the EU relies upon oil for a high proportion of its energy

Botlek oil terminal at Rotterdam

requirements. The low-cost oilfields exploited in many parts of the world are supplemented by ocean-going supertankers of 100 000 tonnes and over dead weight. These carry crude oil to the principal estuaries of Western Europe, at which point the oil is refined and then carried by pipeline, road or railway. This is a well-integrated production–supply pattern, largely under the control of the major Western oil companies during the 1960s, which encouraged a huge expansion of low-cost industrial production. The pattern of oil refining in the EU is almost entirely of coastal, riverside or estuarine refineries with ocean terminals for crude-oil input (fig. 2.7). As consumption increased, refining capacity enlarged dramatically reaching 884 million tonnes by 1976. However, by this date the oil price rise of the early 1970s had reduced consumption, so the EU encouraged a rationalisation of capacity. By 1989 capacity had dropped to 573 million tonnes, and although by 1993 capacity had risen to 606 million tonnes, this was mainly due to the addition of East German refining capacity. Italy has the largest refining capacity (116 million tonnes), reflecting its almost total dependence upon imported oil for energy, followed by Germany, France, the UK, the Netherlands and Spain. The refining capacity of the Netherlands is high and dominated by the Rotterdam–Europoort agglomeration which is at the centre of the transnational pattern of pipelines (fig. 2.7). As well as the North Sea oil terminals, the Mediterranean Sea has become a major focus with oil pipelines reaching north to the Rhinelands from Lavera, Genoa and Trieste. However, since 1973/4 a range of new and complex factors have transformed the position of oil. The rising pace of energy consumption until then was changed by the external situation. The actions of the OPEC cartel to control operations and quadruple prices ended the low-cost advantage of oil and sent the industrial world into recession. Since then the price of oil has fluctuated depending upon the political effectiveness of the cartel in controlling production, and during the 1980s the cartel's power diminished and the price of oil fell markedly again. The EU is now a net consumer of energy, heavily dependent upon imports, and is locked into the global political economy.

One aspect of this complex supply situation is the attempt to diversify sources of supply, so reducing the strategic risk of over-dependence upon any one area. In 1958, the Middle East supplied 77 per cent of the original six EC countries' oil, whereas by 1993 this had fallen to 40 per cent. Today, Africa, including Libya, Algeria and Nigeria, supply 25.5 per cent of the EU's oil requirements, and increasing amounts are coming from Eastern Europe (including the former Soviet Union) and Norway. Exploration within the Union has been intensified. Land deposits of oil have been disappointingly small and there are only small producing fields in the Lacq

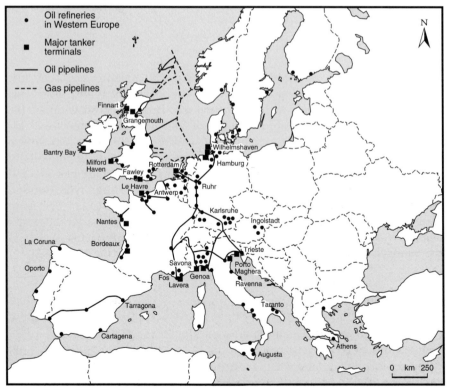

FIGURE 2.7   *EU oil refining capacity*

and Parentis areas of Aquitaine–Pyrenees; at Emsland and Lower Saxony in the North European basin; in the Rhine valley and in the Paris Basin. In the UK there are small fields in the Trent valley and Dorset, but these account for a small proportion of total UK consumption.

Fig. 2.2 (page 37) reflects some success in reducing the role of oil in relation to other energy sources.

NORTH SEA GAS AND OIL

A significant new energy province, the North Sea, emerged during the late 1960s. Combined with the effects of the accession of the UK to the EU, it has had the effect of altering the location of European energy supplies. The centre of indigenous energy production is now in and around the North Sea, the so-called 'Home Energy Zone' (Parker 1979). The economic value of the North Sea is in supplementing EU energy supplies by up to one-third, in reducing oil imports substantially, and in moderating the power of OPEC. If they are taken in their wider context, i.e. the continental shelf, the energy reserves could last well into the next century, although opinions vary considerably.

The source rocks

In the early part of the Permian period (circa 250 million years ago), the Rotliegendes sandstone was deposited in the North Sea area over coal deposits which were the source of natural gas. In later Permian times, the Zechstein Sea, in which large deposits of salts and carbonates were laid down, covered much of the area of north-west Europe and the North Sea. Later the North Sea was a sedimentary basin for hundreds of millions of years, throughout the Triassic, Jurassic, Cretaceous and Tertiary periods, and so has become a vast area of marine deposits, including hydrocarbons, interruptions of which could only have been on a minor scale. The main natural gas concentrations are trapped in porous sections of the Rotliegendes sandstone and below the impermeable salt layers. The oil occurs mainly in the younger rocks where they are thickest in the centre of the North Sea.

The discovery of North Sea wealth

Exploration on the continent of Europe and in the UK, from the 1930s onwards, provided evidence of small oil and gas fields, but there was little encouragement to undertake the expense of searching for and developing resources under the North Sea on this evidence alone. In addition, marine technology in this field has had to develop very rapidly during the last few years to be capable of constructing and maintaining the large semi-submersible platforms necessary for drilling in up to 200 m of stormy seas.

At Slochteren, a village in the Groningen province of Northern Holland, Shell and Esso struck natural gas in enormous quantities on 14 August 1959. Further drillings confirmed the vast size of the find: the estimated reserves of gas in this field are 2400 million tonnes of coal-equivalent. It may seem strange that a major gas field like this one in the Groningen province had remained undiscovered for so long. One reason was the great depth of the gas, over 3 km below the surface.

Studies of the rock structures beneath the North Sea began with an airborne magnetometer survey of the entire area from southern Norway to the Straits of Dover, which indicated broad areas within which hydrocarbons were likely to be found. These are normally dome-like zones in which the oil and gas are trapped beneath impermeable rock layers. The first seismic survey of the UK part of the North Sea began in 1962 as a joint enterprise of Shell, Esso and British Petroleum. In July 1964, the Continental Shelf Act defined the territorial areas of the North Sea for the seven nations bordering it. The boundaries between the areas of the states concerned were defined by reference to a 'median line' (fig. 2.8). Concessions were granted to 23 consortia to drill for natural gas in specified 'blocks' in the UK area, each about 250 km^2 in area.

Natural gas

The first major strike of natural gas was made by British Petroleum late in 1965 in the Rotliegendes sandstone, some 70 km off the Humber estuary. An 80 km pipeline under the sea brought the first experimental quantities of gas from the under-sea wells to Easington on Humberside early in March 1967. A 60 cm feeder main, 120 km long, from Easington across the Humber then fed into the existing Canvey–Leeds methane pipeline. By May 1967, out of some 50 odd wells, 16 had shown significant amounts of gas – a phenomenal score by all past drilling experience.

In 1993, 65 488 million m^3 of natural gas were extracted from 48 offshore gas fields (mainly in the North Sea but also from the South Morecambe Field in the Irish Sea – fig. 2.8). Over half came from the three most prolific fields: Leman, Indefatigable (South) and the Hewett area. The gas is largely supplied from four North Sea shore terminals and one in Barrow-in-Furness (Cumbria).

Natural gas has become a substantial and rapidly growing element in the EU energy pattern during the last decade. The UK and the Netherlands have between them approximately 75 per cent of EU reserves of natural gas. In the Netherlands natural gas now provides 49 per cent of the total primary energy consumption. Dutch natural gas production has now been trimmed back to minimum levels to conserve the remaining reserves. In the EU as a whole it provided 21 per cent of primary energy consumption in 1993. The Shetland Basin, with its large natural gas reserves in fields such as Frigg and

Sleipner, is of great significance in prolonging these supplies and in making natural gas a long-term economic factor.

The oil discoveries

The oil companies discovered significant evidence of oil deposits as well as natural gas in the North Sea. Whilst natural gas is present in the sandstones found to the south of the Humber estuary, oil-bearing layers are to be found in the younger Cretaceous, Jurassic and Tertiary rocks in the Scottish and East Shetland Basin. The northern part of the North Sea is extremely hazardous, especially in winter. Nevertheless, the prospect of large indigenous supplies of oil in Western Europe was such a great attraction that during the latter part of the 1960s exploration drilling rigs began to move north. The major world oil companies have been heavily involved, with 30 consortia working in the area and creating a new marine industrial technology in the shape of the offshore drilling platform. British Coal is involved with the major oil companies in oil exploration as a natural extension of its offshore drilling for coal. The British National Oil Corporation (BNOC or Britoil) was set up to secure government participation but has now been sold to BP as government involvement has been reduced.

Norway and the UK gained the major share of this new natural resource as most deposits of oil lie along the median line dividing British from Norwegian waters. There are smaller deposits in Danish waters. Norway, having a much smaller population, benefits in per capita terms more than the UK, although in any case the whole of Western Europe benefits from having a politically stable source of oil.

Assessing the importance of the oil and natural gas

There is a complex series of physical, economic, geographical and political considerations involved in assessing the significance of the resources.

1 Major economic development has come to the Shetland Islands, Aberdeen and Stavanger. Rotterdam is particularly well-placed to refine North Sea oil.
2 There are over 60 oilfields with recoverable reserves already in production. Some of these such as the Brent field are large by world standards.
3 The UK produces approximately 96 million tonnes of oil per year (accounting for nearly 80 per cent of total EU oil production), is one of the top ten world oil producers, and has become a large-scale oil-exporting country. Production peaked at about 123 million tonnes in 1985/6, dropping to 83 million tonnes in 1991 but increasing again since then, reaching 90 million tonnes in 1993. Remaining recoverable reserves

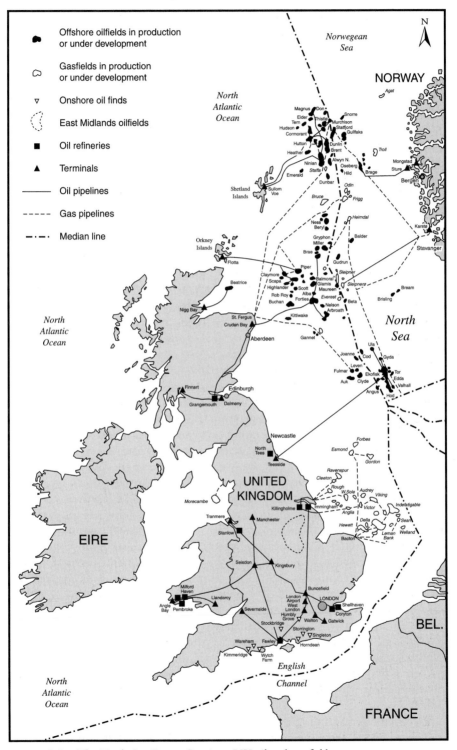

FIGURE 2.8   *The North Sea Energy Province: UK oil and gas fields*

in the 'proven' plus 'probable' categories amount to 1406 million tonnes, while the total remaining potential could be nearly 6000 million tonnes on current estimates. However, offshore fields are more expensive to exploit than onshore fields.

4 The world oil market and price are the key factors in determining the value of North Sea oil. Many of the present fields would not be exploited now had not OPEC increased the price of oil so dramatically in 1973.

5 British government taxation policy in some of the smaller, marginal oilfields is now sufficiently flexible to allow for them to be profitably developed. These marginal oilfields are crucial to the extension of North Sea production. Improving technology should allow for the proportion of recoverable reserves to increase.

6 Policies of oil exploitation illustrate basic geographical differences. Norway, having a small population and major HEP endowment, has taken a much slower approach to oil wealth. In the UK, with its large energy requirement, very rapid exploitation from 1975 onwards has occurred.

ELECTRICITY

The transformation of the primary fuels described in this chapter into the secondary source electrical energy is one of the most important single aspects of the energy revolution. The generation of electricity depends upon the use of coal, oil and natural gas in thermal power stations, together with nuclear power stations and renewable energy sources (fig. 2.11). There are considerable variations between the Member States. In the UK coal provides 60 per cent of electricity generation, and nuclear power 27 per cent. However, gas is forecast to meet 25 per cent of the UK's electricity demand by 1998 (up from virtually nil in 1990) – the so-called 'dash for gas' – due to the government's decision to allow the market to decide on which fuels should be used after privatisation of the electricity industry. The two largest generating companies in England and Wales have cut their purchases of coal from 65 million tonnes in 1992/3 to 40 million tonnes in 1993/4, and this will reduce further to 30 million tonnes by 1997/8. In Portugal some 29 per cent and in Italy some 21 per cent of electricity generation is from HEP and wind power. Italy is heavily dependent upon petroleum (but plans to increase gas-fired electricity production to 25 per cent by 2000), the Netherlands upon natural gas, and in France the dominant contribution is by nuclear power. The generation of electricity illustrates a range of contrasts in development, natural endowments, localised resources and government policies.

Electricity demand in the EU has doubled every ten years since the 1950s. This has been accompanied by a much greater efficiency in production and transmission. The same amount of primary fuel as used in 1958 will now generate 45 per cent more electricity, and the super-grid at 400 kilovolts will now transfer it over large areas with a minimal loss of energy.

Electricity has enormous advantages. It is a clean form of energy, and is the most suitable energy form for automated industrial processes, including robotisation and data processing. Most important of all, the distribution of electricity via the grid over large areas of Western Europe has helped to break down the old pattern of heavy industrial regions restricted to the coalfields in favour of a widespread and flexible distribution of industry.

At present there are four grid systems: Nordel covering Scandinavia, UCPTE covering 12 nations in continental Europe, the British system and the IPS/UPS system of the former Soviet bloc. Only Eire stands alone. Within the system the transmission networks of member nations are synchronised to keep the whole system at the same steady frequency. This has led to the trading of electricity between grid members – e.g. France exports more than 60 terrawatt hours of electricity per year. The four separate systems are also interconnected, e.g. the UK is linked with UCPTE via a cable beneath the English Channel, and the IPS/UPS system also is linked with UCPTE via Austria and Germany. The idea of a single energy market where large industrial users of energy can buy their supplies of power from anywhere in the EU is consistent with the Single European Market.

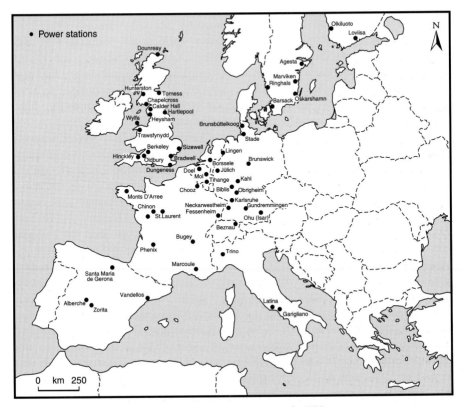

FIGURE 2.9   *Nuclear and hydro-electric power capacity in the EU*

However, the ability to trade electricity is now encountering problems partly due to differences of opinion over the deregulation of electricity. The UK wants competing generators of electricity to sell to a number of buyers by renting out transmission lines, whereas the French are concerned that this will undermine their state-owned industry. Price differences across the EU present many opportunities – e.g. German industrial consumers are eager to import cheaper electricity, and UK generators like National Power and Powergen are keen to sell electricity abroad.

NUCLEAR ENERGY

Nuclear energy was seen by many as the long-term energy source of the future, but there are enormous problems of pollution and waste disposal still to be overcome. Its economics are related to the availability and efficiency of competing fossil fuels. Its great advantages are that its fuel, uranium, is needed in relatively small quantities and is therefore easily transportable. Its main use is for the generation of electricity, that most flexible form of secondary energy. The drawbacks of nuclear energy include safety factors, disposal of nuclear waste and the uncertain research factor. Plutonium, in particular, remains radioactive for periods up to 200 000 years.

Geographical locations for nuclear power stations are dominated by the need for cooling facilities, remoteness from major population centres, and the provision of electricity in energy-deficient areas. Coastal areas and large rivers are therefore ideal. When the pressures of development lead to sites being close to centres of population, such as Stade near Hamburg, then social, political and environmental objections arise.

The UK led the world with its installation of nuclear power stations (fig. 2.9). As a highly industrialised country with an independent military deterrent, major research capability, declining coal production and large oil imports, it has had a long-term nuclear programme since the 1950s. Magnox Mark I reactors were followed by the Mark II, or advanced gas–cooled reactor (AGR), built at Dungeness 'B', Hinkley 'B', Hunterston 'B' and Hartlepool. The second-generation AGRs are much larger than the original power stations, but these have been subject to long delays because of development problems. In 1994 Sizewell B in Suffolk (the UK's first pressurised water reactor – PWR) was completed. There are now only 16 major nuclear power stations in the UK. Three commercial Magnox stations have been shut down and are being decommissioned (Berkeley on the Severn estuary was closed in 1989, and Trawsfynydd in North Wales and Hunterston A in Scotland were closed in 1993). This is in addition to the Steam Generating Heavy Water Reactor prototype at Winfrith which was closed in 1990, the AGR at Windscale which only ran as a research facility for the UK Atomic Energy Authority between 1961 and 1981, and the prototype fast breeder reactor at Dounreay which was shut down in 1991.

Sizewell B nuclear power station in Suffolk

All of the remaining Magnox reactors are likely to be closed by 2005. The nuclear capacity in 1993 contributed 22 per cent of the national electricity supply, but by 2020 nuclear power may only contribute 1 per cent.

Euratom was set up as one of the original institutions of the Common Market, with its aim being the coordination of nuclear-energy production and research. During the 1960s, however, its work was severely curtailed by a lack of funds and by the lack of urgency because of cheap and abundant oil. In 1970 installed nuclear capacity in the EEC was minimal compared to that in the UK.

However, the oil shock of 1973 gave a major boost to nuclear power programmes, and new construction was considered necessary and desirable. Large new installations, particularly in Germany and France, boosted this capacity to 10 000 megawatts by the end of 1977, thus supplying nearly 10 per cent of the total electricity generation. The energy costs of the 1970s, and particularly the rise in the price of oil, stimulated a major programme of research and development.

Nuclear power's contribution to electricity production rose considerably in the 1970s and 1980s, but generating capacity is expected to peak in the latter part of the 1990s. The pattern of development has been rudely interrupted by the nuclear accident at Chernobyl in the former USSR in 1986. The effects of the disaster triggered a slow retreat from nuclear energy. Controversy is widespread and has made it likely that only France and possibly the UK will construct any more nuclear plants in the foreseeable future. The share of nuclear power in energy production is likely to decline in the early twenty-first century as plant is decommissioned. In the early 1990s the German government closed all the nuclear stations in East Germany in response to fears over safety, and one of the new EU members, Sweden, which currently obtains 40 per cent of its electricity from nuclear stations, has declared its intention to close all plants by 2010. A moratorium on new nuclear plants in Spain has left five new stations unfinished until 2000 at the earliest. Only France continues to have a strong commitment to nuclear power. Since 1974, 56 reactors have been built, and it is planned to have 60 by the end of the twentieth century. In 1993, 75 per cent of France's electricity was produced by nuclear power.

RENEWABLE ENERGY SOURCES (RES)

Coal, oil and gas (collectively referred to as 'fossil fuels') and nuclear power are now dominant as commercial energy sources in the EU. This group of fuels comes under the heading of 'conventional' energy supplies. In recent years questions have been raised about the sustainability of an energy policy that relies on finite resources and creates a legacy of environmental pollution for future generations.

The search for alternative energy supplies to 'conventional' energy supplies has focused on the development of 'renewable energy resources' – RES – the main ones being hydro, tidal, wave, wind and solar power, biomass and geothermal energy. These are obtained by harnessing energy in the natural environment, e.g. a wind turbine extracts the natural kinetic energy of the wind and transforms it into electricity and low-temperature heat. Currently, the EU obtains only about 5 per cent of its energy requirements from RES, but during the next century this is expected to increase to meet 8 per cent of total primary energy demand by 2005.

However, the importance of RES in the different Member States varies considerably. In Luxembourg RES are the only indigenous sources available, and in Portugal RES cover 96.4 per cent of primary energy production due to the availability of hydro-power and extensive forests, and limited fossil fuel resources. The contribution of RES to primary energy production is also important in Italy (31.3 per cent), Spain (18.5 per cent), Greece (18.3 per cent), France (14.2 per cent) and Denmark (10.7 per cent). On the other hand RES is well below the EU average contribution in the case of the UK (0.5 per cent) and the Netherlands (1.4 per cent).

Biomass combustion and hydro-electric power have been a significant part of EU energy supply for some time. In the 1970s and 1980s the energy supplied by these sources saw significant growth. At the same time energy supplied from other renewable sources also grew quickly.

Hydro-electric power (HEP) is the largest and oldest form of renewable energy used in the EU. Its contribution to the electrical energy balance of each country varies considerably from 45 per cent in Luxembourg through to 29 per cent in Portugal and 0.1 per cent in the Netherlands. In some countries HEP is very significant; for example, in France, the Alps, Massif Central and Rhône valley (fig. 2.10) are the principal areas of generation. However, the scope for generation is limited as the best sites have already been harnessed and there is often considerable opposition from local people and environmentalists to the flooding of areas often located away from where the power is needed. The three new entrants to the EU are not likely to alter this picture. Proposals to build a large hydro-electric dam on the Danube at Hainburg in Austria were withdrawn in 1985 when protesters objected on the grounds that the riverside forest at the site was one of the last remaining stretches in Europe.

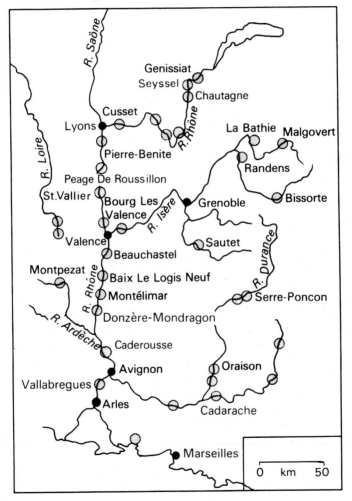

FIGURE 2.10 *Hydro-electric power in the Rhône valley*

Tidal power is best harnessed at sites where there is a funnel-shaped estuary and where a wave occurs as the tide moves up and down. The Rance estuary in Brittany has supplied the French grid system for over 25 years from turbines in a dam near St Malo. A similar scheme is in operation on the Shannon in Eire. There are several other possible sites, with the best found along the west coast of Portugal, France, Eire and the UK. The latter has the potential for over *half* of the total European tidal resources. A barrage across the Severn estuary would generate the equivalent of 2.5 large power stations. Other possible sites include the Mersey estuary and Morecambe Bay. However, again, the number of potential sites in the EU is limited, and there has been considerable opposition from environmentalists to the loss of high-grade wetland sites.

Wave power can be extracted on the shoreline (by constructing devices on cliffs or in gullies), in the near-shore waters (by devices fixed to the sea bed) or in deep water (again, by floating devices). The only devices to have been developed so far in the EU for grid power production have been for shoreline generation, e.g. on the Island of Islay in Scotland, but it is estimated that a country like the UK could generate 20 per cent of its electricity from wave power.

Wind power is a very old form of renewable energy that is seeing a significant revival. It has been developed to a much greater extent than wave power, either from wind farms (such as at Llandinam in Wales) or from individual wind generators (such as on the Greek islands). Denmark is the largest generator of electricity from wind energy in the EU, accounting for 70 per cent of the installed capacity. Sizeable subsidies were given by the Danish government during the late 1970s and early 1980s, which boosted the industry.

Electric wind turbines in Newquay, Cornwall

Solar power has provided an invaluable solution to the problem of supplying hot water (using active solar devices) to temporary tourist populations in remote rural areas of Greece, Spain and Portugal. Climatic conditions in other parts of the EU are not as suitable, but in these cases *passive* solar energy is nevertheless being developed. This involves maximising the entry of solar radiation and preventing the loss of heat so that heat from lighting, cooking and the occupants themselves can be used to assist in the heating of a building. Approximately 40–50 per cent of EU energy is used in buildings, so that such passive solar energy and low-energy design could reduce the amount of energy required quite significantly.

Geothermal energy (using heat from the earth to heat water) is most developed in Italy where over 50 geothermal units are in operation. Natural steam to drive turbines was first used in Italy in 1904, and this is the only country in which geothermal energy contributes significantly to electricity production (but only, however, to the extent of 1.6 per cent). Smaller amounts are produced in other parts of the EU including France (Guadeloupe), Portugal (the Azores), Greece and Germany. However, lower-temperature aquifer sources can also be used, and these provide district heating, as in part of Paris and in the former East Germany.

Biomass (or biofuel) can also be considered under the heading of RES, but as it encompasses many long-standing fuels such as firewood, which have been over-exploited in the past, care must be taken when considering this renewable resource. In Europe during the Second World War more than 1 million vehicles were powered by producer gas (a mixture of carbon monoxide, methane and hydrogen generated by the partial burning of any combustible material with a limited supply of oxygen). New research into many of these old techniques shows that they perform all the tasks of conventional fossil fuels, produce no net increase in emitted carbon dioxide and generally have little pollution emission. A further advantage is that they can make good use of the surplus agricultural land in the EU by providing new income-generating opportunities for farmers.

Within the EU, wood, straw and municipal solid waste are the most commonly used biofuels, with wood forming the greatest proportion. France is by far the largest consumer of wood, taking 45 per cent of the EU total due to the large proportion of wood-burning stoves in rural areas. The main consumer of straw for energy is Denmark where there are over 12 000 straw-burning stoves on farms and over 30 district heating schemes using straw. Biomass provides 5.8 per cent of Denmark's total primary energy requirements, and the government intends to increase this to 9 per cent by the year 2000. The most widely used method of recovering energy from municipal solid waste (MSW) is incineration. The other rapidly expanding major source of energy is landfill gas.

Biogas consists mostly of methane produced from the anaerobic digestion of organic residues. Agricultural waste, sewage and a variety of liquid industrial effluents can be treated anaerobically. The technology required is widespread at sewage works, and it is expected to be used increasingly in treating food-industry waste and slurry from intensive livestock farming.

Member States currently using biogas to any extent are Italy, the UK, Denmark and the Netherlands, due to their livestock farming industries.

The development of energy crops is closely tied to the Common Agricultural Policy (CAP). Set-aside land, which farmers must put to a use other than food production, makes energy crops an attractive option. Wood could be sustainably harvested or coppiced. Biofuels may also be produced from energy crops. The Netherlands is investigating using feedstocks such as elephant grass, poplar wood or straw for gasification to a fuel for use in electricity-generation plants. In Italy biodiesel is being produced from feedstocks of rapeseed and soya.

The conservation, or more efficient consumption, of energy has become just as important as the search for alternative sources. This ranges from the development of reduced-fuel-consumption engines to the recycling of industrial raw materials and combined heat and power (CHP) schemes. Public opinion and international agreement is now demanding sustainable lifestyles into the twenty-first century, and much thought is being given to calculating the real costs of much of our current energy production and consumption patterns. Decisions to restrict private car use and expand public transport are one example of this.

The EU's ALTENER (Alternative Energy) Programme was set up in 1993 to develop RES and is seen as evidence of the EU's firm commitment to promoting sustainable energy sources in the aftermath of the UN's Earth Summit in Rio de Janeiro in June 1992. The Programme has the objectives of increasing the extent of renewable energy's contribution to total primary demand from the current 5 per cent to 8 per cent by 2005, of tripling the production of electricity from RES, and of securing for biofuels a market share of 5 per cent of total fuel consumption by motor vehicles. Other programmes supporting RES include JOULE, THERMIE and VALOREN.

TOWARDS AN EU ENERGY POLICY

The reduction in the importance of coal, matched by a rapid rise in oil consumption and the growing use of natural gas and nuclear energy, together with the local importance of renewable energy sources, has created a great variety of choice of energy sources in the EU of the 1990s (fig 2.2). Since the 1950s energy self-sufficiency has become a thing of the past. This reduction in indigenous supplies leads, however, to a dependence upon global supplies where stability of supply is not assured. The difficulties of formulating a common energy policy have been obvious since the Paris summit meeting of 1972. The irony is that the ECSC and Euratom were two of the earliest agencies of European integration. The abundance of oil and the diversification of energy supplies during the 1960s meant that attitudes to energy planning were unprepared for 1973. The oil crisis and its aftermath provided a great incentive for an energy policy but also illustrated a great divergence of interest amongst the Member States. National attitudes and the balance of energy consumption vary according to resource endowment, trading policy, research and investment. Italy and France are energy deficient and keen to secure access to energy at the lowest possible price. The UK, as a major oil producer, would like to see a minimum price for oil. The Netherlands and Germany would like an open energy market. Spain, Greece and Portugal are energy deficient, and with major economic development programmes, their increasing requirement for energy imports is altering the EU energy balance. The climates and high living standards of Austria, Finland and Sweden mean that they have a high per capita energy consumption, but they are also highly dependent on imported energy, with significant imports from Eastern Europe in the case of Austria and Finland. However, Sweden and Austria are very advanced in their policies towards environmental sustainability.

	Belgium	Denmark	Eire	France	Germany	Greece	Italy	Luxemb'rg	Netherlands	Portugal	Spain	UK	EU (12)
Coal	21.8	88.6	57.1	5.2	54.9	72.2	9.9	nil	31.4	28.9	37.2	59.6	36.4
Petroleum	2.6	4.5	15.7	1.2	3.0	20.4	50.1	5.2	4.4	39.7	8.3	7.6	9.7
Natural gas	13.0	3.6	20.6	0.8	7.1	0.1	16.7	42.1	57.4	0.5	1.3	3.6	7.2
Other	1.9	nil	nil	0.1	0.9	nil	0.9	7.9	1.4	2.0	0.2	0.6	0.6
Thermal power stations total:	39.3	96.7	93.4	7.3	65.9	92.7	77.6	55.2	94.6	71.1	47.0	71.4	53.9
HEP/wind	1.5	3.3	6.6	15.0	4.3	7.3	20.8	44.8	0.4	28.8	17.1	1.9	9.6
Geothermal power	nil	nil	nil	nil	nil	nil	1.6	nil	nil	0.1	nil	nil	0.2
Nuclear power	59.2	nil	nil	77.7	29.8	nil	nil	nil	5.0	nil	35.9	26.7	36.3

FIGURE 2.11 *Electricity production in the EU (12), 1993 (percentage)*

The Commission estimates that world oil prices will continue to rise in the long term, with periodic fluctuations in supply and demand making costs unstable. The North Sea and wider continental-shelf supplies of oil and natural gas are vital for several decades to come, but increasingly will only partially counteract the deficiency in the EU as a whole. The Bremen European Council in July 1978 stressed the need for coordination and a common energy policy. The Commission's medium-term guidelines for 1985 suggested urgent action to support the EU's coal industry, exploration and development of new indigenous sources of oil, gas and uranium, an increase in the role of natural gas, steady development of nuclear generating capacity, and a drastic reduction in the EU's dependence on imported oil. The Council resolution of 17 December 1974 laid down that by 1985 the EU's dependence on imported energy should be reduced from 61 per cent (1975) to 50 per cent, and possibly to 40 per cent. There should be a more efficient use of energy with a corresponding reduction in overall consumption of 15 per cent, an increase in the share of indigenous natural gas to 25 per cent of the primary energy total, an increase in the role of electricity, and the generation of 75 per cent of electricity from indigenous solid fuels and nuclear power. Fig. 2.2 illustrates the real difficulties of achieving these figures. In 1993 oil and coal were still consumed at levels above those in the 1985 objectives. Between 1985 and 1992, primary energy consumption increased by 16.4 per cent – an average annual increase of 2.4 per cent. Over the same period primary energy production increased by only 5.1 per cent. These two factors resulted in an increase in EU net imports of energy of 34 per cent between 1985 and 1992.

The EU's energy policy has undergone something of a change in emphasis over recent years. Where it used to be concerned almost exclusively with security of supply, it now has two further objectives (or pillars): to develop alternative sources of energy (so as to minimise the impact on the environment) and to develop a single market in energy (i.e. to enable consumers to buy their power from wherever they choose).

In terms of security of supply, the Commission predicts that oil will continue to account for the largest share (45 per cent) of the EU's energy consumption up to the year 2000. Over 70 per cent of the oil consumed in the EU is imported. Natural gas is also becoming increasingly important in the energy balance, and over the medium to long term it too will be progressively supplied by imports. The ending of the Cold War and the progression of the peace process in the Middle East give grounds for hope that there will be a sound political framework for establishing stable energy relations. However, energy security cannot be taken for granted, and the Commission is considering cooperative crisis mechanisms, such as the creation of a strategic oil reserve. The European Economic Area agreement (EEA) with the countries of the European Free Trade Area (EFTA) enables the EU to gain access to alternative energy supplies, such as the Norwegian Continental Shelf. The new democracies of Eastern and Central Europe and the Republics of the former USSR are also a potential source of energy, and through the European Energy Charter (adopted in December 1991), it is hoped that economic recovery in the former Soviet Union and Eastern Europe will be triggered by a joint effort to develop the region's energy resources and modernise its energy industries, thus expanding the trade in energy. It is estimated that in Western Siberia alone only 40 per cent of the total potential oil and 43 per cent of the gas has been found and that only 9 per cent of the oil and 3 per cent of the gas has been produced.

The development of alternative energy sources is largely seen as a non-fiscal method of reducing the impact of energy on the environment: in particular, the use of alternative energy sources should limit CO_2 emissions and reduce other pollution problems, for example acid rain and marine pollution. The non–fiscal proposals include a package of initiatives, for example the research and development programme JOULE and programmes such as THERMIE, ALTENER and SAVE (Specific Actions for Vigorous Energy efficiency). The fiscal proposals mainly concern the development of a carbon/energy tax. The main purpose of this tax is to shift demand away from the most polluting fuels. A second fiscal proposal is to reduce the excise duties on biofuels.

The third objective or pillar of the current EU energy framework is the single energy market. The aim is to eliminate barriers to the free flow of energy supplies within the EU. This will have the effect of increasing energy trade between the Member States, and will help to integrate their energy systems. However, progress here has been slow.

The Commission produced a Green Paper on energy policy entitled *For a European Union Energy Policy* in January 1995. The fact that this returns to many of the same issues that have been covered by previous policies suggests that an EU energy policy still has a long way to go.

3

EMPLOYMENT: INDUSTRIAL CHANGE AND THE TERTIARY SECTOR

THE UNITED KINGDOM

The process of employment change is often dramatic, and is related to the initial decline of the primary sector during rapid industrial development and the subsequent transformation of the secondary sector as it is increasingly replaced by the tertiary or quaternary stage. The UK was the world's first modern industrial power, followed closely by Germany and in varying degrees by the other West European powers. A significant characteristic during the nineteenth century was an overwhelming reliance upon heavy and staple industries. In the 1880s the UK produced about 70 per cent of the world's ships; as late as 1907 coal, iron and steel, and textiles accounted for 46 per cent of its gross domestic product and 70 per cent of exports. The twentieth century has witnessed the relative decline of these basic industries, as they are the first stages on the road to a more mature economy. The growing complexity of industrial structure has meant that they have been supplemented by the assembly-line techniques of the car industry, the technical accuracy of the machine-tool industry, consumer-based light industries, and science-based, specialised 'hi-tech' industries. Associated with this is the increasing dispersal of location, caused largely by the freeing of industry from coalfield locations and its tendency to become 'footloose'. This chapter will also examine the rapid growth of employment in the service sector, a phenomenon of recent and variable development in the advanced industrial economies of the EU. There are four principal themes:

(a) free market factors of location;
(b) industrial production, organisation and financial factors;
(c) government intervention and supra-national factors;
(d) the growth of employment in the service sector, including tourism.

FREE MARKET FACTORS OF LOCATION

Industrial location has traditionally been affected most by the availability of energy, capital, raw materials and skilled labour, by market potential, and by transport facilities. It is the changing relative importance of these factors which sets up decline or growth in, and disparities between, regions. The extent of concentration in the nineteenth century on the older coalfield industrial areas (figs. 3.1 and 3.2) illustrates the essential importance of coal as the original location factor, due primarily to its bulk and weight, which prohibited extensive movement, but also because it suffered little competition for over a century. This is explained by Weber (1909), in whose 'least cost location' theory transport costs were usually minimised by location at the source of raw material. Significant areas of 'heavy' industry are still coalfield-located, although they owe their survival and present position partly at least to new factors which have tended to preserve geographical inertia.

The Sambre–Meuse valley, with a ribbon of settlement, coal-tips in the background and factory chimneys adding to the features of an old industrial landscape

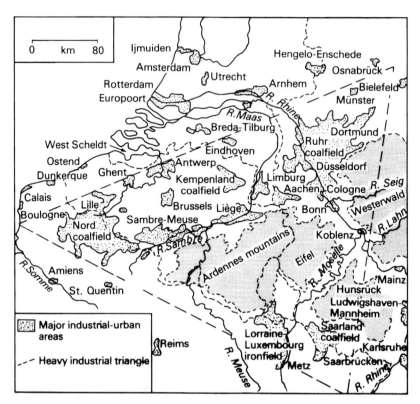

FIGURE 3.1   *The 'Heavy Industrial Triangle' of north-west Europe*

In these coalfield areas there is a predominance of heavy or staple industry, and a tendency to a distinctive single industry, based upon the original local raw materials. Such an emphasis is summed up in the term 'monotechnic'. The Ruhr, the Potteries and Liège all have this characteristic dominant industry, although less so than in the past. The age of development of such areas means they also have a large proportion of old and obsolescent housing and factories in densely populated conurbations.

The United Kingdom coalfields

On a large-scale map of the EU (fig. 3.2) the areas that were dominated by long-established heavy industry are dispersed around the margins of the highland zone of the UK. Individually, however, they are easily definable regions. Dense clusters of industry were found in central Scotland along Clydeside, in the north-east around Newcastle-upon-Tyne, and at Teesside. These were the traditional areas of heavy industry which specialised in iron and steel, shipbuilding, marine engineering, and heavy structural engineering, with chemicals particularly on Teesside. East Lancashire – centred on Manchester – and West Yorkshire were the two areas

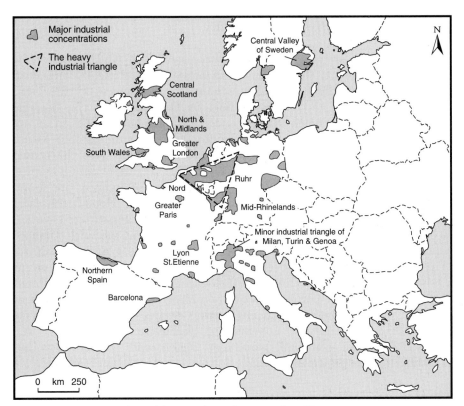

FIGURE 3.2 *Major traditional heavy industrial areas in the EU*

traditionally associated with the textile industry, but the shipbuilding and chemicals associated with Merseyside and the Sheffield steel industry were also close by. The West Midlands conurbation was originally dependent upon the steel and metallurgy of the 'Black Country', but became one of the most varied and complex engineering regions in Europe. One of the most distinctive monotechnic industrial areas in the world, the North Staffordshire coalfield, continues to produce high-quality china, pottery and earthenware goods. It deals with a high-value product in great consumer demand, and herein lies its success. The small North Wales coalfield between Wrexham and the Dee developed a small but important steel and chemical industry. The area was relatively isolated and the medium-sized Shotton steel works on Deeside was closed in 1982 as part of the rationalisation programme of the British Steel Corporation. The South Wales coalfield has been a classic example of intra-regional migration towards coastal locations such as Port Talbot and Llanelli. The end of coal production in the confined valleys of the Rhondda and Taff, combined with the low cost of imported raw materials has led to the industrial concentration of the steel, tin-plate and metal-processing industries along the coast.

The 'Heavy Industrial Triangle'

This zone is the principal area of industrial activity in which most of the coal, staple industries, steel-making and heavy engineering of continental Europe are found (fig. 3.1), and it is bounded at its apices by the Nord coalfield of France, the Ruhr coalfield of Germany, and the Lorraine iron-ore field. The French Nord/Pas de Calais region stretches in an arc from Dunkerque to Lille and through into Belgium as the Sambre–Meuse coalfield (now shut down). Mons, Charleroi and Liège were the central industrial foci in the Sambre–Meuse valley and are still important for textiles, heavy metallurgy, chemicals and glass. Extensions of industry are found north-east in the Kempenland, a more recently developed concealed coalfield that is also now shut down, where Genk and Hasselt are chemical and metallurgical centres. Across the Dutch border was the small Limburg coalfield, around Maastricht, and in Germany lies the small Aachen coalfield. The Ruhr has the greatest concentration of all, and extends from its Duisburg–Dortmund axis south to Cologne and north towards Münster. The southern apex of Lorraine, based upon Minette iron ores and a modern coalfield, includes the steel and engineering centres of Nancy, Thionville and Metz, and extends into Luxembourg. Slightly to the north-east is the Saarland, an old coal and metallurgy region with Saarbrücken and Volklingen as the principal towns.

The Nord/Pas de Calais coalfield

The Nord/Pas de Calais coalfield provides a useful case study which illustrates decline and change in these old manufacturing zones in the twentieth century. In 1962 it had over half its total employment (335 000 out of 607 000) in three staple industries: coal, steel and metallurgy, and textiles. The coalfield, stretching from Bruay to Valenciennes (fig. 3.3) has been badly affected, with coal production falling from 27 million tonnes in 1961 to 15 million tonnes in 1971 and to 2 million tonnes in 1986. The last mine closed in 1991, as it was a very high-cost coalfield. The seams were thin and disturbed, productivity was low and reserves were practically exhausted. The legacy of the area is a cluster of small mining towns known as 'cités minières' with all the environmental disadvantages of obsolescence and a need for urban renewal. The Nord is referred to as the 'Pays Noir'.

The textile industry lies mainly to the north of the coalfield itself at Lille, Roubaix, Tourcoing and Armentières. It was based on wool and cotton and experienced severe contraction, with employment reduced from 224 000 in 1931 to 168 000 by 1954, and to 34 000 by 1991. Foreign competition, a slowness to adapt and introduce up-to-date machinery, and loss of markets to synthetic fibres are the main causes in this decline, resulting in the closure of many small firms and regrouping of others.

The Douai–Valenciennes area was traditionally the centre of the steel and heavy metallurgical industries, with specialised steel and machinery to the

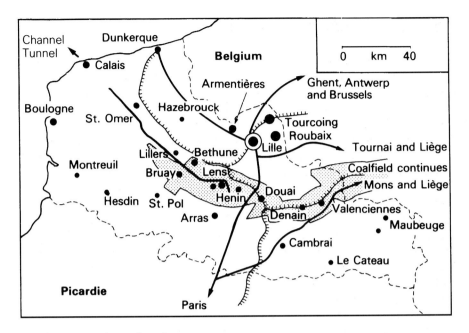

FIGURE 3.3   *Nord/Pas de Calais region*

south in Arras, Cambrai and Maubeuge. Employment has declined, except on the coast where there is a modern integrated steelworks at Dunkerque. Here is the essence of the Nord's problem. The older parts of the coalfield have an over-dependence upon heavy metallurgy. Factories are often small, are in inconvenient situations and use obsolete machinery. There is a lack of light industry and of the specialised high-value products which would help to diversify the industrial structure.

The region needs adjustment and diversification away from basic industries, together with the renewal of its equipment. It has great potential advantages, the foremost of which is that there are 60 million people within 300 km, forming a huge consumer market. A large adaptable workforce has the potential to attract capital investment on a large scale, and many new industrial estates have been sited on the coalfield towns. New industries include plastics, petrochemicals, cars and components, electronics, and consumer durables. The old canal system has been upgraded with deepwater channels taking 3000-tonne barges from Dunkerque to Lille and Paris. In addition, there is the new motorway and rail infrastructure and the link with the Channel Tunnel. The real value of the road and rail network is that it places the Nord athwart the Paris–Lille–Brussels axis. Lille is now at the very centre of a triangle covered by TGV (high-speed trains) encompassing the UK, via the Channel Tunnel, Paris, Belgium, the Netherlands, Cologne and the Ruhr region in Germany (fig. 3.4).

The crisis experienced by the run-down of the coal and steel industries led, in 1992, to Lille developing a strategic plan to capitalise on its transport strengths. The new Lille–Europe TGV station is at the heart of a city-centre

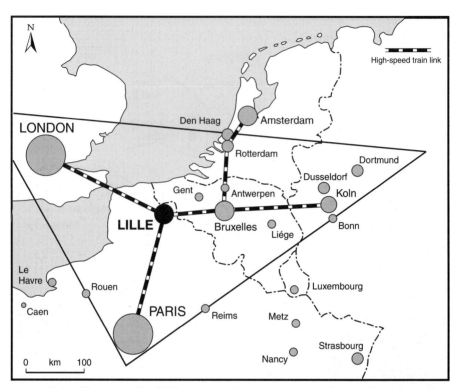

FIGURE 3.4 *The metropolis of Lille in its new European context, related to the high-speed train (TGV)*

development scheme called Euralille. This is an international business centre with exhibition halls, hotels, offices, a shopping centre and a park. Lille aims to encourage the establishment of major tertiary activities such as the regional headquarters of banks and insurance companies relocating from Brussels, Paris or London. The major French bank Credit Lyonnais has established its northern headquarters in Euralille.

Industrial adjustment

There is a continuing major significance for the coal-based industrial areas in spite of the radical changes now taking place. The process of geographical inertia is based largely upon their skilled labour supplies, traditional industrial linkages, fixed capital investment and large urban consumer market. With the commitment which national governments now have to aiding these old industrial regions, and with the EU's regional aid policy, these areas will continue to attract capital investment on a large scale. The problem of the residual staple and heavy industries, and the resulting imbalances, must be corrected by the lengthy process of diversification into new industries.

Of great significance is the position of each industrial area relative to its

The old image of Lille: crowded factories, railways and canal represent the old smoke-stack industrial landscape

national economic core. It is arguable that the Nord/Pas de Calais, Belgian Sambre–Meuse, Ruhr and West Midlands are in a favourable position, lying as they do close to the core areas and in the mainstream of activity. The north-east of England and the Scottish coalfields, both of which lie close to the oil and natural-gas resources of the North Sea, may well have a similar advantage. The North Sea littoral is certainly likely in the future to be a major area of concentration for industrial development and it may well have a revitalising effect upon these older coal-based industrial areas. By contrast, industrial regions lying on the periphery of activity within Western Europe face adjustment in a more difficult context. South Wales, the Basque region of Spain and areas around the Massif Central such as Decazeville, Alès and Commentry have no such advantages of centrality, and the process of industrial adjustment will take longer, and may not be as successful. There are particular difficulties facing those areas of East Germany experiencing de-industrialisation (Saxony has some of the highest unemployment rates).

Modern Lille, the central market square

Bochum in the Ruhr: the Opel car assembly plant

Imports of raw materials: coastal industrial locations

Imports of raw materials are becoming increasingly important. Iron ore, associated with coal in the blackband deposits of the Industrial Revolution, is now left in such small uneconomic quantities that the steel industry imports the bulk of its iron-ore. Only French Lorraine and Andalusia in Spain produce any significant quantity in Western Europe, and this is continuing to decline. Oil is the single most important element of change, but all forms of raw materials which are heavy, bulky and costly to transport overland are increasingly causing industrial concentrations to develop on coastal, estuarine and major waterway sites. Heavy processing industry, including steel, non-ferrous metals, oil-refining, chemicals and petrochemicals, cement and electrical power generation, need to be sited at low-cost importation points, with good facilities for transhipment inland and large flat sites for construction of installations. Ports are increasingly the cheapest points at which receipt, processing, manufacture and distribution can take place (fig. 3.2). These are break-of-bulk points. The sea coast from the Seine to Denmark is the single most important stretch, with Le Havre, Southampton Fawley, Dunkerque, Brugge–Zeebrugge, the Rhine estuary (Rotterdam and Antwerp), Amsterdam, Bremen–Bremerhaven and Hamburg being the main ports. On the Mediterranean coast are Tarragona, the Marseilles–Fos area, Genoa, Tarente, Venice and Trieste (figs. 3.5 and 3.6), whilst in the UK the nodal points for new heavy industry are

Antwerp: A dockside industrial zone based upon break-of-bulk with oil storage and refining, and petrochemicals

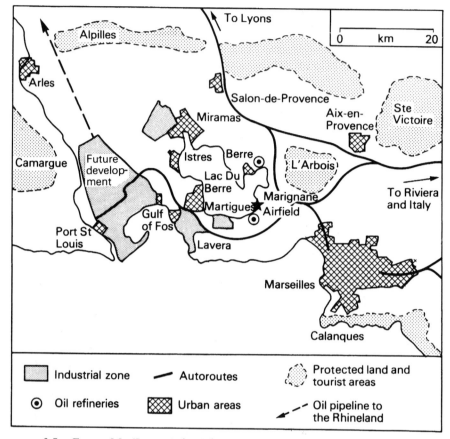

FIGURE 3.5 *Fos-sur-Mer/Lavera industrial zone*

Thamesside, Severnside, Humberside, and Southampton Water. The importance of river ports is illustrated by Rouen, Duisburg and Mannheim, which are centres of major industrial concentrations on waterside sites.

'Footloose' industry: the dispersal process

The liberation of the manufacturing industry from the confined zones of the coalfields and the coastal break-of-bulk points have been achieved by a number of factors acting in conjunction. These are: the widespread cheap transmission of electricity; the development of fast transport links – especially motorways – so that movement of raw materials is cheaper and more efficient; the growth of light industry, precision engineering and science-based industries in which a greater emphasis is placed on skilled labour than on raw materials; and improvements in technology in which the product has a higher value-added content.

Modern growth industries, vehicles and components, electrical engineering, synthetic fibres, electronic and optical equipment, all have a

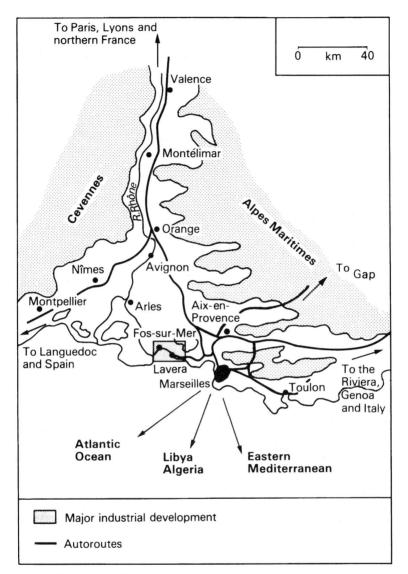

FIGURE 3.6 *The position of Marseilles*

flexible choice of location. Industry has become 'footloose' with many factors being important in the location of factories. Labour costs in a wealthy society such as that of Western Europe are often the single largest element in manufacturing overheads, whilst the consumer goods destined for the market need to be adjacent to that market, or within easy transport distance. Industrial estates are found in almost every town and city, usually as part of a planned expansion of employment during the last three decades when the population was growing rapidly. They have facilities such as road layout, electrical power, water and sewage supply, and standard factory units close to suburbs and housing estates. They often have commercial and retail facilities

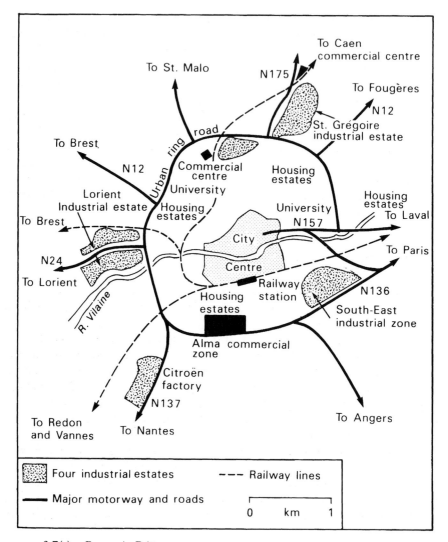

FIGURE 3.7(a) *Rennes in Brittany*

such as hypermarkets, and are sited on the periphery of the town in close proximity to major routeways for improved access.

Rennes in Brittany illustrates modern industrial estate development as an example of industrial dispersal and mobility. It is the capital city of Brittany and lies in a rich agricultural area, the Rennes basin (fig. 3.7(a)). It is a bridge-point on the Vilaine River and has developed as a market, administrative and cultural centre. Its population 30 years ago was about 70 000, but it has experienced dramatic growth since then and now has a population of 245 000. It lies on the main routeways passing into and through Brittany, including the main railway link from Paris to Brest, the north–south road links from St Malo to Nantes, and the east–west roads, the

N24 to Lorient and the N12 to Brest. It lies closest of all towns in Brittany to Paris and is now linked to Paris by the motorways A11 and A81. It was selected by the French government as a growth point for industrial investment in the 1960s. The old city has been encircled by an urban motorway, the Rocade N130, and large industrial estates have developed at access points (fig. 3.7(a)). St Gregoire industrial estate lies at the junction of the St Malo road with the Rocade, the Lorient industrial estate containing the Citroën car works on the western side on the N24, and the south-east industrial estate at Chantepie, whilst to the south on the Route de Nantes lies the second Citroën car works. The Lorient industrial estate is the largest, with a great variety of vehicle components, engineering, light and consumer industry to be found (fig. 3.7(a)). The two Citroën factories employ over 16 000 workers.

Manufacturing in cities

The most significant positive development relating to market and labour-supply factors has been the growth of major manufacturing areas associated with large centres of population, in particular economic core cities and capital cities which are prestige centres acting as the administrative, commercial and financial centres of the country, and the centres of the transport network. Greater Paris, Greater London, Brussels, Frankfurt, Copenhagen and Milan all have one major resource: population. Labour requirements are well-qualified graduates for technical research and managerial staff, and a pool of skilled labour and technicians for the operation of complex machinery.

Mass-market production techniques require areas with a high purchasing power and with an income level above average. Finally, the complexity of modern industry, needing frequent contact and movement by executives, requires good communications and locations near motorways and airports. All these factors have tended to favour the growth of manufacturing in and around the cities of Europe.

The 'minor industrial triangle' of Milan–Turin–Genoa in Northern Italy owes its origins to the accumulation of capital from trade in the medieval city states of the Plain of Lombardy. A range of historical and geographical advantages (see chapter 16) for Northern Italy has meant that it, rather than the national capital city of Rome, has become the industrial core of the country.

Other major city regions are those in the middle Rhineland, such as Frankfurt, and the southern German cities of Munich, Stuttgart and Nuremberg, noted for their wide range of high-value components and precision engineering. The cities of Lower Saxony, particularly Hanover and Brunswick, are important for vehicles and components. In the former GDR, Leipzig and Dresden in the Land of Sachsen and the area around Berlin are the most important industrial cities. Greater Lyons, second city of France in terms of population, stands in the centre of the Rhône–Saône corridor. Originally a

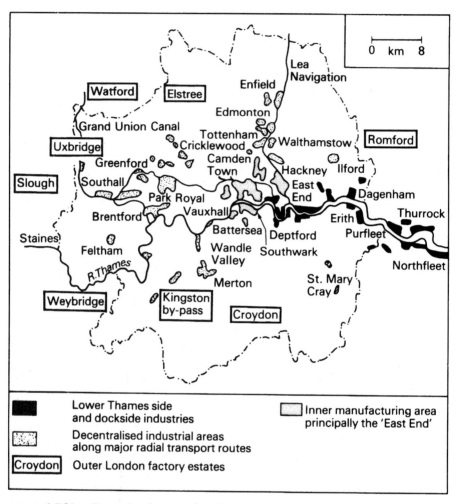

FIGURE 3.7(b)   *Greater London manufacturing areas*

silk manufacturing centre, it has become important for engineering, metallurgy and chemicals, with an impressively varied industrial structure.

Greater Paris and Greater London are capital cities of world rank, and have an extremely varied manufacturing base. Their political, financial and commercial wealth has been responsible for the creation of a 'metropolitan structure of industry'. This includes a complete range of industrial types over the whole city, ranging from the heavy industry of the port areas to the specialised industries of the central area.

The industrial structure of London and its region

A study of six type zones illustrates the factors involved in the concentration of manufacturing in a major capital city (fig. 3.7(b)).

1 **Central London.** The central areas of metropolitan cities contain activities which are a reflection of their position in national life. The manufacture of fashionable clothes, jewellery and other luxury goods is often carried out very close to the marketing centre, as in the West End of London adjacent to Oxford Street and Bond Street. The publishing and printing of periodicals and newspapers is another specialised industry which is carried out in the City of London, although this has been subject to considerable migration out to modern sites in the redeveloped docklands.

2 **Inner London, 'The East End'.** This was another nucleus of London's industry in the nineteenth century, with a crescent of small workshops from Whitechapel through Bethnal Green and Hackney to Finsbury, Clerkenwell and Camden Town. Sixty years ago the bulk of London's industry lay within this area, but considerable migration has taken place out of the cramped quarters and decayed inner suburbs to outer London and the New Towns. The East End is, however, still a major element in London's industrial geography. The main industries are clothing and furniture, food, drink and tobacco, printing and specialised instrumental engineering. The most interesting feature is the distinctive pattern of 'quarters', as in Whitechapel which has small-scale workshops in adapted and congested premises devoted to clothing manufacture.

3 **Thamesside.** This is a most distinctive zone with a role as the transhipment point for the primary processing industries. The docks have migrated down river from the original port in the Pool of London above Tower Bridge past Woolwich to Dagenham and to Lower Thamesside at Purfleet, Thurrock and Northfleet. The evolution of this zone typifies that of all the European estuary-based port areas: the decline of the inner areas and the movement outwards to deep water terminals near the open sea. London docks are now at Tilbury, and the former docks from Wapping to the Royal group of docks are the focus of a very dramatic redevelopment programme, the LDDC (London Docklands Development Corporation). The heavier and more noxious industries are downstream: vehicles at Dagenham, and cement, explosives, paper-making, oil refining, and petrochemicals out through Northfleet and as far as the Isle of Grain.

4 **Radial transport lines.** Decentralisation along main roads and railway lines followed the growth of transportation facilities. Significant industrialisation occurred between 1900 and 1914 in the Lea valley, from Tottenham and Edmonton towards Enfield, with the introduction of workmen's train fares and the growth there of working-class housing. Much of the former East End industry migrated there, in a linkage process along the nearest line of communication. The move from cramped inner areas was also a powerful factor in the growth of these manufacturing sites along radial railway lines. Much of the industry in the Lea valley is a natural continuation of that of the East End: furniture, clothing and shoes, supplemented by electrical engineering. Most of the other areas with

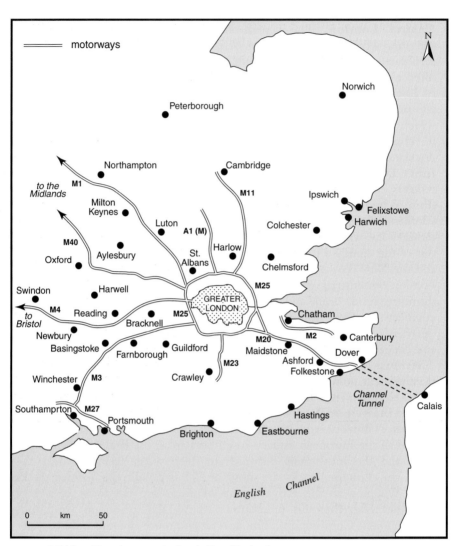

FIGURE 3.7(c)   *Growth centres in South-East England*

factory concentrations, particularly those in West London, depend upon road transport: Colindale and Cricklewood on the Edgware Road; Park Royal, Perivale, Wembley and Greenford along the A40 and Western Avenue; and Brentford, Feltham, Yiewsley and West Drayton along the A4/M4 section to the west of the city. The Great West Road illustrates the great variety of planned factories. Here, engineering products, particularly electrical, are dominant, but there are also consumer goods needing a large market, labour supply and efficient communications (e.g. branded foods, pharmaceuticals, cosmetics, plastic kitchenware, radio and scientific instruments, refrigerators).

5 **Factory estates in Outer London.** A more recent growth, these show many similarities to type **3**, being usually along radial routes, but they

have often been planned to take account of the movement of population out of London, and the associated labour supply. Croydon, Staines, Uxbridge and Elstree are examples, with mainly light- and consumer-goods factories. The movement of industry out into London's new towns is also part of this process. Perhaps the best example of an outer industrial estate is, however, Slough, one of the first trading estates established in the 1930s.

6 **New industry in the city region.** A tendency of an outward dispersal of industry into the smaller towns and rural areas both surrounding and accessible to the city is a feature of the contemporary industrial scene. Higher operating costs, shortage of space and expensive labour costs in the city have led to a relocation of industry along the major motorways and to industrial growth in places such as Reading, Swindon, Winchester, Basingstoke and Newbury. Motorways such as the M4 or M11 are sometimes referred to as the 'sunrise strip' because they provide access to the facilities of London, proximity to London's airports, and a high quality of life, and have a large catchment area for skilled workers. Computers, precision engineering, biotechnology and electronics are amongst the wide range of hi-tech industry which has been attracted to these areas. The 'Cambridge effect', the grouping of hi-tech companies in 'science parks' around the research facilities of the university, has led to Cambridge becoming one of the fastest growing industrial towns in England (fig. 3.7(c)). The crescent of growth stretching from Portsmouth to Oxford, Cambridge and Felixstowe, is being supplemented by the effects of the Channel Tunnel in Kent, Sussex and Surrey.

THE ORGANISATION, CONTROL AND FINANCING OF INDUSTRIAL PRODUCTION

Basic structural changes in industry have often been accompanied by locational changes as the small workshops of the nineteenth century have become the large factories and the vast corporations of today. Many of the problems of industrial areas such as Lancashire or the Franco–Belgian coalfield arise from the decline of staple industries like cotton and their replacement by sophisticated industries such as radio and electronics, often not tied to the same location. The key to structural changes lies in the economies of scale which can be achieved by mass production, integration of the means of production, and large-scale capital investment, research and technology in industry. The large units are exemplified by giant corporations such as British Petroleum, Imperial Chemical Industries or Volkswagenwerk (fig. 3.8). These giant corporations have an important geographical effect in that they tend to intensify core–periphery contrasts. Although they establish branch factories in peripheral regions, their principal investment tends to be directed towards 'leader' regions as they maintain their headquarters and market effort in core city regions such as London, Paris, Amsterdam, Milan and Cologne.

Mass production and the specialisation of labour

The many stages required by the assembly of components, the increasing substitution of labour by machinery, and the concentration of processes in large factories have led to high capital costs and a need for continuing large-scale investment. Integration of related processes occurs as a means of cutting costs of production and increasing efficiency. Horizontal integration is the control by one group of most or all of the productive capacity in one stage of manufacturing. Added to this is vertical integration where in many cases economies can be made by bringing together successive stages of manufacture. Substantial savings in fuel, transport and other overheads give increased efficiency, lower costs of production and economies of scale. Ford Motors (UK) have a vertically integrated plant at their Dagenham factory capable of producing cars through all stages of manufacture and assembly. The synthetic-fibres group Courtaulds illustrates both aspects of integration very well. They have a 'Northern Textiles Division' to coordinate their control of over one-third of Lancashire cotton spindles. In addition, they also control production stages running from the raw materials (wood pulp and chemicals) to the initial production stages (spinning, weaving, knitting and bonded synthetic fabrics) and finishing (dyeing, printing, hosiery, garments and marketing) as well as textile engineering.

The assembly line, which dominates the car industry, the aircraft industry and much of the electronics industry, requires thousands of components which are produced in separate specialist factories and then transferred to the assembly factory. Industrial linkage of subsidiary component factories by transport is therefore essential, with this type of industrial association being known as 'regional swarming'. One of the best examples is the West Midlands conurbation with its associated towns having a high proportion of their industry geared to producing components for the vehicle industries of Birmingham and Coventry. Older industries such as cotton textiles, iron and steel, and shipbuilding, have for decades had a tendency to cluster in their traditional areas, where there are similar linkages.

Giant industrial corporations: multi-nationals

Multi-national corporations (MNCs) illustrate the technological advantages of size: Imperial Chemical Industries (ICI) of the UK has become a significant multi-national corporation which has almost a conglomerate structure. It controls many types of both basic and sophisticated chemical products and has over 30 wholly owned or subsidiary companies in the EU. Its world stature is illustrated by over 200 subsidiary and associated companies in the rest of the world.

Rank	Company	Headquarters	Main activity
1	Royal Dutch/Shell Group of Cos.	UK/Netherlands	Petroleum
2	IRI – Istituto per la Ricostruzione Industriale	Italy	Petroleum, engineering, chemicals
3	Daimler Benz AG	Germany	Motor vehicles
4	British Petroleum Co PLC	UK	Petroleum
5	Volkswagen AG	Germany	Motor vehicles
6	Siemens AG	Germany	Electrical engineering
7	Fiat SpA	Italy	Motor vehicles
8	Unilever Group	UK/Netherlands	Food, chemicals
9	VEBA AG	Germany	Electricity, chemicals
10	ENI – Ente Nazionale Idrocarburi	Italy	Petroleum, engineering, chemicals
11	Elf Aquitaine	France	Petroleum
12	Deutsche Telekom	Germany	Tele-communications
13	Renault	France	Motor vehicles
14	Electricité de France	France	Electricity production and distribution
15	Philips' Lamps Holding NV	Netherlands	Electronics and electrical engineering
16	Alcatel-Alsthom	France	Electrical engineering
17	Hoechst AG	Germany	Chemicals
18	PSA Peugeot Citroën	France	Motor vehicles
19	BASF AG	Germany	Chemicals
20	RWE AG	Germany	Energy production

FIGURE 3.8   *EU (12) top 20 manufacturing and service groups, 1992*

ICI operates in both chemicals and synthetic fibres in a virtual monopoly situation within the UK. The severe competition which ICI faces is from its counterparts in the United States of America, Du Pont and Procter and Gamble, and in Europe from Bayer, BASF and Hoechst. An indication of the role and power of large companies in terms of total national capacity is in the UK where the 50 largest companies produce nearly half the national turnover. An even more extreme example is the Netherlands, where 35 per cent of production is from three companies: Philips Electrical (Eindhoven), Royal Dutch Shell and Unilever NV.

Dramatic changes in structure and size have occurred with increased global competition, the dismantling of tariffs and increased production and movement throughout the EU, creating direct competition and the need for enlargement and rationalisation. In France, particularly, there has been considerable activity as the industrial structure has developed. Two steel giants, Sacilor and Usinor, are now merged into one of the larger companies in Europe. The tables of the largest EU companies and comparable American companies (figs. 3.8 and 3.9) serve to illustrate several significant facts:

Chemicals		Motor vehicles and components	
Rank	Name	Rank	Name
1	Du Pont (USA)	1	General Motors (USA)
2	Procter & Gamble (USA)	2	Ford (USA)
3	Hoechst (Germany)	3	Toyota (Japan)
4	BASF (Germany)	4	Daimler-Benz (Germany)
5	Bayer (Germany)	5	Volkswagen (Germany)
6	Imperial Chemical Industries (UK)	6	Nissan (Japan)
7	Dow Chemicals (USA)	7	Fiat (Italy)
8	Ciba-Geigy (Switzerland)	8	Chrysler (USA)
9	Rhône-Poulenc (France)	9	Renault (France)
10	Johnson & Johnson (USA)	10	Honda (Japan)

Electrical and computers		Aircraft/aerospace equipment	
Rank	Name	Rank	Name
1	IBM (USA)	1	Boeing (USA)
2	Hitachi (Japan)	2	United Technologies (USA)
3	Matsushita Electric (Japan)	3	British Aerospace (UK)
4	General Electric (USA)	4	McDonnell Douglas (USA)
5	Siemens (Germany)	5	Allied Signal (USA)
6	Samsung (Korea)	6	Deutsche Aerospace (Germany)
7	Toshiba (Japan)	7	Lockheed (USA)
8	Philips (Netherlands)	8	Aerospatiale (France)
9	Sony (Japan)	9	Kawasaki Heavy Industries (Japan)
10	Alcatel-Alsthom (France)	10	General Dynamics (USA)

FIGURE 3.9 *Table of world industrial comparisons, 1992 (turnover in ECU millions)*

(a) American companies usually head the world 'league table' by large margins, followed by Japanese companies in sectors such as cars and electrical goods.

(b) Germany, the UK, the Netherlands, France and Italy have the largest companies in the EU, reflecting the mature industrial structure of the European core.

(c) Petroleum, chemicals, motor vehicles and electrical goods are the sectors with most large companies.

(d) Ireland, Greece and Portugal have generally small-scale industry reflecting their peripheral situation and under-industrialised structure.

(e) Belgian industry is on the whole small-scale with the largest company, Petrofina, ranking sixty-ninth.

(f) Spain, too, has a relatively under-developed industrial structure, with state holding companies controlling large sectors of the economy. The largest company INI ranks thirtieth.

The survival and revival of small-scale industry

Industry in the EU is not all controlled by large companies. In fact, much of the industrial structure is small and fragmented, at least by American standards. In the member countries of the periphery, there is still a predominance of small production units, many family firms, a lack of rationalisation and the survival of small workshops. This reflects the fact that the industrial revolution in these countries has been slow, late and incomplete. However, it must be stressed that the survival of small-scale industry has been looked upon much more favourably by governments in recent years. Although the great corporations have advantages of scale and technology, nevertheless they have problems such as labour and management relations. Small companies have flexibility, fewer labour problems, and have a major part to play in the specialised production of components, in light industry, and in providing employment in rural areas. The British government is actively encouraging small factories and workshops in rural areas, through rural development agencies. Many of the new 'sunrise industries' of electronics, computers, data-processing and information technology are in relatively small factories with a limited workforce. They often deliberately locate in small towns and rural areas with a higher quality of life. The agglomeration factor in industry may now be in reverse in many sectors of the economy.

Investment and technology: research and development

Industry has moved into a sophisticated stage of development during the mid-twentieth century. The replacement of many traditional raw materials with synthetics, particularly in plastics and textiles, is one example of this. More important is the influence of high technology with certain sectors of the economy assuming key roles: space satellite technology; aero-engines and aircraft; radio and electronics; nuclear technology; automation systems; information technology; biotechnology and computers. These require vast expenditure on research, which has led to the existence of a 'technological gap' between Europe on the one hand and Japan and the USA on the other and to the invasion of Japanese and American industry into Europe in these key sectors in an attempt to control the fastest-growing industries. Comparisons can be made between the smaller national European companies and the larger Japanese and American ones (fig. 3.9). In the advanced sectors of the economy, four factors are crucial: the relatively small home-market of the EU country and the financial difficulty of sustaining projects to the stage of commercial viability; the reluctance of governments to pay indefinitely for projects costing millions of pounds; the smaller European market in military weapons; and the difficulty of countering the sales capacity of the Americans and Japanese.

European aircraft manufacturers have suffered in particular because of the great market benefit reaped by the Americans from their large military commitments and widespread use of civil aviation. The United States airforce has twice as many aircraft as all the countries of Western Europe. The USA produces 60 per cent of the world's aircraft. Nevertheless, the British, Spanish, German and French governments cooperated in the 'Airbus' project. This has been successful enough to be able to compete with the American aircraft industry.

The electronics and electrical engineering industry is one of the fastest-growing sectors of the economy. American companies dominate the field, and command about 80 per cent of the world sales in electronics, computers and telecommunications. The largest European companies are Siemens of Germany, Philips of the Netherlands and Alcatel-Alsthom of France, but even they are small compared to some of the United States giants. Europe's computer companies need to cooperate to survive. It is in this sector, with its telecommunications and automation systems, essential to the sophisticated economy, that Europe lags considerably behind the USA and Japan.

Related directly to this is the invasion by American and Japanese industry, by the injection of capital and extension of ownership and management. This investment is generally advantageous with the stimulation it brings in new factory growth and employment, higher wages and rationalisation. The real problem is when this leads to excessive outside control of key industries with its implications for dependence upon foreign technology. Cross-frontier EU mergers to create European industrial units of international size and stature serving a home market of 372 million people are necessary. Of course, investment is a multi-layered process, and EU countries, particularly the UK, are now investing in and owning large sections of American industry.

There are significant economic reasons and geographical implications for cross-frontier operations of multi-national companies. Western Europe is an affluent, mature market, with abundant skilled labour. Outside corporations need to overcome EU tariff barriers by manufacturing within its market area. Much American investment lies within the UK and the 'Golden Triangle' or leader regions of the EU. The UK gains because of its 'cultural' proximity to the USA and the absence of language barriers. Belgium is seen as a 'core' country, and the Belgian government has enthusiastically supported American investment. By way of contrast, since the recession of the mid-1970s, many multi-national subsidiary plants previously established in peripheral areas of the EU such as Spain and southern Italy, and based upon cheaper labour costs, have been closed. Production has been transferred to cheaper labour areas of the developing world. Spatially, the operation of multi-national companies illustrates the different economic potential of the core and periphery.

GOVERNMENT INTERVENTION AND SUPRA–NATIONAL FACTORS

Government intervention has occurred principally because of the need for adjustment in the complex economies of the EU countries, and has three basic aims: to control areas of production which are basic to the economy; to support prestige and high-technology industries; and to support declining industrial areas. State intervention reached its maximum extent in the 1970s in the UK, France, Italy and Spain, where extensive government control was seen as the best way to guide the economy.

Nationalised (state-controlled) industries

In the UK nationalised industries included some of the largest employers in the country. In certain areas basic to the national economy, there are advantages in state control. In theory at least, an overall planning view can be secured, national resources are available for investment, and large-scale operations can be funded nationally. An alternative view is that state companies are wasteful of public money and inefficient. Thus there has been a major reduction of the state-controlled sector during the 1980s, with many production industries and service companies returned to the private sector. These include: Jaguar Cars, British Airways, British Telecom, British Steel, Rolls-Royce Aero-engines, British Shipbuilders, British Aerospace, British Gas, water and electricity companies. Even British Rail is now being privatised.

In France the state owns and operates large sections of the economy: the Charbonnages de France (coal-mining, power stations and chemicals); the steel industry; Electricité de France; Gaz de France, SNCF (French

Railways); SNECMA (aero-engines). A variation on direct control is the Renault Car Company where government control is vested in a director-general and day-to-day running is left very much in the hands of the company management. In Italy IRI (Instituto Per La Reconstruzione Industriale) originated as a financial rescue operation in 1933 and has since grown into a state corporation which controls the telephone system (SIP), Alitalia Airways, the Autostrade (toll highways), Finmare (merchant marine), ILVA (steel), and other engineering, textile and chemical companies. Another development has been ENI (Ente Nazionale Idrocarburi), set up with the object of capitalising on the oil and gas reserves in the Po valley and having a monopoly of prospecting in Italy. With its headquarters near Milan, it now controls oil refineries, petrochemical plants, tanker fleets and oil pipelines from Pegli and Trieste to Ingolstadt in southern Germany. In Spain INI is a state holding company set up during the rapid industrial development of the 1960s and 1970s. The state controlled and owned 90 per cent of industrial companies in the former GDR. After unification, the Treuhandanstalt (Trust Agency) was set up to privatise, rehabilitate or close down these companies.

Active intervention and guidance in industry

Active intervention is even more widespread than direct government control. Where larger units have been necessary and the national interest has been at stake, persuasion and guidance has been used. In the United Kingdom aircraft industry, famous names such as Fairey, Avro, Bristol, Supermarine, Vickers and De Havilland were merged into two giants, the British Aircraft Corporation and Hawker Siddeley, subsequently nationalised and then privatised as British Aerospace. Rolls-Royce, the largest British aero-engine manufacturer, could not be allowed to disappear and so the company's bankruptcy in 1971 was annulled by the expedient of a financial takeover by the government. This has now been returned as a profitable company to the private sector. The UK government was a controlling shareholder in British Petroleum, and acquired effective control of British Leyland during the 1970s. The privatisation programme of the 1980s has seen British Petroleum become entirely private, and the Rover Car Group (formerly British Leyland), after a major slimming and rationalisation programme, was sold to British Aerospace in 1988, only to be taken over by BMW in 1994. In industries where there has been persistent intense foreign competition, and an industry has remained at an inefficient level of production with too much labour or is organised in small units more akin to those found in the nineteenth century, regrouping and controlled reduction of output is necessary. Two severe cases have been the UK textile and shipbuilding industries. The Charbonnages de France has established a gradual reduction target in the French coal industry. The French government took control of and regrouped the steel industry to save it from bankruptcy. The establishment of British hi-tech companies such as the computer technology company INMOS (later acquired by Thorn EMI in 1984) has been another aspect of government operation, as was the intervention to assist the Westland helicopter group in late 1987.

Support for declining industrial regions and relocation policies

Specific areas of severe decline have been the major preoccupation of European governments during the past four decades. The efforts of the Italian government to promote industrialisation and to raise living standards in the south have been made through IRI development projects such as integrated steelworks, paperworks, cement works and various land-improvement and marketing schemes. The most important move, however, was the setting up of the Cassa per il Mezzogiorno in 1950 (chapters 10 and 17). In France policies have been aimed at stimulating investment and attempting to persuade industry to move to those areas with contracting staple industries and those which are shedding excess agricultural workers. The Nord/Pas de Calais fits the first category, and the south and west of France the second. In the UK the designation of various development areas has been accompanied by fiscal measures to improve their attractiveness and stimulate industrial growth. Trading estates, and enterprise zones, are all part of the complex operation required to arrest industrial decline. The concept of the regional problem is, however, much wider and is dealt with more fully in subsequent chapters.

European Union industrial and competition policy

This area of operations dates from the early days of the Treaty of Rome, but has become much more interventionist and powerful since industrial problems arose in the 1970s and 1980s. Competition policy-making took on an even higher profile when the Single Market formally came into effect on 1 January 1993.

The principal aspects of this as it affects industrial policy are:

1 the free movement of all industrial goods and services throughout the market;
2 the removal of technical barriers to trade resulting from different national provisions covering quality, measurement, composition, packaging or control of goods;
3 the removal of legal and fiscal barriers, and of tax discrimination throughout the market;
4 the harmonisation of taxes, excise duties and indirect taxation;
5 the convergence of economic and monetary policies within the EMS (European Monetary System);
6 the implementation of research and technical development programmes to strengthen the scientific basis of industry;
7 the establishment of a European company statute, integration of company

law and a European trade-mark and patent system;

8 freedom of movement of capital, freedom of establishment, and the right of persons to engage in business or professions throughout the EU;

9 the opening-up of public markets so that public and local-authority contracts will be open to the EU and not just to national suppliers.

In spatial terms these will assist:

(a) cross-frontier mergers to form companies which can trade in all parts of the EU as a single unit, taking advantage of economies of scale. There has so far been limited progress in this direction. The Leyland-Innocenti vehicle agreement ended in failure. Arbed, the Luxembourg steel group, is one of the more successful examples, having additional control of Belgian and Saarland steelworks. Specific cooperation projects are an alternative, as in the successful Airbus consortium of French, British, Spanish and German aerospace companies.

(b) the restoration of competitiveness in the old declining industries of textiles, steel, footwear, and shipbuilding at a reduced level of production by rationalising plant, and the resolution of social problems by the creation of new employment in the affected areas. There are limitation agreements in imports of textiles, production quotas for steel and retraining of workers whose jobs have been lost.

(c) a reduction in disparities between regions by means of the structural funds such as the European Agricultural Guidance and Guarantee Fund (EAGGF), the ECSC Fund, the European Investment Bank (EIB), the European Social Fund (ESF) and the European Regional Development Fund (ERDF), particularly in areas with severe unemployment.

(d) investment in the high-technology industries of aerospace, electronics, data-processing, telecommunications and information technology, in sophisticated capital equipment such as machine tools, and in new energy sources such as with the nuclear research programme and the JET (Joint European Torus) project for thermo-nuclear energy established at Culham in Oxfordshire. New zones of high-technology industry are fast developing, often in city regions with good motorway access such as the London–Bristol M4 corridor, Greater Paris, and the Rhineland cities of Frankfurt and Stuttgart.

THE TERTIARY OR SERVICE SECTOR

From the mid-1950s to 1973, industrial output in the EU rose two and a half times. The manufacturing industry provides employment for about 29 per cent of the working population, and the EU is an industrial giant alongside the USA and Japan. Nevertheless since the mid-1970s a crisis has developed in large parts of the EU's industrial structure. Large-scale unemployment is widespread and many sectors of industry are under severe pressure. The rise in energy costs since the oil-price rise of 1973, ensuing inflation, rapidly rising labour costs, falling productivity and exchange rate fluctuations mean that the market share has fallen. At the same time competition from recently industrialised countries, often in the developing world, with low wage levels and modern equipment has risen dramatically. This is the new international division of labour which is now taking place. Certain old-established sectors have suffered most, including the steel industry, textiles, clothing, footwear and furniture, paper and pulp manufacture and shipbuilding. Even the automobile industry has suffered from international competition and depressed demand.

The industrial workforce has declined dramatically, particularly in the older industrial centres of the EU such as the UK and France. From 1971 to 1993 France lost 2.3 million industrial jobs, and the UK lost 3.7 million during the same period. However, until recently, industrialising countries in the southern periphery with lower labour costs, such as Greece and Portugal, were still increasing their workforce in industry.

Although there are major variations across the EU, the tertiary or service sector is now the majority employer in all cases (fig. 3.10). Levels in excess of 65 per cent in Belgium, the Netherlands, Denmark, Luxembourg, France and the UK, compared with the relatively low levels of Greece and Portugal, indicate major contrasts in levels of development.

Theorists such as Kondratieff have explained this in terms of a series of 50-year waves of economic activity, where the innovation and expansion of the post-war period lost strength and was followed by a down wave of activity which culminated in the recession and inflation of the 1970s and 1980s. One solution to this is the move into innovative hi-tech industrial functions including electronics, telecommunications, office automation, and aerospace sited in science parks in pleasant, amenity-rich world-city regions with skilled workforces and high purchasing power. The fringes of south-west Paris and the Southampton–Oxford–Cambridge crescent around London are examples of this.

The other explanation is that in the late capitalist phase in developed countries there is a shift of employment into the service sector and a blurring of the distinction between secondary, tertiary and quaternary employment. From 1971–1993 the service sector in the EU saw a net increase in employment of 43 million people. The centres of tertiary employment are in the national core areas and major cities. These cities are prestige centres, often a capital city such as London, Rome or Paris or the regional cities of Frankfurt, Munich, Barcelona or Milan. They have a large pool of skilled labour, high proportions of well-qualified graduates and highly qualified technical, scientific and professionally trained people. They are the centre of the transport network. Centrality exerts a major influence upon the location of administrative offices, and linkages between businesses, ease of attracting staff and the availability of retail and social facilities are other aspects of the positive advantages of cumulative causality. Young people are attracted to

	Agriculture	Industry	Services
Eur 12	7.4	28.6	64.0
Belgium	2.9	28.9	68.2
Denmark	5.1	26.5	68.4
Germany	3.3	37.0	59.7
Greece	20.8	23.6	55.6
Spain	9.9	30.1	60.0
France	5.2	26.9	67.9
Ireland	13.2	27.1	59.7
Italy	7.7	32.1	60.2
Luxembourg	3.2	27.0	69.8
Netherlands	4.0	23.3	72.7
Portugal	11.8	32.5	55.7
UK	2.1	27.8	70.1

FIGURE 3.10   *EU (12) employment by sector, 1994 (percentage) (source:* Eurostat*)*

the city and look for 'white collar jobs'. The city acts as the administrative, commercial and cultural heart of the country or region.

The range of tertiary employment may be classified as follows: insurance, banking and commercial services; professional, medical and law services; trade storage distribution; retail services; transport and shipping services; public utilities, publicity and sales activity; information services; scientific, education and research establishments; national and local government; cultural, travel and tourist services; offices of private industry and head offices of international corporations.

The financial sector in many EU countries was traditionally split up into various activities. However, a progressive liberalisation of the financial professions within the EU has allowed banks to play a direct role in the placement and brokerage of shares and bonds, as well as in related activities. At the same time, links between the banking and insurance professions have grown. Some insurance companies now offer credit services and payment facilities, while banks in turn offer insurance products.

A substantial degree of internationalisation in the provision of financial services has been made possible by deregulation and the revolution in communication technology. Nevertheless, London remains the centre of the financial market, in terms of both stock-market capitalisation and the volume of transactions, although Paris and Frankfurt have significantly increased their market share.

The information-services sector includes telecommunications, software and computing services and electronic information services. It is estimated that in the EU the information business already accounts for more than 5 per cent of GDP, and it is expected to be one of the largest and fastest-growing business sectors in the EU with the convergence of the telecommunications, data-processing and media industries. The main EU telecommunications network operators are Deutsche Telecom Bundespost, British Telecom, France Telecom, SIP of Italy and Telefonica of Spain. Deregulation in some Member States has led to competition in areas such as the mobile-communications market (e.g. between Racal Vodafone, Cellnet and Mercury in the UK). From 1998 all EU members, with few exceptions, will be obliged to open the market for basic telecommunication services.

London's central area

Central London is defined by Victoria Station and the Houses of Parliament on the south, Hyde Park and Paddington Station on the west, Regents Park and Euston Station on the north, and the Tower of London on the east (fig. 3.11). This large area, one of the greatest foci of commerce in the world, attracts companies because of the prestige of the address, the close contacts with other forms of business, and the facilities for national and international trade provided by road, rail and air transport. The most important area is the square mile of the City of London around the Bank of England which is devoted to banking, commerce, insurance, shipping and the commodity markets. There is also Fleet Street, the Inns of Court and the Temple, and the theatre area of Piccadilly and Leicester Square. By the river

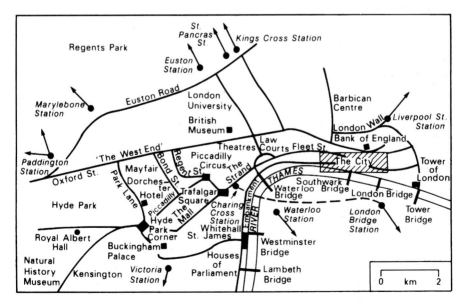

FIGURE 3.11   *Central London*

lies the distinctive administrative zone of Whitehall and St James with its public buildings, parks and palaces. Mayfair with its embassies and squares, the 'West End' retail zone of Oxford Street, Bond Street and Regent Street, and the University of London in Bloomsbury add to the picture. London is a world centre for commercial, administrative, legal, professional, cultural and diplomatic purposes. It is also a world-famous tourist city, with facilities including the museums of South Kensington, the Tower of London and the hotels of the West End. London's employment pattern is dominated by its tertiary occupations.

Tourism

Travel has been a long-term element in human activity for leisure as well as business. However, tourism, as such, is of relatively recent origin. Tours by English Victorian ladies began in the 1860s, but the increasingly mass character of tourism dates from 1945 and has moved rapidly from a national to an international scale. The most rapid growth in numbers of people was during the 1970s at a rate of over 12 per cent per annum, and by 1975 over 80 million people were visiting the Mediterranean coasts, where by far the greatest volume of tourism takes place. In 1992 the EU received 188 million tourist arrivals.

The reasons for this dramatic increase fall into several categories. Rising living standards in the EU, including both increasing amounts of surplus income and increased leisure time, are important. They are linked to important changes in psychology and social habits fostered by the effects of mass media. There is the need to escape from day-to-day pressures to a range of holidays which include the family holiday at the seaside, the cultural and historic tour, the cruise, and the physical pastimes of mountaineering, trekking and winter sports. The seasonal rhythm has been extended massively from the summer into the winter period. Infrastructural improvements are also important, ranging from hotel accommodation to self-catering and camping facilities. The single most important factor by far, however, is increased access. The railways, once crucial to the Victorian tours, have been overtaken by car ownership, the cross-channel ferry services and now the Channel Tunnel, and the European highway network, so that the French Riviera is easily accessible from the UK within 24 hours. Even more so, however, the development of Mediterranean tourism, particularly to Spain, Greece and Portugal, is related to the expansion of air transport and particularly the charter flight and package tour. The 'fly-drive holiday' is an interesting variation on these themes.

The location of tourist centres in Western Europe may be summarised by (fig. 3.12) and classified as well-established historical and cultural cities such as Florence and Seville; capital cities such as London, Berlin, Rome or Paris; winter sports in the Alpine region; scenic walking areas such as the

Auvergne, Black Forest and Ardennes; and the south-facing coastlands of the Mediterranean which stretch from Malaga to the Greek Islands. The great diversity is based upon the dramatic physical and climatic ranges within the environment, and the variations in holiday demand.

Tourism is significant in terms of the core–periphery division in the EU. It is responsible for large-scale capital transfer from the tourist demand areas of the north-western core to the peripheral Mediterranean coastlands. Employment generated by tourism in Spain involves over 10 per cent of Spain's employed population, accounting for 800 000 direct jobs and a further 540 000 indirect ones. Development has thus been encouraged in areas which have no other economic value beyond their specific environment of sun and beach or snow and mountain. The development that has taken place involves the multiplier effect with the reconstruction of the natural environment with hotels, water-supply, sewage and drainage facilities, transport infrastructure and a range of other buildings and services. Governments have used these to positive advantage in the stimulation of regional development. In spite of the advantages of tourism in regions of little alternative economic value, there are disadvantages to the local region from the tourist economy. Employment is seasonal, old social amenities have

The City of London: European and global financial and commercial centre

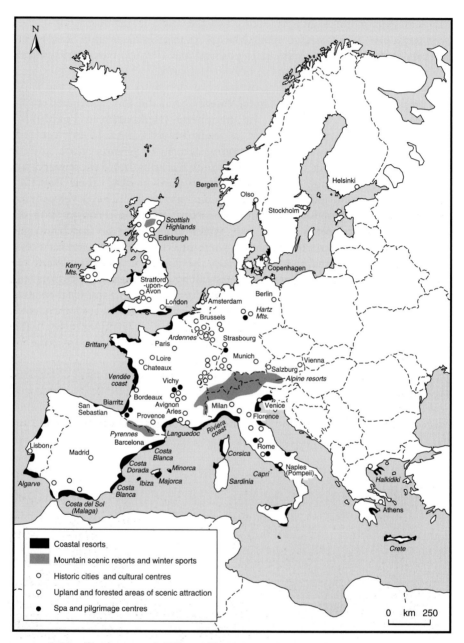

FIGURE 3.12   *Tourist centres in Western Europe*

been broken up, and there are often environmental impacts which may just be visual, e.g. the high-rise ribbon development along the coast at Benidorm in Spain, or of a more serious nature, e.g. inadequate sewage treatment and marine pollution, or deforestation in the Alps that exacerbates the avalanche problem. The international system of multi-national hotels, air charter companies and travel agencies are responsible for the influx of tourist cash, but often the profits of the enterprise are returned to the core and do not remain in the tourist region.

Tourism in Mediterranean France

Provence–Côte D'Azur has been an important tourist area since the mid-nineteenth century when the French Riviera became an attraction for wealthy English tourists. The opening of the railway from Paris in 1865 was a major stimulus to the Riviera and to the development of the now old, established resorts of Nice, Monte Carlo, Cannes and St Tropez. In addition in Provence are the Roman cities of Arles, Orange and Nîmes and the medieval cities of Avignon and Aix-en-Provence with their cultural and historic attractions, and Roman sites like the Pont du Gard aqueduct. The Camargue, the marshy section of the Rhône delta, has been established as a regional park. Tourism has developed along the whole of the Riviera coastline and extends eastwards into Liguria in Italy. Provence–Côte D'Azur has been one of the major growth areas of France in the last 40 years, with some 40 per cent of the 'second homes' in the country, and it has been able to exploit its greatest advantages. These are a scenic, mountainous coastline with sheltered bays, hot sunshine, a southerly aspect, and proximity to the wealthy areas of northern Europe with good, well-developed communications. There are over 14 car sleepers weekly from Paris, and excellent motorway links via the Rhône valley. The traditional hotel accommodation has been supplemented by caravans and camp sites and the

Cannes on the Côte D'Azur

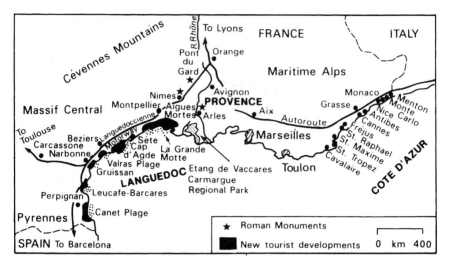

FIGURE 3.13   *Tourism in Mediterranean France*

Riviera coast has become badly congested. The Avignon–Nice autoroute, 'La Provençale', now helps to alleviate traffic congestion.

Congestion on the Riviera coast and in Provence first turned attention towards the western side of the Rhône valley, the Mediterranean coast of Languedoc, an under-developed area with over 200 km of empty sandy coastline. There were few roads and few towns of any size except Montpellier. The whole region was underdeveloped, depending upon monoculture production of large quantities of poor-quality wine. From 1963 onwards, Languedoc was the focus of a French-government planning project for coordinated development. The development company for Lower Rhône–Languedoc (CNABRL) has controlled the development of Languedoc. The modernisation and diversification of agriculture has involved irrigation schemes using the Rhône near Arles, and the Herault and Orb rivers. There are major irrigation projects around Beziers, Montpellier and Nîmes. There is a great increase in cultivation of intensive crops such as apples and market garden crops, and a reduction in vines. A most important development has been the construction of the motorway, the 'Languedoccienne', which has ended the relative isolation of the coast. There have been pest-eradication programmes, afforestation projects, and an improved water-supply system. Six tourist units have been developed with accommodation for 450 000 tourists. Local development corporations construct local roads, recreation and urban services, parking facilities, marinas and hotels, camping villages, and apartment accommodation. Two large projects are most important: Leucate near Perpignan and La Grande Motte–Port Camargue (fig. 3.13). The latter is next to the regional park of the Camargue, and the airports at Nîmes and Montpellier. It has accommodation for 42 000 people and a marina for 1000 boats. The transformation of this region into a tourist attraction has been described as the creation of the 'French Florida'.

TRADE: THE WORLD'S LARGEST TRADING GROUP

The EU is now the world's most significant trading group and in 1991 the EU (12) was responsible for 22 per cent of world imports and nearly 20 per cent of world exports (compared with 18 per cent and 16 per cent for the USA – the next most important).

There are considerable variations in the relative importance of trade to each country. In 1991 the Netherlands and Belgium/Luxembourg, with their commercial traditions, had an export trade which was equal to 46 per cent and 60 per cent respectively of gross domestic product (GDP). This is far higher than the equivalent figure of 18 per cent for the UK and 25 per cent for Germany, usually considered as essentially exporting countries (fig. 4.1). Greece and Spain have lower proportions with trade accounting for 12 per cent of GDP, in both cases reflecting the long period of isolation of Greece and Spain from European and world markets. The distinction between trade surplus countries like Denmark and deficit countries such as Greece may be seen.

WHY SUCH A LARGE INVOLVEMENT?

The reasons for this large involvement in foreign trade are complex, but may be identified under three headings:

1 **Widespread industrialisation** was based in the nineteenth century upon mineral resources which have become depleted to the point of exhaustion. The mineral resources of the EU, though extensive in some commodities such as coal, are incomplete, with major deficiencies in certain crucial areas, such as petroleum, high-grade iron ores and non-

97

	Exports (million ECU)	Imports (million ECU)	Exports approximately % of GDP
Germany	323 947	314 735	25.4
France	184 746	200 118	19.0
Italy	136 755	147 197	14.7
Netherlands	108 212	110 899	46.0
Belgium – Luxembourg	95 013	102 321	59.7
United Kingdom	147 213	169 437	18.0
Ireland	19 534	16 833	55.7
Denmark	29 298	26 674	27.8
Greece	7015	17 411	12.3
Spain	51 351	72 666	12.0
Portugal	13 158	21 089	23.7
EU (12) total	1 116 242	1 199 380	22.0
World	5 609 256	5 354 375	

FIGURE 4.1 *EU (12) and world trade, 1991*

ferrous metals (fig. 4.2). Many of the more accessible coal seams have been worked out, so the coal is now difficult to exploit and is high-cost, and the remaining French iron ores have an iron content of only 30 per cent. There are adequate reserves of salt and potash and the reserves of natural gas and petroleum in the North Sea will redress the balance considerably for a time. Nevertheless the basic picture is one of deficiency in raw materials, with a corresponding reliance on large-scale imports (20 per cent in 1991).

2 **A heavily urbanised population with a high standard of living.** Resources are used at an ever-increasing rate in industrialised societies, and there is an underlying propensity to import semi-finished materials for further processing, together with finished manufactures, which add to the range of choice open to the consumer (fig. 4.3). Wealth generates imports and the richer the society the greater is the reliance upon a complex movement of imports and exports of all categories.

3 **Food is an important element in the EU's import trade**, despite a potential self-sufficiency in temperate foods. In 1991, 8 per cent of imports were of foodstuffs, including temperate foods from the USA and Australia, and tropical foods from Africa and Asia (fig. 4.4). This illustrates the importance of the former colonial territories, and explains their status as associate trading partners of the EU. The Yaoundé Agreements of 1963

and 1969, followed by the Lomé Conventions of 1975, 1979 and 1984, were preferential trade and aid treaties. The most recent Lomé Convention (Lomé IV) was signed in 1989 to cover the period 1990–2000.

THE SINGLE MARKET AND INTRA–COMMUNITY TRADE: TRADE CREATION

The Single Market theoretically allows goods, services, people and capital to circulate freely throughout the Member countries, the basic prerequisite for this being free trade, and the abolition of all internal customs duties, tariffs and

	EU 12 production	Main producers	% of world production
Coal	193.7	United Kingdom, Germany	5.6
Crude oil	114.4	United Kingdom	3.6
Copper	0.3	Portugal	3.0
Iron-ore	33.1	France, Spain	3.5
Bauxite	2.2	Greece	1.9
Salt	23.6	Germany, United Kingdom, France, Netherlands, Italy, Spain	14.3
Potash	6.3	Germany, France, Spain	28.5
Lead	0.3	Ireland, Spain, Greece	7.6

FIGURE 4.2   *Selected resources of the EU (12), 1991 (million tonnes)*

	Imports (percentage)				Exports (percentage)			
	EEC 6		EU 12		EEC 6		EU 12	
Commodity group	1958	1977	1986	1991	1958	1977	1986	1991
Foodstuffs	25	14	12	8	10	10	10	8
Fuel and raw materials	46	28	18	20	10	9	9	5
Manufactured goods	29	58	70	72	80	81	81	87

FIGURE 4.3   *External trade — main commodity groups (by value)*

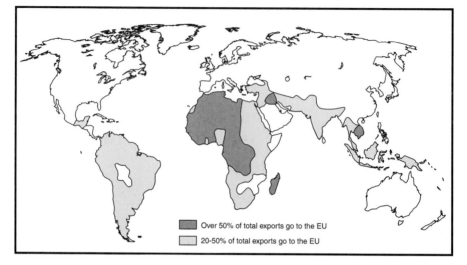

Over 50% of total exports go to the EU

20-50% of total exports go to the EU

FIGURE 4.4   *The EU's share in the exports of the developing world*

quotas. This has effected a very rapid expansion of trade within the Single Market. The original Six completed the abolition of all internal tariffs by 1969, but new members have adjusted gradually to the EU levels via transition periods. A single market of almost 372 million people now extends from Finland to Crete. The real expansion of trade relating to this is in intra-community trade, and the period from 1958 to 1972 saw a substantial trade increase between the Member States, with trade growing in value during this period at an annual rate of over 15 per cent. Although the recession slowed this process down for a time, since 1975 the value of trade has continued to grow. The individual Members raised their proportion of trade with each other from 25 per cent to 57 per cent (fig. 4.6). Those with the highest levels of integrated trade have either a limited base to their domestic economies, such as Ireland, or a tradition of European trade such as the three Benelux countries. All have benefited: Italy has become an exporter of fashion clothing and consumer durables; France and the Netherlands have greatly expanded their exports of agricultural produce; and Germany's persistently favourable balance of trade is due principally to the opening of EU markets to its efficient industry. The UK has a vastly increased market for the products of its specialised engineering, chemical, vehicle, electronics, telecommunications and aerospace industries. Germany is now the UK's single largest export market, and the EU now takes 54 per cent of the UK's exports. The European market is one in which the UK must succeed if she is to thrive as a major industrial and trading nation.

The direction of British trade was already swinging strongly towards the industrialised markets of Western Europe during the 1960s (fig. 4.5). After the enlargement of the EEC in 1963 the UK, Ireland and Denmark rapidly increased their interdependence with the other EU countries (fig. 4.6). The

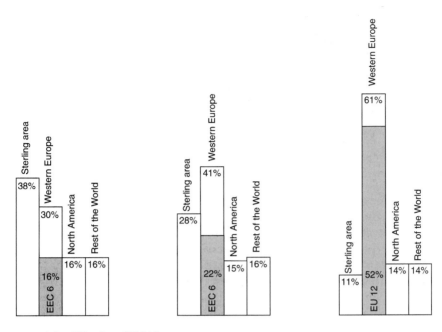

FIGURE 4.5   *Direction of British exports*

Mediterranean enlargement of the 1981–6 period involved a lengthy
transition period whilst the tariff barriers behind which Spanish industry had
sheltered during its development were gradually removed. Nevertheless,
Greece, Spain and Portugal have also increased their interdependence with

	1957	1971	1986	1992
Belgium/Luxembourg	44	63	70	71
France	21	50	64	66
Germany	24	47	54	55
Italy	21	42	55	59
Netherlands	41	55	61	59
United Kingdom	16	22	50	51
Ireland	–	69	73	72
Denmark	–	32	53	55
Greece	–	–	58	63
Spain	–	–	51	60
Portugal	–	–	59	74
EU 12 (average)			59	62

FIGURE 4.6   *Intra-EU trade. Percentage of total imports coming from other Member countries*

the rest of the EU since their accession. Intra-EU trade is the means by which the special expertise and comparative advantages of each Member country may be used with greater efficiency to achieve interdependence and convergent economies.

THE CUSTOMS UNION AND EXTERNAL TRADE:
TRADE DIVERSION

At the same time as the Treaty of Rome provided for the reduction to zero of internal tariffs, it also required all Members to conform to a common external tariff (CET). This was accomplished in 1968 for the original Six Members. New Members have been absorbed gradually through transition stages over a number of years. This is a Customs Union and was the distinguishing feature of the EEC. This may be compared with the purpose of EFTA, which was to promote free trade between its members, with each country keeping its trade relations with third countries quite separate. The EU has formed a single trading unit without internal barriers and with a common external tariff wall. Essentially, therefore, it is creating a single economic unit from 15 separate ones. The common external tariff deals with external trade relationships, that is, with the rest of the world. Although in global terms the CET is set at low rates, the average for industrial goods being 6 per cent and there are trade arrangements with some associated countries at zero rates, this does involve some *trade diversion* from other countries. The CET tends to replace imports from non-Member countries with suppliers within the Customs Union. Thus the benefits of *trade creation* in the enlarged markets have to be set against *trade diversion* from non-Members.

The character and direction of external trade is summed up as follows. Twenty-eight per cent of imports are of raw materials and foodstuffs, whilst 72 per cent are manufactured goods. Eighty-seven per cent of exports are of manufactures, and 13 per cent are primary products (fig. 4.3). There is thus a large, complex, and increasingly multi-lateral movement of manufactured goods throughout the developed world. About 80 per cent of total trade by value is with the industrialised and wealthy countries within the EU and the rest of Western Europe, and with North America and Japan (fig. 4.7). There is a major imbalance of trade in imports from Japan. Trade with the rest of the world overall accounts for about 20 per cent of the total (including about 2 per cent with former East European countries). The majority of this is with Economically Less Developed Countries (ELDCs), although a large proportion of that includes a heavy reliance upon imports of petroleum from OPEC. Although rather less oil is now imported because of North Sea supplies, this will change as the North Sea supplies diminish.

The real value of a trading group such as the EU is that because of its high rate of growth and development, it has the ability to create and sustain a large volume of world trade and to provide the aid for development which is

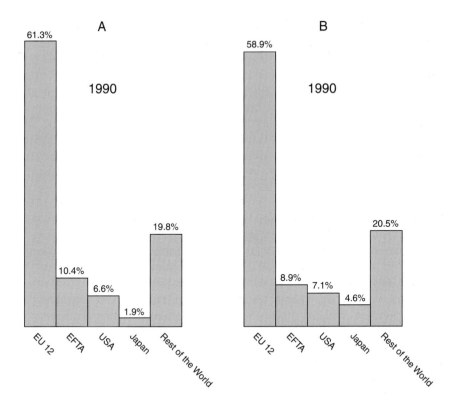

FIGURE 4.7   **(A)** *EU (12) exports (percentage) by area of destination*
(B) *EU (12) imports (percentage) by area of origin, 1993*

needed. This is the very significant *trade-creation factor*. In fact, many studies have shown that the generally low levels of the CET have not led to trade diversion on the scale which might have been thought. The Treaty of Rome stated that 'Member States aim to contribute ... to the harmonious development of world trade, the progressive abolition of restrictions on international trade, and the lowering of customs barriers'. The enlargement of the EU has been a major factor in creating and maintaining a more outward-looking trade and external policy. Historically, Europe has had traditionally privileged links with the developing countries, and the accession of the UK with its traditional involvement in world affairs has done much to strengthen those ties.

Trade and external relations

The development of a world trading interest is based upon the European special relationship with former dependent territories. In 1964 the Yaoundé Agreement came into operation with 18 African countries setting up a free trade zone and arrangements for financial aid. At the same time, the early

Association agreements with Greece and Turkey were signed. The very important 'Kennedy Round' on tariff reductions in 1968 marked the emergence of the EEC as a trading unit and a negotiating entity on the world scene. The EU has now embraced a commercial role and external relations. It has developed an extensive system of generalised preferences for many types of products, and has a complex network of association and trading agreements with many groups of countries. One of the most important is the already-mentioned Lomé Convention, with 70 African, Caribbean and Pacific ex-colonial territories better known as the ACP countries. This was first signed in 1975 and renewed in 1984, and the most recent Convention (Lomé IV) was signed in 1989 to cover the period 1990–2000. The Convention covers free trade for virtually all products from ACP countries, cooperation and development aid. Ninety-nine per cent of exports from the ACP countries enter the EU free of duty and there are special arrangements for products such as rum and sugar. In return, EU exports to ACP markets enjoy most-favoured nation (MFN) status. The Convention also includes an export-earning stabilisation scheme – Stabex – for states heavily dependent upon several primary export products. The Stabex scheme worked like an insurance scheme against bad years. A minimum income is guaranteed to ACP countries for their exports of 48 products including cocoa, coffee, tea, peanuts and sisal. In 1979 this was supplemented by SYSMIN (also referred to as MINEX), a similar stabilisation scheme covering a range of ACP exports including manganese, phosphate and bauxite, tin and iron ore. The current Lomé Convention will run for ten years, twice the duration of its three predecessors, thus giving greater stability to EU–ACP relations. It provides for ECU12 billion of aid in the form of grants, loans and interest-rate subsidies over the first five-year period. This represents an increase over Lomé III of some 20 per cent in real terms.

Aid terms have been improved in an effort to reduce ACP indebtedness. All EU aid is now non-repayable except for risk capital and EIB loans. A ban on the import and export of hazardous waste and radio-active waste between the EU and ACP countries has been agreed. At the same time the EU has become more rigorous in its policy of reducing or suspending aid to countries guilty of human-rights violations.

There are also agreements with the EFTA countries. EFTA (the European Free Trade Association) was created in 1960, and since 1973 there has been a free trade area in manufactured goods between the EU and EFTA. Over the years a considerable degree of economic integration has taken place between the EU and EFTA in the form of direct investment, joint ventures and technical cooperation. The geographic proximity of the EFTA countries has given rise to many other areas of common interest, such as transport and the environment. Taken together, the EFTA countries are the EU's largest export market (fig. 4.7a).

The progressive creation of the Single European Market led the EFTA countries to review their relationship with the EU. Austria, Finland and Sweden presented formal applications to join the EU, but other EFTA members took up the aforementioned idea of a 'third way' for EU–EFTA relations – i.e. not the existing free trade relationship or full EU membership. This 'third way' became known as a 'European Economic Space', and after some difficult negotiations the European Economic Area (EEA), linking EU and EFTA countries in the world's largest free trade area, took effect in 1994. The single-market principles and policies of the EU have been extended, as far as possible, to the whole of the EEA. There is free movement of goods, services, capital and persons on the basis of EU legislation in return for a financial contribution from the EFTA countries to reduce regional and social disparities in the EU. Switzerland withdrew from the EEA before it came into effect after the Swiss people rejected it in a referendum. This has affected the position for Liechtenstein as she has a customs union with Switzerland.

The Maghreb countries of Tunisia, Algeria and Morocco and the Mashreq countries (Egypt, Jordan, Syria and Lebanon) plus Israel are linked to the EU through cooperation agreements covering trade, industrial cooperation and technical and financial assistance. The agreement with Israel provides for free trade in industrial products.

The EU has association agreements with Turkey, Cyprus and Malta designed to lead to the progressive establishment of customs unions with the EU. The agreement with Turkey goes a step further, envisaging the possibility of Turkey's ultimate full membership of the EU (Turkey formally applied in 1987). Cyprus and Malta applied to join the EU in 1990, and the Commission's view of these applications is that the problem of the division of Cyprus should be resolved first and that Malta should take important steps to modernise her current economic and financial structures.

The Mediterranean Basin is rapidly becoming part of the EU's economic sphere of interest. It is a major supplier of primary products and lying as it does on the southern flank of the EU, is clearly an area of strategic interest to Western Europe. 'Geopolitical reasons in themselves make an impressive case for the necessity of a coherent European Community policy on the Mediterranean. A glance at the map proves it. Look first at the Balkans and then at the edge of the Atlantic. Take in the Dardanelles and the petrol-producing region of the Near East; remember too that the Mediterranean is the inescapable north–south axis for links between Europe and Africa. We must question whether the Community could survive a serious disturbance in the Mediterranean region ...' (Lorenzo Natali, European Commissioner with responsibility for Mediterranean affairs, 1981).

The EU has accepted that it has, out of enlightened self-interest, a particular responsibility for the social (and thus political) stability of the Mediterranean region. It should therefore contribute to the region's economic and social development. This responsibility has increased following the 1990 Gulf War. The EU is also aware that immigration pressures could build up from these countries if the pace of their economic development proves inadequate to meet the needs of their growing populations.

Significantly, the EU's developing spheres of economic interest lie principally with its former dependent territories, with the other industrial countries of Western Europe, and within the Mediterranean Basin. However, since the collapse of the Berlin Wall, the EU has been actively involved in providing aid to ease the harsh impacts of the transitional period for the former East European countries. This aid has political as well as economic aims as the fear exists that should reforms prove disastrous the people may turn to their former Communist leaders. Direct aid is seen as a way of supporting the democratic spirit in Central and Eastern Europe. In addition to this, there is also the threat of large-scale immigration into the EU. By helping the former East European countries to help themselves, the EU is investing in immigration control. EU relations are particularly close with the neighbouring 'Visegrad Four' (Poland, Hungary, the Czech Republic and Slovakia) who would have to bear the brunt of any mass immigration from countries further east such as the former Soviet republics.

PHARE (Poland/Hungary: Aid for Restructuring Economies) was one of the first aid programmes agreed in 1989, and since then it has been extended to other East European nations. A new type of association agreement called 'Europe' association agreements was devised for the East European countries. The first of these were agreed with the Visegrad Four, and others have also been concluded with Bulgaria, Estonia, Latvia, Lithuania, Romania and Slovenia. The EU also has more limited trade agreements with Albania, extending its generalised system of preferences (GSP) previously reserved for the ELDCs, and has negotiated so-called Partnership and Cooperation agreements with some Commonwealth of Independent States (CIS) members – Russia, the Ukraine, Byelarus, Kirgizstan and Moldova. The aid programme to the CIS is known as TACIS (Technical Assistance to the CIS). Hungary, Poland, Romania, Slovakia, Latvia, Estonia, Lithuania, Bulgaria and the Czech Republic have formally applied for EU membership.

Some EU industries are particularly concerned about the increased flow of East European goods in the EU market. The 'sensitive' areas of iron and steel, farm products, chemicals, textiles, clothing and footwear are all suffering from overcapacity, yet these areas are Eastern Europe's greatest export potential, accounting for between 35 and 45 per cent of all the region's exports. If the 'sensitive' areas were not protected by the EU, the lower labour costs of the East European countries (in Poland the average hourly rate in the manufacturing sector is only one-tenth of that in Germany) would undermine already declining industries.

Other barriers to trade

The creation of the Single European Market has led to fears of a 'Fortress Europe' as the EU has become the largest trading bloc in the world. The USA believed that Europe would no longer be 'open for business', using trade barriers to restrict US trade. There were also concerns about the high level of EU imports into the USA. On the other hand the EU has experienced a trade deficit with Japan, and protectionist measures have been introduced. The eighth round of international trade-liberalisation talks began in 1986 in Uruguay under the auspices of GATT (the General Agreement on Tariffs and Trade), and were seen as the greatest and most complex trade negotiations so far. GATT talks aim to increase world trade by reducing tariffs and quotas on as wide a range of goods and services as possible. Although 107 countries took part in the Uruguay round, the main players were the EU and the USA (EU Member States do not negotiate within the GATT as individual countries but are represented by the EU – all agreements reached by the EU must then be implemented by all Member States).

The Uruguay round of GATT not only had to tackle the issue of increasing protectionism – partly due to falling rates of economic growth and rising unemployment in the 1970s and 1980s – but also had to tackle new areas including agriculture. At the commencement of the Uruguay round, the cost of agricultural protection world-wide was running in excess of £100 billion a year.

By 1990 prospects for a successful outcome to the talks looked poor. The EU would not accept the US proposals (supported by the Cairns Group – an organisation of 14 leading agricultural exporters including Australia, Canada and Argentina) for a 75 per cent reduction in domestic agricultural production subsidies and a 90 per cent reduction in export subsidies. The talks were suspended and relations between the USA and the EU deteriorated despite the implementation of a 30 per cent reduction in production subsidies by the EU. However, in 1992, agreement was reached between the USA and EU on agricultural trade (the 'Blair House' agreement), paving the way for the completion of the Uruguay round in 1993.

5

TRANSPORT: MOVEMENT ON A CONTINENTAL SCALE

The historical legacy

Transport in the EU is a complex network of systems which have evolved over a long period of history, under national conditions of development, and as a response to market forces, generally with a lack of strategic planning. The primary axes were dependent upon historic trade routes such as the east–west Hellweg, and the Rivers Rhine and Rhône beside which great cities such as Cologne and Lyons developed. During the Industrial Revolution the rapid development of waterway and railway networks was most marked in the coalfields and Heavy Industrial Triangle. The national basis of operations meant that unique systems developed within national frontiers, and the transport infrastructure between countries was poorly developed and fragmented up to the Second World War.

The Treaty of Rome and subsequent enlargements of the EU have increased to a continental scale the planning of transport operations and highlighted the urgent need for integration of the transport networks. Increased speeds have reduced the time needed to cross Europe and it is often better to think of travel in terms of time rather than distance. The Italian Riviera is two hours away from London by air or 24 hours by road or rail and sea. Economic, political, cultural and tourist contacts have expanded rapidly.

At the same time there is a growing complexity of transport systems and an associated need for efficient linkage and integration. Canals and railways, long dominant in long-distance movement, have been supplemented or supplanted by motorways, although a developing high-speed train network is seeing the return of rail transport. Air travel is very significant for medium- and long-distance passenger and tourist transport, and there is significant competition for cross-channel and other short-distance sea routes

	Inland waterways		Railways		Merchant fleet	Civil aviation	Road freight	Road network
	Length in use (km)	Tonne-kilometres (millions)	Length of line operated (km)	Freight Tonne-kilometres (millions)	1000 tonnes gross	Passenger kilometres (millions)	Million tonnes (1991)	Length (km)
Germany	4636	75 239	40 816	79 793	5552	48 934	na	639 805
France	8500	8631	33 555	50 632	4230	54 232	1395	915 651
Italy	1366	neg	16 016	21 680	7730	28 634	900	303 523
Netherlands	5046	34 755	2753	3038	849	32 046	384	105 817
Belgium	1948	5018	3432	9348	256	6203	299	133 749
Luxembourg	37	338	275	709	1581	na	na	5203
UK	1192	184	16 881	17 274	6017	124 052	1547	386 546
Ireland	neg	neg	1944	603	198	2274	na	92 362
Denmark	neg	neg	2344	1858	5781	4042	na	71 042
Greece	neg	neg	2484	606	24 542	7262	187	81 191
Spain	neg	neg	12 560	12 499	3224	27 117	na	158 801
Portugal	124	neg	3054	1783	708	7671	267	66 095

na = not available
neg = negligible

FIGURE 5.1(a) *EU (12) comparative transport data, 1992*

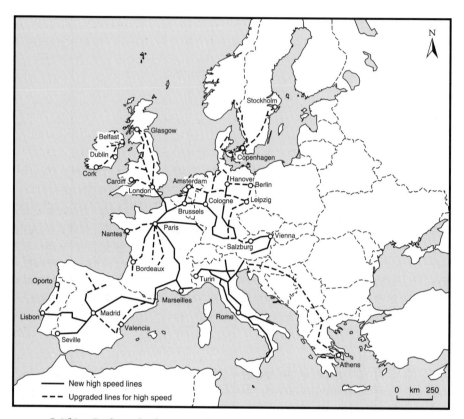

FIGURE 5.1(b)   *Railway development – high-speed lines (developed and planned)*

between ferry, hovercraft, jetfoil, air and rail (e.g. the Channel Tunnel). The internationalisation of all these is illustrated by the container revolution, long-distance coach services, channel ferry services, railway car sleepers, by technological feats like the Channel Tunnel project and the trans-Alpine tunnels and the development of the Euro-route systems of motorways.

There are also other specialised elements which form part of the totality of movement in the EU. Movement of capital, goods, liquid fuel, and labour are considered in other chapters.

RAILWAYS

The railways were built largely in the nineteenth century industrial period, and often reflect national patterns with the main lines radiating from the capital city to the frontiers. Very few were built with an international viewpoint in mind, but a standard gauge was adopted across Europe, which has proved beneficial because of the twentieth-century growth of inter-city cross-frontier services.

Despite their inflexibility, high capital costs, and substantial competition from other forms of transport, railways still play a major role and in recent years have seen a revival, although there are wide variations between the Member States (figs. 5.1(a) and 5.3). The highest density is in north-west Europe with its industrial and urban concentrations. France has a very comprehensive network of railways and these carry the highest number of passengers and the second greatest tonnage of freight after Germany. The relatively large area of France and the long distances benefit rail haulage. Government support has been substantial since the railways were completely rebuilt after 1945. French Railways (SNCF) is a public service with competition from road haulage reduced by restrictive licensing. Germany's railways carry similar amounts of freight and passengers, and have a very dense network relative to area, but are less important relative to other forms of transport, specifically waterways. The system is currently being privatised, with the Bundesbahn in the western Lander amalgamated with the Reichsbahn in the eastern Lander as DBAG (Deutsche Eisenbahn-Aktiengesellschaft). However, this is part of an integrated approach by the government to tackle current and future transport problems with the use of road tolls for goods vehicles. Italy has a small network of railways compared to its area, partially a result of the retarded growth of the system up to the 1930s. The great length (1000 km) of peninsular Italy, the rugged nature of the relief and the inability of much of the area south of Lombardy to sustain a high level of traffic were all factors in this retardation. Although the railways are now state-operated, they still constitute a minimal system compared with the northern Member States.

The UK's railway system has experienced considerable reduction. A relatively small land area, high densities of population and a well-developed network of roads combined to emphasise the disadvantage of the railways as a relatively inflexible form of transport. The railways have had to operate in open competition with, and have lost ground to, the roads both in passengers and haulage. The UK was over-endowed with railways owing to the 'railway mania' of the nineteenth century, when much duplication of railway lines occurred. This very dense network has been reduced during three periods of rationalisation. By the 1930s these were four large companies: London, Midland and Scottish; London and North Eastern Railway; Great Western Railway; and Southern Railway. In 1948 the system was nationalised as British Rail; and during the 1960s the Beeching Report and subsequent pruning reduced the track by about one-third to 17 000 km. The UK network has a greater density than France, but it is considerably less used, particularly for freight. It is currently in the early stages of privatisation.

In other EU countries the use of rail systems varies according to other factors. Belgian railways are a high-density system and are quite well used for freight which is indicative of the general level of industrialisation; by contrast that of the Netherlands is a smaller system because of the competition from its extensive waterways. Spain, Portugal, Ireland and Greece have a low-density network indicative of retarded industrial and urban development. All

EU countries have experienced a marked relative decline in the amount of freight carried by rail since the late 1960s. Nevertheless, in volume–distance terms, the railways are still very significant, particularly in France and Germany (figs. 5.1(a) and 5.3). Their continuing importance depends on the movement of bulk freight, inter-city routes and suburban commuter services.

The recent revival of the railway systems, as environmental concern increases and as road and air traffic approach saturation point, has required major investment in new technology and substantial government subsidies. Of course many lines will be upgraded rather than being entirely new. Nevertheless, the railways are increasingly being seen as a stimulus to growth in the peripheral regions. It has been shown that high-speed railway lines between major city regions over medium distances compete very economically with other forms of transport. In France, the South-East TGV has been operating from Paris to Lyons and Marseilles since 1981 and has proved a great success. It is now extended to Valence. The Atlantic TGV opened in 1989 for Le Mans, Rennes and Nantes, and in 1990 the link to Bordeaux was completed. The North TGV (linking with the Channel Tunnel) is also complete (with a link to the South-East TGV) and there are plans both to extend services, including links to Marseilles and Strasbourg, and to link the South-East TGV with Geneva and Turin. Other countries such as Spain (Madrid to Seville and Barcelona), Italy (Naples–Rome–Florence–Milan), and Denmark (Copenhagen–Fredericia), are developing high-speed lines (fig. 5.1(b)).

In Germany high-speed rail links are planned as part of the programme to unify the country. There are five main schemes: Berlin–Hanover, and then on to Dortmund, the Ruhr and Cologne; Berlin–Hamburg/Lubeck/Rostock; Berlin–Stuttgart/Munich; Saxony/Thuringia–Rhine/Ruhr; and Saxony/Thuringia–Rhine/Main. The Berlin to Hamburg link is called Transrapid, and will be built and run entirely by private enterprise. Each of the schemes involves track improvement and electrification which will lead to reductions in journey time – e.g. the journey from Berlin to Hanover will be reduced from four hours to one hour and 45 minutes when the ICE trains commence in 1997. The most expensive of these projects links Nuremburg with Berlin via Bamberg–Erfurt and Leipzig–Halle, thereby creating an important axis between the high-tech industries of southern Germany, the industrial regions of middle Germany and the capital, Berlin.

One of the most significant developments is the North European project involving several countries. The project is to link Paris, London, Brussels, Amsterdam, Cologne and Frankfurt using both the Channel Tunnel and new sections of line designed for speeds of 300 km per hour, together with upgraded sections. A new high-speed link from the Tunnel to London through Kent is planned, and British Rail are also considering links to the north of England and Scotland, by-passing London. In addition, the Dutch railways are planning to make improvements in Amsterdam/Rotterdam–Cologne services via Utrecht on the main Amsterdam–Milan trunk route.

The Channel Tunnel itself should help to increase the amount of rail traffic in the EU, although this will depend on the completion of an improved rail network. Channel ports could lose an average of between 30 and 35 per cent of accompanied roll-on, roll-off (Ro-Ro) traffic, but unaccompanied Ro-Ro freight should be less affected. The share of freight using rail in the EU is expected to rise by 10 per cent at the expense of road, particularly for long-distance journeys. For passenger travel, rail is expected to attract two million passengers a year from air, with particular benefits for inter-city business travel. The train can become particularly attractive for journeys between 300 and 600 km (on the Paris–Lyon route, air traffic's share of passenger traffic declined from 30 to 9 per cent after the introduction of the TGV).

Inland Waterways

The importance of inland waterways is related to the occurrence of large navigable rivers and the lack of physical barriers. Denmark and Ireland have no commercial waterways of any significance. In Italy only the River Po and its tributaries are of any value for freight as the rest of the peninsula has rugged terrain with short mountain torrents and few rivers of any size. The Iberian peninsula offers few possibilities for navigation. The UK has limited use of inland water transport for a variety of reasons which include topography, the limited size of barges characteristic of the early narrow canal system, and the disuse into which it fell after its virtual destruction by railway competition.

Those countries of the North European plain drained by the Rhine and its tributaries, however, have the natural basis for an extensive canal system (fig. 5.2). Eastern France, Belgium, the Netherlands and Germany depend to a large extent upon inland waterways for the transport of bulk cargoes such as oil, iron ore, coal, grain and petroleum products. Germany's economic axis trends north–south along the length of the Rhine and movement is primarily between the industrial areas along its banks. Duisburg, Frankfurt and Cologne are the most important inland ports.

The importance of the Rhine can be seen in the total German tonnage carried by waterways (fig. 5.1(a)). In fact, the majority of inland shipping activity in the EU is accounted for by goods transported on the Rhine. Nearly 300 million tonnes are transported annually on this main artery. A free market situation prevails on the Rhine. The Act of Mannheim of 1868 guarantees free shipping on the Rhine and its arteries for all ships with flags belonging to countries signatory to the Act (Germany, France, the Netherlands, Switzerland, Belgium and the UK).

In the Netherlands 38 per cent of all freight is carried by water (fig. 5.3), reflecting the traditional character of the country, but also underlining its position at the mouth of the Rhine, with Rotterdam as the great entrepôt of Europe. In Belgium, the Scheldt and Meuse Rivers, and the Albert and

FIGURE 5.2   *Inland waterways associated with the Rhinelands*

Juliana Canals form a very important link between Antwerp, the Rhine and north-eastern France. To France the main value of inland waterways is the linkage of the Paris Basin via the Seine to the coast, via the Oise/Nord Canal to Lille, and via the Marne and Moselle system with Lorraine, Strasbourg and the Rhine. Although the French canal system is very extensive, much of it is outdated, confined to the north and east of France, and, by comparison with railways, is under-utilised. However, in 1994 plans first proposed in 1961 were revived to build a 229 km canal linking the Rhine and the Rhöne for completion by 2005. The Rhine–Rhöne link will follow the course of the smaller 150-year old canal and will enable ships carrying up to 4500 tonnes to travel from Rotterdam to the Mediterranean.

In 1992 the Rhine–Main–Danube Canal was opened, and it has already exceeded initial expectations on volumes carried. The opening of this canal, creating a waterway that passes through ten states (the Netherlands, Germany, Austria, Slovakia, Hungary, Croatia, Serbia, Romania, Bulgaria and the Ukraine), led the EU to regulate the use of the Rhine to prevent ships from East European countries coming up the Danube and stealing business (e.g. low-priced Polish operators were undercutting German companies).

Demand for inland waterway transport is likely to continue to grow as German unification and the opening-up of East European economies stimulate trade. However, the decline of both the steel industry (with its coal and ore cargoes) and the building industry (with its sand and gravel cargoes) has led to excess fleet capacity. The EU policy is to reduce the fleet size and improve the quality of vessels and service. There is pan-European coordination for the scrapping of vessels and the introduction of more efficient and less polluting boats on better canals with lower energy costs since an alternative to road transport is a priority for EU transport policy. In Germany inland waterways in the former GDR need considerable renovation – e.g. some 12 per cent of the locks on the Elbe waterway are not functioning. There are also plans to connect Berlin/Magdeburg with the North Sea ports of Hamburg and Bremen by improving navigation on the Elbe–Havel canal and the Mittelland canal.

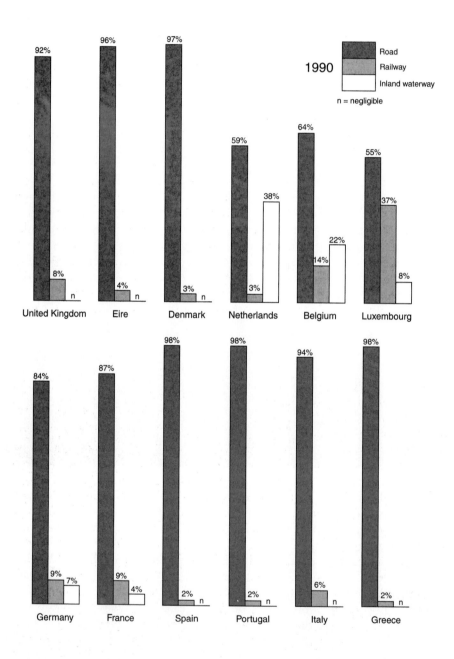

FIGURE 5.3 *Percentage of inland freight carried by each type of transport, EU (12), 1990*

ROAD TRANSPORT

All countries of the EU have a well-developed network of roads but there is a marked difference between the much higher densities in the 'core' countries of the north-west and peripheral countries such as Spain, Portugal and Greece (figs. 5.1(a), 5.5, 5.6). Greece, Spain, Portugal, Denmark, Eire, Italy and the UK are proportionately the greatest users of road transport with over 90 per cent of all freight being carried by road. Since the 1960s the creation of fast motorway links within and between the EU countries has done most to make road transport the principal means of transporting freight. In Italy the reasons are largely historical, since until the 1930s there was a very poorly integrated system of railways, with no through routes over the 1000 km from north to south, and very great difficulties east–west across the Apennines. This minimal network was associated with late unification and weak industrialisation of Italy up to the 1930s. To cope with the rapidly expanding economy since 1945, and aided by modern technology, the Italians have constructed an excellent Autostrada system with some superb feats of engineering. Perhaps the most famous is the Autostrada Del Sol, which links Milan to Naples with many bridges, tunnels and dramatic views. The long north–south distances have been overcome by motorways, but even more significant is the construction of motorways and tunnels through

Autobahn through the Spessart uplands near Frankfurt, Germany

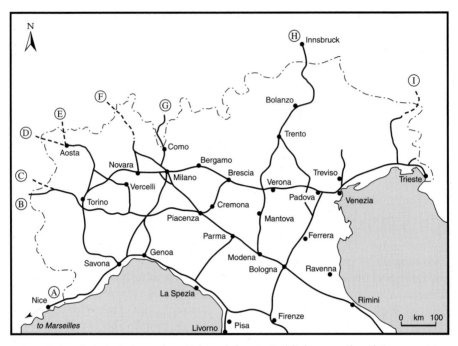

FIGURE 5.4   *Autostrada in northern Italy and the principal links across the Alpine mountains system*   **(A)** *Riviera coastal motorway to Marseilles and the Rhône valley*   **(B)** *Frejus tunnel to Chambery, Grenoble and Lyon*   **(C)** *Mt Cenis pass to Chambery and Lyon*   **(D)** *Mt Blanc tunnel to Chamonix and upper Rhône valley*   **(E)** *Grand St Bernard pass to Lake Geneva*   **(F)** *Simplon pass to Switzerland*   **(G)** *St Gotthard pass to Zurich*   **(H)** *grenner pass to Innsbruck and Munich*   **(I)** *Villach (Austria) Salzburg–Munich route*

the Alps which have done much to end the relative isolation of Italy from the trunk of Europe (fig. 5.4). Along the Riviera to France from Genoa, from Turin to the Frejus tunnel or up the Val D'Aosta and through the Mont Blanc Tunnel, from Milan northwards to the Simplon and St Gotthard Passes, and from Verno northwards to the Brenner Pass, the Italian Autostrada are linked by fast routes to the rest of the EU.

Although Italy's network is a critical element in its economy, the German autobahn system is more extensive and was originally constructed as part of the economic recovery programme before 1939. Following the post-war division of Germany, the main trend became north–south based essentially upon two lines of movement (fig. 5.6(b)). The Rhineland was the primary artery, linking the Ruhr with Bonn, the Saar, Frankfurt, Mannheim and Stuttgart. A second line ran from the North Sea ports of Hamburg and Bremen south to Hanover, Brunswick and Kassel, and thence to Nuremburg and Munich. East–west routes linked up these two axes at major urban nodes. However, after unification there has been a need for more effective east–west links. A new Hanover–Braunschweig–Magdeburg–Berlin autobahn is to be built, with another linking Nuremburg, Leipzig and Berlin.

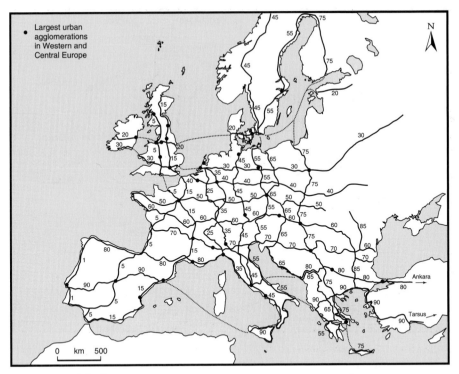

FIGURE 5.5 *The E-route motorway system*

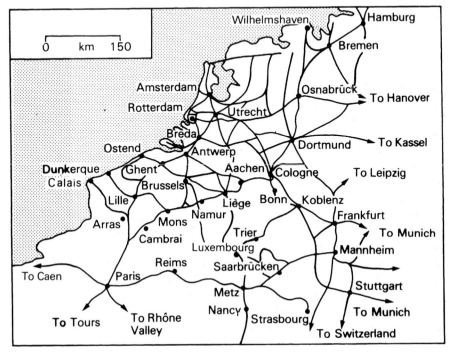

FIGURE 5.6(a) *Motorway links within the Triangle*

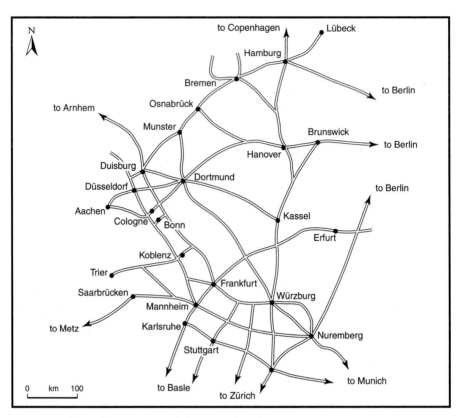

FIGURE 5.6(b)   *The German autobahn network with major cities*

The other EU countries have motorway systems which reflect their axes of greatest activity. The importance of London and Paris is illustrated by the concentration of roads and motorways upon these two cities. In the UK the radial pattern based upon London is supplemented by a figure 'H' which is centred upon the industrial Midlands. This links the industrial areas of Northern England and Scotland with London, South Wales and the Bristol area. The French system is based essentially upon links from Paris to the Lower Seine, Lille, Dunkerque and the Nord, and south to Bordeaux, Lyons, Marseilles and the Côte D'Azur (fig. 5.5).

Belgium and the Netherlands have a greater mileage of motorways in proportion to area than any other part of the EU. This reflects three significant geographical facts: a high level of economic activity; a high density of population; and their position as the focal zone of the EU (fig. 5.6(a)).

The motorway system of the EU reflects several important geographical relationships – the new mobility and affluence of the population with nearly 125 million private cars, nearly one car for three people. It is one of the ideal ways in which the EU can develop a modern integrated cross-frontier system of transport. Most significant of all, however, is its influence in changing industrial location. Those areas with accessibility have become favoured zones for footloose industrial growth. The Frankfurt–Mannheim–Stuttgart corridor, the Autostrada Del Sol and the M4 corridor in the London city region have become excellent examples of industrial- and service-sector growth. These are the new 'sunrise' areas and 'industrial boulevards' of the EU.

However, as the pattern of road provision in the EU is diverse (Ireland has one motorway compared with the German network which is the second largest in the world), it is difficult to agree on a consistent road policy. The motor-vehicle industry is important to the EU economies because it employs so many people – in Germany it employs about 7 per cent of the workforce – but motor vehicles also have a major impact on the environment. Over a ten-year period a typical car produces a considerable amount of waste, including 44 tonnes of carbon dioxide, 5 kg of sulphur dioxide and 47 kg of nitrogen dioxide. Motor vehicles cause delay and stress to millions of commuters and truckers, and between 1970 and 1988 more than half a million people were killed in road-traffic accidents in the EU. Yet policies which discourage road travel and encourage public transport are damaging to the motor-vehicle industry. This dilemma explains why the EU is on the one hand encouraging research into greater efficiency and traffic limitation and on the other hand encouraging further development of the road network such as new Channel Tunnel access routes and trans-Alpine crossings.

AIR TRANSPORT

Air transport is concerned principally with the international movement of passengers, but at the same time there is considerable domestic and intra-EU movement. Freight traffic is increasing rapidly, and London Heathrow is now one of the busiest freight transit points in the UK. Airports are substantial contributors to regional development and public revenues. They contribute to employment in three ways: first, through direct employment at the airport by the airport itself and the activities carried out by companies operating at the airport: second, through the indirect impact of services related to the airport's business – e.g. hotels and tour operators; and third, there is the impact of induced employment which results from a multiplier effect from both the direct and indirect impacts. A case study for employment at Copenhagen Airport showed that 35 per cent of it was direct employment and that 27 per cent was indirect, but that the balance of 38 per cent was due to induced employment.

Some indication is given (figs. 5.1(a) and 5.7) of the relative importance of national air-fleets, passenger density and principal airports. Although there are over a hundred major airports in the EU, six city regions dominate air traffic. London Heathrow, supplemented by Gatwick, Luton and Stansted, is the busiest passenger airport in the world. Its major problems, common to all

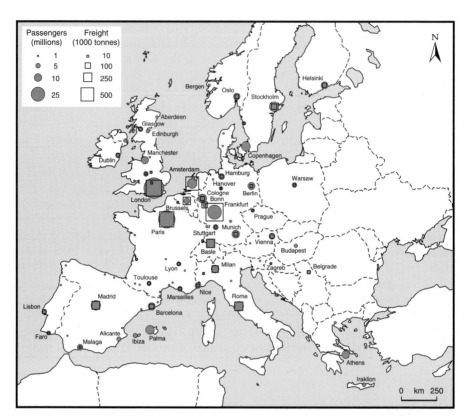

FIGURE 5.7(a) *Major EU airports (source:* Association of European Airlines, 1990*)*

Schiphol airport, Amsterdam, one of the busy airports of Europe

London Heathrow	45.2	Barcelona	10.3
Frankfurt	30.7	Athens	10.1
Paris Orly	25.2	Brussels	9.4
Paris De Gaulle	25.2	Milan	9.4
Gatwick	20.0	Gran Canaria	7.0
Rome	19.1	Berlin	6.7
Amsterdam	19.1	Nice	5.9
Madrid	18.4	Dublin	5.8
Stockholm	13.0	Lisbon	5.6
Copenhagen	12.4	Malaga	4.9
Manchester	12.4	Glasgow	4.8
Düsseldorf	12.3	Stuttgart	4.8
Munich	12.0	Marseille	4.7
Palma de Mallorca	11.9	Lyons	3.9

FIGURE 5.7(b)   *EU airports, 1992 – total number of passengers (millions)*

large airports, is the congestion when several large passenger jet aircraft arrive in close proximity, the continual need for expansion of or additional terminals, the position peripheral to the city with the need for transfer of passengers, and the environmental problems of large airports in residential areas. The significance of London is related to the UK's traditional international relationships, whilst Paris, Amsterdam, Madrid, Frankfurt and Rome reflect a combination of the nodality of capital cities and core regions, together with their position as transit points between Europe and the rest of the world. A large number of regional airports such as Munich, Brussels and Milan have developed, because of vastly increased air traffic, to supplement the major airports. One of the most important and fast-growing airline operations has been tourist charter flights, largely to the Mediterranean. Forecasts show that the combined passenger traffic of the EU's 27 largest airports will grow to over 697 million by 2005.

SEA TRANSPORT

Shipping is related mainly to trade, and here, although the original Six had a substantial merchant shipping fleet, the accession of Greece to the EU completely changed its character (fig. 5.1(a)). One of the largest merchant

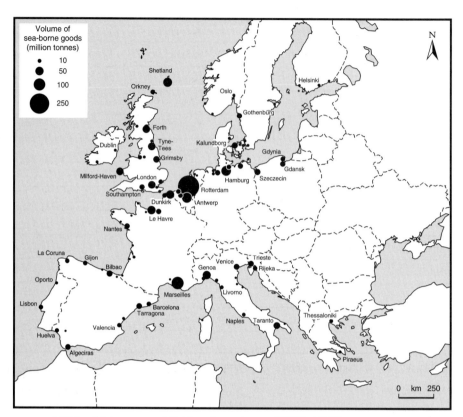

FIGURE 5.8(a)   *Major ports and freight volume (source:* IBFK, 1990)

Container wharf at Pernis-Eemhaven, Rotterdam

	Total
Hamburg	1968
Bremerhaven (Bremen)	1278
Le Havre	858
Marseilles–Fos	481
Dunkirk	70
Genoa	310
Rotterdam	3666
Antwerp	1549
London (Tilbury)	382
Tees-Hartlepool	109
Felixstowe	1434
Grimsby-Immingham	244

TEU = Twenty Foot Equivalent Units

FIGURE 5.8(b)   *Container traffic at major EU ports, 1991 (1000 TEUs)*

carrying fleets in the world flies the Greek flag. It is a function of international trading traditions that this significance is so marked, and it contrasts with the mainly continental character of the original Six. In addition the accession of the UK, Denmark, Sweden, Finland, Greece and Ireland has meant that intra-EU sea traffic, hitherto largely coastal, is now an essential part of movement between Member States. Approximately 30 per cent of intra-EU trade is carried by sea.

The map of ports and sea traffic (fig. 5.8(a)) shows the area of greatest significance. The North Sea coast and English Channel, from the Tyne to Southampton and from Le Havre to Hamburg (and Copenhagen), have the greatest number of large ports and carry most passengers and freight. These are amongst the busiest sea lanes in the world, and are another significant reflection of the high level of economic activity in the northern part of the EU. In addition, there are major ports on the Atlantic coasts of the UK and France, and the Mediterranean ports act as input points to the EU from the south.

Most of the EU's large ports can be characterised as importing ports as incoming traffic is much higher than outgoing. There are only a few ports where exports exceed imports – Calais and Rouen are two examples. In each Member State one or a few ports specialise in liquid bulk traffic, e.g. Le Havre and Marseilles in France, Wilhelmshafen in Germany and Trieste in Italy. Specialisations also exist for dry bulk traffic – Bremerhaven and Lubeck in Germany and Limerick in Ireland are examples. Some ports, such as Calais, Dublin, Valencia and Felixstowe, can be characterised as general cargo ports.

A most significant change in port geography has taken place during the last 40 years. Changes in the patterns of sea-borne trade, the growth of the channel passenger ferry services and advances in technology are all reasons for this. Increase in vessel size and the development of containerisation and

Country	Total traffic (million tonnes)	Main ports	Cargo handled (million tonnes)
Belgium	164.2	Antwerp	101.4
		Zeebrugge	30.8
Denmark	38.4	Copenhagen	9.4
Germany	203.5	Bremen-Bremerhaven	30.7
		Hamburg	65.5
		Wilhelmshafen	17.9
		Lübeck	16.5
Greece	23.8	Thessaloniki	14.0
		Piraeus	9.8
Spain	223.7	Bilbao	27.4
		Tarragona	23.7
		Barcelona	18.3
France	302.5	Marseille	89.4
		Le Havre	57.2
		Dunkirk	40.7
Ireland	25.4	Dublin	7.7
Italy	327.2	Genoa	42.0
		Trieste	35.5
Luxembourg	–	–	–
Netherlands	374.7	Rotterdam	290.8
		Amsterdam	31.2
Portugal	51.1	Lisbon	16.5
UK	427.9	London	49.5
		Tees-Hartlepool	42.8
		Grimsby-Immingham	38.2
		Milford Haven	35.7
		Southampton	31.5
EU (12) total	2162.4		

FIGURE 5.8(c)   *Ports of the EU (12), 1991*

roll-on, roll-off facilities (Ro-Ro) (fig. 5.8(b)) have led to a decline of traditional port cities based upon estuary or lowest bridging point sites, such as Amsterdam and London, and the development of and concentration at downstream deep-water terminals. London–Tilbury and Marseilles–Fos are examples of these large deep-water Euroports.

There are a number of 'Euroports' which are international in character, handle a large tonnage and serve a substantial part of the whole EU. The Single European Market is enabling large companies to rationalise production, concentrate on achieving economies of scale and locate at places convenient both for assembling their raw materials and for distributing to the whole EU market. Antwerp has the highest centrality index of all north European ports, followed by Rotterdam, Amsterdam, Zeebrugge and Dunkirk. The New Zealand Apple and Pear Market Board selected Antwerp as its main port of entry for EU distribution, and Cargill, the American grain and animal-feed processor and transporter, also selected Antwerp for its oil-seed-crushing and refinery location. Rotterdam is by far the largest Europort, although its tonnage figures are relatively distorted by the very large amounts of petroleum which it receives. It has been the world's largest port for over 30 years due to its connections with its hinterland by way of a high standard of road, rail and inland waterways – particularly along the River Rhine – and because of its geographical location on the North Sea. Other major Euroports are Antwerp, Bremen, Le Havre, Hamburg, London, Tilbury, Marseilles–Fos, Genoa, Barcelona and Lisbon (fig. 5.8(c)). A feature of most EU countries is that trade is dominated by one or two of these major Euroports. In the case of the UK, there is a great difference. As well as London (Tilbury) and Felixstowe, there are over 70 small and medium-sized ports (related to the maritime traditions and favourable estuary locations around the UK shores) which handle the country's trade. Many of these ports are benefiting from the use of small feeder vessels used to take goods closer to their final destination by cheaper water transport. The main UK ports to benefit from this transhipment from larger to smaller ports are those on the east coast closest to the main Euroports. Solid fuel, animal-feed raw materials and fertilisers are now transported through ports such as Colchester, Wivenhoe and Brightlingsea. The volume of container traffic gives a good illustration of the dominant ports, and also shows those ports which have grown rapidly in recent years to take advantage of the cross-channel growth in trade. These include Dover and Felixstowe, but ports in the south and east have all generally benefited from the growth in European trade and trans-shipment. By contrast, ports in the west and north have declined with the reduction in relative importance of deep-sea cargo trade. Liverpool is one such example.

PRINCIPAL LINES OF MOVEMENT: CORE AND PERIPHERY

The transport system as a whole within the EU is dominated by several corridors in which the rate and density of movement is at an extremely high level (fig. 5.9). There are two primary north–south axes: the French corridor from Le Havre to Paris via the Seine, and thence to Lyons and Marseilles via the Rhône valley; and the Rhine corridor from Rotterdam via the Ruhr to south Germany. These are supplemented by the Stuttgart–Munich, Frankfurt–Main valley, Berlin–Hanover and Hamburg–Bremen–Ruhr axes,

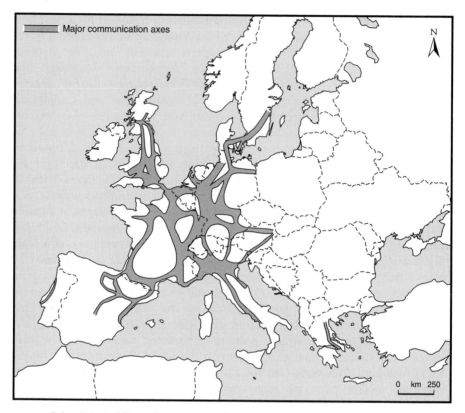

FIGURE 5.9   *Principal lines of movement within the EU*

and are linked to each other via the Belfort corridor and the Nord–Brussels Sambre–Meuse valley. To the north the main UK axis from Lancashire to the south-east region is linked to the rest of the EU by the Channel sea lanes, whilst to the south the Italian line from Milan–Turin–Genoa is integrated into the main stream by means of trans-Alpine routes. To the east is the Danube corridor. The concept of an EU core will be developed subsequently, by showing that the main stream of movement is determined with a zone joining Manchester, Southampton, Paris, Marseilles, Milan, Frankfurt, Rotterdam and Leeds.

By contrast, the peripheral regions such as Ireland, Iberia, southern Italy and Greece tend to have localised or isolated movement patterns, for a range of physical, spatial and historical reasons.

The populous regions of the Euro-core with their access to markets, labour, finance, etc. gained immensely from the strengthening during the post-war period of these major European axes of movement or 'Euroroutes'. Evidence suggests that the effect of transport integration and high-speed-rail developments will be to reinforce access to the core regions at the expense of the periphery. Economic activity will be stimulated and reinforced in the Eurocore, and although new sub-axes will emerge such as the Lyons–Grenoble–Marseilles axis, generally the improvement of transport facilities will have a limited effect upon peripheral regional growth. In effect the core regions will be enhanced whilst the periphery will be further peripheralised.

THE TREATY OF ROME AND TRANSPORT POLICY

The divergences that have emerged in the transport systems of the EU indicate the legacy of a number of separate national transport systems, which, though connected, do not operate as a single integrated system. There is a compelling need for EU action in the formulation of a coherent transport policy. It is set out in the Treaty of Rome that 'the community should establish a common transport policy to enable the free movement of people and goods over national boundaries'. A Common Transport Policy (CTP) was formulated as early as 1961 but in practical terms had accomplished little until recently owing to the reluctance of national governments to allow real and practical progress. The two most important objectives are the establishment of fair competition and a regulated transport market. To promote fair competition there is the need to formulate a uniform system of transport taxation, with licensing rules which will allow lorries to make journeys throughout all Member countries, and a standardisation of working hours and conditions. This involves the use of the *tachograph*, the automatic meter which monitors the lorry's journey. One of the most difficult problems has been the standardisation of overall lorry weights. It is intended to achieve a regulated transport market by controlling freight rates; by maintenance and stabilisation of the railway system; and by a common scheme of containerised freight to integrate the road, rail, inland waterway and sea transport network. It is likely that future policies will continue to look at the coordination of air and sea transport, because the enlarged EU is no longer linked by a continuous land surface and distances are much greater. Rhine shipping is such a major feature in the economy of five of the Member States that some form of integration is necessary. The coordination of air traffic control is now a serious issue.

The most important practical step, however, towards fast, uninterrupted movement and the completion of the Customs Union amongst the Member countries has been the adaptation of separate motorway systems into a European classification. The 'E' road system (fig. 5.5) links the major trunk roads and motorways across national frontiers. Some intra-national routes have already been carefully coordinated, for example, the Dutch motorway from Rotterdam to Utrecht and Arnhem which connects with the German autobahn system in the Ruhr and Rhineland (fig. 5.6). The South Belgian motorway from Liège to Namur, Charleroi and Mons connects directly with the French system either south to Paris or north to Lille and Dunkerque. The Antwerp–Liège motorway joins the Germany system at Aachen. The European Commission encourages consultation procedures which allow for this cross-frontier integration. The European Investment Bank has also contributed to many projects of this type such as the Brussels–Paris motorway, the Val d'Aosta–Mont Blanc and Grand St. Bernard tunnels and motorways, and the Brenner Pass route linking the Italian Autostrada system at Verona with the German system south of Munich.

The partial implementation by national governments of the CTP has been criticised by the EU institutions, but the policy was thrust into focus by the moves towards the Single Market in 1992. The Commission published an action programme to improve the economic and social cohesion of the EU by establishing European transport networks. It is encouraging the harmonisation of technical standards to ensure inter-operability (being able to operate a transport service in all Member States because the same technical transport standards apply throughout the EU). The action programme also includes financial measures to ensure that the EU budget gives higher priority to trans-European networks (TEN). The improvement of international links, such as those between France and Germany, the improvement of links to the peripheral regions, particularly to the Mediterranean regions and islands, the reducing of bottlenecks in and around major cities, such as London and Paris, and the overcoming of natural obstacles by means of the Channel Tunnel project to improve access (figs. 5.9 and 5.10) for the British Isles, are foremost on the agenda.

Journey time from London (hours)

To	1989	1995
Paris	$5\frac{1}{2}$	3
Brussels	5	$2\frac{3}{4}$
Amsterdam	$10\frac{1}{2}$	$5\frac{1}{2}$
Luxembourg	$8\frac{3}{4}$	6
Bonn	9	$6\frac{3}{4}$
Copenhagen	$19\frac{3}{4}$	17
Rome	$24\frac{3}{4}$	$21\frac{1}{2}$
Madrid	$25\frac{1}{2}$	21

FIGURE 5.10   *The Channel Tunnel: effect upon accessibility between the UK and the Continent*

6

THE IRON AND STEEL INDUSTRY:
INTEGRATION AND RATIONALISATION

This chapter and the next will give some detailed consideration to particular industries and their changing locations and structure. The steel industry, automobiles, textiles and chemicals have been selected because they have made a very significant contribution to the West European economy, and because they exemplify many of the processes of change which have been discussed in Chapter 3.

The steel industry is an important index of the relative wealth and stage of development of any particular country. It is traditionally a major employer of labour and requires high capital investment, and therefore has a tendency to locational inertia. Steel is a basic material which is used in almost every part of industry, transport of all types, construction and engineering, both heavy and sophisticated. It is therefore greatly involved in the complex patterns of modern industry.

The EU is one of the world's major steel producers (fig. 6.1) and this chapter analyses its development in terms of four themes: the growth of national industries up to 1945; government intervention and control; the supra-national factor; contemporary locational and structural changes.

THE DEVELOPMENT OF THE UNITED KINGDOM STEEL INDUSTRY

The early nineteenth century

During the Industrial Revolution coal was the critical determinant of location. Those coalfields developed which had coking coal, clayband iron ores and limestone available. These raw materials were heavy and of low value in proportion to bulk and were costly to transport very far. In addition, early iron and steel technology was relatively inefficient, requiring large quantities of coal in proportion to iron ore, and the means of transport available could not cope with such a situation. For these reasons the coalfields were unrivalled sites for steel-making, amongst them South Wales, Durham, and the 'Black Country' of the West Midlands.

The 1870s to 1930s

Improvements in iron-smelting techniques, allowing a more efficient use of smaller quantities of coal and, therefore, lower fuel costs, made it less essential for steel-making to be tied to the coalfields after the mid-nineteenth century. Two new steel-conversion processes also contributed to this trend. The Bessemer converter in the 1850s was modified by Gilchrist-Thomas so that high-phosphorus iron ores could be utilised thus allowing increasing use of the abundant, though lean, ores of the Jurassic scarplands of Cleveland, Lincolnshire and Northampton. In 1873 the open-hearth furnace enlarged the scale of steel-making and was to dominate the scene until the 1950s. The iron-ore fields became location sites for new steelworks, established on 'greenfield sites' (entirely new locations with no previous industrial characteristics). Corby, opened in 1935, was a good example of this, and together with Scunthorpe, became a major iron and steel manufacturing zone in the first half of the twentieth century.

The increasing complexity of location was compounded by changes in the supply of raw materials which began during the early twentieth century. Imports of foreign ores from Sweden, Canada, Spain and North Africa increased rapidly, partly because of larger ore-carriers, and partly because of the higher ore-content of foreign ores, two or three times as high as the lean Jurassic ores of Northampton. There was a growing tendency for steelworks to be located at ports and estuary sites around the coast. The natural growth points became the South Wales coast between Cardiff and Swansea; Teesmouth; the Dee estuary and the Manchester Ship Canal. These coastal zones adjacent to already-existing coalfields and iron- and steel-producing regions were in an excellent position for the low-cost assembly of all necessary materials. Teesmouth was a good example, having an abundant supply of ore in the nearby Cleveland hills, coking coal from south-west Durham 40 km away, limestone from Weardale, flat estuarine land for the construction of large factory areas, and, most important, the estuary, which allowed the import of rich Spanish and Swedish ore.

The decline of formerly important areas was beginning, but was complicated by the effects of the Great Depression of the 1930s. Inertia kept the original locations on the coalfields in existence but their long-term operating efficiency was low. They were often in small congested works, with exhausted iron ore and uneconomic coal, and requiring imports with high transport costs. The Ebbw Vale Steelworks was one such case, closed

	1964	1971	1973	1974	1976	1977	1981	1987	1991	1993
Germany	37.3	40.3	49.5	53.2	42.4	39.0	41.6	36.2	42.2	37.6
France	19.8	22.8	25.3	27.0	23.2	22.1	21.2	17.4	18.4	17.1
Italy	9.8	17.5	20.9	23.8	23.4	23.3	24.8	22.9	25.2	25.8
Belgium	8.7	12.4	15.5	16.2	12.1	11.3	12.2	9.8	11.4	10.2
Luxembourg	4.6	5.2	5.9	6.4	4.6	4.3	3.8	3.3	3.4	3.3
Netherlands	2.6	5.0	5.6	5.8	5.1	4.9	5.5	5.1	5.2	6.0
EC (Six)	82.8	103.2	122.7	–	–	–	–	–	–	–
UK	24.7	24.2	26.6	22.4	22.4	20.5	15.3	17.1	16.5	16.7
Denmark	neg	0.5	0.5	0.5	0.7	0.7	0.6	0.6	0.6	0.6
Ireland	neg	0.1	0.1	0.1	0.1	0.1	0.3	0.2	0.3	0.3
Greece	–	0.4	0.8	0.7	0.6	0.6	0.9	0.9	1.0	1.0
Spain	–	7.8	10.8	11.7	11.1	11.2	12.9	11.7	12.8	13.0
Portugal	–	0.4	0.5	0.4	0.5	0.5	0.6	0.7	0.6	0.8
EU (12) total	–	136.6	162.0	168.2	146.2	138.5	138.5	125.9	137.6	132.4

FIGURE 6.1   *EU crude steel production (million tonnes) (source:* Eurostat*)*

during the 1930s slump and reopened in 1938 largely as a social measure to help combat the serious long-term unemployment problem in the mining areas of South Wales. This structural problem of reconciling the development of new growth areas, whilst maintaining employment in run-down regions as a social service, has continued to affect the steel industry to the present day.

Post-1945

By 1945 the UK steel industry had completed the second stage of its evolution. It was a large-scale industry with a network of factories in seven traditional regions (fig. 6.2). There was, however, an unintegrated structure and much duplication of products. Control was in the hands of many private companies, often in small factories, undercapitalised, and with obsolescent equipment. The processes of change begun in the 1930s were continued and intensified: the movement to the coast; technological change and increasing advantages of size gained by amalgamation and concentration in large factories; and the residual areas of steelworking maintained by inertia and increasing state intervention. Port Talbot and Llanwern, in particular, are examples of favourable sites for large integrated steelworks built on extensive areas of flat land and using low-cost imports at deep-water access points.

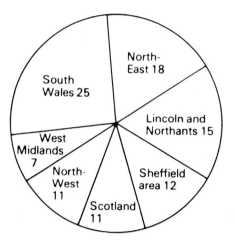

FIGURE 6.2   *UK steel production – percentages by traditional regions, 1970*

Inland sites have appeared increasingly uneconomic, a conflict of interest emerging over many old steel-working areas where government intervention has often delayed the closure of unprofitable works for social reasons. Ebbw Vale, Consett, Corby, Bilston and Workington are all examples of these. On the other hand, some areas have adapted by making special, high-quality steel. Sheffield is such an example.

New processes

Technological progress has continued rapidly with two new factors: the basic oxygen process and electric arc furnace. The separate processes of iron-making, steel-making and finishing are increasingly being integrated in large works. Internal costs are lower and economies of scale and greater efficiency are achieved. The open–hearth furnace has now largely been replaced by the basic oxygen converter which combines three great virtues: the rapidity of the Bessemer converter; the scarp-consuming ability of the open-hearth furnace; and a facility for continuous casting and large-scale production. Two such converters can produce 4 million tonnes of steel per year. The entire UK capacity could thus be obtained from ten converters in five steelworks. The likely pattern for the future is therefore concentration in larger units. In 1969 open-hearth furnaces still accounted for 51 per cent of capacity, and the basic oxygen converters only 34 per cent. By 1991, 71 per cent of steel was produced in oxygen converters, with electric arc furnaces – used for very-high-quality and alloy steels – providing the remaining 29 per cent.

Nationalisation

The final element is government intervention. There were once 13 major steel companies, some very large, such as the Steel Company of Wales, but there was too much product duplication, wasteful internal competition and a lack of scale required for international competition. In 1967 the steel industry was nationalised and the British Steel Corporation was formed out of a merger of 14 companies, with a few private-sector companies concentrating on alloy and special steel products. In 1973 a ten-year development strategy was embarked upon and a major reorganisation plan was carried out by the British Steel Corporation. This included the creation, in 1975, of a subsidiary, BSC (Industry) Ltd, to invest in creating new employment in areas affected by steel closures. The strategy included the following:

1 Reorganisation on a product basis, with area specialisation creating greater efficiency. Wales specialised in strip and sheet metal steel, South Teesside became the headquarters of general steels, and Sheffield of alloy and special steels.

2 A major investment programme concentrated upon modern plants such as the Teesside complex and coastal terminals like Hunterston.

3 A large new fleet of ore-carriers was developed to gain from the economies of large-scale sea transport; Port Talbot (150 000 tonnes capacity), Immingham (100 000 tonnes), Redcar (200 000 tonnes) and Hunterston (350 000 tonnes) were developed as ports for this purpose.

4 Rationalisation and modernisation meant the retention of five main heritage (traditional) bulk-steel-making areas. These were the five large integrated plants at Teesside, Scunthorpe, Port Talbot, Llanwern and Ravenscraig. At Sheffield and Rotherham the capacity for stainless steel, alloy and special steels was maintained. Although closure of bulk steel-making occurred at Shotton, Ebbw Vale, Corby and Hartlepool, nevertheless important finishing processes were maintained. Corby had a major tube-making works and Shotton cold rolling mills and a steel coating plant.

The collapse of demand for steel in 1975 caused BSC to accelerate its closure programme, and in 1977 the ten-year strategy was abandoned. For much of the period after 1975 the industry was operating well below capacity, and by 1988 the industry had undertone a major rationalisation and privatisation programme (BSC was privatised in 1988 to become British Steel PLC), combined with investment in new plant and technology. However, capacity has been reduced by 19 per cent between 1975 and 1992 in line with current demand. Production in 1992 was 16 million tonnes.

The Anchor Steelworks at Scunthorpe

A reduction in the workforce has accompanied modernisation. This has involved a substantial reduction from 257 000 (1967) to 196 000 (1973), 88 000 (1981), 53 000 (1988) and 41 800 (1993).

The modernisation of steel-making plant has affected some areas adversely, a continuation of the problem first seen in the 1930s. East Moors (Cardiff), Consett, and Bilston were old obsolescent plants which have been closed. In terms of traditional regions (fig. 6.2) the West Midlands, North-West and Scotland have been phased out from steel production. Ravenscraig, the last major steel plant in Scotland, produced its last steel in mid-1992, was mothballed until 1995 and is now being dismantled following the failure to find a buyer.

STEEL ON THE CONTINENT: THE DOMINANCE OF THE 'HEAVY INDUSTRIAL TRIANGLE'

Germany: the Ruhr

Prior to the establishment of the EEC, the steel industry on the Continent was related almost entirely to the central coal belt and its associated supplies of iron ore. The original definition of the 'Heavy Industrial Triangle' (fig. 6.3) is based upon the Ruhr, the Nord/Pas de Calais and Sambre–Meuse coalfields, and the southern apex of Lorraine. The Ruhr rose to importance during the mid- and late nineteenth century with large quantities of high-grade, easily extracted coking coal, and clayband iron ore. The Siegerland iron ore and limestone was close by, and after the Franco–Prussian war of 1870–71, when Lorraine was under German occupation, the Ruhr used large quantities of Lorraine iron ore. The River Rhine and its extensive canal system including the Dortmund–Ems, was an excellent vehicle for cheap imports of iron ore. Finally, the growth of the Ruhr as a major urban and industrial area helped generate its own market of numerous steel-using industries such as those manufacturing locomotives, armaments, rolling stock, heavy engineering products and light engineering products such as cutlery. By 1938 Germany produced 22 million tonnes of steel, nearly 70 per cent of which came from the Ruhr. By 1974, in spite of a setback immediately after the Second World War, the Ruhr was producing 34 million tonnes of steel. Even with the reduced production levels since 1974, it still produces 56 per cent of Germany's total. Some idea of the concentrated nature of the German steel industry in the Ruhr is given by the fact that this great volume is produced in a conurbation of some

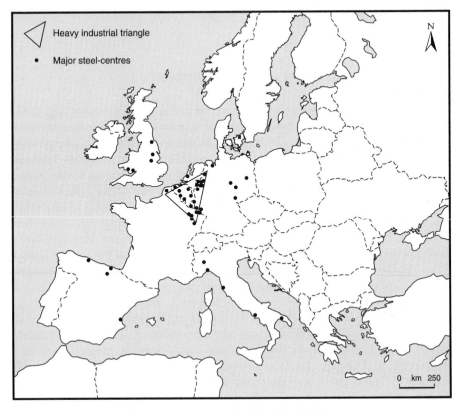

FIGURE 6.3   *Major steel-producing centres in the EU (12), 1994*

60 km by 16 km in extent, mainly in large integrated plants at Oberhausen, Rheinhausen, Duisburg and Dortmund.

France: Nord/Pas de Calais

The French steel industry is much less concentrated, but one major area has been the Nord/Pas de Calais coalfield. There were three traditional districts: Denain–Valenciennes, the centre of the heavy industry; Boulogne and Isbergues on the Aire canal; the minor production centres of Maubeuge and Hautmont in the Sambre valley. These small-scale steel works were in the congested older areas of the coalfield, and the centre of production has now moved to the large coastal integrated works at Dunkerque.

Belgium

Across the Belgian frontier lies the Sambre–Meuse coalfield. Both the coal and haematite iron ores outcropping along the valley were the initial location factors for a very considerable heavy industrial zone. La Louvière–Charleroi in the centre and Liège–Seraing at the eastern end of the coalfield retain a large proportion of Belgium's steel industry, now in a few large integrated works.

Lorraine, Luxembourg and the Saarland

The major home iron-ore-producing region in the EU is Lorraine (fig. 6.4). This developed after 1870 based upon the exploitation of the Jurassic iron ores. These lean ores (up to 30 per cent iron), with their high phosphorus content, became economic only with the invention of the Gilchrist-Thomas process. This stimulated the movement of steel manufacturing to the iron-ore field by the early twentieth century, similarly to that of the UK. Lorraine is a major French steel-making area with 28 per cent of total production. Considerable rationalisation and modernisation of small factories has occurred. Iron-ore output has fallen to 5 million tonnes per year (fig. 6.6), and now provides only a partial supply of the raw material for steel-making. There is also the small but productive Lorraine coalfield. Even so, Lorraine imports coal from the Ruhr. The export of iron ore to the rest of the EU is increasingly difficult because of competition from imported high-grade ores. The Ruhr, Belgium and the Nord no longer use Lorraine ore and its use is confined to its own region, the Saar and Luxembourg. The Lorraine steel-making area stretches from Nancy in the south through Hagondange and Thionville to Longwy. In Luxembourg, a large steel industry for a small country is based upon the northern extension of the Lorraine ore-field. There are three steelworks near the southern border with France (fig. 6.4), but large imports of coal are needed to sustain the industry. The Saarland

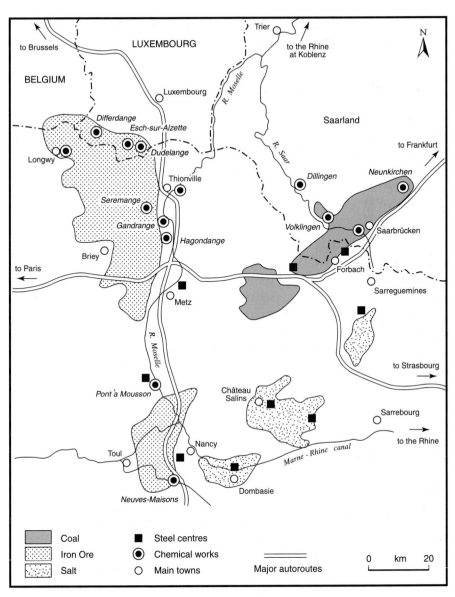

FIGURE 6.4 *Lorraine, Luxembourg and the Saarland*

coal basin is the third major steel-producer in the region, producing steel at Saarbrücken, Volklingen and Neunkirchen.

Other steel-making centres away from the Rhinelands

The areas so far discussed in the Heavy Industrial Triangle are the traditional national steel-making regions of Germany, France, Belgium and

Luxembourg, which although adjacent to one another, developed entirely separately. They are all based upon highly concentrated reserves of coal and iron ore, but historical rivalries over the national frontiers which dissected this natural resource zone created fears during the nineteenth century that each steel industry was too close to the frontier for strategic safety. The best example of this geographical unity but historical separation is the essential complementarity of the Ruhr and Lorraine, whose logical exchange of raw materials was for long prevented not only by transport problems but also by national rivalry and high tariff barriers. One result of this has been the development of steel-making capacity, albeit on a small scale, in regions away from the frontiers which were felt to be strategically safer, particularly in France and Germany. In France the Massif Central has scattered deposits of coal and iron ore and had the added strategic advantage of being within the heart of the country, safe from attack. The St Etienne region around the Loire coalfield was the cradle of the Industrial Revolution in France and, until the end of the nineteenth century, was the leading area of steel production. To the north lies the small Blanzy coal basin with Le Creusot as another 19th-century steel and engineering area. Other small coal basins with industrial pockets lying around the Massif Central are Commentry and Decazeville. An interesting example of these small, dispersed and often very specialised industrial pockets is the cutlery centre of Thiers, between St Etienne and Clermont Ferrand. This pattern of inland dispersal was accentuated by the growth of centres such as Caen, where a steelworks was based upon local iron ore, and Grand Quevilly below Rouen on the Seine, using imported iron ore. In the Upper Isère and Arc valleys between Grenoble and Albertville, a specialised steel industry using hydro-electric power has developed. In Germany the steelworks at Peine and Salzgitter in Lower Saxony had been originally developed in 1938, partially upon the iron ore and coal of the Harz foreland of Lower Saxony. These areas maintained their position during the inter-war years because of favourable government policies, but have become increasingly insignificant in terms of contemporary steel-making capacity. In the former GDR, the Land of Brandenburg became a centre for the steel industry, using imported scrap iron and coke; other centres of production were based in Saxony Anhalt, Thuringia and Saxony. Much of this production is now being restructured, with significant reductions in employment.

By the 1950s two new factors similar to those already referred to in the UK were to play an increasingly important part in further development. These are the ECSC and technological changes, which together have substantially changed patterns of location and structure.

Sidmar Zelzate steelworks, Ghent, showing a large converter in operation

THE EUROPEAN COAL AND STEEL COMMUNITY (ECSC)

The European Coal and Steel Community (ECSC) came into effect in July 1952 primarily as a common market in coal, steel, iron ore, scrap, pig iron and coke. Its effect upon the coal industry was referred to in the previous chapter, but in the steel industry it has helped to give a European perspective and a long-term view of supply and demand. It has assisted in lowering freight rates; ensured conditions of equal competition and a regular supply of raw materials; created a single market and price levels; led to modernisation, rationalisation and expansion of production; raised the living standards of workers; assisted new steelworks development projects with investment grants; and encouraged intra-community mergers.

The abolition of frontier tariffs, national subsidies, and transport-rate discrimination has greatly increased interdependence and intercommunity trade. Lorraine, for instance, had a natural geographical advantage for marketing its products in the adjacent parts of south Germany, and from 1956 to 1961 it increased its sale of rolled steel products there fourfold. The transport costs of Ruhr coke fell by 30 per cent in the ten years up to 1962.

In 1952, just before the ECSC began, scrap cost $22 per tonne in the Netherlands, but in Italy up to $55 per tonne. The ECSC has been responsible for large reductions in transport charges across frontiers and for smoothing out cost variations between Member States.

The stability and large home market within the ECSC encouraged long-term planning and an increased growth potential, and there was a huge expansion of production. Between 1952 and 1964 the EEC steel output more than doubled to 83 million tonnes and, by 1973, the enlarged EC of nine produced 150 million tonnes, substantially more than the USA. The investment loans, research activities and regional social policies of the ECSC were together partially responsible for guiding the location of at least two new steel plants (fig. 6.5). The Sidmar steelworks on the Ghent–Terneuzen canal at Zelzate in East Flanders was built in 1962 in an area of economic depression. The Taranto steelworks in southern Italy was constructed with a view to it becoming an initial growth pole for metal-fabricating industries and for industrial employment in this underdeveloped area.

The large EU market of 372 million people has replaced raw materials as the dominant location factor.

THE CONTEMPORARY PATTERN OF STEEL–MAKING IN THE EU

The locational attraction of the coalfields has diminished with better iron-ore sintering and preparation, and with improved fuel economy there has been a fall in the amount of coke needed per tonne of pig iron. From the early 1960s it became progressively less economic to use home iron ore, which has a low iron content, and there was a great increase in imports of cheap, high-grade foreign ores of some 60 per cent purity. Lorraine and Andalusia in Spain are the only substantial home ore producers left (fig. 6.6). Germany finds it cheaper to import most of its iron ore. The Netherlands and Italy also depend upon imported coal. The coastal steelworks at Dunkerque consistently uses cheap imported coal from Poland and the USA. For the EU as a whole imports of iron ore from external countries now dominate supplies. The use of bulk carriers enables these raw materials to be carried cheaply by sea. The increasing use of scrap, particularly in those heavy industrial districts which produce a surplus for re-using, is shown by the fact that it is used for a third of Germany's, and nearly 60 per cent of Italy's, steel.

Coastal locations

The continuous wide-strip steel mill and the basic oxygen process were the two other very significant developments which assisted the cumulative

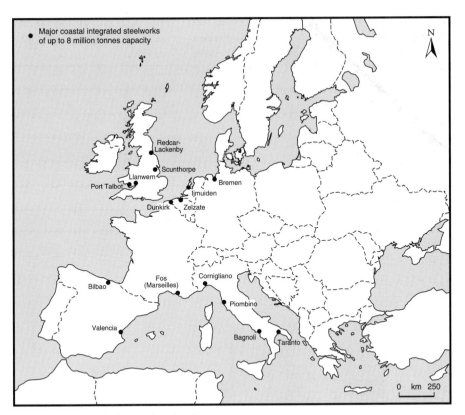

FIGURE 6.5   *EU (12) coastal steelworks*

movement to the large integrated coastal steelworks (fig. 6.5). These new locations have developed as a response to the increasing need for imports and deep-water ore-terminals, together with the availability of large bulk-carriers, and the need to eliminate transport costs to the interior. They are all large and many have a potential capacity of up to 8 million tonnes with berthing facilities for large ore-carriers. The first concentration of these is along the North Sea coast from Dunkerque to Bremen, and the second along the Mediterranean coast from the Rhône delta to Italy. Most of the Dutch steel production comes from the Ijmuiden works, built at the end of the North Sea canal, with a capacity for 6 million tonnes of ingot steel, rolling mills and a tinplate factory. It has a dock capable of handling 80 000-tonne ore-carriers. The only limitation to the Ghent (Zelzate) plant is that the Ghent–Terneuzen canal, by which it is linked to the West Scheldt, can take only 60 000-tonne ore-carriers. The Bremen works uses the Weserport facilities 55 km downstream for bulk ore-carriers. The Dunkerque works (6 million tonnes of steel) has facilities for 100 000-tonne carriers and, with Ijmuiden, these two have the greatest potential in a situation where import-handling efficiency is critical.

	Home production				Iron content of home ores (%)
	1976	1981	1986	1993	
Germany	3.0	1.6	1.0	0.8	14
France	45.5	21.8	14.7	4.9	30
Italy	0.6	–	–	–	–
Spain	–	–	6.4	1.2	45
Luxembourg	2.1	0.4	–	–	–
United Kingdom	4.6	–	–	–	–
Total EU (12)	55.8	23.8	22.1	6.9	35

FIGURE 6.6   *Iron-ore production in the EU (million tonnes)*

Italy

Piombino coastal steelworks, Livorno, Italy

The Italian steel industry vividly illustrates the dramatic growth and locational changes of the past 30 years. Prior to 1945, with negligible raw materials, steel-making was confined largely to northern Italy near the sources of hydro–electric power and the steel–using industries for scrap. This area has maintained its importance through heavy investment and the large markets of the Italian industrial triangle based upon Turin and Milan. Sesto San Giovanni, Turin, Bergamo and Brescia have a number of specialised steelworks producing quality steel in electric furnaces. There was a small works at Piombino, adjacent to Italy's only supplies of iron ore, on the Island of Elba. Total Italian production in 1953 was only 3.5 million tonnes. Since the early 1960s, however, production has increased at a phenomenal rate: in 1964 production had reached 9.8 million tonnes per year and by 1968 17 million tonnes. Production figures for 1993 rate Italian steel production substantially higher than that of France and the UK (fig. 6.1). Post-war reconstruction patterns have involved heavy state participation and control. The state has a controlling interest through the holding company of ILVA, which now controls some 60 per cent of total production. The unemployment problem of southern Italy was a major factor in the opening of the Taranto steelworks in 1964, with handling facilities for 100 000-tonne bulk ore-carriers, and it was planned that this should be the nucleus for the metal-fabricating industries in Bari and Taranto. The programme of development has been based upon coastal steelworks which import iron ore, scrap and coal very cheaply, and now four large integrated plants, Cornigliano, Piombino, Bagnoli and Taranto, produce the bulk of Italy's steel (fig. 6.5).

Spain, Portugal and Greece

The Spanish steel industry was largely developed in the 19th century upon the coal and iron-ore reserves of the Basque coastlands, but increasingly now relies upon imports. Development was small because of the peripheral nature of the Spanish economy in relation to Western Europe, but there has been intensive development of the steel industry since the Second World War. Major investment was made during the 1960s and 1970s by the regime of General Franco, assisted by West German and American investment with the aim of developing a modern steel industry. Bilbao is able to import scrap iron ore and coal cheaply by sea. There is also a modern integrated plant at Valencia on the east coast. Spain, now producing 13 million tonnes of steel per year, is a good example of heavy state involvement in the industry. The Portuguese and Greek governments have also created small steelworks at Seixal near Lisbon and Piraeus near Athens respectively, as part of the national development programmes and for import substitution purposes.

The Heavy Industrial Triangle

Although the movement to the coast has been very substantial, the Heavy Industrial Triangle still accounts for a major proportion of steel-making on the continent. The tremendous concentration of steel-making capacity in the Ruhr has substantial advantages with its large coal reserves, adjacent consumer markets, dense communications networks and local sources of scrap. Lorraine remains a major factor in French production plans. A new steelworks has been built at Dillingen in the Saar. Enormous capital investment is required for the development of entirely new 'greenfield sites', and this is another reason for the maintenance of traditional steel-making regions. They have, in addition, a positive advantage which accrues directly from the establishment of the ECSC and Common Market. The triangle now has a new role. It is the most centrally placed industrial area within the EU with good, short, internal lines of communication, the principal source of raw materials and a huge urban market and supply of labour. The canalisation of the Moselle has benefitted Lorraine (fig. 6.4), particularly with its dependence upon Ruhr coke via a waterway from which frontier tariffs have now disappeared. The effective disappearance of the frontiers has given this region a new advantage: the natural unit which has always been prescribed by geography but denied by history. Its complementary resources can now be used in a coherent manner, focussed upon the major artery of the River Rhône and its tributaries. The advantages of this Rhineland core region, with increased integration, have encouraged its maintenance as the single most important steel-making region of the EU (fig. 6.3).

Changing geography

However, the geography of the steel industry has changed considerably. The old core of steel-making in the Heavy Industrial Triangle has been supplemented and extended northwards towards the coastal regions around the North Sea, and southwards to the Mediterranean coasts.

State involvement

Considerable importance in decision-making still rests with the national governments and there is an increasing state involvement in both control and planning. Modernisation and rationalisation has involved relocation and amalgamation of companies, larger steelworks and an increasing domination by large corporations (fig. 6.7).

France

Three specific French projects have been significant:

(a) substantial investment in the Lorraine steel industry for manpower reduction, rationalisation and modernisation, including raising the capacity of Gandrange to 4 million tonnes;
(b) the doubling of the capacity of Dunkerque to 8 million tonnes;
(c) the construction of the Solmer plant at Fos-sur-Mer near Marseille, with 8-million-tonnes capacity, as part of the development plan for the Lower Rhône region.

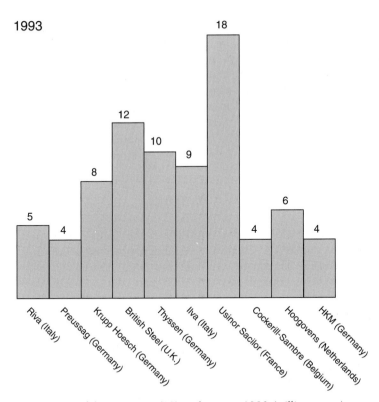

FIGURE 6.7 *Output of the major EU (12) steel groups, 1993 (million tonnes)*

This has completely changed the locational balance of the French steel industry, which is now dominated by two large coastal steelworks. Its structure is also changing rapidly with rationalisation: it is now dominated by the state-owned Usinor Sacilor which accounts for over 90 per cent of bulk steel output. There are still a number of small companies as a legacy from the days when the isolated metallurgical centres of the Massif Central and Alpine region flourished. Although many closures have been inevitable, survival has been based upon specialisation in special steels (Pechiney-Ugine produce French special and alloy steels). The French steel industry ran into considerable difficulties during 1978 and the French government was forced to nationalise it in an effort to rationalise its structure and increase productivity standards. This involved closure of inefficient plants and a large reduction in the workforce. Lorraine, heavily dependent upon the steel industry, has been badly affected, particularly in towns such as Longwy and Thionville, which have become depressed areas.

Mergers and large steel groups

The largest steel groups in the EU in terms of output are Usinor Sacilor of France, Thyssen of Germany, British Steel, ILVA of Italy and Krupp Hoesch of Germany. Other Member countries have experienced reorganisational change in varying degrees. The Luxembourg-based company Arbed also controls integrated steel plants in the Saarland and Belgium (through its subsidiary, Sidmar of Ghent) and has become a multi-national steel and engineering company with continuous casting facilities in Thuringia in the former GDR. Germany, the largest producer of steel in the EU (about 38 million tonnes in 1993), has a number of other major companies: Preussag, HKM, Metallgesellschaft, VIAG, Degussa, Eko-Stahl and Klocknerwerke. In Belgium Cockerill-Sambre emerged as the largest group.

The steel crisis from 1975 onwards

The rapid expansion of the steel industry in the 1960s was continued into the first half of the 1970s. This was accompanied by basic locational changes, and an increasingly integrated structure and larger size of steelworks. From no less than 113 companies in 1958, 60 per cent of production is now controlled by just *ten* large companies. Modernisation has continued with new investment and the closure of almost all open-hearth and Bessemer furnaces. In 1991, 76 per cent of UK steel was produced from basic oxygen converters, and 24 per cent from electric arc furnaces.

The steel industry, however, was badly affected by the recession which began with the oil crisis of 1973. Steel output fell from a high point of 156 million tonnes in 1974 to 126 million tonnes in 1986 (fig. 6.1). The projected EU capacity for the 1980s was originally over 200 million tonnes, but this was completely unrealistic. In 1981 EU steel production was running at only 63 per cent of capacity, and each country experienced severe problems with closures of steelworks, and labour redundancies. Even the Ruhr reduced production by 25 per cent. BSC slimmed its capacity most of all and closures of outdated plant proceeded, with gross capacity of 18 million tonnes being concentrated at five integrated steel plants. It was then returned to private ownership (1988) as British Steel PLC. The Belgian/Luxembourg steel industry was badly affected. These are two small countries with a high per capita steel production which was very important to their economy. There were too many small producers and much of the steel industry was in inland locations which tended to be more costly. The industry was restructured around two major companies: Cockerill-Sambre, located in the old heavy industrial zones of Liège and Charleroi, and Arbed, based in Luxembourg.

As an example of the process of integration into the declining EU steel industry, Spain in particular has encountered great problems. The state steel company ENSIDESA has been granted EU aid to restructure and modernise, reducing capacity and involving job losses of over 25 000 since 1983, particularly in the northern coastal provinces and Bilbao.

The causes of decline in steel-making were many and complex. There has been over-investment in the industry during the boom years of the 1960s. There was massive surplus capacity in the economic recession from 1973 onwards as demand fell sharply. The oil price rise that created the recession severely affected the EU steel industry as it used large amounts of energy. European steel was high-cost compared to many of the newer low-cost Third World producers of steel (the Newly Industrialised Countries – NICs) due to their cheaper labour costs, and this was exaggerated by the oil price rise. The dominant position of steel in the economy of developed countries had been severely eroded because of new raw materials and substitutes which could replace steel. The Japanese steel industry, with investment in robotics, was a major competitor. High-technology industries require less steel than the older industries. Steel followed industries such as textiles and shipbuilding into the category of a 'declining industry'. Not only did the NICs discover that it was cheaper for them to buy home-made steel rather than more expensive steel from the EU, but EU industries themselves were also beginning to import cheaper steel from foreign suppliers.

During this period of crisis EU steel companies increased production and offered discounts, leading to cut-throat competition, further price cuts and bankruptcies. To prevent the industry from fading away, governments put in subsidies despite the fact that this was strictly forbidden under the Treaty of Paris which created the European Coal and Steel Community (ECSC) in 1951. The EU decided that it had to act to prevent the market from breaking up through state aid. The first response came in 1977 from Etienne Davignon, the Commissioner for Industry. The Davignon Plan involved compulsory minimum prices for some products, voluntary production quotas and voluntary export restraints (VER) limiting imports from non-EU markets (the first VER agreement was with Japan in 1975). However, as the situation continued to worsen in the 1980s the 'Manifest Crisis' clause of the Treaty of Paris was invoked. This meant compulsory quotas, EU inspectors and fines for companies that broke regulations. The European Commission took steps to reorganise the industry as it realised that the long-term future of the steel industry could not be guaranteed by protective measures. It favoured the amalgamation of all bulk steel-making into a new pattern, which would involve extensive mergers and result in a few major steel groups each producing up to 12 million tonnes per year. Examples were the merger between Usinor and Salicor in France and the creation of ILVA in Italy. The steel industry had to modernise and regain its competitiveness. This meant taking advantage of new technology and reducing costs. Some of the technological advances included the electric arc steel furnace (which has enabled the development of mini-mills), continuous casting (around 90 per cent of EU crude steel is now produced by this method compared with 30 per cent in 1980) and the basic oxygen steel process. Although these technological advances reduced energy costs, the main saving was through redundancies. Between 1980 and 1990, the EU steel industry saw a 43 per cent reduction in the workforce, with the UK and France affected most. This restructuring process brought about a 19 per cent reduction in the EU's production capacity for crude steel.

Despite the considerable reduction in the production capacity and workforce, the restructuring of the 1980s was not completed. The sudden improvement of the market in 1988 as demand picked up, together with governments continuing to grant subsidies, enabled the less competitive manufacturers to survive. The buoyant economy up to 1991 obscured the need for change, and the decline of steel prices over the next three years took the industry by surprise. Prices in 1993 were about 30 per cent below the levels of 1990, pushing many firms into loss and making it impossible to write off plants which ought to have been closed. Many steel-making plants were unused, with the industry working at below 70 per cent of its capacity.

In 1993 steel producers recognised the need for major changes and were left to carry out their own restructuring with support from EU resources (in contrast to the imposed controls under the 'Manifest Crisis' of the 1980s). There was general agreement that up to 26 million tonnes of hot-rolled-steel production facilities and more than 30 million tonnes of crude steel capacity should be closed, leading to a loss of over 60 000 jobs. The ECSC budget would provide a Steel Social Programme to ease the impact of redundancy. Imports from Central and Eastern Europe, which were particularly affecting the German market, were controlled.

By 1994 capacity reduction had fallen well short of target, and there was resistance from Italy and Spain to reducing state subsidies. Germany asked for support for a rescue package for the East German producer Eko Stahl, and a powerful local campaign prevented the closure of the loss-making Klockner works near Bremen. Demand has now risen again with an improvement in prices, so that it is unlikely that further reductions will occur until the next crisis. In 1995 British Steel bought the UK's second largest steel company United Engineering Steels, signifying a possible expansionary period for an industry that has been in recession since the early 1970s.

However, non-subsidised producers continue to worry about subsidies to loss-making competitors, and there is concern about the impact of mini-mill competition from the USA and Japan. Mini-mills are relatively small companies with annual capacities ranging from 0.15 to 1.2 million tonnes of finished products. They are involved in the production of more specialised products, and play a significant part in the management of industrial waste, converting cheap scrap into quality steel products. Mini-mills make steel in plants a quarter of the size of the blast furnaces and rolling mills of the giant integrated firms and therefore require only a quarter of the capital investment. The mini-mills owe their success to their flexibility and capacity to adapt production to market demand. Japan and the USA are currently switching to this technology, and although mini-mills account for a substantial share in total steel production in certain Member States, e.g. Italy and Spain, 70 per cent of EU steel production comes from integrated companies which allow economies of scale but little flexibility of production.

7

OTHER INDUSTRIES: AUTOMOBILES, TEXTILES AND CHEMICALS

THE AUTOMOBILE INDUSTRY

The automobile industry has a central role in the complex industrial economies of Western Europe. It is a major user of raw materials and a large-scale employer. In France it absorbs 50 per cent of the production of rubber, 50 per cent of the shaped aluminium, and 21 per cent of sheet steel and machine tool production. About 4 million people gain their living (directly and indirectly) from the industry in the EU. Its real growth has been since 1945 as a reflection of consumer demand, and as a symbol of prosperity it has been seen as a propellant or growth-pole industry in the city regions where it has a significant multiplier effect. It is an assembly-line and component industry with horizontal integration resulting in a few large companies dominating production. The geographical location of the industry near large centres of population does not usually correspond to the older heavy-industry areas (fig. 7.1).

Development of the industry

The European motor industry originated in the 1890s with names such as Daimler, Lanchester and Panhard. In 1896 the Daimler Company began production in Coventry, but the industry had a slow undistinguished growth up to 1914, when it was primarily a small-scale producer of high-cost goods for a restricted market. Even until the slump of the 1930s it remained best known for a large number of specialist quality companies such as Lea Frances of the UK and Ferrari of Italy.

But during the 1930s, the character of the industry was changing. The economic depression wiped out many firms and mergers had occurred on a large scale. In the UK the number of manufacturers declined from 88 in 1922 to 31 in 1931. By 1937 the UK had become the second world producer next to the USA. Mass-production methods were introduced during the 1930s and the growth of per capita income was another indication of the imminent development of the consumer boom which was to come after 1945. The very rapid growth since 1945 corresponds to the initial demand for and development of the family car. Since then there has been replacement demand and now a third stage with the proliferation of the second family car. There is now one vehicle for every three people in the EU, but car-ownership figures vary widely across the EU, from nearly two vehicles for every three people in Germany to one vehicle for every six people in Greece and Portugal. The industry developed very rapidly between 1950 and 1980 and is consequently modern in characteristics. Factories are usually housed in one-storey modern buildings, and, with the large amount of space needed for storage and parking, usually cover a wide area. They are often on 'greenfield sites' (e.g. Wolfsburg, Germany) and some distance from city centres where space is readily available. Communications by road are invariably good and siting on by-pass roads is common. The car assembly factories on the A45 at Coventry and on the Rocade highway at Rennes in Brittany are good examples of this.

The structure of the vehicle industry

The assembly line involves the concentration of a wide range of supplies which come from subsidiary manufacturers. These provide basic materials such as pressed steel, rubber, glass, etc. and a host of manufactured components and accessories including electrical equipment and brakes. These specialist sub-contractors have traditionally been independent of the vehicle companies which are their main outlets and, therefore, vertical integration in the industry is almost non-existent. Indeed, the trend is towards 'de-verticalisation', and even Mercedes-Benz, famous for its high own-sourced content of almost two-thirds, is seeking to reduce this to 45 per cent. There are exceptions to this. Renault and Fiat have their own steel and metallurgy supplies; and Krupp Hoesch, essentially a steel-maker, also produces commercial vehicles. In general, however, the major component manufacturers are independent and exert a considerable monopoly. Between 1987 and 1992 there were around 350 mergers and acquisitions in the European motor-components industry, so that there are now only two main suppliers of dashboards (Magneti-Marelli and VDO-Mannesmann) and three main suppliers of brakes (Bendix, Teves and Lucas-Girling). With a great number of independent suppliers there is therefore a real necessity for efficient distribution. This leads to a tendency for a number of vehicle industry zones to develop, made up of linked component manufacturers and car assembly plants concentrated in and around city regions. This regional swarming has the advantages of short distances for the transport and distribution of components, a pool of skilled and semi-skilled labour, and easier technical cooperation. It is seen to best advantage in regions such as the West Midlands, Lower Saxony, the Paris region, the Rhinelands and Milan–Turin. However, in the last few years European companies have significantly reduced the number of suppliers they deal with directly from an average of 1200 in 1990 to 800 in 1993, reflecting the trend to emulate the Japanese companies that generate trust by single-sourcing almost everything. Nissan deals with under 200 companies, while Volkswagen deals with more than 1400.

Location

Each nation's vehicle-producing areas are often city regions in national core areas whose large populations provide the natural market (fig. 7.1). The UK has a traditional concentration in the West Midlands, particularly at Coventry and Birmingham. There is a distinct tendency for factories to be sited on the outer fringes of the city, away from the congested centres. In the Greater Paris region the largest companies have factories in the suburbs or satellite towns. Renault has its main works at Billancourt, but has other factories at Nanterre and Clichy to the north-west, at Rouen and Le Havre on the Lower Seine, and Orleans and Le Mans. There is also

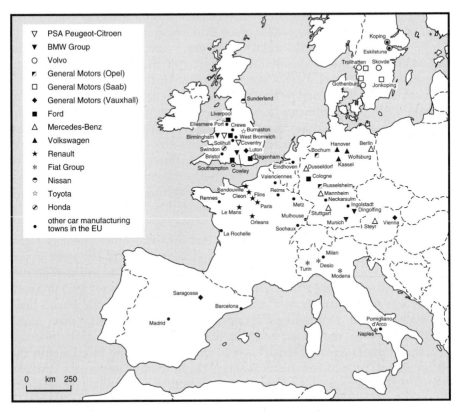

FIGURE 7.1   *The motor vehicle industry – principal locations in the EU*

Peugeot-Citroën at Reims and Poissy. However, there has been a significant locational change in the French motor-vehicle industry, with decentralisation occurring in response both to government intervention and to rising costs and shortage of space in the Greater Paris region. There are also anomalous situations such as the Peugeot factories at Montbeliard in the Jura and Mulhouse in Alsace, which continue to operate successfully from there as high managerial and technical skills overcome their apparent disadvantage of location.

Germany illustrates a modification of this pattern: Daimler-Benz at Unterturkheim and Sindelfingen near Stuttgart, and at Mannheim and Gaggenau in the middle Rhineland; General Motors (Opel) at Russelsheim (Frankfurt); BMW at Munich; Porsche at Stuttgart; and Ford at Cologne. All these indicate the importance of the cities of south Germany and the Rhinelands. The largest single vehicle enterprise, however, Volkswagen, does not conform to this particular model. Wolfsburg was an early example of relocation of industry in 1937 to the then centre of Germany, partly for strategic reasons and partly as a policy of dispersing Ruhr industry. It was located next to the Mittelland canal, the main waterway from the Ruhr to Berlin. The reputation and efficiency of the company have allowed it to expand its operations, the Volkswagen factory now employing over 50 000 people. It has expanded to nearby Hanover, Brunswick and Kassel, and Lower Saxony has become the country's second vehicle region with 40 per cent of output, equivalent to that of the Rhinelands.

To summarise, the EU vehicle industry is principally located in the following areas: the Midlands and south-east of England; the Paris region; Barcelona and Madrid, Lower Saxony and the Rhinelands. Nevertheless, the industry has been encouraged to move into areas of high unemployment in certain cases. Governments have used the car industry as a target for decentralisation and to aid the restructuring of old industrial regions. The Italian government has used the car industry in its industrialisation programme for the Mezzogiorno. The Turin-based car manufacturer, Fiat, chose Melfi in Basilicata as the site for its new factory to produce the Punto. Fiat's choice of the site was partly due to generous government grants and partly due to the lower wage costs (14 per cent below those of Turin) and the willingness of the workforce to accept new working practices. Melfi is also in an area clear of Mafia influence. Fiat has three other assembly plants in the south (at Avellino, Pomigliano and Cassino), and by 1994 it was producing more cars from its southern factories than from Turin. The UK government encouraged factories to be established on Merseyside, in South Wales and at Bathgate in Scotland, and this continued with the Nissan plant at Washington in North-East England. In France and Germany there is also a movement to the older coalfield areas which need a new industrial infrastructure. Peugeot-Citroën has a factory at Lille in the Nord region and it has also set up two factories at Rennes, the development pole for Brittany. In 1939, 75 per cent of the French workforce in motor-vehicle manufacture was in Paris, compared with 30 per cent in 1992. Opel has a factory at Bochum in the Ruhr, and Ford at Saarlouis. In Germany a relatively new development has been the link with establishments both in former East Germany, notably Volkswagen with Trabant in Zwickau (which they subsequently closed, transferring the workforce to a new site at the Mosel), and elsewhere in Central Europe – e.g. Skoda in former Czechoslovakia. It is often politically useful but not geographically logical to move industries out of their traditional centres. Government intervention often runs in the face of the advantages of regional swarming.

The major vehicle companies

Horizontal integration has become almost complete. The assembly lines and mass-production units are dominated by a few large companies, with resulting economies of scale. In the UK in 1993 four groups dominated: the Ford group (including Jaguar) produced 22 per cent, General Motors 18 per cent, Rover (now a subsidiary of BMW) 14 per cent and the Peugeot group 12 per cent. There are several small, but significant, luxury manufacturers, such as Rolls-Royce. On the Continent there is a similar picture. In Germany Volkswagen dominates the market, with 28 per cent of total production and a very considerable export market, followed again by Opel (General Motors), Ford and Daimler-Benz. France has two major groups, Peugeot–Citroën (30 per cent), and the Renault company (27 per cent). Italy, however, has the most marked concentration by one company. Fiat produces 45 per cent of Italy's cars, and controls Lancia, Alfa Romeo, Maserati, Innocenti and Ferrari.

The EU car industry in its global context

Motor vehicles are an important element in the EU's trade. With the progressive abolition of tariffs during the 1960s and 1970s intra-EU trade increased spectacularly and it has now risen to almost 36 per cent of total production. However, during the last decade there has been increasing import penetration from Japan, which now takes 12 per cent of the EU market. American involvement in the European vehicle industry is very significant, but varies from 40 per cent control in the UK and 35 per cent in Germany, to 12 per cent in France and Italy. This American involvement, the Japanese export assault upon the European market, and the advantages of scale mentioned earlier, are the principal reasons for the existence of a few large EU companies which can compete in the world scene (fig. 7.3).

In the 1980s the vehicle industry entered an uncertain period. The market became increasingly saturated and competition severe. The instability underlying the oil industry in the 1980s led to a search for more economical cars. First Rover and Fiat and later Peugeot and Renault found that over-optimistic investments had left them with too much capacity, too many workers and unsustainable levels of overheads. Faced with too much capacity chasing too few customers, they accepted the need to retrench to survive. This involved both restructuring within firms and mergers between

The Volkswagen factory at Wolfsburg, Germany

firms. There was a swing to automated production, labour shedding in old plants and lower manning levels on new production lines – e.g. Renault's plant at Palencia in Northern Spain has an annual output of 100 000 vehicles but only 3300 employees. Employment in the EU was reduced by 20 per cent and productivity increased by more than 40 per cent. Greater mechanical reliability was sought and new models introduced to match imports in terms of performance, equipment and comfort. Mergers included those between Peugeot and Citroen in France and Volkswagen and Audi in Germany.

One important change that resulted from the experiences of the early 1980s was the withdrawal from ownership by national governments. SEAT and Alfa Romeo were the first to be sold off, the German government sold its stake in Volkswagen in 1987, and the UK government privatised Jaguar in 1985 and Rover in 1988.

Spain alone in the EU experienced a rapid development programme in the 1980s. Spain is now the EU's third largest producer (fig. 7.2). The principal reasons for this were an import tariff barrier of 37 per cent before joining the EU and an aggressive government-sponsored expansion policy aimed at import substitution with the aid of foreign investment particularly from the USA and Germany.

In the second half of the 1980s EU production staged a marked recovery (fig. 7.2), and output at the end of the decade was a third higher than at the start – a comparable performance to that of Japan and far better than that of North America. Production-capacity shortages began to occur, encouraging a general interest in Eastern Europe as a production area.

However, in mid-1992 the recession struck the EU motor-vehicle industry, and in 1993 new car sales fell by more than 15 per cent to the lowest total for eight years, creating the biggest year-on-year decline of the post-war period. Production of cars is now only just above 1973 levels. In Germany production is down 6 per cent from the 1991 post-unification boom levels, and in the UK and Italy production has stagnated. This has led to a further period of restructuring – e.g. Volkswagen, after suffering a loss in 1993, has reduced its workforce by 27 000 at its six domestic plants, and Ford of Europe has reduced its workforce by 15 per cent. Further concentration has occurred, e.g. the takeover of Rover by BMW in 1994. Restructuring is also taking on new forms, however, as producers dispose of in-house components operations to outside suppliers to allow themselves to concentrate on the core operations of the design, development and assembly of vehicles.

The EU produces 36 per cent of world car output (fig. 7.2), but the industry is rapidly changing as the EU moves to become an open car market by 2000. In order to avoid very strict controls, Japan entered into voluntary restraint agreements with five EU countries: the UK, Italy, Spain, Portugal and France. These national agreements cannot be retained now that the Single European Market is operating, and so the Commission has, with great difficulty, negotiated alternative arrangements. These allow for the level of Japanese imports to the EU to be frozen at the current level of 1.2 million a year, but all restrictions on car and light commercial vehicle imports from Japan are due to be removed at the end of 1999.

European producers are being forced to act quickly to close the competitive gap behind their Japanese and North American rivals and to counter new producers such as South Korea (Hyundai, Kia and Daewoo). Imports from Japan came to a mere 45 000 cars in 1970, but they rose to 743 000 in 1980 and exceeded 1.2 million a year in the early 1990s. This growth was in spite of two obstacles: a major deterioration in the exchange rates for European currencies against the yen, and the protectionist measures taken by France and particularly Italy to exclude Japanese imports. To counter this last measure, Japanese producers have built transplant factories in the EU so that the vehicles they produce are not classed as imports and can therefore be sold throughout the Single Market. The move into Europe is largely a move into the UK which has proved attractive because of the 'open door' policy of the British government. The 'Big Three' (Honda, Nissan and Toyota) are now firmly in place, but the French and Italians are aggrieved at the British policy, with the UK being described as a 'Trojan Horse' or 'Japan's fifth island'. However, Nissan and Suzuki have production operations in Spain, and Mitsubishi, in a joint venture with Volvo and the Dutch government, is producing vehicles at Born in Southern Holland.

The expansion of the Japanese 'Big Three' means that manufacturing capacity could outstrip sales by between 2 and 3 million by the late 1990s. The response of the EU producers is to develop new leaner production practices such as the just-in-time (JIT or 'Kan-banning' as it is sometimes called) Japanese philosophy whereby components are not stockpiled months in advance but ordered when required (this has the advantage of removing

		Cars			Commercial vehicles			
	1967	1973	1985	1991	1993	1967	1986	1991	1993
Germany	2296	3642	4165	4660	3753	187	266	356	237
France	1777	3202	2817	3188	2836	233	423	423	320
Spain	–	–	1230	1774	1505	–	132	308	261
Italy	1439	1823	1389	1633	1117	103	162	245	150
Netherlands	49	94	106	85	80	7	14	14	6
Belgium★	164	260	987	1430	1438	25	50	51	42
UK	1560	1747	1048	1237	1146	384	225	217	193
Portugal★	–	–	60	60	78	–	28	77	52
Denmark★	nil	nil	1	1	1	nil	1	1	1
Eire	nil	nil	nil	nil	nil	nil	1	nil	nil
Greece	nil	nil	nil	nil	nil	nil	nil	nil	nil
Luxembourg	nil	nil	nil	nil	nil	nil	nil	nil	nil
Total	7285	10 768	11 803	14 068	11 954	939	1302	1692	1262

★ includes vehicle assembly by subsidiary companies

FIGURE 7.2 *EU (12) motor vehicle production and assembly (thousands)*

Volkswagen	16.3
General Motors (USA)	13.0
PSA Peugeot Citroën	12.1
Ford (USA)	11.8
Fiat	11.1
Renault	10.5
BMW	6.4
Others	18.8

FIGURE 7.3 *EU car companies, 1993 (percentage of EU market)*

storage costs); to move from 'brown' to 'green' engines (not just to the so-called 'crisis' cars like the Peugeot ECO 2000 – capable of over 160 km to the gallon – but also to alternative power plants that release less carbon dioxide emissions); to move into luxury-car production (General Motors has acquired Lotus) and to develop East European markets (Volkswagen has embraced the transplant factory as a means of expansion, exploiting the East European markets with a 70 per cent stake in the former Czechoslovakian Skoda works in an attempt to emulate its successful 'takeover' of the Spanish SEAT).

However, Nissan in Sunderland have already taken JIT a step further by developing 'synchronous supply' which has cut inventory times to 10 minutes in some cases. This is only possible because the synchronous suppliers are virtually next door to the main plant in Washington and are computer-linked. As each painted body arrives on the final production line, it carries a coding tag with all the specifications of colour, size, etc. At each station this tag triggers a computer message to the supplier requesting a precise part for that body. Ikeda Hoover, the seat makers, have 45 minutes to make and deliver the seat 1.6 km away. The company delivers 12 sets of seats to the exact place on the line every 20 minutes. The seats and other parts are delivered in special frames, which are returned for reuse, eliminating the need for extra packaging.

A final challenge facing motor-vehicle producers is that environmental problems could result in measures to reduce the use of passenger cars, diverting people to public road and rail transport or other forms of transport. Congestion resulting from the failure to extend and improve the road network could also deter growth.

THE TEXTILE AND CLOTHING INDUSTRY

The textile and clothing industry is an old staple industry, a major exporter and one of the most important single industries in the EU. It has a workforce of over 2.7 million (with 143 000 enterprises, of which 117 000 have less than twenty employees), representing nearly 9 per cent of total manufacturing employment. It is, however, beset with problems of foreign competition, a relatively slow growth of domestic consumption, and an outmoded structure associated with its nineteenth-century origins. Its precursor, the cottage industry, has retained a residual influence in the survival of sub-divided processes and the tendency to small-scale factory units, with a poor degree of integration. It is often, therefore, described as a declining industry and has faced great problems of adjustment during the present century.

Location

There has been a tradition of heavy regionalisation and concentration in localities originally favoured with water power, coal and the local availability or import facility of the raw material. On a European scale there are a number of major textile zones in terms of the numbers employed (fig. 7.4):

Flanders and the Rhineland; Bavaria; Lombardy and Piedmont; Veneto; the sub-Pennine region of Lancashire and Yorkshire; Norte in Portugal; and Catalonia in Spain. However, if the number of people working in textiles and clothing as a proportion of the total workforce is mapped, then a different picture emerges. Regions with over 30 per cent of industrial employment in textiles and clothing are Norte, Central Macedonia, Western Greece and Castile–La Mancha, and many of the regions with lesser proportions are also in Greece and Portugal, indicating a link between the less prosperous Member States and the textiles and clothing industry. Several smaller, though significant areas, often medieval in origin, have survived by specialising in high-quality fabrics or by developing a monopoly in a particular material or process.

Flanders–North Rhineland

Astride the Franco–Belgian border lies one of the traditional textile areas in Europe, important since the Middle Ages. It stretches across the Plain of Flanders from Lille into Belgium between Courtrai and Ghent. From its earlier concentration on local wool from the sheep grazed on chalk

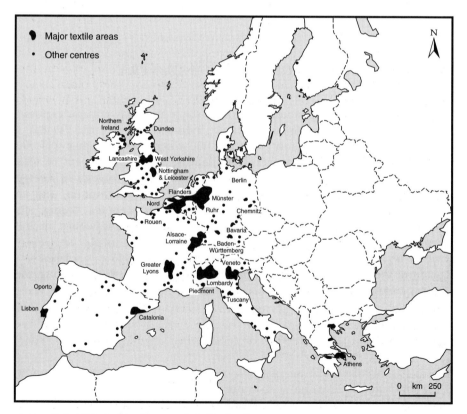

FIGURE 7.4 *Principal textile manufacturing locations*

escarpments, and linen using flax from the Lys valley, it changed into a complex modern industry. Cotton, nylon and mixed fibres are produced at Lille, Roubaix–Tourcoing, Armentières and La Bassée, but fine linens, carpets, hosiery, clothing and furnishing fabrics are also manufactured, and outlying centres include Amiens, Abbeville and Cambrai. In Belgium about half of the total number of cotton spindles were in or around Ghent, but the Scheldt–Dendre valley towns of Oudenaarde, Ranse, Tournai and Geerardsbergen were also important. Courtrai produced fine linen from Lys valley flax, though most flax is now imported from France and Poland. The industry has moved into Brabant and Brussels, producing carpets, blankets and fashionable clothing. The original woollen industry has now largely migrated to Verviers in the Ardennes to take advantage of the soft water and local wool.

The textile areas of the Netherlands and Germany are a natural eastward extension. In the Netherlands the industry developed from the trading activities of the Hanseatic league along the Rhine, in the towns of Breda, Tilburg, Arnhem, Nijmegen and Rotterdam/Dordrecht. During the twentieth century there was an eastward extension to the eastern heathland towns of Hengelo, Enschede, Emmen and Twente, where nylon and rayon production is carried out. In adjacent Germany lies the 'Baumwollstrasse' of North Rhine/Westphalia, where a combination of Ruhr coal and the traditional crafts of towns such as Krefeld and Mönchen-Gladbach have produced a specialised textile industry which occupies towns around the fringes of the Ruhr. Krefeld's original speciality of silk and velvet has been supplemented by nylon and terylene. The cotton industry was centred upon Wuppertal, Mönchen-Gladbach and Bocholt. Düsseldorf and Cologne were important too, and the area extends northwards to Nümster and Bielefeld, which specialised in linen.

Lombardy, Upper Piedmont and Veneto

The bulk of the Italian textile industry is concentrated along the northern Alpine fringe of the Po valley, stretching from Biella through Milan, Bergamo and Vicenza to Padua. The principal concentration of cotton manufacturing is within a radius of 60 km from Milan, in the industrial satellite towns of Varese, Gallarate, Busto Arsizio and Legnano. There has been quite intense regional specialisation, particularly in the silk manufacturing arc of Como, Varese and Treviglio, and the concentration of woollens and worsteds in the Biellese and Bergamasque sub-Alpine valleys. Immediately to the south of Milan, the towns of Vercelli, Magenta and Pavia manufacture synthetic fibres. Another woollen and knitwear area is based upon Padua, Vicenza, Schio and Valdegno, in Veneto Province.

The Lancashire/Yorkshire sub-Pennine region

The rise of the textile areas of northern England was caused by the coincidence of several factors in a unique situation, which led to the establishment of two areas which dominated world textile production in the nineteenth century. The natural factors were the suitability of the Pennines for sheep-rearing, abundant lime-free water, numerous sites for water power, coupled with a high relative humidity, and power from the Lancashire coalfield. These were augmented by crucial human factors. These were the energy of pragmatic non-conformists and entrepreneurs, and their ability to accumulate capital, the inventions of textile machinery by Kay, Arkwright and Crompton, and the lack of guilds in this area. The construction of port facilities, canals and railways as the expansion of these industrial areas got under way, and as imports of raw materials became necessary, was a further factor of concentration.

There was an extraordinary degree of specialisation in Lancashire, and in 1931, 84 per cent of all cotton operatives in the UK were in East Lancashire and the adjoining part of Yorkshire. Manchester was the commercial centre, bank and warehouse. Spinning was localised in an arc of towns close to Manchester, and weaving more particularly in the group of towns north of the Rossendale Fells and in the Ribble valley. The finishing trades (bleaching and dyeing) and clothing were not quite as localised, factories tending to be limited to one or other activity, which led to small production units and a lack of integration.

West Yorkshire developed an equally concentrated woollen textile region, based upon the Leeds–Bradford conurbation. Here the principal specialisation was in the type of product rather than, as in Lancashire, in processes. Long wools for worsteds predominated in Bradford and the north-west of the region, and short wools for woollen products in the south-east, whilst carpets were made at Halifax, and Leeds was the ready-made clothing centre. Bradford was the financial and commercial centre of the industry.

Catalonia, Spain

Barcelona, once capital of the Catalan kingdom, is the most important manufacturing city of Spain. It is an industrial, commercial and financial centre, but its wealth was originally based upon its port, the cotton trade and the development of the textile industry. Water power was a major factor of textile development in Catalonia and has now been replaced by modern hydro-electric plants in the Ebro valley. Cotton, wool and synthetic fibres are manufactured in Barcelona and a ring of satellite towns – Badalona, Manresa, Granollers, Mataro and Sabadell. Textile machinery is also one of the range of engineering industries in the city. Although the textile industry is widely spread throughout Spain and other cities such as Bilbao, Catalonia is the greatest single concentration, with over 3000 small factories.

Other areas

1 **Alsace–Lorraine:** This originated as a textile area in the medieval period. The Vosges mountains provided local wool, soft water and

fast-flowing streams, and the industry has survived in factories around Epinal, Mulhouse, Belfort and Colmar, chiefly with cottons, thread, fine linen and hosiery.

2 **Greater Lyons:** Silk-making originated in the fifteenth century from exiled Italian merchants and 80 per cent of French output still comes from this area. Rayon and nylon has developed to supplement the natural silk.

3 **Bavaria and Baden-Württemberg:** The cities of south Germany have a traditional cotton textile industry at Stuttgart, Karlsruhe and Augsburg.

4 **Peninsula Italy:** There is a significant woollen area in Tuscany (Prato and Florence in the valley of the River Arno) and at Rome. Woollens have been supplemented with synthetics established by large companies like Snia-Viscosa. Local raw materials are an advantage, with mulberries supporting silkworms in the Marche and eucalyptus being grown for rayon production. In the south large factories were set up under the auspices of the Cassa per il Mezzogiorno at Caserto and Frosinone (Naples) and Pisticci (Taranto).

5 **The East Midlands Hosiery Belt of England:** This is dominated by Leicester and Nottingham, but stretches south in the valley of the River Soar around Hinckley, and north to Mansfield. This area expanded rapidly in the 1960s, because of the expanding market for knitwear and the ease with which synthetic fibres can be used. Around Nottingham it is associated with the original lace industry and the early working of silk and cotton, and around Leicester with woollens.

6 **Northern Ireland:** Ulster is a world-famous linen-manufacturing region. Belfast dominates the industry, but Lurgan, Lisburn, Portadown and Ballymena are also important. Although competition from cheaper goods and the decline in demand for high-quality specialist linen has taken place, the industry still has an important export market and a large development of synthetics has taken place.

7 **Dundee, Scotland:** Linen and jute are the two products of this very specialised town. Dunfermline damasks and Paisley fabrics are other famous specialities.

8 **Kidderminster in Worcestershire, England:** This town is a specialised carpet centre, based originally upon local wool and now dependent upon skilled labour and upmarket products.

9 **Rouen:** This is an isolated cotton-manufacturing town originally based upon raw cotton imports through Le Havre.

10 **Portugal:** Local wool and imported cotton form the basis for the textile industry in Portugal. Lisbon, Oporto and Coimbra are the principal centres with woollens, cotton and garment manufacturing, but there are several hundred small factories spread through most of the major towns. In the Norte (North) region, textiles account for 19 per cent of employment, with a particular concentration in the Vale do Ave where some 120 firms employ more than 30 000 workers. In the Centro (Centre) region some inland towns are very dependent on textiles – e.g.

the textiles industry provides more than 70 per cent of industrial jobs in Castelo Branco and Guarda. The long coarse wool (*churra*) produced in the north goes mostly to make rugs and carpets, whilst the finer merino wool of the south produces woollen cloths.

11 **Greece:** In Greece the textile industry is spread throughout the country with hundreds of small firms, but there are concentrations in Central Macedonia, where the department of Imathia has a highly developed cotton industry, and in Western Greece where there is a concentration in the town of Patras.

Decline and adjustment

The EU textile industry has the most modern production facilities in the world and is still a world leader in design and creativity, but despite these assets the industry has seen a significant decline in recent decades. Employment in the industry declined throughout the 1980s by more than 30 per cent. The UK was badly affected, with one estimate that in 1990 there were 100 job losses every working day. The cotton industry, particularly in Lancashire, has shown the classic symptoms of decline and the need for restructuring an old industry. In the nineteenth century Europe dominated world textile production, and as late as 1900 the UK accounted for 50 per cent, and the other EU nations for 35 per cent of world textile exports. The huge fall in British exports this century was caused by the developing nations of Asia, formerly its export markets, beginning to build up their own textile industries. Lancashire felt the loss of markets most heavily because of its high degree of specialisation in cotton fabrics which were particularly oriented towards the export trade. By the 1920s the inherent disadvantages of Lancashire had become apparent: the lack of local raw materials; static home demand; the near impossibility of competing with the cheap labour of India, China, Japan and Hong Kong; and an increasingly obsolete industrial structure with old machinery. Production dropped and unemployment rose. There was, therefore, no alternative for Lancashire but to rationalise the structure of the industry, to improve efficiency, and to reduce capacity and the workforce at a socially acceptable rate.

In many other parts of the EU there has been a similar pattern of events. The French and Belgian textile industry is still characterised by its small production units and long domestic traditions. During the 1960s France had about 5000 mills employing nearly half-a-million workers. Changes in the international division of labour were being seen within Europe, with declining production in the mature north-west European countries being matched by a shift of production to lower cost centres in southern Europe. During the period 1965–77 over 900 000 jobs in textiles were lost in north-west Europe, whilst at the same time nearly 300 000 were created in Italy, Spain, Portugal and Greece. In Italy the production of woollens and hosiery, in particular, expanded rapidly. Since 1977, however, contraction has been

	1958	1971	1981	1986	1991	1993
Germany	607	499	336	258	274	na
France	518	425	293	228	187	161
Belgium/Luxembourg	172	121	68	59	52	27
Italy	481	542	476	409	na	437
Spain				217	146	127
Portugal				75	167	142
Greece				59	40	75
Netherlands	103	76	33	22	20	10
United Kingdom	815	622	395	246	174	161
Ireland	neg	42	19	11	11	na
Denmark	neg	20	15	15	7	13
Total	2696	2347	1635	1599	1078	1153

na = not available

neg = neglible amount

FIGURE 7.5   *EU (12) changes in employment in the textile industry (thousands)*
(source – Eurostat)

particularly rapid, with all countries of the EU experiencing factory closures
and falling employment. The mill towns of the Nord and Alsace–Lorraine
have been badly affected, with the textile workforce of the Nord region
reduced from 170 000 in 1951 to 60 000 in 1982, and to 34 000 in 1991.

The economic crises since 1973 have particularly affected the textile
industry, because a period of falling demand has coincided with a sharp
increase in imports of inexpensive textiles from low-cost, developing
countries. In the EU as a whole, over 3500 factories have closed and nearly
1.2 million jobs have been lost since 1971 (fig. 7.5). To allow time for
modernisation and reorganisation, the EU has negotiated import-limitation
agreements (quotas) with some 30 low-cost textile-producing countries
under the multi-fibre arrangement (MFA). This is a system set up in 1974 to
protect the textiles and clothing industries in the Economically More
Developed Countries (EMDCs) from cheaper products from Economically
Less Developed Countries (ELDCs). The MFA was only envisaged as a
temporary arrangement, but it has been renewed three times. The
agreement now is to phase it out over a period of ten years from 1995 in
return for a commitment from textile-supplier countries to adhere more
closely to strengthened General Agreement on Tariffs and Trade (GATT)
rules.

There is now a definite trend towards larger companies and a greater
integration of production to gain the economies of scale. In the UK in 1946

there were over 1300 registered companies, but now there are three large groups, including Courtaulds and Coats/Viyella. Courtaulds has accomplished a substantial amount of horizontal integration. Coats/Viyella (by far the largest European textile company, in terms of both turnover and employees) are represented in all processes of the industry from spinning through to clothing production, and is a good example of vertical integration. In the high-income European countries, the numerous fashion changes, which require quick decisions and manufacturing changes, are best taken by such large well-capitalised companies, although even they can be overtaken by very rapid changes. Although a much greater degree of horizontal and vertical integration has been achieved in the UK, many of the southern EU producers, such as Greece and Spain, still have a predominance of small-scale and family firms. Portugal, in particular, has an unintegrated structure with several hundred small factories that are labour intensive, and use domestic production techniques. However, rationalisation is rapidly occurring here with funding from the EU under the RETEX programme as firms face competition from ELDCs. RETEX funds are available not to help the industry update production methods but to create alternative employment. It is estimated, therefore, that a third of Portugal's textile and clothing plants will close during the 1990s, with 60 000 job losses.

Although the picture of textiles is one of overall decline, not all branches of the industry have experienced the same rapid decline as cotton. Production of woollens has remained virtually static whilst that of synthetic fibres has dramatically increased. Woollens have had a greater ability to specialise in high-quality fabrics and to concentrate on the high-value domestic market. The woollen industry was never quite so dependent upon the export market as cotton, and thus had fewer potential contraction problems. Wool can be blended easily with synthetic fibres and has benefited from the rapid rise of the carpet and hosiery industries. The volume of knitted goods has doubled since 1960.

Synthetic fibres

Synthetic fibres have exercised a decisive influence upon the character of the textile industry during the twentieth century. Their principal role has been as a supplement to, or substitute for, natural fibres. They are lower in price and are much more versatile, capable of being blended to varying degrees with natural fibres. There is a great range of synthetic fibres of chemical origin, including in the UK Nylon, Terylene, Courtelle and Acrilan, and their variants in France (Crylon) and Germany (Dralon). Rayon is a cellulose wood-pulp product, but is of declining importance compared with the synthetic coal- and oil-based fibres.

Production of synthetics has risen dramatically within the last 30 years. It is now much greater than that of natural fibres (fig. 7.6) and this has partially masked the fall in production and manpower which has taken place in these natural fibres. The widespread introduction of synthetic fibres has had a significant effect upon the traditional textile areas. The new ranges and qualities of the synthetics have helped resuscitate the industry and have given a new lease of life to old manufacturing areas. The cotton towns of Lancashire are an example of the residual strength of the industry in the area where specialisation developed to its greatest extent. After 50 years of decline, it now looks as if the recent improvements in machinery including the new ring loom, and the new ranges of synthetic fabrics, have given the area new life. The industry has moved to new locations, often in the areas of petrochemical production as at Teesside (Billingham and Wilton), and into development areas as at Pontypool, but in the main, it has succeeded in maintaining its heavily regionalised character. Geographical inertia has played a large part in this as the textile regions have always been heavily capitalised in plant, machinery and skilled labour.

The widespread substitution of synthetic fibres has had another important effect. Mixtures of fabrics such as polyester–cotton and wool–Terylene are increasingly rendering the traditional divisions within the industry obsolete. The influence of markets has become more important as half of the textile industry's output of cloth goes directly into consumer clothing. Rapid fashion changes have thus dictated a much closer identity of interests between the branches of the industry. The old processing distinctions are

	Wool fabric	Cotton fabric	Synthetic fibres
	1991	1991	1992
Germany	30	158	981
France	44	126	125
Belgium/Luxembourg	4	56	321
Netherlands	2	na	
Spain	19	83	293
Portugal	11	74	74
Italy	165	178	711
United Kingdom	39	31	291
Ireland	na	na	109
Denmark	2	na	40
Greece	15	53	12
Total EU	331	759	2957

na = not available

FIGURE 7.6   *EU (12) textile production (thousand tonnes) (source – Eurostat)*

breaking down, and spinning, weaving, knitwear and clothing manufacture are increasingly part of one organism, the vertically integrated company. This has involved new capitalisation, rationalisation, amalgamations and the introduction of new production techniques. Most significant of all has been the growing association of textiles with the chemical industry, particularly petrochemicals and synthetic fibres.

The large chemical and petrochemical synthetic fibre groups became financially involved because they produced raw materials on a large scale for the textile industry. It was therefore natural that they should secure their outlets by controlling the means of production and marketing. This led to the acquisition of textile companies. Imperial Chemical Industries set up British Nylon Spinners, and Courtaulds absorbed British Celanese in 1957. Both ICI and Courtaulds PLC are now important components of the textile industry in the UK. In Italy Snia-Viscosa is in association with Montedison, the chemical group; Hoechst of Germany is entering into arrangements with textile companies.

A radical reorganisation of the textile industry has been taking place, particularly in the mature north-west European producers. The response to world competition is rationalisation and integration, the substitution of capital for labour, greater specialisation in upmarket products, innovation in fashion and design, flexibility in production and modern marketing techniques. Many producers in the EU have entered into alliances for specific products with Japanese and other foreign companies – e.g. Hoechst of Germany has linked with Teijin of Japan. This should help strengthen the EU presence in Japan and give access to Asian markets. It will also enable companies to pool research and development costs.

In the 1980s production became concentrated in Asian countries, and design tended to concentrate in the EU where designers such as Karl Lagerfeld of Chanel in Paris and Giorgio Armani in Milan began to dominate the design scene. German companies started the trend of sourcing their merchandise from low-cost countries, i.e. contracting out manufacturing to countries like the Philippines where labour costs and other overheads were very low. East European countries are likely to be the cheap production countries of the 1990s. However, some low-cost producers have become politically unstable, and delivery problematic, so it may be that production may revert to the EU where rising unemployment could provide cheaper labour.

THE CHEMICAL INDUSTRY

The chemical industry developed very rapidly in Western Europe during the 1960s and 1970s. The West German chemical industry grew by an average of 20 per cent per annum between 1950 and 1970, twice the growth rate for West German industry as a whole. However, in the first half of the 1980s stagnant production and overcapacity led to a considerable restructuring of the industry. This involved significant redundancies and reductions in capacity, but it enabled the industry to start off from a much stronger base when the economic environment improved from 1983 onwards. In the late 1980s the chemical industry again experienced strong expansion, but from 1990 the industry has again stagnated due to the effects of recession and overcapacity.

The industry occupies a key role in the complex industrial economy largely because it supplies raw materials upon which industry depends. In the UK, for example, only about 20 per cent of the products of the chemical industry enter the home consumer market directly, whereas at least 65 per cent are used by other sectors of industry. The textile industry has long depended upon chemical bleaches and dyestuffs, but more recently synthetic fibres from petrochemicals have partially replaced the traditional natural materials and have helped to resuscitate and transform the range and quality of textile products. The footwear industry depends on tanning materials, synthetic resins and rubber, and now, increasingly, plastics. Fertilisers and crop-production chemicals are another rapidly developing sector of the industry. The heavy chemicals division produces acids and alkalis, and pharmaceuticals (drugs, medicines, cosmetics, photographic goods, soaps and toiletries) are manufactured as high-value specialist, lighter chemicals, more specifically for the consumer market.

This great complexity of products is matched by a variety of locations (fig. 7.7). There are three broad types of location: at a raw material and energy source; at the point of import or trans-shipment of bulky raw materials; and near the market for the product. All three factors may operate at different periods of time.

Raw materials and energy

Coalfield locations

The coalfields provide a major concentration area as coal was initially both a raw material and a source of energy. Although coal is no longer the key source of energy and raw materials, the centres of heavy industry continue to provide a major inertia focus for chemical manufacturing. The major chemical manufacturing regions on the Continent are the Ruhr, Saar, Sambre–Meuse, Limburg and Kempenland coalfields. Lignite provides the raw material for much of the chemical industry in the former GDR, and although many chemical plants have been closed due to pollution problems, there are still important centres at Berlin and Cottbus (in the Land of Brandenburg) and in the chemical triangle encompassing Halle, Merseburg and Bitterfeld (in the Land of Saxony–Anhalt). The Heavy Industrial Triangle plays a significant part in the chemical industry. In the Ruhr, the main chemical centres are Duisburg, Düsseldorf, and Leverkusen near Cologne. The coke-oven plants produce heavy chemicals, including coal tar, benzene, ammonia and sulphuric acid. There is also production in the north of the Ruhr at Marl–Huls, where natural gas is piped from the Ems gasfield. Synthetic rubber, ammonia, and petrochemicals are produced near Maastricht in South Limburg. In the Sambre–Meuse valley, Liège is the centre for heavy chemicals, and in northern France the former coalfield towns of Béthune, Lens and Douai produce aniline dyes, ammonia and acids.

Other mineral sources

A specific mineral resource may determine the location of a chemical industry: for example, sulphur extraction from natural gas at Lacq and St Marcet in the Pyrenees; the potash deposits at Mulhouse used for fertilisers; salt deposits in Lorraine (Dombasle and Sarralbe); and gas at Cortemaggiore in the Po valley. Perhaps the largest area of this type is in Lower Saxony around Hanover, where oil, potash and salt account for the large-scale manufacture of fertilisers. In Italy there are many dispersed locations, including the processing of sulphur at Ragusa in Sicily, and in Emilia-Romagna, and potash at Campo-Franco. In Spain the Basque coast has considerable non-ferrous metal deposits, and these have given rise to heavy chemicals at Bilbao, whilst Oviedo and Gijon have fertilisers, glass and ceramic factories. The mineral deposits of the Sierra Morena in southern Spain have given rise to chemical industries at Linares, Seville and Huelva in the Guadalquivir and Rio Tinto valleys.

Hydro-electricity

The availability of hydro-electricity is another localising factor. In Italy there are plants at Terni in the Appenines, Crotone in Calabria, and at Bolzano in the Alto-Adige for nitrate fertilisers. In France an electrochemical industry has developed in the Durance valley (Argentiere), at Grenoble in the Isère valley, and in the Pyrenees, south of Lourdes.

Import and trans-shipment points

Oil refineries and petrochemicals

The influence of cheap transport has often led to the expansion of existing centres which were originally based upon raw materials. Oil refineries have become the principal locational factor for the petrochemical industry; cheap transport by inland waterway or pipeline is also important. In the UK the expansion of existing centres has occurred where the original coal factor is complicated by others. The Merseyside chemical area stretches from St Helens through Runcorn and Widnes into Cheshire at Northwich, and was originally based upon the saltfields of mid-Cheshire and the Lancashire coalfield. The oil refinery at Stanlow, the glass industry of St Helens, the

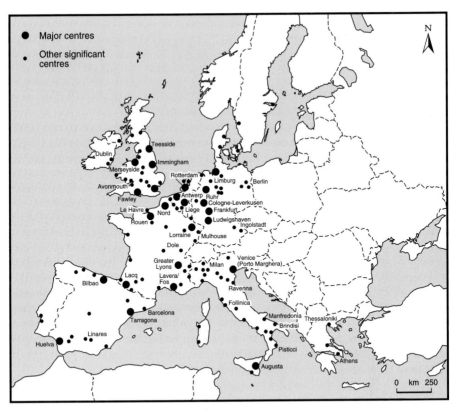

FIGURE 7.7   *EU (12) chemical industry locations*

supplies of bleaches and dyes needed by the textile industry, the cheap import facilities of Liverpool and the Manchester Ship Canal for tropical vegetable oils, as well as limestone from Derbyshire, compounded matters so that the industry related to a whole series of factors.

Teesside is a similar example where the main centres, Billingham and Wilton, are linked by a pipeline under the Tees for movement of petroleum by-products. Anhydrite and salt from beneath the Tees estuary and also coal from Durham were the main raw materials at first. Much of the real impetus for the vast growth of the Wilton complex, making plastics, Terylene, and other synthetics, however, was the development of Teesside as a major oil-refining and petrochemical centre.

In many cases trans-shipment points at deep-water estuaries, or along large rivers, have become initial growth points. The oil refineries of the Rhine delta at Rotterdam and Antwerp, produce petrochemicals. The Dutch towns of Arnhem and Nijmegen along the Rhine have chemicals and rubber works. Similar developments have occurred at Marseilles, Thameside, Humberside, Hamburg, Le Havre and Southampton Water. Italy has developed petrochemical locations at her major ports: Genoa, Naples, Augusta in Sicily, and Bari.

Inland areas

The best example of an inland transportation break-point is the mid-Rhineland, centred upon Frankfurt, Mannheim and Ludwigshaven. The Rhine axis reflects the ease of importation along a major waterway. The complex of Badische-Anilin/Soda-Fabrik AG (BASF) is at Ludwigshaven and is one of the largest in Europe.

The oil and natural-gas pipelines extending from Rotterdam to the Ruhr and Frankfurt, the south European pipeline from Trieste to Ingolstadt, and from Marseilles to the Rhine at Karlsruhe (fig. 2.7) are of importance for the location of chemical factories.

Market locations

Branches of the chemical industry are widely distributed in the major cities. Here are found the lighter, higher-value chemical products which require a good labour supply and consumer-market proximity. Paris, Brussels and London are the largest centres with pharmaceuticals and cosmetics. Lyons, Nottingham, Cologne and Manchester are others. In Italy, the single most important area is the Milan–Turin axis. Milan employs one-third of the total chemical workers in Italy, manufacturing a very wide range of products for the very large consumer market in northern Italy.

In addition to the consumer market, in many cases the market for associated products is an important factor. Examples are the crop-protection chemicals and fertilisers made at Hanover and Brunswick, close to the intensive agriculture of the Borde of Lower Saxony, and cities such as Ghent, Turin and Lyons which produce dyestuffs for the textile industry.

The structure of the chemical industry

The chemical industry has experienced extensive research and development (R&D), automation, and capital investment. EU companies spent around 4.8 per cent of their turnover on research and development (R&D) in 1990. In specific sectors of the pharmaceutical and agrochemical industry, the figures may be twice that percentage. The most innovative fields of R&D include bio-technology and new materials (advanced composite materials, polymers, plastics and ceramics). The industry tends to be organised in very large units which are capital-intensive and owned by a few giant companies (six of the world's top chemical companies are EU-based). Although there are nearly 33 000 enterprises in the EU, the chemical industry remains very concentrated, with 8 per cent of the enterprises representing almost 80 per cent of turnover. There has been a spectacular increase in the size of the factory units, particularly in the field of petrochemicals, with the benefit of economies of scale. A strategy of merger (such as that of Agfa of Germany and Gevaert of Belgium) and acquisition has also been followed to restructure the industry during recession. This has created a series of strategic alliances and asset swaps – e.g. ICI swapped its polypropylene operations for BASF acrylic operations.

Each EU country has at least one major chemical group which exercises a partial monopoly, but the scale of operations does vary considerably. In Germany, the three largest firms (Hoechst, Bayer and BASF) share most of the industry and are also the largest chemical companies in the EU, whereas in France there is much less concentration with over sixty firms sharing at least half the market. The UK is dominated by ICI which is the sixth largest chemical company in the world and is a multi-national with many subsidiaries in Western Europe and the rest of the world (fig. 3.9). In 1993 it was de-merged into two companies to form a 'new' ICI (industrial chemicals, paints, materials and explosives) and a separate company Zeneca (pharmaceuticals, agrochemicals, seeds and speciality businesses). Another feature is the influence of the major oil companies such as Shell, BP and Esso which exercise control over the raw-material sources for petrochemicals. Shell Chemical, a subsidiary of the major oil company, is one of the top chemical groups in the EU and the world. With regard to product segmentation, the German, Dutch and French industries are more oriented towards basic chemicals and plastic materials, while the UK and Italy have a greater share of pharmaceuticals and a few other everyday consumer products.

The chemical industry benefited enormously by the dismantling of tariffs and increase in intra-EU trade in plastics, synthetic rubber and artificial fibres. The EU is the world's leading exporter of chemical products with exports more than twice the size of those of North America. Markets for chemical products have developed rapidly particularly in East Asia, Brazil and the Middle East although new producers have appeared in these regions creating increased competition. High-value-added goods are increasingly concentrated in the EU, whilst lower-value production is transferred by the multi-nationals to developing-world locations. However, the major share of world production remains in the hands of European and American groups. The importance of the industry can be measured by the fact that American investment is very high. Probably a quarter of the total American investment in Western Europe is in the EU chemical industry.

8

AGRICULTURE: THE COMMON AGRICULTURAL POLICY

A HIGHLY PRODUCTIVE FARMING REGION

The EU is one of the most productive agricultural areas in the world, and large parts of its landscape have become almost totally humanised after centuries of continuous cultivation. Sections in the regional chapters which follow are devoted to the variety of farming landscapes and products, for instance: the productivity of the 'pays' of the Paris Basin; the efficiency of the dairy farming and specialised horticulture of Denmark and the Netherlands; the rich croplands of northern Italy; the Rhineland vineyards; and the subsistence farming of the Mezzogiorno.

Scale and diversity

The largest single advantage of the EU is its scale. The large market of almost 372 million people is a tremendous incentive to farmers, but of even greater significance is its latitudinal extent. The EU (15) stretches from latitude 35 to latitude 70 degrees north and covers an area capable of producing most foodstuffs apart from those which require tropical conditions. France is a major producer of wheat and maize, Germany of pork products, the UK and Spain have the largest numbers of sheep and goats, and Italy provides a large proportion of the EU's rice. These are just a few indications of the range of products within these latitudinal limits.

There are, however, great variations between the Member States in the importance attached to agriculture (fig. 8.1). In peripheral countries such as Greece, agriculture accounts for over 14 per cent of GDP and there is a large proportion of the workforce employed in agriculture (fig. 8.10). In the UK agriculture occupies only 2.2 per cent of the working population, but

	Agriculture (% of gross value added GDP) (1992)	Food and agriculture imports (% of total imports) (1993)	Food and agriculture exports (% of total exports) (1993)	Net importer or exporter of food (1993)
Germany	1.2	11.7	6.1	Importer
France	2.9	11.9	16.0	Exporter
Italy	3.6	16.8	7.4	Importer
Netherlands	3.6	16.0	25.4	Exporter
Belgium	1.8	13.0	11.9	Importer
UK	1.4	11.6	7.8	Importer
Ireland	8.9	11.4	22.9	Exporter
Denmark	3.0	16.7	29.4	Exporter
Greece	14.2	15.5	33.1	Exporter
Spain	3.0	15.7	16.6	Exporter
Portugal	3.2	16.0	8.2	Importer
Luxembourg	1.8	16.7	11.9	Importer

FIGURE 8.1   *Agriculture – the importance to each member country (source –* Eurostat*)*

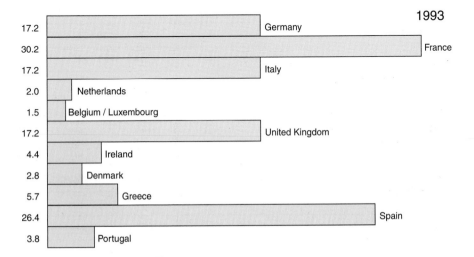

FIGURE 8.2   *The total agricultural area 1993 (million hectares)*

UK farmers supply about 55 per cent of the country's food. Agriculture is therefore a valuable and very cost-effective part of the UK economy, playing a part out of all proportion to its manpower. In Germany and Belgium agriculture provides only 1.2 and 1.8 per cent of GDP respectively for, like the UK, they are heavily industrialised and all three are importers of food. Portugal and Italy are also net importers of food. Denmark, Ireland, Greece, Spain and the Netherlands are net exporters of food. France has the largest agricultural production in the EU, emphasising its large areas of farmland (fig. 8.2) and position as 'The Granary of Europe' (fig. 8.3).

Land utilisation figures (fig. 8.4) show that Denmark and Portugal have the largest proportion of arable land, followed by Germany, France and Spain. Ireland, the UK and the Netherlands are predominantly pastoral reflecting their maritime climatic characteristics. The proportion of tree crops (vines and olives) illustrates the characteristic production of the Mediterranean countries. This adds yet another element to the scale, complexity and diversity of the agricultural scene, which will now be examined in greater detail.

	Crop production (1000 tonnes)					Livestock numbers (1000)		
	Wheat	Barley	Maize	Rice	Sugar beet	Cattle	Sheep and goats	Pigs
France	29 324	8995	14 966	125	4633	20 328	11 451	12 564
Germany	15 766	11 006	2656	–	4352	16 207	2474	26 514
UK	12 890	6038	–	–	1434	11 605	29 571	7704
Italy	8171	1634	8029	1331	1419	7704	11 724	8244
Denmark	4349	3407	–	–	521	2180	102	10 345
Netherlands	1035	252	95	–	1133	4794	1653	13 709
Belgium	1463	425	168	–	1043	3100	138	6903
Luxembourg	49	68	–	–	–	202	8	66
Eire	597	975	–	–	177	6265	6125	1423
Greece	2143	415	2099	137	307	629	15 958	1099
Spain	5002	9520	1699	310	1213	4962	27 239	18 219
Portugal	422	99	568	76	3	1345	4206	2547

FIGURE 8.3   *Selected figures of agricultural production, 1993 (source:* Eurostat*)*

Climate and agricultural regions

Climatic and physical factors have the effect of creating four main agricultural zones (fig. 8.5).

---

1 **North-west Europe** is exposed to westerly winds from the Atlantic, and the normal climatic regime is therefore wet and variable throughout the year, with mild winters and cool summers. This maritime climate is characterised by a mixed farming regime with a bias towards a grassland and stock-rearing economy and specialised dairy farming. This is common on the coasts and lowlands of Ireland and in the UK, Normandy, Brittany, the polders of the Netherlands and Schlering-Holstein in the north German lowlands. Denmark is a special case: only 9 per cent of the cultivable land is under grass, although it is within the coastal maritime belt; 45 per cent is under mixed cereals grown as stockfeed. This intensive method of feeding cattle indoors on grain is a more cost-effective way of producing dairy products.

2 **Towards the interior of the Continent** the transitional continental climate has colder, though fairly short winters, but has sunnier, hotter summers than the coastlands. With a lower overall rainfall, arable farming is much more important and cereals tend to dominate. This climate is combined with the presence of extensive lowlands, covered with fertile loess (limon), in areas such as the Paris Basin, Flanders, Picardy and the Börde of Westphalia and Lower Saxony stretching into south-east

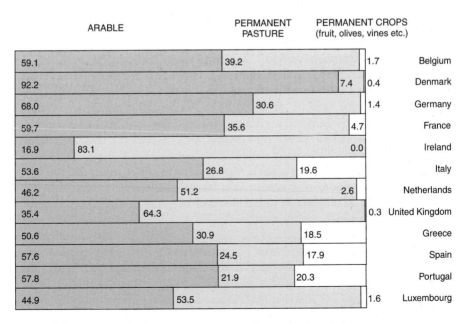

FIGURE 8.4   *EU (12) land use – percentage of agricultural area, 1993*

Rotation grassland. Friesian cattle, silos and modern farmhouse buildings in Flevoland, Netherlands.

Germany, giving rise to the EU's grain and sugar-beet producing area. East Anglia belongs to this agricultural type as it has the lowest rainfall in the UK. The additional advantage of an extensive chalky boulder–clay lowland has made it the UK's principal area of cereal cultivation. The Basin of Aquitaine has a long growing season and is climatically almost part of the French Midi. The plain of Lombardy is transitional rather than truly Mediterranean in climate, and both Aquitaine and Lombardy have a rich and varied pattern of agriculture with market gardens, orchards, vineyards and cattle pastures. More than half the land is, however, under cereals, particularly wheat and maize and, therefore, this area merits inclusion as part of the EU's major arable farming regions.

3 **The dissected plateaux and Alpine mountain zones** stretch across much of the interior of Europe. Agriculturally, these are marginal farming areas lying at an altitude of between 300 and 2000 m and characterised by a cool, damp climate, considerable rainfall and winter snow, together with exposed conditions and thin soils. The hill-farming and stock-breeding of the Pennines, Lake District and Welsh mountains, is a valuable element in the UK stock-rearing economy. The Ardennes, Black Forest and Rhine Highlands have extensive forests which provide valuable timber. There are large areas of pasture and moorland with low rural population densities. The French Massif Central is more varied with areas of forest, interspersed with areas of rye, oats and buckwheat cultivation, whilst on

Arable land on the Belgian High Plain, viewed from the site of the Battle of Waterloo

the south-western margins are the limestone 'Causses' which traditionally have provided grazing for sheep, producing the famous Roquefort cheese. The Iberian peninsula of Spain and Portugal is the most extensive semi-arid zone in Western Europe with large areas of mountain and plateau. One-third of Spain is rough grazing or waste, with large parts of the Meseta plateau and the central Sierras given over to sheep-grazing and goats. Cattle rearing is more common in the humid west and north, in Galicia and the Cantabrian mountains.

The Alpine fold mountains provide another variation on this theme. The high western regions, with heavy precipitation, have fine stands of timber, but the main form of livelihood is usually stock-rearing based upon the alternate use of alpine and valley pastures in the classic transhumance system. In sheltered valleys, as for example north of Grenoble in the Isère valley (the Gresivaudan), are vineyards and orchards, whilst in more remote areas subsistence farming and depopulation is the usual pattern. A large part of the Italian Appenines is basically suited to tree crops such as the olive and vine, but 40 per cent of

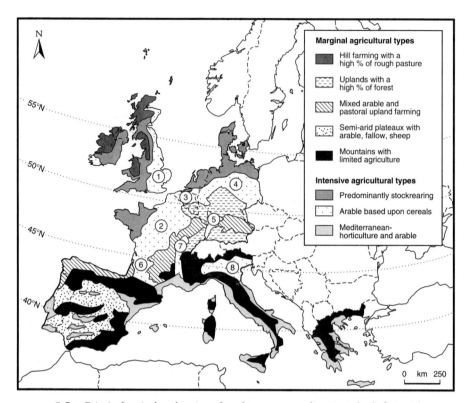

FIGURE 8.5 *Principal agricultural regions (based upon macro-climatic and relief criteria)*
(1) East Anglia and the lowlands of eastern England   (2) Paris Basin and scarplands
(3) Flanders and High plain of Belgium   (4) Börde of Westphalia and Lower Saxony
(5) Rhine–Main valley   (6) Basin of Aquitaine   (7) Rhône–Saone valley   (8) Plain of
Lombardy

peninsular Italy is too steep for cultivation anyway, and soil erosion in the
past has seriously damaged its capacity for agriculture of any kind.

4 **The southern coastal fringes of the EU**, including the Midi of
France, the huertas of southern Spain, the Greek coastal plains and the
Italian lowlands, have the traditional summer drought of the
'Mediterranean' regime, but areas of lowland are very limited, and usually
protected by high backing mountains.

   The agriculture varies so much with local conditions that the classic
Mediterranean complex of olives, vine and cereals is only a very basic
picture, and increasingly intensification is occurring where irrigation is
available. The region of northern Italy (chapter 16) which stretches from
the Ligurian Riviera into Lombardy, illustrates this variation. Intensive
horticulture, viticulture, fruit and floriculture is common on irrigated and
terraced coastlands, with intensive crop and cereal production and cattle
rearing in the interiors.

Local variations due to micro-climatic effects, aspect and market demand

Whilst the description of these four basic climatic divisions and their agricultural responses are useful in describing the latitudinal range of agricultural production available in the EU, nevertheless there is a mosaic of diverse farm types within this broad picture. Specialised agriculture depends upon locally favourable circumstances and is found in restricted areas (fig. 8.6).

Viticulture

Although the large-scale areas of viticulture lie in the Mediterranean regions including Languedoc, southern Spain, Provence and much of Italy, nevertheless there are locally favoured environments which allow the vine to flourish much further north.

The northern limit of the vine lies approximately from the River Loire to Koblenz on the Rhine. The sheltered slopes of the Rhine Gorge and Rift valley, the warm soils and southward-facing scarps of the Champagne

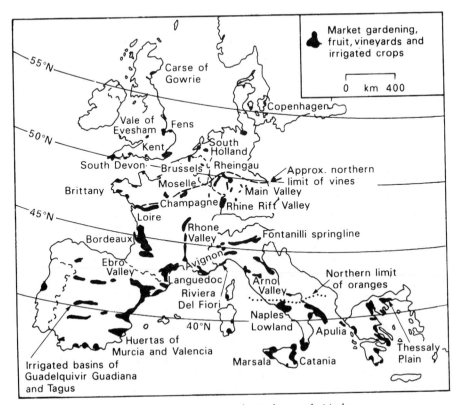

FIGURE 8.6   *EU (12) specialised and intensive horticulture and viticulture*

Pouilleuse near Reims, and the southward-facing Côte D'Or in Burgundy are included in these specialised high-quality wine-producing areas.

The Vale of Evesham

The Vale of Evesham in south Worcestershire experiences a warming effect with mild winters and early springs because of the funnelling effect of the Bristol Channel upon the westerly winds. As a result it is an important area in the UK for the intensive cultivation of fruit and vegetables.

Brittany

In Brittany the cultivation of primeurs (early vegetables) is made possible around the coast in sheltered bays such as St Malo, Roscoff and Quimper. The mildness of the winters and early springs are associated with the Westerlies and North Atlantic Drift.

The Netherlands

Much of the intensive horticulture of Randstad, Holland, with its vegetables, glasshouses, and bulb cultivation, is on mixed soils where sand has been blown inland from coastal dunes over the peat to create a fertile, easily worked soil. The nearby urban markets in the Netherlands itself, Germany and the UK have also been a major stimulation.

Vineyards of the Côte D'Or near Nuits St Georges, south of Dijon

Urban markets and transport

In addition, economic factors have become increasingly predominant. The food requirements of the large city populations have created 'Von Thunen' type conditions, and land is intensively farmed immediately around the city. The perishable and highly-priced fruit and vegetables are freed from transport costs of any magnitude and are in close proximity to their urban market. The environs of Paris, London, Hamburg and the Randstad illustrate this. A modification of this occurs where transport provides an easy and inexpensive route to the market. The cultivation of *primeurs* (early fruit and vegetables) in the Rhône delta near Avignon is not only due to early springs and intensive irrigation, but also to the development of fast access routes to Paris.

Self-sufficiency

The diversity of land-use across the Member countries gives a picture of considerable integration. The EU has combined 15 countries into a unit capable of producing the majority of its own food. These countries, together, have a broad self-sufficiency in food, adding great strength to each Member country (fig. 8.7). For example, the grain-producing area of East Anglia is not sufficient to feed the UK's large population, but the EU as a whole *can* produce enough grain. The large areas of agricultural land and the range of climate types stretching from northern Scotland to Sicily and

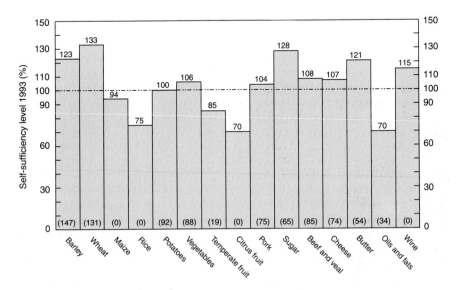

FIGURE 8.7   *Self-sufficiency of the EU (12) in food products, 1993. (Figures in brackets are the comparative levels for the UK alone)*

183

Malaga, make the EU product greater than the sum of its parts. The law of comparative economic advantage operates so that the UK as a traditional grass and livestock region is a producer of beef, pigmeat, and dairy produce. The Mediterranean areas such as Spain, Greece and Italy (fig. 8.8) have a climatic monopoly within the EU in the production of sub-tropical crops such as vines, olive oil, rice and citrus fruits, and advantages in tomatoes and early vegetables. Denmark is a major supplier of dairy produce. The potential self-sufficiency of this large and productive area is the key to an understanding of the Common Agricultural Policy and is the reason for the early importance attached by the EU to a policy for control and restructuring of farming and food production.

Farm structure and land tenure: the traditional picture

There are very large differences in the cultural traditions, social systems and farming techniques of the Member States, and it is these variations which illustrate many of the problems inherent in the EU's farm policy.

Land tenure and farm size (fig. 8.9(a)) vary considerably. At one end of the scale large parts of Spain and the south of Italy have tiny peasant holdings (*minifundia*) alternating with vast estates owned by absentee landlords (*latifundia*). The underdeveloped latifundia, with their typical extensive monoculture of wheat and day-labour system, exist alongside peasant smallholdings of under 1 ha on two or three widely separated patches of land. Even today about 70 per cent of the total agricultural holdings of Italy and Greece are under 5 ha in size (fig. 8.9(b)). Of course, particularly in the traditional economies of the Mediterranean countries, the peasant farm is the very significant supporter of the family unit in rural areas. In the modernised and wealthier farming areas of Lombardy a normal system of tenant occupation on farms nearer the average size occurs. France, on the other hand, has a tradition of owner-occupation and the average farm size is 25 ha, but there are real differences between regions. In the north-east most farms are over 30 ha, whilst Brittany, Aquitaine and much of the Midi have a majority of farms under 12 ha in size. The tendency to small farms, which are difficult to work for profit, is compounded by the system of widely scattered holdings which are a remnant of the medieval open-field system and a legacy of the European code of equal inheritance. Germany is also characterised by a proportion of small farms, and in Bavaria and Swabia particularly these are often fragmented. An additional complicating factor is that many farms combine part-time agriculture with commuting or with tourism. In the Netherlands, however, many of the farms on the reclaimed polders are state-owned and rented out to the farmer in consolidated plots of land. By contrast, the UK has a more mature farm structure with the average farm size at 70 ha (fig. 8.9(a)) and, more significantly, it has the greatest number of large farms over 400 ha in the EU, often run as a company by a manager. Again, however, major regional contrasts are shown by the predominance of small family mixed farms in the north and west, such as the

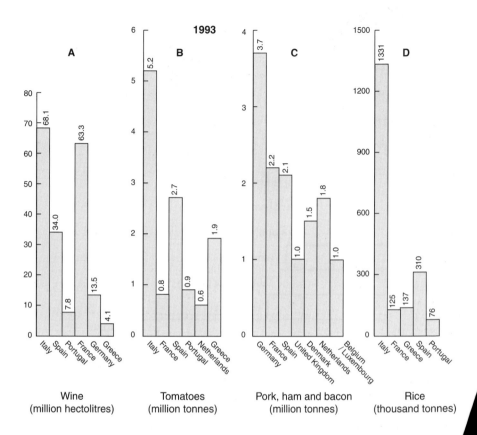

FIGURE 8.8 *Production of selected specialised crops, 1993.* **(A)** *Wine (million hectolitres)* **(B)** *Tomatoes (million tonnes)* **(C)** *Pork, ham and bacon (million tonnes)* **(D)** *Rice (thousand tonnes) (source:* Eurostat*)*

Pennines and central Wales, and the large cereal farms of eastern Engla owned as capitalist estates by finance houses or insurance companies.

Many areas of the EU had too large a farm population for efficie During the 1950s the original Six had a very significant problem with having 6.5 million people or 41 per cent of its workforce on th (fig. 8.10). This was a remarkable picture of regional contrasts in a developing industrial country which yet retained a large rural economy. Even the Netherlands, a much more efficient agricultural had 14 per cent. By contrast the UK had 5 per cent of its population employed in farming. Many of the older peasant France and Italy had an innate conservatism and lack of ent change, and had difficulty raising and investing the capital mechanise efficiently.

The tremendous variations in yields from one part of the have been a major problem (figs. 8.11 and 8.14). Tr Netherlands had a consistently high yield of commodities reflection of intensive efficient farming, and of orientat

1986

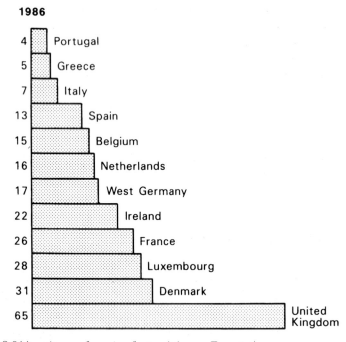

FIGURE 8.9(a)   *Average farm size (hectares) (source:* Eurostat*)*

...ups	Denmark	Germany	Greece	France	Italy	Netherlands	United Kingdom	EU (12) total
	29	70	20	67	25		11	49
	17	19	12	17	19		13	16
	22	8	18	9	23		16	13
	25	2	31	5	28		26	14
	7	1	19	2	5		34	8

of agricultural holdings by size groups (selected), 1989 (source:

ncy.
Italy
land
rapidly
peasant
country,
working
farmers of
usiasm for
required to
EU to another
ditionally, the
uch as wheat, a
on to the food

populations. Denmark developed the most
world and the UK's yields, particularly in its
high. By contrast the yields for major crops
lf the levels of those in the Netherlands.
vels is made by comparing the British
eople; the Dane for 17; and the
ine people. A model summarising
ices the concept of the core and
Van Valkenburg (fig. 8.13). An
the following criteria: average
yields; and yields for eight selected
duction area across the north European

plain focused upon the Rhine delta and adjacent areas. Conversely, there are peripheral regions in which agriculture is much less favoured, including some of the Mediterranean region, south-western France, the Atlantic fringes and parts of Sweden and Finland.

The problems of size and fragmentation, together with an excessive farm workforce, inadequate mechanisation, backward farming techniques and low yields, were widespread, causing considerable imbalance in the rural sector. When the EEC was formed in 1958 half its farmland was in need of consolidation. It was to take advantage of the benefits of scale to produce sufficient food and to improve the structure of farming throughout the whole Community that the Common Agricultural Policy was formulated.

THE COMMON AGRICULTURAL POLICY

Protectionist policies in agriculture are not new: most governments in Western Europe have always protected their farmers for a range of social, economic, strategic and political reasons. Farming tends to be high cost, and protection of the home producer against cheaper world competition, thus maintaining a certain level of self-sufficiency, has always been deemed to be necessary. Structural reorganisation and land reform have also been a long-term aim of governments who have also felt it politically necessary to retain the support and votes of the rural community. World markets for agricultural products are notoriously unstable and unpredictable, depending upon the weather and fluctuations in supply and demand. In addition, rural farm incomes are traditionally lower than those in industry and the service sector, and farming is the dominant occupation in remote and physicall difficult regions, which therefore need considerable assistance.

One of the earliest examples of EU policy-making was the establishme of the Common Agricultural Policy in 1962. From the end of the Sec World War there was a paramount need for the security of food supply t maintained and the original Six in the EU saw the CAP as a mea achieving early success in integration policies. France and Germany sa a 'quid pro quo' for French food surpluses set against German in products in the new common market. The CAP is a system of prote which the EU food market is regulated. Its objectives, defined in A of the Treaty of Rome, are to increase agricultural productivity, t fair standard of living for those people in the agricultural sector, markets in a high-risk business, and to ensure reasonable consum thus establishes a zone of EU preference in one of the w food-producing areas, in which its farmers and growers can p cent of the food needed by the 372 million consumers.

The policy is administered by the European Agricultural Guarantee Fund (EAGGF), the words of which spell ou practical functions: the guidance and improvement of farm

the guarantee or protection of the farmer's income by means of a common price support system. The central aim of the policy is to establish a single market for all farm products. This means that national, fiscal and physical barriers to trade must be abolished, with unrestricted intra-community free trade. There must be stabilised and guaranteed prices at the same level throughout. Easy access to all parts of the EU by fast transport routes would thus reduce to a minimum the costs of transport. This ideally means success for the most efficient producer and the effect of favourable environmental factors should make itself increasingly felt. Under the law of comparative economic advantage this should mean that regional specialisation in agriculture will be the norm. UK farmers would specialise in dairy products, lamb, beef, pork and poultry as well as cereals, because the combination of arable and grassland and a livestock economy is particularly fitted for the prevailing climatic and physical conditions. Conversely, Italy and southern France have great climatic advantages in horticulture and a monopoly in vines, olive oil and citrus fruits. Thus, each region produces at its own level of advantage, giving regional interdependence in farm products. The potential self-sufficiency which has already been mentioned for the fifteen countries is enormously strengthened by this specialisation in each region.

During the early years of the EU, there is no doubt that the CAP was a potent force and a success story for an integration policy. Protection etween the Member States was swept away and the basic features of a single ʳket in farm products was established. With high financial returns to ʳs under the common price support system, production increased ᵗially through the 1960s.

upport system

ɲf the farmer's income

ᵉ farmer's income has always been one of the major
ɔn Agricultural Policy. It is recognised that it is more
᷄ incomes at a level comparable with those of the
ʳ. The reason lies partially with the composition
ᵗ that France and Italy in particular have always
ᵂerful farming section in their population
ᵈ upon the CAP to act as a compensatory
markets to German industrial products.
ᵉ, the guarantee policy, works in the
ᵉm is applied to each product and a
ᵗmates a fair return for an efficient
ᵗ can therefore sell on the open
but if the price slumps there is
᷄tervention organisation, run by
ᵗ. This intervention price is about 8
᷄ a type of 'floor' or reserve price. In

ⁿᵗ
ɔnd
᷄o be
ns of
ᵂ it as
dustrial
ction in
rticle 39
ensure a
᷄o stabilise
ᵉr prices. It
ᵂrld's major
ᵈoduce 90 per
Guidance and
its two major
ᵖroduction and

addition, if a foreign producer wishes to sell food within the market, they have to pay a levy at the frontier which raises their prices to the level of the target price, thus excluding any low-cost imports from undercutting the EU farmers' products. So the farmers' incomes are protected at an artificial level, the target price, but there is one safeguard for the consumer. If the market price for a product goes over the target price, competition from imports will bring it down to the target level again, thus providing a measure of price regulation.

To pay for this price support, the Member countries pay to the Fund the levies which they have received from food imports, customs duty receipts and a proportion of their receipts from value-added tax. In effect, the indirect taxes paid by the consumer are the source of the farmers' guaranteed protection.

Agricultural guidance and reform

The other positive function of the Common Agricultural Policy is guidance and reform.

Since 1950 there has generally been a dramatic improvement in the agricultural structure. Several factors are involved and it is difficult to identify relative importance. Initially, there can be no doubt that the stimulating effects of the large internal market had a major effect, particularly upon France, whose export of agricultural produce doubled between 1966 and 1971. Two-thirds of these exports were to Member countries. Equally, the policies of national governments have had a considerable effect. The 'Cassa per il Mezzogiorno', the comprehensive plan designed to aid the Italian south with industrial development, also carried out substantial measures of farm improvement and modernisation. The French 'Remembrement' policy was officially introduced as early as 1941, with the object of consolidating severely fragmented farmland which covered much of the country. It has been only partially successful, largely in areas like the Paris Basin, with its open-field system. In the more traditionalist west and south, such as Brittany, Aquitaine and the Massif Central, where it was needed much more, there was considerable resistance to change. Official agencies called SAFER and FASASA were set up in 1960 and 1962. These buy land which is used to consolidate fragmented holdings and to enlarge smallholdings into viable units. They also encourage farmers in western France to retire at age 60, and retrain people leaving the land for other employment. Finally, a national network of agricultural markets was set up to improve distribution throughout France. In addition a third very significant factor has been rural–urban migration, particularly in France, Germany and Italy. During the 1960s this massive rural exodus was a major factor in slimming the agricultural workforce. Some mountain areas of marginal farming like the Jura, Vosges and Massif Central are in danger of becoming depopulated. French government policy changed to promote a balanced agriculture with different stimuli, depending on regional needs.

Cheese making in Holland

Hill farmers are now given bonuses to increase their cattle herds, and grants are made to young farmers who will settle in areas with population below the minimum desirable level (11 people per km^2). On the other hand, in areas like Brittany where there are too many farmers, there are inducements to retire or amalgamate. There is room for the small family farm giving a living to three or four people. The large, highly mechanised grain farms of the Paris Basin need entirely different conditions from those required by the smaller, highly efficient dairy farm of 50 cattle, typical of Holland and Denmark. In addition funds have been allocated by the European Investment Bank and the EAGGF for dairy processing, fruit and vegetable processing plant, and retirement pensions for older farmers. The combined effects of economic forces, national policies and the guidance policies of the Common Agricultural Policy have been a transformation in the farming structure over the past 20 years.

The percentage of the population employed on the land has been substantially reduced (fig. 8.10). The total EU (12) workforce fell from 19 million in 1950 to 11.5 million in 1966, and to 7.2 million in 1993, although differences are still marked. In terms of productivity, cereal yields have at least doubled (fig. 8.11). Large increases in mechanisation and the use of fertilisers also have been recorded (fig. 8.12). Irrigation, land drainage and intensification of production techniques, with new capital investment in livestock breeds, crop strains and fertilisers, have resulted in a marked reduction in the amount of land and labour needed to produce a given amount of food.

Cooperative wine producers in Provence

Percentage of workforce employed in agriculture

	1950	1958	1965	1971	1972	1974	1976	1981	1986	1993
Belgium	11.3	9.0	6.1	4.4	4.2	3.7	3.4	3.0	2.9	2.5
France	28.3	23.3	17.0	13.2	12.9	12.0	10.9	8.6	7.3	5.1
Germany	24.7	15.0	11.0	8.3	7.8	7.3	7.1	5.9	5.3	3.0
Italy	41.0	33.0	24.7	18.9	18.2	16.6	15.5	13.3	10.9	7.5
Luxembourg	24.0	17.0	13.5	10.1	9.3	6.6	6.1	5.6	4.0	3.0
Netherlands	14.1	12.0	8.0	6.9	6.9	6.6	6.5	5.0	4.8	4.6
United Kingdom	5.1	4.0	3.2	3.0	3.0	2.8	2.7	2.8	2.6	2.2
Denmark	–	22.0	–	10.9	9.8	9.6	9.3	8.5	6.2	5.4
Ireland	–	38.0	–	26.9	25.7	24.3	23.8	19.2	15.8	12.7
Greece								30.3	28.5	21.3
Spain									16.1	10.1
Portugal									21.9	11.7

FIGURE 8.10 *EU (12) agricultural workforce changes (source:* Eurostat)

Problems for the CAP

Since 1968 a whole range of problems have emerged for the CAP.

Surpluses

The price support system, by giving high financial returns to efficient and inefficient farmers alike, gave them a continual impetus to increase output, and raised production to surplus levels by the late 1960s. Dairy products in particular were very prone to these, and the intervention cost of buying and storing large quantities of food became very substantial. The 'butter mountain' was the first major sign of this, but was followed by 'cereal mountains' and 'wine lakes'. The perception of the CAP became one of a high-cost and wasteful system. The problem was essentially that the regulated commodity price which protected a smallholder in the Massif Central encouraged efficient farmers in the Paris Basin to raise output and profits, thus creating a spiralling problem. The Mansholt plan, published in 1969 by the then Commissioner for agriculture, was the first attempt to solve these problems. It recommended that in the medium term up to 1980, up to 5 million workers should be withdrawn from farming and either receive pensions or be retrained for other employment. Also, 5 million ha of marginal land were to be taken out of agriculture and used for afforestation, leisure parks and nature reserves. The aim was to further cut the workforce, eliminate the marginal high-cost producer, raise efficiency, lower target prices, and eliminate surpluses. Its real significance was to indicate that the CAP needed to evolve into a social and economic policy for poorer rural regions. However, Dr Mansholt was really ahead of his time, and very little was done to control the spiralling costs of farm support.

The CAP and trade agreements

The EU is substantially self-sufficient in many major foodstuffs (fig. 8.7). Nevertheless, imports of food have increased substantially owing to a considerable rise in living standards. Tropical fruit and vegetable oils are the main deficiencies. Cereal imports, particularly, have soared since 1958 because of their use as feedstocks for animals. The position is complicated further by the export of soft wheat, of which the EU has a surplus, and the larger quantity of imports of hard wheat. The protective nature of the CAP does cause disagreements with countries such as the USA, over the different standards of imported goods, and on the 'dumping' of surplus products for a cheap sale, where these affect the internal producers. There is periodic raising of tariffs or exclusive orders. It even happens within the EU, as for example in the 'lamb war' when France refused to accept UK lamb imports in an attempt to protect its sheep farmers.

A logical extension of the Common Agricultural Policy is the augmentation of the EU's temperate products with those tropical foodstuffs which it cannot produce for climatic reasons. Many ex-colonies, particularly

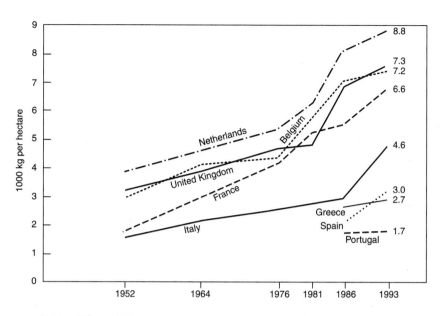

FIGURE 8.11 *Wheat yields*

	Use of fertilisers (kg per hectare)				Tractors (1000s)		Use of fertilisers: regional variations
	1965	1986	1989	1990	1950	1990	
France	91	181	199	186	140	1465	Over 200 kg per hectare in the Paris Basin
Netherlands	239	346	290	277	23	197	Over 450 kg per hectare in the market gardening areas
Italy	49	111	107	105	61	1440	
Spain		58	67	65	15	740	

FIGURE 8.12 *Use of fertilisers and machinery*

in Africa and the Caribbean, are associated with the EU. In 1963 18 African states, most of them ex-colonies of France, became associates at the Yaoundé Convention. Since then, however, many of the UK's former colonies have also become associated, culminating in the Lomé Agreements of 1975, 1979, 1984 and 1989. The associates obtain tariff-free entry into the EU for their staple commodities, and they also obtain aid for development projects through the European Development Fund. The EU has an assured supply of primary products and tropical foodstuffs, and a preferential market for its manufactured goods (Chapter 4 trade).

The United Kingdom and the 1973 enlargement

Within the EU a clash of interests developed with regard to the agricultural policy and there have been many underlying tensions. Germany and the UK are heavily industrialised and urbanised, and population has outstripped food production since the nineteenth century. They are thus large-scale importers of food, and by means of import levies, they both make large contributions to the Common Agricultural Policy funds. The UK, in particular, because of its very efficient farming system, obtains few development grants from the CAP for structural reforms. France and Italy on the other hand are large-scale food producers and France is a large food exporter. Ireland, though a small volume producer, has a small population and is therefore a major exporter of dairy produce. These last three Members have acute structural problems and gain immensely from the guaranteed prices, export subsidies, large internal market and grant aid implicit in the Common Agricultural Policy. The Netherlands and Denmark are two Members whose agricultural exports exceed imports and this reflects their traditional specialisation and efficiency in dairying and horticulture, combined with a small population.

The UK, in general, finds the Common Agricultural Policy unfavourable to its own interests. The circumstances of her unique position with early industrialisation, limited land resources and a large urbanised population led to the adoption of a cheap food policy from the 1840s onwards. Under a policy of free trade, cheap imports from anywhere in the world were allowed to enter the country and most of these were from territories originally under British control. UK farmers (high-cost producers, relative to those of Canada and New Zealand) were compensated with deficiency payments which made up the difference between their high costs and prices, and the price levels of the lower cost imports. The farmer stayed in business with a subsidy, the imports entered freely at a low price level, the taxpayer paid the difference, but the consumer enjoyed very low retail prices for food. This was a fine arrangement for a country with a small farming population, needing essential food imports and also controlling vast agricultural areas of the world. This situation was transformed during the Second World War and since. The need to increase production and self-sufficiency during the wartime period 1939 and 1945, the current 'agricultural revolution', and the acceptance that governments have an obligation to manage and maintain an efficient national food production machine, had led to a much greater contribution by British farmers to an overall national self-sufficiency in eggs, milk, potatoes, barley, pork and poultry.

The UK has abandoned its former position as a free-trade importer from the Commonwealth and the rest of the world, and entered one of European protection. Farmers in the UK are generally in a very good position. With guaranteed markets and prices their efficiency has meant a great stimulation of production upon integration into the large European market which is aiming for substantial self-sufficiency. Specialised groups such as the horticulturalists have problems because of climatic disadvantages, but in general the UK farmer has experienced increased demand for and high production of cereals and livestock products. However, there is the problem of late entry to a system designed for different needs. The ultimate aim of the Common Agricultural Policy is that the agricultural strength of the whole shall be the basis for the specialisation and reform of all the parts, and that the integration of 15 countries will create a strong food and agriculture system which can supply all the needs of 372 million people. However, for the UK, the advantages are finely balanced. The consumer is within a managed price system where prices are high, but supplies of food are plentiful, stable and of good quality. The UK obtains only small benefits from the guidance fund because its agriculture, with the exception of hill-farming, needs little assistance or restructuring. The contributions which the UK pays into the budget because it is a major importer of food have been the cause of continuing tensions and negotiation.

Inflation and currency problems

The situation has deteriorated since 1973. The Mansholt reform proposals for medium-term improvements were overtaken by events, with dairy products, cereals and sugar in structural surplus, and the guaranteed prices to farmers out of control. Rapid inflation since 1973 was largely responsible for the increasing cost of the Common Agricultural Policy price support mechanism. The second problem related to the accounting mechanism of the CAP. The common price system required a set of internal exchange rates to convert national currencies to a common denominator. These were 'Green Currencies' or agricultural money, and examples were the 'Green Pound' and 'Green Franc'. The ECU (European Currency Unit) has developed from this. With the currency chaos of the 1970s and floating exchange rates, the national currencies were revalued. The periodic changes in value of the pound, French franc and German mark were not accompanied by similar changes in the value of the 'green rates'. The 'Green pound' was therefore different in value from the real pound and the 'common prices' throughout the EEC diverged considerably. As a result, the EEC had to introduce a system of MCAs (Monetary Compensation Amounts) which offset the difference between the 'green rate' and the real exchange rate.

The Mediterranean enlargement

The agricultural problem regions, Italy and south-western France, continued to have physical difficulties, fragmented holdings, remoteness, inadequate infrastructure and low productivity. Their special needs were considered in the Mediterranean aid package of 1978, with a range of measures for irrigation, advisory and cooperative services, and upland forestry measures. At that time the Mediterranean region contained 17 per cent of EU farmland, 18 per cent of farm production and 30 per cent of farmers, indicating low labour productivity. Measures adopted by 1981 included irrigation in the Mezzogiorno and Corsica, the development of a farm advisory service in Italy and Southern France, flood protection in the Herault valley of Southern France and support for cooperative ventures in Italy. Such schemes qualified for 25 per cent and occasionally 50 per cent contributions from FEOGA.

However, after the entry of Greece in 1981 and Spain and Portugal in 1986, the agricultural situation deteriorated again. EU agricultural output was raised by one-quarter, and the agricultural workforce rose from 7.3 million in 1981 to 10 million in 1986 with the new entrants. Their Mediterranean products added to existing imbalances in wine, fruit, olive oil and tomatoes. Conflict arose with existing producers in France and Italy, adding to political tensions. Structural problems were enormous, with little or no land reform having taken place in Spain and Portugal. The economic divide between rich and poor farmers became even more extreme than before.

After 1983 the Integrated Mediterranean Programmes (IMP) recognised the problem by coordinating aid to the whole Mediterranean region from the EAGGF, and the Social and Regional funds for agricultural modernisation and diversification. Expenditure on this six-year programme started in 1985 and was designed to improve job opportunities and raise income levels in the still strongly rural areas on the southern margins of the EU where farmers faced difficult environments and outdated land-tenure structures. The IMP operated over the five most southerly planning regions of France, most of Italy and virtually all of Greece. It excluded highly developed urban areas such as Athens and major tourist zones. Maximum intensity of support was given to highland and lowland areas in Greece, Southern Italy, Sicily, Sardinia and Corsica, with limited assistance being applied to central Italy and south-west France. Of the money, 40 per cent was spent on improving agricultural production and making it more market-orientated, 33 per cent on creating alternative rural employment opportunities (e.g. in tourism and craft industries) and 27 per cent on funding afforestation, fishing and training schemes.

Contemporary issues

To a certain extent the Mediterranean orientation of the CAP in the late 1970s and early 1980s rectified the northern bias of the earlier phases of the CAP, but more fundamental issues also needed rectifying. By the mid-1980s the CAP still took over 60 per cent of the EU budget, depriving funds needed for industrial decline and urban problems. Food production was in structural surplus in many sectors and the intervention and price support system had tended to continue these costly surpluses. However, there were major regional imbalances between the EU's farming regions. The CAP illustrated some inherent contradictions. It was basically a strategic food policy. Whilst its economics could easily be questioned, it was increasingly

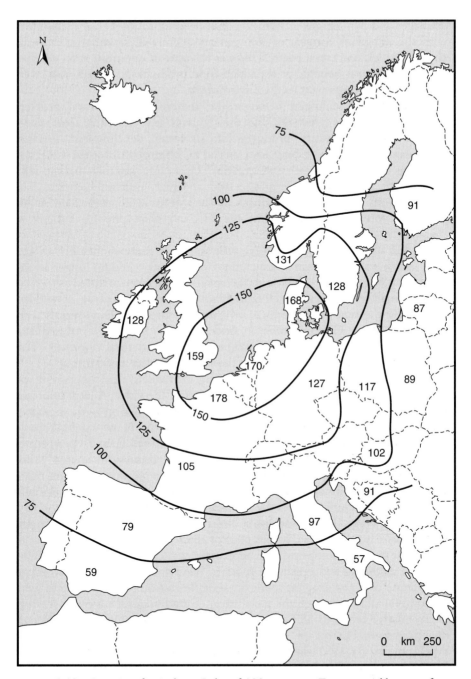

FIGURE 8.13 *Intensity of agriculture. Index of 100 = average European yield per acre for eight major crops (source –* Van Valkenburg*)*

taking on the role of a social and regional policy.

Alongside this emerged a range of crucial environmental questions. Damage to delicate eco-systems through use of fertilisers, irrigation and land drainage, and by changes in farm structure leading to the cereal mega-farms with the attendant dangers of soil-erosion, merely illustrated the dramatic changes which had taken place. This was the start of questions as to whether the medium-term benefits of expanded food production, at high cost, were worth the long-term costs to the environment.

Clear contrasts emerged between the remote marginal rural problem zones with negative pressures, and the dynamic lowland rural areas where there were very positive pressures for economic development, exurban residences and alternative rural land uses. The original aims of the CAP had largely been achieved with the creation of a large internal market with specialised commercial farming and virtual self-sufficiency. The contradictions and rigid mechanisms of the system were embedded in the political interests and structure of the EU and were proving difficult to change.

In 1983 a series of revisions were proposed by Commissioner P Dalsager, who said that the CAP was a luxury the Community could no longer afford. They may be summarised as 'a policy of lower market-oriented prices . . . helping small and medium-sized farmers to modernise and adapt . . . without stimulating the output of products in structural surplus'. His proposals were taken further by Commissioner F Andriessen in 1985 who stressed that farmers were stewards of the landscape, wildlife and rural resources. This indicates the changing perceptions of the role of farmers and farming.

In February 1988 at the Summit meeting in Brussels, final agreement was made on a comprehensive and binding reform of the CAP. A legal limit was placed upon farm price support with controlled annual growth so that it would reach no more than £20.7 billion in 1992. Thus, expenditure in agriculture as a percentage of the EU budget would fall from 70 per cent to 55 per cent by 1992. There were quotas and production ceilings called 'stabilisers' for all products which, if breached, triggered price cuts and taxes. This included, for instance, a 10 per cent cut in milk quotas, and 13 per cent reduction in guaranteed prices for beef. Alternative land use such as forestry, received subsidies. There was also a 'set-a-side' scheme under which arable farmers were paid to leave 20 per cent of their land fallow, or convert it to grazing or non-surplus crops. The agreement was combined with a doubling of aid to declining and inner-city regions. Nevertheless, despite these efforts to restrain costs, the amount spent on agriculture from the EU budget went on rising steadily, although the proportion of the budget spent on agriculture fell in relative terms to 58 per cent in 1992. However, this merely reflected the increase in outlays on other policies – particularly regional and social development. By 1991 the CAP was in a position where it was no longer bringing the essential support to farmers, particularly small farmers and those in less favoured regions of the EU. The CAP was getting into an impasse: farmers were making sacrifices but consumers and taxpayers were not drawing any advantages from their efforts. Retail food prices had gone on rising but the prices paid to farmers had been nearly static since 1985. In some parts of the EU, land was being over-exploited with the intensive use of fertilisers and pesticides, while in more marginal farming areas the rural exodus was accelerating. The 'set-a-side' policy was being questioned as farmers tended to set-a-side the least productive land and then farm the rest more intensively.

Radical action was therefore proposed by the Commission in early 1991 and approved in June 1992. The emphasis changed from the maintenance of high guaranteed support prices to a policy of direct aid for farmers. Central to this action were price cuts for key products linked to the withdrawal of land from production, with farmers being directly compensated for the resulting loss of income. The EU also undertook to develop environmental protection as an integral part of the CAP.

Cereal prices are being reduced by 29 per cent over three years starting in 1993/94. This reduction should bring them close to current world market prices. A minimum import price is being set for cereal imports to maintain a reasonable margin (about 40 per cent) of EU preference. However, farmers are able to obtain direct income-support subsidies (calculated on the basis of the average yields in each farming region) as compensation, but they must withdraw 15 per cent (set-a-side) of their arable land. This set-a-side requirement does not apply to the smallest of EU cereal farmers (those with 20 ha or less). Land which has been set-a-side can be used for non-food purposes like the production of cereals for bio-fuels. The change-over from price support to direct income support brings the cereal sector in line with the principle applied to other products such as oilseeds, processed vegetables, olive oil and tobacco.

Beef prices are being reduced by 15 per cent, and the reduction is being compensated by extra premiums being paid if farmers raise beef cattle on open grazing land, thus encouraging extensive farming rather than intensive factory farming. The guaranteed price for milk products has been frozen for three years and a 1 per cent reduction in national milk-production quotas agreed. There are also quotas for sheep and controls on tobacco production.

Accompanying these measures is an improved early-retirement programme for farmers aged 55 or above, so that younger people can become involved in agriculture, the encouragement of environmentally sensitive farming, finance for afforestation programmes and measures to encourage the management of land taken out of production.

The 1992 reforms should make the cost of the CAP more bearable to Member States, and more of the money will go on direct support to farmers and less on stocking surpluses and on subsidising exports on world markets. For the first time funds are based on different levels of compensation in different regions, allowing communities with the greatest need to receive funding. The reforms should encourage the preservation of rural heritage and the countryside, and the owners and users of land will be expected to do more than just grow food: farmers will diversify into tourism, arts and crafts, and small-scale manufacturing. However, conservationists are worried that set-a-side will encourage some farmers to adopt new uses for their land which are not compatible with landscape conservation, e.g. golf courses or caravan sites. In 1994 the set-a-side scheme was reformed further. Farmers could either set-a-side a different 15 per cent of their land each year

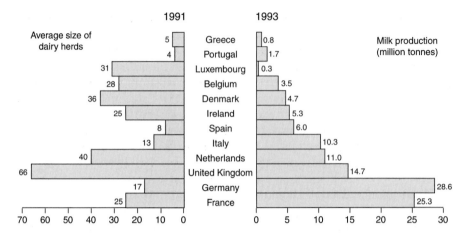

FIGURE 8.14 *Dairy herds and milk production*

(rotational set-a-side) or set-a-side for a five-year or 20 year (ecological set-a-side) period. Conservationists favour the latter as it creates more time for flora and fauna to become established.

FREE TRADE AND TRADING GROUPS

The view of the classical economists such as John Stuart Mill was that international trade between nations led to a more efficient deployment of world resources by assisting countries to specialise in the production of those goods in which they possessed a comparative economic advantage. The ideal was therefore a global multi-lateral free-trade situation, but in practice this has rarely existed for very long.

In the nineteenth century, largely under the influence of the UK, there was an extension of 'free trade' throughout the world. This meant that food and raw material supplies from large-scale producers in the newly discovered continents could be purchased at low cost, largely for the benefit of the rapidly industrialising Western World. At the same time, manufactured goods from Europe were exported on a large scale. During the twentieth century there has been a move towards protectionism as all newly independent countries have sought to protect their own developing industries by placing protective tariffs on goods formerly bought in Europe. Equally, they have looked elsewhere when freed from the necessity of trade with the former colonial power. This is shown in the decline in the proportion of UK exports going to the 'sterling area' (largely synonymous with the Commonwealth) (fig. 4.5). As high as 80 per cent during the nineteenth century, these exports declined to 38 per cent (1960), and by 1993 to 11 per cent.

Here is the essential basis for combining the resources of the small, highly industrialised nations of Europe on a continental scale. The EU gives them a guaranteed home market of almost 372 million people which is a huge internal trading unit with an industrial base and capability for vigorous competition in export markets. It is a 'regional economic grouping' which depends upon a substantial and uninterrupted flow of goods and services. It is therefore in the common interest that barriers to international trade be as low as possible and this has been partially achieved through GATT (General Agreement on Tariffs and Trade) and the international conferences such as the Kennedy Round.

The EU operates as a trading unit on two planes: internal free trade in a common market of the Member States; and a customs union in external trade.

THE FUTURE LANDSCAPE AND THE CAP

The principal geographical patterns will remain very much as now. Regional specialisation should intensify, with each country producing what it does best. The UK will continue to remain a mixed livestock-cereal economy, with specialist dairy and meat products, according to the law of comparative economic advantage.

Although less land is needed for efficient food production, its concentration in fertile lowlands such as the Paris Basin and lowland England, will be tempered by other pressures upon these areas such as urban expansion, roads and airports. There is a case for supporting types of production which pay greater respect to ecological principles, such as medium-technology farming in which less stress is given to maximum output, and where the landscape is conserved in its natural state. A major reduction in imports of feedstock for dairy farms would be a result of this.

The marginal lands will see rather more change. Forestry is one obvious alternative with conifers for commercial use but broad-leaved species also have an important part to play. Forestry is associated not only with timber production, but also with water supply, recreation space, and tourism. Regional and national parks, such as the Camargue in France are multiple land-use zones. Conservation of mountains, distinct environments, forests, heathland and wetlands requires careful control of the ecological balance.

The CAP has to reflect a compromise between food importers such as the UK and Germany, and food exporters such as France and Greece. Its pricing policies must take account of the needs of the farmer, the consumer and the landscape. The maintenance of the rural population and the service infrastructure requires the CAP to keep a major guidance role as a social and regional policy.

9

POPULATION: THE AXIS OF CITY DEVELOPMENT

DIVERSITY

In January 1995 the EU had a combined population of 372 million people, and included Germany with nearly 82 million, three large countries each with populations of nearly 60 million (the UK, France and Italy), Spain, with 39 million, nine smaller states, and the tiny Grand Duchy of Luxembourg (fig. 9.1). This economic grouping, stretching from Finland to Crete, includes a great number of ethnic and linguistic types. The peoples of Italy and France, traditionally known as Latin or Mediterranean, speak languages belonging to the Romance group, whilst the northern part of the EU is dominated by the Teutonic group of languages (German, English, Scandinavian and Dutch). The Roman Catholic Church in the south is broadly associated with the Romance language groups and more specifically with Spain, France and Italy, whilst there is a similar link between Protestantism and the areas around the North Sea. There is, therefore, a broad distinction between the northern and southern sections of the EU on the basis of religion, language and culture.

In general, the language divisions are those of national frontiers, but there are several complicating factors. Minority languages exist alongside major national languages as in the case of the Welsh, Gaelic, Breton and Basque areas. Along the Franco–German frontier zone in Alsace and Lorraine is a German-speaking minority, and the whole Rhineland area in the past has been a zone of contention between the two major groups, French and Germanic. In Belgium there is a division along linguistic lines between the French-speaking Walloons in the south and the Flemings in the north. However, these distinctions have begun to lose their former psychological importance, and the economic pressures of the twentieth century, combined with political maturity and a desire for peaceful cooperation and federation, have created 'unity within diversity'. There is of necessity a system of official languages in the EU – French, English, German, Italian, Spanish, Portuguese, Greek, Dutch, Danish, Finnish and Swedish, the first two being in most common use.

DISTRIBUTION AND DENSITY OF POPULATION

Distribution of population tends to reflect relative regional advantages, and indicates the countries with the highest degrees of industrialisation, population, wealth and urbanisation (fig. 9.2). In summary, there is a densely populated core and sparsely settled periphery.

Using national statistics, the Member States may be divided into four groups (fig. 9.3). The Netherlands and Belgium have a very high population density with over 300 people per km². The Netherlands has the highest

	Population (1/1/95)	Percentage in agriculture (1994)	Percentage in industry (1994)	Percentage in services (1994)	Percentage of population urbanised (1994)
Belgium	10 131 000	2.9	28.9	68.2	97
France	56 027 000	5.2	26.9	67.9	73
Germany	81 553 000	3.3	37.0	59.7	87
Italy	57 248 000	7.7	32.1	60.2	67
Luxembourg	407 000	3.2	27.0	69.8	89
Netherlands	15 423 000	4.0	23.3	72.7	89
UK	58 276 000	2.1	27.8	70.1	90
Denmark	5 216 000	5.1	26.5	68.4	85
Ireland	3 577 000	13.2	27.1	59.7	58
Greece	10 442 000	20.8	23.6	55.6	65
Spain	39 170 000	9.9	30.1	60.0	77
Portugal	9 912 000	11.8	32.5	55.7	36
Finland	5 099 000	8.6	26.3	65.1	63
Austria	8 040 000	6.9	35.4	57.7	56
Sweden	8 816 000	3.4	25.0	71.6	83

FIGURE 9.1   *EU (15) population, employment and urbanisation*

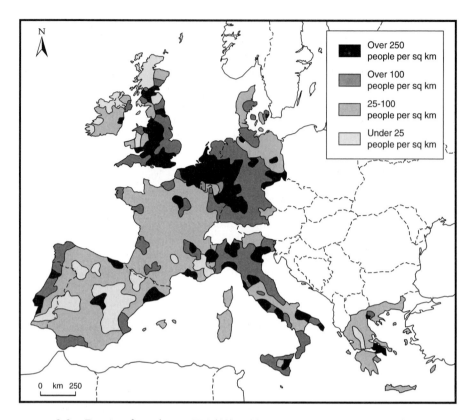

FIGURE 9.2   *Density of population, EU (12), 1991*

density of all with its population concentrated in the Randstad conurbation. Belgium's population is highest around the Brussels–Antwerp area, with similar concentrations throughout the commercial cities of Flanders, and the Sambre–Meuse coalfield.

High densities of population are recorded in the UK, Germany and Italy, and increasingly in Luxembourg, but there are considerable regional variations. The Italian population concentrations in the Lombardy lowlands, Ligurian coast, and the Rome–Naples area contrast with the sparsely populated Alps and Central Apennines. Germany and the UK have major concentrations in their industrial zones and city regions. These favoured zones of population concentration, the German Rhinelands and the English lowland (fig. 9.2), contrast significantly with many upland areas in both countries which have extremely low densities. Luxembourg has the thinly populated Ardennes in the north, but Luxembourg City and the steel-making district in the south have a moderately high density (250 per km^2).

Denmark, Portugal, France, Austria, Greece and Spain have relatively low overall densities of under 130 people per km^2, reflecting their greater agricultural and rural character. France has a remarkably even distribution of population, and apart from Paris there are few concentrations of any great extent. Even the Nord and Lorraine heavy industrial areas never reached the same degree of population density as comparable areas in Germany or the UK. In the Iberian peninsula the well-watered Atlantic coastal lowlands of Portugal have favoured a relatively dense agricultural population, whilst in Spain there are large stretches of underpopulated arid mountain plateaux. Three urban industrial concentrations exist around Madrid, Barcelona and Bilbao. Copenhagen is a significant exception to the rule in Denmark.

Ireland has a long tradition of rural depopulation, lack of mineral resources and a peripheral position in relation to Europe as a whole. The only centre of any size is the capital, Dublin. In Austria, 20 per cent of the population lives in the province of Vienna, with the lowest population in the western mountainous provinces of Tirol, Salzburg and Voralberg (excluding the cities of Salzburg and Innsbruck) and in the south-eastern province of Burgenland. For Sweden, 85 per cent of the population lives in the southern half of the country. Finland has the lowest density of all.

ECONOMIC STRUCTURE AND POPULATION PATTERNS

Population density is one indication of the rate and scale of economic activity, but equally valid indices are employment characteristics and the degree of urbanisation. The proportions of the population employed in agriculture, industry and services measure fairly accurately the stage of evolution which any country has reached (fig. 9.1). The percentage of the population which is urbanised indicates a sophisticated lifestyle associated with a mature economy. The relative proportions for each sector of the economy in the EU countries can be compared with those for the USA which has a declining proportion of employment in industry, and a high proportion of employment in the tertiary sector. The UK closely approaches the American situation with a well-developed tertiary sector, efficient agriculture, a declining industrial sector and a high degree of urbanisation. The Netherlands, Belgium, Luxembourg, Sweden and Germany have similar characteristics except that Germany has a larger industrial sector. In all these north-west European countries there is an advanced social and economic infrastructure associated with a high standard of living and urban lifestyle. France, Denmark, Italy, Finland and Austria have developed rapidly during the last 40 years, but still have an enlarged agricultural sector. There is a different emphasis when examining Portugal, Spain, Ireland and Greece, which have much larger agricultural sectors, an underdeveloped tertiary sector and often a lower degree of urbanisation. Indeed, an examination of primacy (the percentage of urban population in the largest city) shows major differences across the Mediterranean basin. Italy and Spain have a balanced, mature urban hierarchy, with only 7 per cent and 12 per cent respectively of

Country	Population per square kilometre
Netherlands	372
Belgium	331
United Kingdom	239
Germany	228
Italy	190
Luxembourg	155
Denmark	121
Portugal	107
France	106
Austria	96
Greece	79
Spain	78
Ireland	51
Sweden	19
Finland	15

FIGURE 9.3   *EU (15) density of population, 1994 (source:* Eurostat*)*

the urban population in the largest city. In Greece (Athens, 30 per cent) and Portugal (Lisbon, 22 per cent) the percentage is much higher, illustrating the rapid contemporary rural and urban migration which has been concentrated heavily into the capital city region creating an unbalanced spatial structure. Athens is a rather unfortunate example of the rapid transformation without planning constraints of what 40 years ago was a relatively small city of half a million people. Now there is a considerable unattractive urban sprawl which has surrounded the ancient city. These differences illustrate a complex gradient of economic types ranging from the core countries in the north-west of the EU to the less developed peripheral countries of the EU.

National averages tend to blur the differences between contrasting regions of economic sophistication or underdevelopment, and some idea of these extremes may be gathered from the figures which compare sample EU regions (fig. 9.4). Concentrations of population in south-east England and Greater Paris, and North-Rhine Westphalia contrast with the very low populations of Limousin, Crete, Alentejo and Basilicata. The service employment levels in Paris, Brabant (Brussels), south-east England and Liguria, and the industrialised Piedmont, Lower Bavaria, Thuringia and North-Rhine Westphalia are of equal significance. Here the essential contrasts between regions can be seen: wealthy urbanised regions with a high

	Total population	Agriculture (%)	Industry (%)	Services (%)	Population density (km²)
Ile de France	10 861 600	0.4	25.3	74.3	904
Piedmont	4 301 900	6.8	41.9	51.4	169
Basilicata	610 400	20.3	24.1	55.6	61
Liguria	1 670 800	3.9	24.0	72.1	308
Normandy (Lower)	1 403 300	9.1	31.1	59.8	80
N Rhine/Westphalia	17 594 500	2.0	42.4	55.6	516
Brabant (Brussels)	2 258 300	1.6	22.9	75.5	673
Limousin	718 500	13.5	28.4	58.1	42
North Holland	1 605 200	5.0	27.0	68.0	141
Lower Bavaria	1 101 100	10.5	42.5	47.0	107
S E England	17 703 400	1.2	25.6	73.2	650
Crete	543 900	45.0	15.9	39.1	65
Alentejo	538 600	22.0	28.5	49.5	20
Castilla La Mancha	1 716 700	16.0	37.2	46.8	22
Thuringia	2 684 000	10.0	53.0	37.0	165

FIGURE 9.4 *Regional characteristics, 1992 (source:* Eurostat*)*

level of service-sector employment; industrial conurbations with a high percentage of employment in industry; rich farming areas with high rural populations; and isolated marginal farming areas barely able to sustain even low population levels.

AREAS OF POPULATION DECLINE

The rate of decline of rural, peripheral or upland regions varies considerably. In the UK rural depopulation has been going on since the sixteenth century and has produced a farming population which is less than 3 per cent of the total workforce, as well as a high level of urban concentration. Peripheral mountainous areas are still losing people in spite of government schemes to introduce employment and improve facilities. Since the 1930s the principal losses have been in the Scottish Highlands, and the uplands of the Cheviots, Pennines, the Lake District and Wales.

In France, regions like the Massif Central have a complex internal

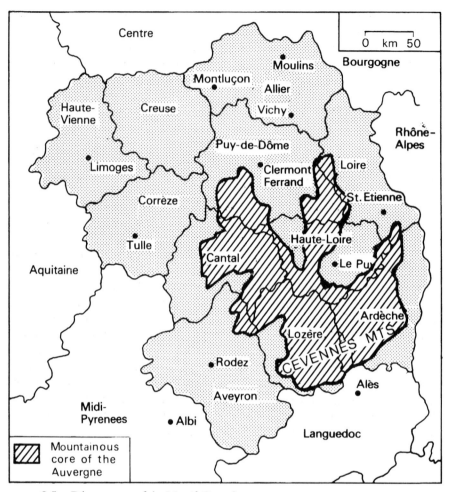

FIGURE 9.5 *Départements of the Massif Central*

population movement. Although population is lost from the central areas, there is often a concentration into lowland fringes and valleys within the zones as a whole. The Massif Central (fig. 9.5) is still losing people from its mountainous spine, particularly the *départements* of Haute-Loire, Cantal, Aveyron, Lozère, Corrèze and Creuse. The valley of the Allier in the north, containing Moulins and Clermont Ferrand, has seen considerable growth, although the population is currently stagnating. Clermont Ferrand is practically a 'company town' of the Michelin Tyre Group, and also gains by being in easy communication with Paris. Limoges and St Etienne are other old industrial towns on the margin which are minor growth areas.

In Belgium, the Ardennes are within commuting range of the Liège conurbation to the north, and towns such as Dinant, Bastogne and Spa have experienced growth in a new dormitory role. In addition, there is the development of 'second homes' in the Ourthe valley, and upland regions like the Ardennes may well be repopulated, as they are becoming a major leisure area (fig. 13.6).

There are great differences between northern and southern Italy (fig. 9.6). The out-migration from the Mezzogiorno has been a sustained response to the overpopulation, low standards of living and poor employment opportunities. Much of the movement has been to Piedmont, Lombardy and Liguria, but in addition there has been a major movement into Germany and other EU countries, a result of the free movement of labour allowed within the EU. Between 1950 and 1990 the Mezzogiorno lost over 4 million people, although since 1980 migration has been much reduced and even – in Sicily, for instance – reversed (Chapter 17).

In Greece, the rapid development of the Athens–Piraeus lowland, which now has 34 per cent of the total population of the country, is an example of the excessive 'pull' of primate capital cities to the detriment of peripheral areas of the country.

Old and exhausted coal-mining areas are also responsible for pockets of either population decline, relative stagnation, or unemployment and dislocation. Commuting is a partial answer. The Belgian Borinage is an example where many ex-miners travel daily to Charleroi and Brussels. The small high-cost coal-fields of the margins of the Massif Central, Montluçon, Decazeville and Commentry are now under a complete closure plan which will intensify migration from the whole area. In the former mining valleys of South Wales, migration and commuting to Cardiff and the coastal area has taken place. In the north-east of England there is heavy migration from the old Durham mining villages to new towns such as Washington and Peterlee. The Nord Pas de Calais region of France has similar problems, losing over 180 000 people between 1980 and 1990 (fig. 9.11).

AREAS OF POPULATION GROWTH

Population growth areas lie around the major nodes of industry, services and transport, the city regions, and in new residential and leisure areas.

Low-cost assembly points on major estuaries and transport nodes such as Rotterdam, Antwerp, Hamburg, Marseilles and Teesside have become the growth points for such industries as oil refining, petrochemicals and other basic industries. The West Midlands, at the central point of convergence of the UK motorway system, possesses a varied and regenerating range of industry and services.

The capital cities of core regions of the Member States have experienced continuous population growth since the mid-nineteenth century. Their attraction lies in their functions as administrative, cultural, service and prestige centres. They lie at the focal point of the national transport network, and have two significant resources: a pool of skilled labour and a huge market. They are examples of the ultimate factor behind multi-million

Mont Gerbier in the Massif Central of France: a rugged volcanic upland of marginal farming and rural depopulation

city growth: the non-basic or self-sustaining capacity of the large population concentration. London, the Randstad, Brussels and Paris are good examples.

The Rhine valley of Germany has experienced sustained population growth (fig. 9.6) but illustrates a variation on the capital-city-concentration theme. Germany has a political history of many independent states each with its capital city, but the unification of Germany has fundamentally affected spatial patterns of population distributions and composition. Greater Berlin, with a population of almost 3.6 million, is now the largest city in Germany and is expected to grow in size especially as a result of its designation as the capital and seat of government. In the Lander of the old West Germany (partly reflecting the federal principles of the Republic) there is a uniform distribution of central places of medium and large size, each well connected by a dense network of road and rail links, so that in the Rhine valley, for example, no one city dominates completely. Thus various cities in the Rhine valley enjoy specialised, yet interrelated, functions: Bonn as administrative centre; Frankfurt and Düsseldorf as financial centres; Duisburg as the major port; and Cologne and Mannheim as major commercial and industrial cities. In south Germany Munich, Stuttgart, and Nuremberg enjoy extensive regional status. However, in the new Lander of the former GDR the settlement pattern has been considerably modified by the operation of the centrally planned economy of East Germany (GDR). Consequently, towns and cities have become densely populated, while rural regions are thinly settled. The suburbanisation process was much less pronounced in the former GDR, so that the difference between urban and rural areas is much more distinct. In addition, the new Lander of the former GDR have very few large central places as East Berlin tended to dominate. A further complication is that the choice of capital for each of the new Lander has been contentious – e.g. in Mecklenburg-Vorpommern, the city of Schwerin (with a population of 130 000) was chosen in preference to the Hanseatic port of Rostock (with a population of 250 000). In Italy, the principal manufacturing and core region lies in the northern triangle of Milan, Turin and Genoa. Nevertheless, the historic, cultural and administrative functions of Rome, and the regional importance of Naples, ensure their continuing growth.

Population growth in coastal and other environmentally attractive areas is associated with wealth, holidays, retirement, mobility and the phenomenon of the 'second home'. Large areas of the English south coast have become continuous suburban developments as towns like Bournemouth and Poole, and the Bognor Regis and Brighton group, coalesce. They are the new leisure-service centres. On a larger scale is the pattern of linear growth along the Côte D'Azur from Cannes to Monte Carlo and along the coast of the Ligurian Riviera (fig. 9.11).

Region	Net migration (1960–75)	Net migration (1980–90)	Net migration (1991)
North-Rhine Westphalia	+897 998	+328 000	+154 600
Baden-Württemberg	+732 301	+358 000	+159 400
Hessen	+704 578	+179 000	+76 700
Piedmont	+644 369	+8800	−600
Lombardy	+866 846	+80 800	+6100
Liguria	+184 761	+17 000	−2700
Brabant	+188 846	−2300	−3400
Lower Saxony	+251 401	+179 600	+90 600
Limburg (Netherlands)	+686	−1200	+1600
Campania	−430 992	+10 900	−27 200
Calabria	−425 382	−12 900	−11 900
Mezzogiorno (total)	−2 355 725	+109 500	−68 600

FIGURE 9.6 *Migration flows in sample regions (source:* Eurostat)

THE CONURBATION AND CITY REGION

The most characteristic feature of contemporary Europe is the extent and scale of city growth (figs. 9.8 and 9.9). The percentage of the population which is urbanised is above 70 per cent in all EU countries except Portugal, Ireland, Greece, Italy, Finland and Austria.

The pattern of small nucleated cities of the medieval period was succeeded in the nineteenth century by the conurbation, a sprawling structure composed of a number of coalescing industrial towns. The city of Stoke-on-Trent comprises six towns based originally upon the North Staffordshire coalfield and the pottery industry, and is a good example of a polycentric agglomeration of industrial towns. Rhine–Ruhr, Lille–Roubaix–Tourcoing and Greater Manchester (fig. 9.7) are much larger examples. The twentieth century has witnessed such an increase in mobility that people often now live up to 60 km out of the city and commute daily to work. The lifestyle of the city is a great attraction, and its retail, commercial, administrative and cultural services expand so that congestion becomes the great problem in the city centre. Replacement of obsolescent property and changes in residential and employment patterns has meant displacement of people to the city margins, with new housing estates and a vast expansion in the total city area.

The term 'city' is an insufficient description. Paris city has 2.2 million people; the Paris region includes the city and four départements. It extends over nearly 2000 km^2 and has a population of 10.7 million. The London planning region, bounded approximately by a radius of 60 km from Charing Cross station, is really three concentric zones. The Greater London conurbation, with just under 8 million people, forms the core and inner

Monte Carlo on the Côte D'Azur: centre of the French sun-belt and rapid population growth

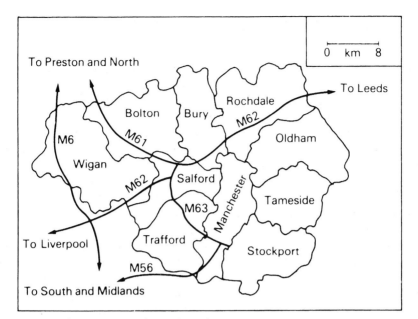

FIGURE 9.7   *The Greater Manchester city region*

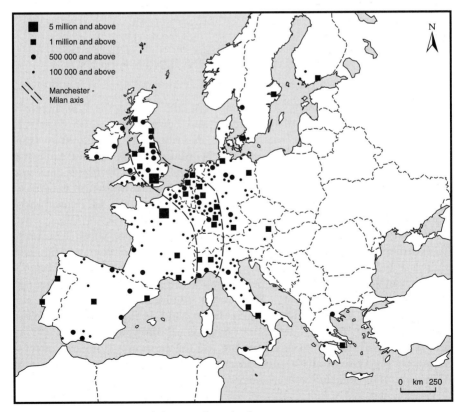

FIGURE 9.8   *Major cities and the axis of city development*

ring, and is surrounded by the green belt, a successful device which has substantially arrested continuous growth. The outer ring consists of old centres such as St Albans and Guildford, and new towns such as Stevenage and Crawley, established after the 1947 New Towns Act. The rapid suburbanisation of this outer ring has proceeded apace, so that this is now a part of London's 'commuter belt'. The effects of city growth now reach far beyond the London planning region, however. The whole of south-east England and East Anglia from the Wash to the Solent has 34 per cent of the total population of the UK.

Such regions of dynamic growth are 'city regions' dominated by the central city and surrounded by industry and housing, leisure areas and open space. On the fringe there are old-established towns, metropolitan villages and non-contiguous residential areas and new towns. These are all linked to the services, employment facilities and lifestyle of the city by fast suburban communications. The four largest city regions in the EU (fig. 9.9) are Rhine–Ruhr, Greater Paris, Greater London and Randstad. These are primate cities of world rank and complex metropolitan regions. They are followed by a group each with populations around the 3–5 million mark; Madrid, Milan, Berlin, Barcelona, Athens, Rome, and Naples. The very great number of medium-sized cities with populations over 600 000 demonstrates fully the substantial degree of urbanisation which now exists.

THE AXIS OF POPULATION CONCENTRATION

There are two central areas of concentration (fig. 9.2). In the UK there is a quadrilateral stretching from Manchester and Leeds to the south coast. On the Continent there is a triangle best described by joining lines from Stuttgart to the coast at Dunkerque and Hamburg. These are not exclusive, and areas external to these such as Greater Paris, Lyons, Northern Italy and Rome are important subsidiary nodes. If a high rate of migration is taken as the most significant factor, the Mediterranean coastlands of France show sustained growth over a long period.

The main axis of city development thus stretches from South Lancashire to Northern Italy, often referred to as the Manchester–Milan axis (fig. 9.8). This is a wide belt which essentially crosses the English lowlands and extends to the heavily urbanised North Sea coastlands stretching from Lille through Belgium to the Randstad. The River Rhine has three great city agglomerations: Rhine–Ruhr, Rhine–Main, and Rhine–Neckar. Though broken by the Alpine mountain chain it re-emerges in the Plain of Lombardy, with its traditions of city life and the economic core area of Italy. Some 60 per cent of all the million cities in Europe are found in the UK, Germany, Italy and the Netherlands.

CONTEMPORARY POPULATION CHANGE: A SUMMARY

In Western Europe this may be understood by reference to three principal themes. After the traditional or pre-modern stage up to the late eighteenth century there was the demographic transformation of the Industrial Revolution in which rapid growth of population and an expanding workforce was absorbed by rapidly expanding manufacturing industries in the cities and industrial areas. This was a period of population concentration and rural depopulation. The rapid changes in population have slackened since the 1960s and during a modern phase during the 1970s and onwards there has been a population state much closer to equilibrium, with birth rates falling, the population ageing and migration patterns becoming much more complex with a particular difference emerging between north-western Europe and southern, or peripheral, Europe.

The EU enjoyed rapid growth in both population and economic terms during the period from 1950 to 1970. All countries of the EU experienced this growth in varying degrees. The German economic miracle was a term associated with the growth in population in West Germany to 61 million people. During this period the German economy gained some 7 million labour migrants as refugees from the East European countries poured in and as workers from Yugoslavia, Turkey and southern Italy also entered the country, attracted by its booming economy. France gained large numbers of people from French North Africa and in the case of the UK there were migrants from Ireland and the Commonwealth.

In addition to this international migration there was a large-scale natural increase. The post-war baby boom reached its second peak in the mid-1960s. One of the major economic pressures which was operating was that of rural de-population. The movement towards more efficient farming, rationalisation, modernisation and intensive production of food was associated with the growth of manufacturing, mass production and the tertiary economy in the city regions. Consumer wealth and a rapidly growing transport system have vastly increased population mobility and intensified this trend. The movement away from isolated rural, peripheral or upland environments towards the more favoured industrial regions is known as urban concentration and rural de-population. This is complemented by the economic pull factor exerted by the metropolitan cities, core areas and expanding service infrastructure and is exemplified by the economic growth of the Rhineland cities of Germany and by the drift to the south-east in the UK. Four out of five of the EU's inhabitants now live in 'urban places' – a significant increase over the level of urbanisation that existed over 40 years ago (65 per cent in 1950).

However, during the 1980s it became recognised that in many EU countries, larger metropolitan areas had been losing population to smaller urban regions ('counter-urbanisation'). In the UK between 1971 and 1981,

Urban area	Population 1992 (thousands)	EU rank
Rhine–Ruhr	10 419	1
Paris agglomeration	8662	2
London region	7825	3
Randstad	6169	4
Madrid	4846	5
Milan	3670	6
Berlin	3590	7
Barcelona	3400	8
Athens	3097	9
Rome	2985	10
Naples	2905	11
Stuttgart	2852	12
West Midlands conurbation	2326	13
Frankfurt-on-Main	2300	14
Greater Manchester	2281	15
Lisbon	2131	16
Vienna	2045	17
Hamburg	1924	18
Brussels	1845	19
Mannheim–Ludwigshaven	1800	20
Oporto	1695	21
Clydeside	1648	22
Leeds–Bradford	1543	23
Stockholm	1471	24
Munich	1465	25
Copenhagen	1337	26
Lyons	1262	27
Turin	1114	28
Marseille	1087	29
Valencia	1060	30
Helsinki	1005	31
Lille–Roubaix	950	32
Dublin	921	33
Antwerp	917	34
Genoa	786	35
Tyneside	761	36
Palermo	755	37
Seville	754	38
Gothenburg	720	39
Thessaloniki	706	40
Bordeaux	686	41
Hanover	680	42
Merseyside	663	43
Sheffield	644	44
Bremen	622	45
Nuremberg	617	46
Zaragoza	614	47
Nottingham	612	48
Toulouse	608	49
Liege	601	50

FIGURE 9.9   *Rank-size of EU urban areas*

the six largest cities lost population fastest while 52 rural areas gained most rapidly. The East Anglia economic planning region became the fastest-growing region in terms of population increase, with people attracted to small urban areas like Cambridge and Norwich with their attractive environments and high 'psychic income'.

It was anticipated that this shift away from the larger urban concentrations would accelerate, but this does not appear to have happened, though there is some evidence of a reversal of population growth in some of the EU's largest cities.

Since the mid-1970s the rates of population increase have slowed very markedly. In 1990 the population grew by only 0.2 per cent – compared with 0.5 per cent for all Economically More Developed Countries (EMDCs) – and in 1994 live births were estimated at 4.1 million – i.e. a birth rate of 10.9 per cent (down from 11.2 per cent in 1993). The birth rate has fallen most dramatically in the southern Member States and in Eire. By the late 1980s countries like Greece and Italy had the lowest rates of natural increase in the EU, and the total fertility rate of the EU (1.45 children per woman) has also declined. Although this rate varies between Member States, with Italy now the lowest (1.19) and Sweden the highest (1.89), the main trend has been the *convergence* of the demographic characteristics of the various EU countries. However, there has been a recent trend in some EU countries, particularly Denmark, Luxembourg and Finland, for the total fertility rate to increase. The rates of natural increase slackened in the richer countries of the core of north-west Europe. There are many complex reasons for this including changing age structure (people aged over 65 already represent 14 per cent of the EU population) and the position of women in society. The most specific reason was the onset of the economic recession from 1973 onwards. The decline in industrial production and consequent unemployment has led to a reduced demand for labour migrants, the drying-up of the process of international migration and the phenomenon of return migration where the so called *Gastarbeiter* or guest workers in Germany are no longer welcome. In the Netherlands there has been a marked downgrading of future estimates of population growth.

Italy illustrates an interesting contrast within its national boundaries. Northern Italy is well developed and part of the mainstream economy of Western Europe and illustrates the same population characteristics. However the Mezzogiorno still retains many demographic traits typical of the pre-modern period. It has persistently high birth rates which are associated with geographical inaccessibility, a predominance of agricultural employment, low urbanisation rates and low female economic activity rates.

Nevertheless, fig. 9.6 shows a reversal of the out-migration from the Mezzogiorno as a whole, and out-migration from Calabria has slowed. On the other hand, population gain from net migration in the north is much reduced, with figures for Piedmont showing a net loss in 1991.

However, while the birth rate has been plummeting, life expectancy at birth in the EU has become one of the highest in the world – 73.2 for men, 79.6 for women in 1993. The combination of a declining birth rate and substantially increased life expectancy led to increasing concern in many Member States in the late 1980s, and to the production by the EU in 1990 of its first report on demographic trends. The report highlighted a number of issues and particularly asked whether society was capable of looking after the growing number of old people who would need help, whether the new pensioners (most of whom would still be healthy and well-educated) would be allowed to contribute to society and whether the job market would be able to adapt quickly to a much older workforce. The report also pointed out that, after 1992, old people would be as free as any other group to move around the EU, and that their selective in-migration could pose particular problems for favoured retirement areas such as coastal settlements.

A further significant change in the demographic growth of the EU has been the role of migration. Between 1945 and the early 1960s there were Member States like France, Germany and the UK whose economic growth depended upon a workforce recruited from abroad, and there were others who were major exporters of labour, particularly Italy, Spain, Portugal and Eire. After the economic downturn of the early 1970s there was a significant decline in labour immigration as many EU countries tightened their immigration policies. The need for labour also changed to one increasingly feminised or more skilled, or both, as manufacturing declined and service industries grew. In recent years most long-term work permits for entry to the UK have gone to workers transferred by their employers, with about 80 per cent going to professional and managerial workers. Labour demand is often now in sectors such as financial services and computing. These are mainly inaccessible to the mass of migrants. Their jobs are in marginal types of activity like agriculture, domestic service and catering, or in the 'underground economy' – low skilled, low paid and informal.

The problems of work shortages for these migrants has been compounded by an increase in racism in the EU Member States and growing support for political parties from the far right (the French National Front won 15 per cent of the vote in the first round of the presidential elections in 1995, and actually topped the polls in Marseilles, Mulhouse, Avignon and Metz). In Germany the influx of migrants from Eastern Europe has caused particular problems in the former GDR where unemployment has been rising. However, many of these migrants are asylum seekers. Asylum is applied for by people seeking to be recognised as refugees within the meaning of the 1951 Geneva Convention. Between 1987 and 1992 asylum applications rose considerably, with Germany as the most popular destination because of its very liberal asylum policy and Sweden the second most popular. Under the terms of the Maastricht Treaty, Member States have to cooperate on immigration policy, and the EU has harmonised and tightened its rules on asylum-seeking, leading to charges of it adopting a 'Fortress Europe' policy and of encouraging racism. The application of the policy has been made easier by the cooperation of national police forces through Europol. Between 1992 and 1994 net migration has almost halved, and during 1994 net migration declined by 26 per cent in Germany which experiences half of the total migration of the EU. Only Sweden showed a marked increase.

Case-study: France

Up to 1975 the core regions experienced the greatest volume of population increase. In France this is illustrated by fig. 9.11. Only three regions persistently gained population on a large scale: Paris, Provence–Côte D'Azur and Rhône Alpes. These three absorbed half the total population increases from 1945–75, by which time they contained over 35 per cent of the total population of France. Net migration losses were recorded in the Massif Central, an impoverished and isolated upland region in Western France, basically an area of contracting agricultural employment with few alternative sources of employment, and in the old industrial area of the north-east where contracting employment in coal-mining, heavy metallurgy and textiles was combined with a slow replacement by new industries.

From the mid-1970s onwards the spatial expression of this was considerably modified. In the first place the collapse in employment in traditional industries such as coal, steel, shipbuilding and textiles, and the recessionary pressures on the economy, dampened down buoyancy in areas which had been 'core' in the 1960s. A good example of this was Lorraine in eastern France in which the depressed steel and engineering industry led to considerable emigration during the late 1970s and 1980s. Within the city

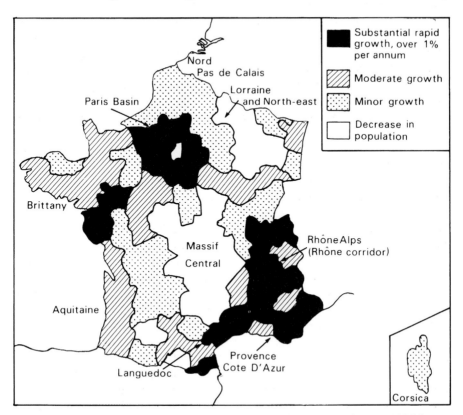

FIGURE 9.10   *France – population change 1975–82 (source –* INSEE (census 1982)*)*

regions a process of de-concentration and counter-urbanisation began. The process of inner-city decline and slum-clearance schemes, together with increasing affluence, car ownership and the need for more space for residential purposes and the decentralisation of employment to the edge of the city region, all combined to mean decentralisation from the cities to the suburbs, away from the larger cities to small and medium-sized settlements down the urban hierarchy, and from the older settled industrial areas to the accessible rural areas. Migration patterns became much more complex.

The 1982 census in France reflected these trends. In the first place there was the beginning of regeneration of growth in areas which had been characterised by population decline for well over a century. These included Brittany which was now much more prosperous partly due to tourism, the Alps and parts of the Massif Central which were more accessible. There were, however, still broad areas of countryside beyond the reach of urban influence which were still in decline. Those mountainous areas of the Massif Central which were still losing population included particularly the départements of Haute Loire, Cantal, Aveyron, Lozère, Correze and Creuse (fig. 9.5). The industrial départements of the North and East were losing population, as were the inner départements of the City of Paris. The 1990 census showed a continuation of these trends (fig. 9.12), although the cities have seen renewed population growth, particularly in the south in cities like Toulouse and Montpellier and in regional capitals like Nantes and Dijon. Nevertheless, the population is still spilling out into surrounding rural communes. It is in Paris that the most interesting changes have taken place. The Paris region now has a negative migration total and this partially reflects the success of the French authorities in checking the rate of growth of the city. Growth has been concentrated in the five new towns on the edge of Paris and in the accessible rural areas up to 100 km out of the city. The

	Net total migration			Total population 1991 (million)
	1954–75	**1980–1990**	**1991**	
Ile De France	+1 152 000	−127 400	−8800	10.8
Lorraine	−31 939	−135 300	−13 300	2.3
Nord/Pas de Calais	−202 907	−184 000	−15 500	4.0
Brittany	−76 559	+55 300	+6400	2.8
Auvergne	−24 931	−4700	−200	1.3
Languedoc-Roussillon	+330 000	+215 900	+21 600	2.2
Provence- Côte D'Azur	+969 568	+295 200	+25 400	4.3
Rhône-Alpes	+516 105	+134 200	+17 800	5.4

FIGURE 9.11   *France – population change 1954–90*

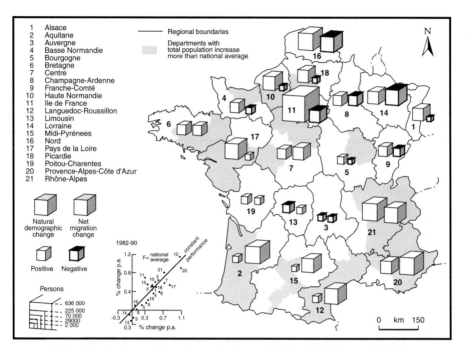

FIGURE 9.12   *Regional population changes in France 1982–1990 (Source:* INSEE, *census 1990)*

population growth of the Mediterranean regions continues with their attraction for tourism and retirement in addition to the important industrial developments around Marseilles. Not only the Côte D'Azur but also the area of the South-East Rhône valley around Provence and the coast, the so-called 'sun belt', has seen consistent growth. Those towns and cities with the most long-standing growth include Cannes, Antibes, Aix-en-Provence, Montpellier, Avignon and Toulon.

Another important area of consistent growth is the city region of Lyons with strong growth in the Alpine–Isère–Rhône corridor, and in particular the cities of Grenoble, Annecy and Lyons itself.

Within the stages of urbanisation (urban concentration, suburbanisation and now counter-urbanisation) we may see the contrasts within the urban system of Western Europe. The population contrasts which have been shown allow us to consider the existence within the EU of a dynamic core and a problem periphery.

10

REGIONAL DISPARITIES: CORE AND PERIPHERY

INTRODUCTION

Much of Western Europe has experienced substantial economic growth and greatly increased prosperity since 1945. More varied energy sources, increased farm production, greater industrial efficiency, greater mobility, a larger volume of trade, greater purchasing power and a wide variety of consumer goods, all create an impression of prosperity. The principal problem, however, within this wealthy society is that of 'dualism'. This is the propensity to uneven growth and the emergence of marked contrasts between natural growth areas and problem regions. Thuringia in Germany has less than 40 per cent of the average income per head in the EU, whilst the Hamburg region has 196 per cent. The basic reason for these disparities, in part at least, is the operation of the Common Market itself. Increased cross-frontier competition, and operation of the large free market amongst 372 million people, means that stronger competitors gain at the expense of weaker ones. Industry tends to move to the area which will allow it to operate at maximum efficiency and with the highest profit. There is recognition that the free market has to be distorted to a certain extent to aid the weaker regions, and that, for example, Italy's Mezzogiorno needs assistance to enable it to compete with the factories of Milan and Turin. The establishment of the principle that less intensive, inactive or declining areas require considerable aid or reconstruction, is one of the very significant innovations in the modern industrial state. It has become an important policy-making area in the EU.

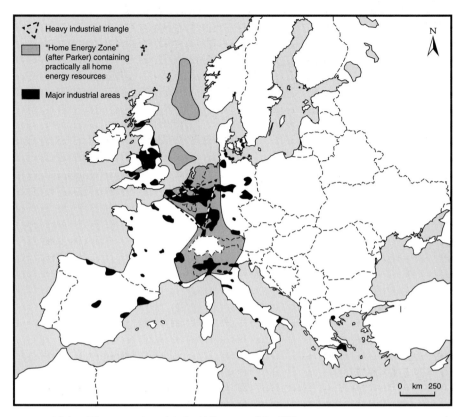

FIGURE 10.1 *Home energy and industrial zones of the EU*

THE ECONOMIC HEARTLAND

The preceding chapters have attempted to illustrate a major theme: the contrasts between the economic heartland and the peripheral regions of the EU.

1 In **agriculture**, the area of large-scale, intensive and efficient food production centres upon the polders, boulder clays and loess lowlands of the North-West European Plain and South-East England (fig. 8.13).

2 The **Home Energy Zone** (fig. 10.1) includes the coalfields of the UK and the Heavy Industrial Triangle which produce 90 per cent of the EU's coal and lignite. Three-quarters of EU hydro-electricity comes from the Alpine zone of south-eastern France and Italy, which forms the southern portion of the Home Energy Zone. If the reserves of gas and oil in the North Sea are added, then the vast bulk of the EU's home energy supplies will continue to be found along a north–south axis which includes the North Sea littoral and the Rhinelands. This is the 'Home Energy Production Zone' of G Parker.

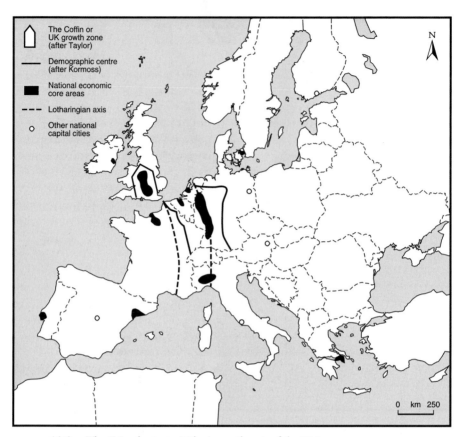

FIGURE 10.2   *The 'Manchester to Milan' growth axis of the EU*

3 **Manufacturing industry** (fig. 10.1) is concentrated in the German
  Rhinelands, eastern France, Central Belgium and the Rhine delta, with a
  very large proportion of the EU's coal, iron ore, steel, refined oil,
  engineering, chemicals, textiles and vehicle production. To this industrial
  triangle must be added the Manchester–London axis, Greater Paris and
  the Milan–Turin core, for although physically separate, they form a
  logical extension of the central industrial axis.
4 **National core areas** of six major EU countries lie within this zone
  (fig. 10.2). EU decision-making lies between Brussels, Luxembourg and
  Strasbourg.
5 **Mobility** is at its height along the Rhineland routeways (figs. 5.2, 5.5 and
  5.6) and the waterway system of the Rhine and its tributaries is both
  physically and psychologically the central artery of the EU, containing its
  greatest seaport, Rotterdam.
6 **The demographic heart of the EU** (fig. 10.2) lies within an area
  delimited by Boulogne–Nancy–Stuttgart–Hanover–Amsterdam (Kormoss,
  1959). In the original six-member EEC, this area had 20 per cent of the
  land area but 40 per cent of the population, and contained some 80

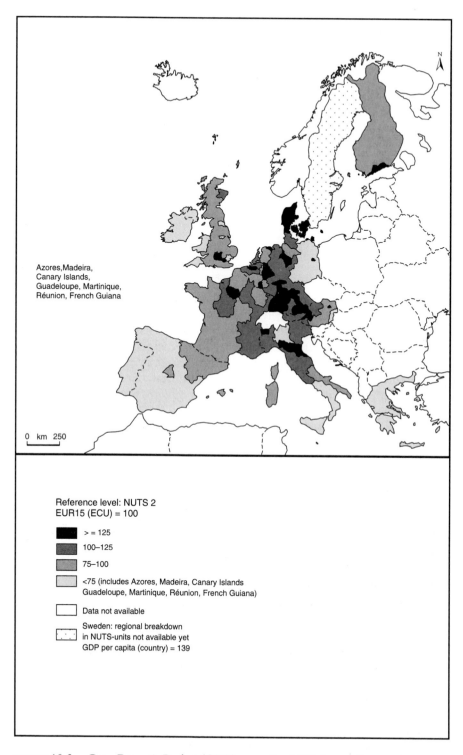

Azores,Madeira,
Canary Islands,
Guadeloupe, Martinique,
Réunion, French Guiana

0 km 250

Reference level: NUTS 2
EUR15 (ECU) = 100

■ >= 125

▨ 100–125

▤ 75–100

□ <75 (includes Azores, Madeira, Canary Islands
Guadeloupe, Martinique, Réunion, French Guiana)

□ Data not available

⁘ Sweden: regional breakdown
in NUTS-units not available yet
GDP per capita (country) = 139

FIGURE 10.3   *Gross Domestic Product (GDP) per capita, 1992 (source:* Eurostat)

million people. The map of population density (fig. 9.2) confirms this picture of a heavily populated core. If the UK 'coffin' (after Taylor) (fig. 10.2) is added, the existence of a population heartland in the Rhineland stretching across the North Sea into England is a reality.

7 **Wealth,** as measured by gross domestic product per capita, is another index which illustrates the relative wealth of much of the central part of the EU, and in particular the national core areas. By contrast, the peripheral areas of Iberia, Greece, southern Italy, eastern Germany and Ireland are at substantially lower levels of income (fig. 10.3).

The Rhineland

Geographically perhaps the most significant part of this heartland is the Rhineland, partly because of its centrality, but also because it illustrates the profound consequences of political unity upon economic strength. The Rhineland was for long denied the unifying forces from which most of the European nation states emerged. The states were either grouped around a cultural heartland as in France, or sheltered behind natural physical frontiers as in England. Even Germany and Italy, which emerged late as nations, had a cohesive culture and were brought to nationhood by the political cores of Prussia and Piedmont respectively. Moreover, Italy had the advantage of natural frontiers, and Germany a political and military force of great strength in the Hohenzollern kings of Prussia.

By contrast the Rhineland is a zone of physical convergence without any natural frontiers and, denied any political cohesion, became a buffer state between two strong cultural heartlands. By the Treaty of Verdun, 843 AD, Charlemagne's Empire was dismembered into three parts: the Western Kingdom evolved into modern France; the Eastern Kingdom of the Saxons became the Holy Roman Empire and later Germany; and the Middle Kingdom or Lotharingia (fig. 10.2) was a narrow corridor inbetween. It covered the present area of Belgium, the Netherlands, Luxembourg, the German Rhinelands and the Saarland, Alsace–Lorraine, Switzerland, Burgundy, and northern Italy. These emerged at various periods as smaller and less powerful states. Belgium was under Spanish and later Austrian rule and was a late developer into statehood in 1832. The Netherlands became independent in the sixteenth century. Switzerland, a confederation with four official languages, but with a majority of German-speaking people, debated whether to join the German Zollverein during the nineteenth century, as did the Grand Duchy of Luxembourg. Alsace–Lorraine and the Saarland, and specifically their mineral resources, have been a major source of friction between Germany and France over the last 150 years, and have changed hands on a number of occasions. The Rhinelands have been a contentious zone for centuries; a zone of convergence, political change and instability; the cockpit of Europe.

The locational advantages of the Rhineland are now realised. Its mineral resources, industrial zones, great urban centres, waterways and network of other communications have been allowed to realise their potential because of the development of the EU. From being an unstable frontier zone, its economic unity 'always prescribed by geography, always prevented by history' (the Schumann Declaration) has become real. The frontier image and the restrictions of politically separate economies have been removed by the EU. The cohesion provided by a well-integrated system of transport links, the proximity of the majority of home energy and heavy industry production and the possession of three national core areas (fig. 10.2), has made the Rhinelands the keystone of the EU's economy. In place of the unstable Rhinelands of nineteenth-century Europe, a 'super core' region on a continental scale has emerged.

THE ECONOMIC REGIONS OF THE EU

The consideration of the economic heartland leads into a more detailed analysis of four types of regions: dynamic growth centres; stable diversified areas; older industrial regions with varying degrees of maladjustment; remote peripheral areas with harsh environments.

Regions of dynamic growth

These are regions with a high level of economic activity, having experienced sustained population growth, a rapid industrialisation rate, and a high degree of urbanisation. The Rhinelands and three other national economic cores – Greater Paris, the upper plain of Lombardy and the Manchester–London axis – together constitute this economic heartland (fig. 10.2). There is a case for adding others of more recent rapid economic growth, such as Hanover–Brunswick, Baden-Wurttemberg, Upper Bavaria, Bremen, Hamburg, Rhône–Alpes and Greater Copenhagen, which form extensions not too far removed from the central axis. Economic life revolves around the 'city region' and, as illustrated in the previous chapter (fig. 9.8), the principal great cities of the EU lie within a broad axis stretching between Manchester, Paris, the Rhineland and Milan. However, the very nature of rapid growth is associated with the questions of pollution and congestion. Rotterdam and the Lower Rhine have considerable pollution problems, whilst the growth of metropolitan areas such as the Randstad and Paris poses enormous planning problems.

Stable diversified regions

Large tracts of accessible land close to the core areas have few economic problems. These are balanced communities in which a prosperous agricultural base is combined with moderate urban growth, light industry and a wide range of service employment. Market towns and cathedral cities act as the focal points of these regions, in which economic growth is less rapid and can be absorbed more easily. Stability and diversity are the keynotes here. Most new development comes from the new mobility which motorways and other forms of fast transit have brought. The diffusion of industry and the development of new residential areas and commuting have brought these regions into easy contact with the core areas and have given them a new prosperity. Much of East Anglia, and the lowland counties of England fall into this category. Amiens, Reims, Troyes and Orléans act as centres for rich agricultural hinterlands in France, as do Wurzburg and Bamberg in Germany and Piacenza and Verona in the plain of Lombardy.

Old depressed industrial regions

Many industrial areas can be found close to the 'axial growth belt'. These areas, such as the Nord, Saar and Sambre–Meuse coalfields, the Ruhr and Saxony, have structural problems related to the decline of industries of nineteenth-century origin like coal, steel and textiles. There is dependence upon imported raw materials and a narrow industrial base. There is also often an unattractive environment of dereliction and obsolescent buildings. Although these are problem regions within their own national context, on a European scale they are relatively much less significant and restructuring is aided considerably by their position close to the growth axis. Central Scotland, South Wales, north-east England and the Basque country are examples of areas more remote from the main regions of growth in the EU, and the contraction of heavy industry has been exacerbated by their distance from the major European markets.

The maladjustment stems from a loss of economic vitality, but with investment, new industries can be brought into these areas. These are usually labour-intensive, light and consumer-goods industries which use the existing abundant labour supply. Retraining of the workforce and the provision of new houses, roads and services is necessary to replace the obsolete and unattractive environment. There is great potential but industrial restructuring and adjustment is needed.

The under-developed periphery: remote regions and harsh environments

The most serious problem areas are those relatively under-developed regions which are physically harsh, are remote, and have a marginal agricultural base and a lack of industrial employment. Occasionally there are small pockets of mineral resources which have stimulated development, such as the small coalfields of the Massif Central and tin-mining in Cornwall, but after a short period of prosperity, contraction and the resulting unemployment have only aggravated the local situation. Persistent out-migration from these regions can be a common symptom of their problems.

(a) Southern Italy (the Mezzogiorno) is a typical example. It is remote from the main stream of economic activity, and has a desiccated environment, inefficient agriculture, over-population, inadequate transport and a limited local market owing to the low living standards. The rugged and semi-arid nature of much of Spain, Portugal and Greece, and difficulties of communication, give rise to uneven development between their different regions. Historical and economic problems show a striking resemblance to Italy's Mezzogiorno.

(b) The Massif Central, the Highlands of Scotland, Ireland and much of northern England generally are remote upland areas with harsh environments. They are plateaux and moorlands, with marginal farming and scattered settlements, and are geographically isolated. The Central Hercynian uplands, the Ardennes, Eifel and Vosges, are of the same general type, though more heavily forested.

(c) The Dutch and North German heathlands of Groningen, Oldenburg and Luneberg have infertile acid soils and a poor agricultural environment.

(d) In Thuringia, the upland environment has combined with the political isolation (up until recently) of being close to the former East European frontier zone.

(e) The remoter regions of Sweden and Finland, including Norrland in Sweden and Ita-Suomi in Finland, offer difficult environments for economic development.

(f) Burgenland has the highest rate of unemployment in Austria, a reflection partly of its historical development – i.e. as a region in the former Austro-Hungarian empire, sandwiched between prosperous Vienna and Budapest, that became a peripheral location on the Hungarian border after 1921 (it was a late addition to the new Austrian state) – and partly of its agricultural base.

NATIONAL REGIONAL POLICIES

The development or revitalisation of these peripheral or depressed regions has been accepted as a necessary policy in Western Europe since before the Second World War, and the problems created by the unification of Germany have underlined the need to continue such policies. However, the intensity of the problem varies greatly, as does the approach. In the UK schemes began as early as 1934 to aid mining and industrial areas with high unemployment and developed into a wide-ranging system by the 1950s. In

France the highly centralised government system set up a coordinated national economic planning system from 1947 onwards. In the Netherlands, planning has been dominated by the imbalances caused by urban density in the Randstad, and in Ireland industrial investment has been encouraged by the state since 1949. In Italy, the intractable historical, political and socio-economic problems of the south stimulated a massive programme of regional assistance in the shape of the Cassa per il Mezzogiorno in 1950. By contrast, in Spain, Portugal and Greece, there has been a minimal attempt at regional planning although state involvement in economic planning has been significant. State intervention has also been important in Austria and the Scandinavian Member States – e.g. in Sweden, there has been a long tradition of support for remote communities.

Economic potential in the European Union

The spatial structure of the EU economy may be examined in the light of a number of factors which include: the loosening of industry from traditional and energy-based locations; the enhanced significance of transport for reduction of distribution costs and lower unit costs of production; and the progressive removal of physical and fiscal barriers to the free flow of goods created by the movement towards economic integration. This has led increasingly, over the past 40 years, to the concentration of productive resources into a limited number of areas in the geographical centre of the EU, and particularly in the land area of the original six Member States.

The core–periphery concept has been applied to the EU by Clark (1969), and Keeble (1982), by means of accessibility coefficients based upon regional income data and distance costs, giving an index measure of a region's relative potential for economic activity (fig. 10.4). The EU (12) in the late 1980s showed an extensive plateau of high economic potential in north-west Europe, with the Rhinelands as the most favoured region, but significant outlying peaks around the original national core area of the Paris basin and south-east England, and the plain of Lombardy. By contrast, the southern, western and northern peripheries were marked by extensive areas of low potential, particularly in Ireland, Iberia and Greece. The Aegean islands and Portugal had the lowest absolute values. The unification of Germany has not really altered this pattern as eastern Germany is peripheral to the core areas, but the addition of Austria, Finland and Sweden has created further outlying peaks, particularly the urban regions of Vienna, Helsinki and Stockholm.

This observed pattern has been analysed by Friedmann and Myrdal who suggest that processes of diffusion of wealth to the periphery may be hindered by a whole range of political and economic processes. The concentration of political and financial power in core areas means that they retain a disproportionate amount of new investment, that economic activity is encouraged to locate near its market in the heavily populated core regions with their existing wealth surplus, that selective migration from peripheral

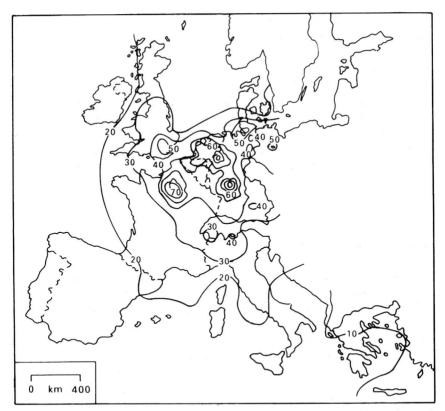

FIGURE 10.4   *Index of economic potential in Western Europe (source – Keeble et al 1982)*

areas loses them their skilled labour and young enterprising people, and that the benefits of improvements to the transport infrastructure means an 'increasing peripheralisation of the periphery' as improved access benefits the core region first and foremost. These four processes amongst others, are behind Myrdal's concept of 'backwash', that is the tendency for a flow of factors back to the accessible core where the process of cumulative causation works positively to enhance the existing surplus.

An effective regional policy is therefore considered economically and politically necessary in order to redistribute resources from the core so that the benefits of the EU economy may be transmitted to those less prosperous regions of the periphery.

Expenditure on regional policy increased immensely during the 1960s and 1970s. All countries relied heavily on positive inducements such as capital grants and loans, subsidies on capital and current expenditure, tax concessions, training grants and the provision of infrastructure. This important principle was intended to move 'work to the workers' in the designated assisted regions. The UK also applied a policy of negative controls in the South-East region for industrial and office building until the 1970s in an attempt to move development away from the congested South-East into northern development areas. This policy was also followed by France and the Netherlands in an attempt to limit growth in cities such as Paris and the Randstad. A fashionable strategy in the 1960s was the 'growth pole' aimed at encouraging the development of backward areas, and relieving congestion in major metropolitan areas. Based partially upon the ideas of Francois Perroux, this made use of the idea of investment in urban areas of 'propellant' industries. Significant use was made of the concept in Italy and France.

Two major problems have persisted. First, regional development is a slow, complex process, and many policies such as the Cassa per il Mezzogiorno in Italy were created with ideas that the problem of the south could be solved within ten years. However, large disparities still exist between north and south (chapter 17). The time-scale of regional development is extremely long. Second, within the growth pole, the 'propellant' industries such as steel, and car assembly, were intended to stimulate the growth of ancillary specialist component and service industries which in themselves would stimulate employment. This again would stimulate local demand setting up the multiplier effect. There is evidence that this effect has been much lower than expected, particularly since the recessions of 1973, 1980 and 1991. Hence the term 'cathedrals in the desert' has been applied to some of these large projects in southern Italy and France.

UK Development Areas

The British classification was a three-fold division into special development areas, development areas and intermediate areas. Originating in the 1930s, government policy was coordinated in 1966 by an Act which placed 40 per cent of the population of the UK under development schedules. It included the whole of Britain north of a line drawn from Liverpool to the Humber and west of the Welsh border. These development areas were designated usually on the basis of a rate of unemployment above the national average. Industrial companies were encouraged to move into the area with grants for factory construction, working capital, and machinery installation. The special development areas included severely declining coalfields which received more substantial assistance.

It has been questioned as to whether regional aid in the UK has been spread too thinly over large areas to be effective. Since 1982 there has been a change of emphasis, and the large-scale extent of the development areas was dramatically reduced and reclassified in 1984 and 1993 (fig. 10.5(a)). The concept of the growth pole has been adopted, where assistance is channelled into areas with a high growth potential. These include western Scotland, Clydeside, Tyne and Wearside, Merseyside, South Wales, West Midlands, Humberside and even areas in south-east England including Thanet and Hastings. In addition, enterprise zones in areas with high unemployment have been designated. These enterprise zones include Clydebank, the lower Swansea valley, Rotherham, Dudley and north-west Kent.

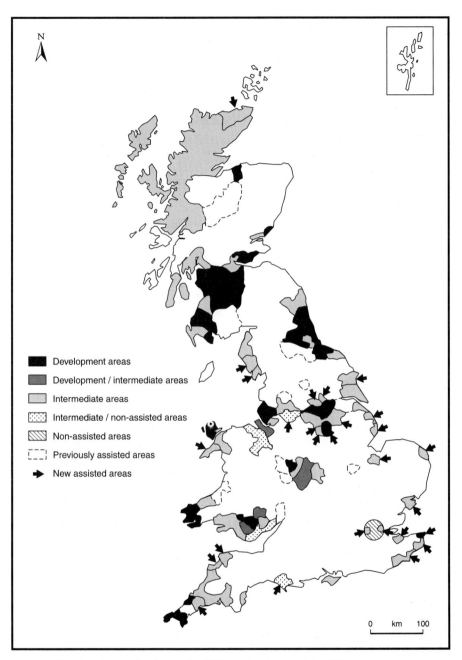

FIGURE 10.5(a)   *Regional policy in the UK – assisted areas, July 1993*

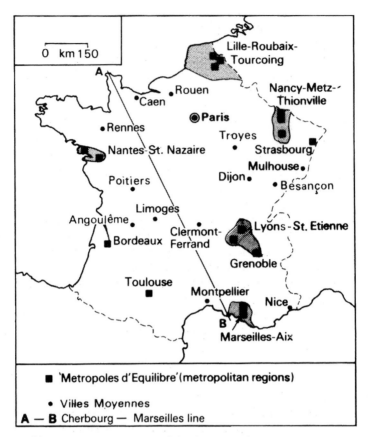

FIGURE 10.5(b) *France – city regions and development poles*

France

French planning policies are extremely well developed with a series of five-year plans, under the direction of DATAR, in answer to three major problems. These are:

(a) the need to develop the under-industrialised sections of the country west of the Cherbourg–Marseilles line (fig. 10.5(b)), to make agriculture more efficient, and to develop the industrial and service infrastructure;

(b) to renovate older industrial areas such as the Nord and Lorraine;

(c) to correct the imbalance caused by the dominance of Paris. The excessive concentration of administration, commerce, industry and wealth in the capital has created a serious gap between Paris and the other French regions, referred to by J F Gravier as 'Paris et le désert francais'.

Planning has taken five main forms:

(a) **Twenty-two planning regions** were created by combining the small départements into larger regions so that planning could be coordinated on a larger scale. These planning regions include Aquitaine, Burgundy, Languedoc and Brittany and are reminiscent of the ancient French provinces.

(b) **Industrial conversion grants** provide finance for the conversion and renovation of industry in the older coal-mining, textile and steel areas and to assist relocation away from Paris to centres like Rennes, Toulouse, Nantes and Clermont Ferrand. Since 1984, 15 special development poles have been set up to attract investment into the worst affected industrial areas such as Lorraine.

(c) **Rural planning agencies** coordinate planning in rural areas. The French call this 'Aménagement du territoire' (management of territory). Finance is given for 'Remembrement', the reorganisation of farms into larger, more efficient units, for improvement of farming techniques, more efficient marketing and the development of cooperatives. Forest management is encouraged. Planning corporations exist for overall management of development in tourism, agriculture and services such as CNABRL in Languedoc. National parks such as the Cevennes, and regional parks like the Camargue, have been created. Brittany and the Massif Central are areas of 'rural renovation'.

(d) **Paris Region** development plans: PADOG (1960), the Schema Directeur (1965) revised in 1969 and 1975, and the Livre Blanc L'Ile de France 2000 (1990) (Chapter 19).

(e) **Metropoles d'equilibre** are cities which have been selected for expansion as administrative, commercial, industrial and cultural centres to counter-balance Paris (fig. 10.5(b)). There are eight of them, such as Marseille and Toulouse, designed to act as 'growth poles'. 'Grand projects' such as the industrial pole of Fos–Marseille are designed as showpieces for French planning (figs. 3.5 and 3.6). A further number of intermediate regional centres have also been selected for development, particularly to attract tertiary employment.

After 1975 there was a drastic modification of the territorial planning programme as France was affected by economic recession. Since 1981 in particular there has been much more attention paid to smaller-scale, local regional projects and to the conservation of town centres.

CURRENT REGIONAL POLICIES IN MEMBER STATES

Since the late 1980s traditional forms of regional policy have been in decline for most northern Member States. The worst situation is in Denmark where all regional development grants, loans and authorities were abolished in January 1991. In Germany, regional policy in the western Lander has been

RESERVE NATIONALE DE CAMARGUE

LE VACCARES
6500 HECTARES
PROFONDEUR : 0,5 A 2 M.
SALINITE VARIABLE :
. 1979 : 4 G/L . CARPES , SANDRES
. 1985 : 25 G/L .CREVETTES .
ATHERINES . PLIES
ALIMENTATION : PLUIES
EAUX AGRICOLES

The Camargue Regional Nature Park in the Rhône Delta

reduced as regional development priorities have been re-oriented towards the new Lander of former East Germany. UK regional policy has also been diluted, and in the Netherlands the availability of regional aid has been restricted to a small area in the north of the country. Budgetary reductions in France during the 1980s, furthermore, have made it impossible to offer incentive awards at the advertised rates.

On the other hand regional policies in the southern or more peripheral – or both – Member States have generally been more stable and have even expanded in scope, value and expenditure. Nevertheless there are also some problems for regional policy in these countries. The recession of the early 1990s has caused budgetary difficulties in countries such as Greece and Ireland, leading to a reduction in spending on regional and industrial support, and there are more serious problems for Italy where a combination of political and economic crises has created an uncertain future for Italian regional policy.

Nearly all Member States are more selective in the award of regional aid, and many have followed the UK in reducing the geographical coverage of their policies. This amounts to as much as one-third reduction in Germany and two-thirds in the Netherlands. Other reductions have taken place in Belgium and Denmark. However, in the southern Member States and Ireland there has been no geographical reduction. Both Greece and Portugal provide regional aid across the whole country, and in Ireland and Spain the designated areas have actually been extended. Nevertheless, the southern States are applying regional aid in a more targeted way. Spain has a complicated system of four grades of designated area and three types of development zone, creating up to eight different rates. In Italy the formerly uniform Mezzogiorno has been subdivided into three different regions.

EU REGIONAL POLICIES

Throughout the buoyant period of economic growth, most regional development was left in the hands of national governments with their own specific regional problems. One of the articles of the Treaty of Rome was concerned with 'aid to promote the economic development of regions where the standard of living is abnormally low and where there is serious unemployment'. However, most financial assistance was given through structural funds such as the EAGGF or the ECSC. The Common Agricultural Policy, through the guidance section of the EAGGF, gave specific aid to farming in less-favoured areas. This included farm modernisation, infrastructure, irrigation and intensification schemes, and training for farm workers, which had a significant impact in peripheral areas such as the Mezzogiorno. The ECSC, initially set up to integrate and increase coal and steel output, became increasingly concerned with modernisation and rationalisation of production, retraining of redundant workers, construction of housing, and schemes to attract new industries into the depressed areas.

After 1973, with the accession of the UK, Ireland and Denmark, and the onset of economic recession, unemployment and the new international division of labour, a major change in attitudes took place. The three new Member States, and particularly the UK, insisted that a regional aid system

	Total (million ECU)	Percentage of total
Spain	13 981	18.7
Luxembourg	83	0.1
Germany	8076	10.8
France	9221	12.4
Italy	17 482	23.4
Netherlands	1243	1.7
Belgium	1614	2.2
United Kingdom	10 660	14.3
Ireland	1369	1.8
Denmark	3519	4.7
Greece	1834	2.5
Portugal	5532	7.4
Total	74 614	100

FIGURE 10.6   *EIB loans, 1990–94*

should be established by the EEC. In May 1973 the Thomson Report (produced by the Commissioner for regional development, George Thomson) identified types of problem areas and announced the establishment of a Regional Development Fund (ERDF). This marked a key change in direction by the EEC. Several important new structural funds and agencies were established to aid regional development, and these continue to operate, although there have been some important changes.

(a) **The European Investment Bank (EIB)** is an autonomous public financial institution based in Luxembourg that works closely with the Commission and Member governments. It is financed entirely by Member States, and its aims, as laid down in the Treaty of Rome (Articles 129 and 130), are:

(i) to grant loans for projects in under-developed regions of the EU such as the Mezzogiorno. The Taranto steelworks, and Naples-to-Reggio railway are examples of projects that have been funded.

(ii) to grant loans and assistance for the modernisation, extension and reorganisation of particular industries and for the development of energy supplies.

(iii) to finance projects of joint interest to Member States, which may be difficult to finance by one Member country alone. The cross-frontier motorways (Nice to Genoa or Paris to Brussels) are an example of this kind of project, or the trans-Alpine Mont Blanc tunnel between Italy and France. The improvement of communications between Member States is of key interest to the EU.

During the 1960s EIB loans were used primarily for roads, motorways and other infrastructure developments, but since 1973, 75 per cent of its efforts have gone to designated assisted areas in the EU. Italy, Spain, the UK, France, Germany and Portugal have become the major beneficiaries (fig. 10.6). The fund has been augmented by the NCI (New Community Instrument) which gives loans for priority energy and industrial projects. In addition, substantial loans are now given to smaller firms, in line with encouragement for entrepreneurial skill and new competition in the market.

(b) **The European Social Fund (ESF)** gives aid to specific sections of the population, in particular stimulating training and employment for young people, women, the handicapped, and migrant workers. The declining steel, textile, shipbuilding and clothing industries have been assisted in restructuring and rationalisation by the retraining of workers for other employment. Small-business and new technology enterprises have been given assistance to provide much-needed new employment in the problem regions. The ESF has had a greatly enhanced role in the high unemployment situation of recent years. Two-thirds of the Fund's resources go to correct structural weaknesses and to improve employment in the less developed parts of the EU.

(c) The Regional Development Fund (ERDF). After the 1973 enlargement of the EEC to nine, pressure for regional aid increased for a series of reasons such as serious regional imbalances in countries like the UK, the peripheral nature of Member States like Ireland, the energy crisis and the onset of economic recession, the development of high unemployment in formerly prosperous regions, and the recognition of the inner-city problem. The introduction of the Thomson report in May 1973 was followed by a protracted argument over the funding of the proposed regional policy. In a period of economic recession it was difficult to persuade weaker states to set up another costly fund. Eventually the Regional Development Fund became operative on 1 January 1975, with an initial grant of £600 million over three years. The criteria upon which regions were to receive aid were as follows:

(i) a lower gross domestic product than the EEC average, plus at least one of (ii), (iii) and (iv);
(ii) heavy dependence on agricultural employment in declining industries with at least 20 per cent of local employment in such a category;
(iii) a persistently high rate of unemployment over a number of years;
(iv) a high and sustained rate of emigration (10 per 1000 each year) averaged over a long period.

The concept of 'additionality' was important. Money received from the ERDF was not to be used instead of pre-existing national financial commitments to regional development: it had to complement or top up such national measures – i.e. it was additional.

By 1975 the Regional Development Fund was allocated on the basis of agreed quotas to the Member States with the greatest regional imbalances. Thus Italy received 39 per cent, the UK 27 per cent, France 17 per cent and Ireland 6 per cent.

The EU had little or no discretion in trying to influence the identification of regions in Member States. As a result, the notion of what constituted a 'region' differed markedly from one Member State to another. Some regions were defined by their degree of political and legal autonomy (such as the German Lander) while others were economic planning regions (such as Wales and Northern Ireland in the UK).

From 1978 onwards there were improvements in the fund and greater flexibility. The fund was doubled to £1.2 billion and a small non-quota section was added which gave assistance to specific regions outside the quota allocation. The European Commission also put forward proposals for assistance to shipbuilding towns in the UK, for steel centres in the UK, Belgium and France, and for the Mezzogiorno. Greek entry in 1987 necessitated a reallocation of the quotas as follows: Mezzogiorno 44 per cent; the UK northern and western regions 29 per cent; Greece 16 per cent; Ireland 7 per cent. After 1985 there was a greater concentration of regional assistance, and the quota system gave way to a priority funding of the most

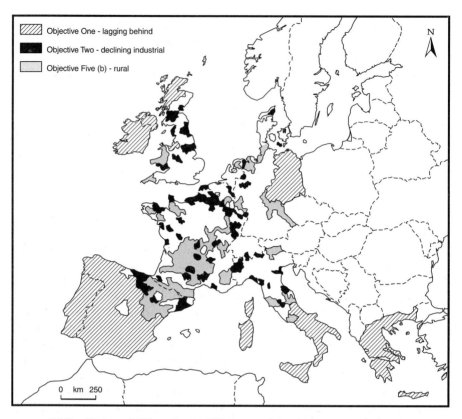

FIGURE 10.7   *Regions eligible under the EU Structural Funds (source:* Drake*)*

backward regions which contained some 50 million people. These included Ireland, Northern Ireland, the Mezzogiorno, Greece, Portugal, Corsica and much of Spain. One significant innovation was the Integrated Mediterranean Programme (IMP) which initially operated from 1985 to 1990. This coordinated aid from the EU to the new Member countries, Spain, Portugal and Greece, but also to the Mediterranean regions of southern central Italy, and parts of southern France. It paid particular attention to agricultural modernisation, forestry, rural diversification, and tourism.

In 1988 a major reform of the EU's Structural Funds was undertaken. The need for this reform stemmed from two major developments in the two years previous to this. At the beginning of 1986 the accession of Spain and Portugal had significantly intensified regional disparities within the EU, and in 1987 the Single European Act (SEA) recognised that economic and social cohesion within the EU formed an essential part of the completion of the Single Market. This necessitated a more effective coordination of regional policy instruments and a greater concentration of resources on the regions in most need and facing the most serious structural adjustment problems.

The 1988 reform was therefore based on three principles: first, to transform structural policy into an instrument with real economic impact; second, to use a multi-annual approach for expenditure planning to ensure

Member States of the stability and predictability of EU support; and third, to implement a partnership with all the parties actively involved in structural policy, especially the regional authorities. More specifically, there was a shift from individual project support to programme financing, a commitment to greater coordination between the activities of the three Structural Funds, and an increased budget which was concentrated on the most disadvantaged regions of the EU. The concept of additionality was continued, but the Structural Funds were doubled from ECU 6.3 billion in 1987 to ECU 14.1 billion in 1993. The Commission identified five key objectives for these Structural Funds: the development of regions lagging in development (Objective One), the conversion of regions in industrial decline (Objective Two), the combating of long-term unemployment (Objective Three), the adjustment of agricultural structures (Objective Four) and the development of rural areas (Objective Five).

The Maastricht Treaty of 1992 renewed the emphasis placed by the EU on economic and social cohesion and provided for the introduction of a Cohesion Fund to assist the most disadvantaged Member States in convergence to Economic and Monetary Union (EMU) – i.e. Spain, Portugal, Ireland and Greece. The Treaty also modified the Structural Funds still further. A further review of assistance took place in 1993, and among the changes were an adjustment to the Structural Fund Objectives for the period 1994–99. The earlier Fourth and Fifth Objectives have been merged – they are now Objectives Five (a) and (b) – and a new Objective Four introduced: the retraining of workers. Only Objectives One, Two and Five (b) apply to regional policy (fig. 10.7) because Objectives Three, Four and Five (a) apply throughout the EU. Objective One is the priority, with 70 per cent of the Structural Funds allocated to it in the period 1994–9.

Apart from these changes, the system is similar to that set up in 1988. The allocation of the funds in an assisted area is decided by a partnership of local or regional authorities, the government of the Member State involved and the Commission. This group produces an agreed Community Support Framework (CSF) which outlines exactly how the money will be spent in the region. About 9 per cent of the Structural Funds are reserved for Community Initiatives (CIs) for tackling specific problems that are transnational and not covered by the CSFs. There are several of these, including TELEMATIQUE (to promote the use of advanced telecommunications in Objective One regions), RECHAR (assistance to areas affected by coal-mine closures), REGEN (for the construction of gas and electricity distribution networks in Objective One regions) and INTERREG (to encourage cross-border links such as a Spanish–Portuguese national park or the development of canal links between Eire and Northern Ireland).

There have always been considerable criticisms levelled at the Structural Funds. The amount of money available has always been small. In 1984–5 the fund used only 8 per cent of EU expenditure, which was tiny by comparison with the large amounts of money spent on agriculture. Inflation and recession rendered the amount of aid available relatively even less effective than before. By 1988 the Structural Funds took up 17 per cent of EU expenditure, and by 1992 this had risen to 27 per cent. However, this still represents less than 0.5 per cent of the total GDP of all the Member States, and may be insufficient to reduce, let alone remove, regional disparities. There are also concerns over the environmental impact of many of the projects funded by the EU.

Nevertheless, there are the beginnings of much greater cohesion as the regional bodies respond to the encouragement for them to take a more active part in development. The Consultative Council of Local and Regional Authorities, which was set up in 1988, is involved in regional policy processes and liaises closely with the Commission and its various Directorates-General. In addition, regions themselves have increasingly set up offices in Brussels in order to lobby the institutions of the EU. The Rhône–Alpes region was the first to do this, and others have followed including the metropolitan authorities of Manchester and Birmingham and the Welsh Development Agency. The Maastricht Treaty has set up the Committee of the Regions (COR) where representatives of regional and local authorities have an advisory status similar to the Economic and Social Committee. The Commission must consult COR over certain matters, including Structural Funds; Trans-European Networks (TEN) in the areas of transport, telecommunications and energy; and economic and social cohesion.

Member States, regions and cities are gradually becoming aware of the necessity of planning beyond national boundaries. In France, DATAR has been carrying out a large-scale programme of studies for the period up to the year 2000 with the objective of providing a basis for policy. The studies analyse the expected changes in society and their spatial impact from a wider European point of view. The most common form of regional cooperation network are the cross–border associations of local authorities that have been established along many of the EU's internal borders. The most advanced are along the Dutch–German border, such as the Euregio or Ems-Dollar organisations. The 'Four Motors of Europe' (Rhône–Alpes, Baden-Wurttemberg, Lombardy and Catalonia) have agreed to pool resources in certain fields such as scientific and technological research. The strategic plans of Barcelona ('Barcelona 2000') and of Charleroi are examples of the European challenge being taken up at the level of cities and urban areas.

As this 'Europe of the Regions' emerges, it will be increasingly necessary to re-examine the geographical pattern of differences and to adjust EU assistance accordingly. The further addition of new members, such as Cyprus or Malta, and the impact of economic developments in East European neighbours will also require evaluation of existing regional policies. Increasing integration in the EU and growing interdependency between its regional economies mean that planning in relative isolation in Member States or regions will no longer be possible.

11

NORTH–RHINE WESTPHALIA:
CROSSROADS OF EUROPE

Notern-Rhine Westphalia is the administrative region (fig. 11.1) which contains both major growth elements and problems of industrial restructuring, and is situated along the principal growth axis of the EU.

THE RUHR COALFIELD: DEVELOPMENT

The Ruhr coalfield is one of the world's best examples of a heavy industrial region based upon coal, although crises in the coal and steel industries of the EU from the mid-1970s have created a dramatic restructuring in the region. Nevertheless, the region still produces 26 per cent of the hard coal and 16 per cent of the steel of the EU (12), and it makes a significant contribution to the oil-refining, petrochemicals and heavy engineering industries. It lies close to the centre of the so-called 'growth zone' of the EU. Its development began from the eleventh century onwards when the medieval cities of Cologne, Duisburg, Essen and Dortmund originated as trade centres along the 'Hellweg', the ancient east–west line of migration through Europe. With the increasing importance of the Rhine routeway, the Ruhr has been a major route focus for hundreds of years. In addition, iron-making was practised immediately to the south in the forested Sauerland. Although coal was mined from very early times, it was in the 1830s that the first shafts were bored in the concealed coalfield areas to the north of the River Ruhr, and since that time mining activity has been moving steadily northwards into the Emscher and Lippe valleys.

The 'take off' period was the 1870s when the 'Fettkohle' or coking coal in the Ruhr was found to be of extremely good quality and suitable for the improved iron furnaces. The unification of Germany in 1871 was

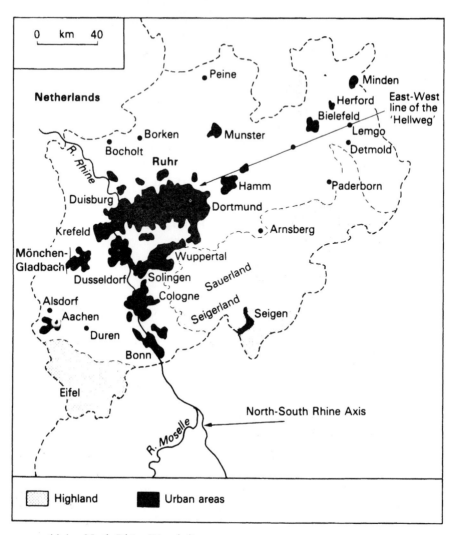

FIGURE 11.1   *North-Rhine Westphalia*

responsible for a great burst of confidence, railway construction and industrial expansion, with coal-mining increasing from 5 million tonnes in 1870 to 60 million tonnes in 1900. With the construction of the Dortmund–Ems and Rhine–Herne canals, the advantages of the Rhine were improved considerably for heavy industry based on local coal and water-borne raw materials. By 1913 coal output had reached 115 million tonnes and iron and steel production 7 million tonnes. The Ruhr's great industrial significance is shown by its resilience in twice recovering after a great deal of its capacity has been either destroyed or dismantled. After the First World War coal output reached 127 million tonnes and iron and steel 13 million tonnes in 1938, and after the Second World War coal output reached the peak post-war production level of 125 million tonnes in 1956 (fig. 11.3).

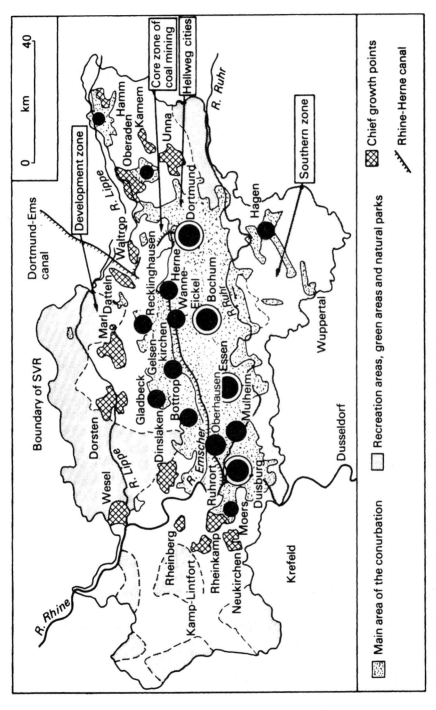

FIGURE 11.2 *The former Ruhr Planning Region (SVR) with four major planning zones*

A distinctive feature of the Ruhr is its great density of settlement. It is an amalgamation of over 20 towns and cities, a complex conurbation or polycentric city stretching east–west from Hamm to Geldern and north–south from the River Ruhr to the Lippe (fig. 11.2). The area once controlled by the Ruhr Planning Region (SVR) contains over 6 million people, great cities like Dortmund, Essen and Duisburg, and 18 'free cities' in all. In addition, Cologne, Düsseldorf, Bonn and many other associated cities make up the Rhine–Ruhr Conurbation of some 10 million people – the largest conurbation in the EU.

The decline of coal

The extent of the coalfield can be seen in fig. 11.2. The real problem has become the increasing depth at which mining has to be carried out. The coal seams dip to the north and the nineteenth-century 'adit' mines are exhausted, whilst the average depth of mines today is nearly 1000 m in the northern concealed part of the coalfield. The progressive migration northwards into the deeper mines has resulted in increasing costs at a time of competition from other cheap energy sources. The Ruhr is in a much better position than most established coalfields in Western Europe, because its coal is by no means exhausted. There are proven resources of 65 000 million tonnes. There are two other circumstances in which it is much superior to other coalfields. The first is in the great variety of types of coal, over 50 varieties, and the second is the extremely high level of productivity achieved by large-scale mechanisation. However, the Ruhr has been affected by the same factors as the other major coalfields in the EU since the 1960s. The diversification to often cleaner and more efficient energy sources and the increasing import of cheaper coal coupled with a decline in the major coal-consuming industries such as steel meant that coal production had fallen to below 110 million tonnes by 1967 and 52 million tonnes by 1993. The mining workforce has fallen from 500 000 in 1956 to 70 000 in 1993; the number of pits has fallen from 99 in 1964 to 14 in 1993 (fig. 11.3). Associated with this has been a remarkable rise in productivity as inefficient mines were closed or amalgamated and the larger mines remained, with productivity rising by over 50 per cent, thus consolidating the Ruhr's productivity lead in the EU.

There has been an accompanying structural reorganisation. Twenty-six of the coal companies amalgamated in 1969 to form Ruhrkohle AG, which now controls 94 per cent of total hard coal production in the Ruhr basin. Ruhrkohle has diversified its business so that 39 per cent is now in environmental technology, trading, power engineering and construction. Steag, its largest non-coal subsidiary, operates power plants for district heating and offers related environmental and engineering services. Ruhrkohle Umwelt specialises in waste management and the cleaning-up of contaminated sites (including sites in the former GDR) and has moved into plastic recycling.

However, these are not labour-intensive alternatives, and a real social problem has been that the mine closures have affected employment patterns tremendously, with over 400 000 coal miners being made redundant since 1950. More significantly, the Emscher valley (fig. 11.2) has suffered more than the other areas. The impact has been concentrated by the nature of the coalfield. The area south of the River Ruhr has long lost its mining capability as the shallow 'adit' mines of the nineteenth century ceased to be used; the area north of Dinslaken and Recklinghausen contains the newer, deeper and more modern mines. The central Ruhr towns of the Emscher valley such as Gelsenkirchen and Bottrop have been affected most, as their employment and economy was based almost exclusively upon coal-mining, to a far greater extent than in the other parts of the conurbation.

A reduced workforce, fewer collieries, the operation of the coalfield as a single unit, and greatly increased mechanisation have made the Ruhr a highly productive coalfield. The existing mining infrastructure is now robotised and automated with very high technology. However, the level of coal production still depends on substantial state subsidies, partly through the so-called 'coal penny' imposed on household electricity bills that ensures a market from the electricity industry for domestic coal, and partly through the agreement requiring German steel makers to use subsidised German coking coal. The coal industry in the Ruhr is therefore protected to a certain degree, but pressure from the EU and a ruling in Germany that the 'coal penny' system was unconstitutional has led to a reduction in subsidies. In addition, steel makers no longer want to be tied to expensive German coal. This will continue the process of mine closures and reductions in employment (fig. 11.3).

Industrial change

Structural problems facing the Ruhr are not confined to the coal industry. The steel industry has been adversely affected by the higher cost of Ruhr coal as compared to cheaper American coal and by competition from the coastal steelworks, which rely upon imported iron ore. Since 1974 production has fallen (fig. 11.3), in common with other areas in the EU, largely because of the recession in world demand for steel and the competition from low-cost producers outside Western Europe. Steel-making has migrated heavily to the points of greatest cost-effectiveness, that is, the Rhine water frontage on the west, and to the Dortmund–Ems and Rhine–Herne canals in the east. Steel-making has ceased in the central parts of the Ruhr, at Bochum and Essen, and the Krupp plant at Rheinhausen was closed in 1993. Special electric steels are manufactured at Remscheid, Krefeld and Bochum.

The comparative advantages of water-front locations, owing to the very substantial imports of Swedish iron ore, coal and other raw materials via the Rhine, has affected the present-day location of the Ruhr steel industry. In addition, there has been considerable reinvestment in new steel plant and reorganisation into larger units, Thyssen being the largest firm. Companies like Krupp Hoesch are now associated with the Ijmuiden works of Hoogovens on the Dutch coast, thereby gaining the advantages of scale. The central area, at Bochum and Essen, has become a steel-using area with vehicles, mechanical engineering, metal fabrication and electrical engineering; growth industries such as electro-technical, chemicals, plastics; and consumer industries such as clothing. Essen has a number of substitute metal industries such as aluminium and zinc-smelting.

The other major case of industrial decline has been textiles and clothing. Its workforce has dropped from over 350 000 in 1965 to less than 150 000 in 1993. However, the heavy chemical industry has had remarkable success in adapting to changed circumstances. The loss of the chemical industries on the Middle Elbe after the partition of Germany gave considerable benefit to the Ruhr. The industry has abandoned its traditional dependence upon coal and coke by-products, and since 1950, oil has been the major raw material transported by pipeline and by the Rhine routeway from Rotterdam. The growth of oil refineries and petrochemicals at Marl-Huls and Gelsenkirchen is associated with this. Light, high-value chemical industries such as pharmaceuticals have rapidly developed.

The decline of the coal and steel industries led to the decline of other closely linked engineering industries, and to a rise in unemployment from a low point of less than 1 per cent in 1970 to a peak of more than 15 per cent in 1987/88. These reductions in employment encouraged people to leave the Ruhr, and between 1961 and 1988 over 550 000 people moved out of the Ruhr, producing a 9 per cent decline in the population. Unemployment still remains above the national average, but the net emigration has ceased and there has been a net inflow of immigrants (mostly German speakers from Eastern Europe) due to the net increase in employment since 1985.

Settlement and planning

The other main problem is the unplanned, high-density and obsolescent environment. The development stages of the coalfield are largely responsible for the nature of urban development. The Ruhr may be divided into four main zones: the southern zone; the Hellweg; the core coal-mining zone; and northern development zone (fig. 11.2). The regional planning authority for the Ruhr (SVR) has been replaced by the KVR (Kommunalverband Ruhr), an association of local authorities, and these have been active in promoting schemes for balanced industrial development, new housing schemes, new town redevelopment, green areas, leisure parks and reclamation of tips and spoil heaps. Its activities vary, however, according to the needs of the four zones.

The southern zone coincides essentially with much of the valley of the River Ruhr and the low hills to the south. Here very few coal mines and little heavy industry remain, and population is much less dense than in other parts of the Ruhr. The area consists of the southern residential suburbs of

Year	Coal production Million tonnes produced	Year	Steel production Million tonnes produced
1850	1	1860	0.1
1870	5	1913	7
1900	60	1938	13
1913	115	1957	18
1938	127	1965	23
1956	125	1970	28
1965	115	1974	34
1970	96	1977	25
1974	84	1981	26
1977	74	1986	24
1981	77	1993	21
1986	68		
1993	52		

Year	Operative coal mines	Year	No of coal miners
1850	200	1950	500 000
1890	175	1956	494 000
1950	150	1964	325 000
1961	120	1969	183 000
1964	99	1974	150 000
1969	57	1977	128 000
1974	45	1981	111 000
1977	32	1986	85 000
1981	28	1993	70 000
1986	26		
1993	14		

FIGURE 11.3   *Ruhr coal and steel production*

Essen, Bochum and Dortmund, reservoirs on the River Ruhr, and four large leisure parks which have been laid out to serve the cities to the north.

The Hellweg cities of Duisburg, Essen, Bochum and Dortmund are large, well-developed urban areas with good shopping facilities, cultural and historic cores, and with important commercial interests, company head offices, tertiary activity, and a high proportion of professional people. They are therefore wealthy urban communities, although surrounded by extensive housing areas of monotonous design or obsolescence and by heavy industrial areas. Their problems, therefore, involve planning for high-density living, but they present much less of a problem than the area immediately to the north.

The core coal-mining zone along the Emscher valley has the greatest problems. Rapid nineteenth-century growth meant that villages such as Gelsenkirchen grew into monofunctional mining towns with heavy industry. Others such as Oberhausen, Recklinghausen, Herne and Bottrop had proportions as high as 50 and 60 per cent in mining employment. Both air and water pollution are problems and the Emscher is one of the worst polluted rivers in Western Europe. As much as 40 per cent of the land is old mining land and is often derelict. Obsolescent housing, unsightly heavy industry and the absence of green space are the principal features of the area, quite apart from the economic problem of redeployment of its labour and considerable migration into the outer areas of the Ruhr.

To the north lies the development zone. This is the most recent coal-mining area stretching northwards towards Münster (fig. 11.1) and although the mines are deep, the pits are large, modern and efficient. This is the newer concealed coalfield, lying at a depth of up to 1300 m, and the coal is often converted at the pithead into electricity for the industries further south. Heavy industry has not developed here to any large extent but instead there are many light and consumer industry factories. The zone's share of the Ruhr total population is only about 15 per cent, and so there is considerable space for development. Major growth points for both new towns and industrial complexes are Wesel, Dinslaken, Dorsten, Marl-Huls and Datteln (fig. 11.2).

OTHER MANUFACTURING TOWNS

There are a number of important sub-zones and groups of towns which are outside the KVR area, yet which have close associations with it (fig. 11.1).

1 The first group comprises the textile towns on the west bank of the Rhine. Krefeld is a traditional centre for silk and velvets, and Mönchen-Gladbach and Rheydt have textile machinery works, and clothing factories.

2 To the south-west lies the city of Aachen with its small coalfield and the huge brown-coal deposit on the Ville ridge west of Bonn and Cologne, which is open-cast mined.

3 To the south lies the Sauerland and Siegerland and the deep valleys of the Sieg and Wupper cut out of the Rhine plateaux. Here are towns related to the early importance of local raw materials and power, and the later specialisation and geographical inertia which has led to two highly complex manufacturing concentrations. Both the manufacture of high-quality cutlery at Remscheid and Solingen, and locks and keys at Velbert can be traced to the smelting of local iron-ore deposits worked with charcoal from the forests, and these industries survive now because of accumulated skills and specialisation. The old-established textile manufacturing towns of Elberfeld and Barmen were based upon the abundance of water power in the Wupper valley, urban growth having now merged them into the conurbation of Wuppertal.

THE CITIES ALONG THE RHINE VALLEY

It is along the Rhine valley, however, that the greatest growth area is found. That part of the Rhineland which lies immediately to the south of the Ruhr is dominated by three cities: Düsseldorf, Cologne and Bonn (fig. 11.1). Düsseldorf is referred to in Germany as the 'Rhinegold', a term which indicates its wealth and reflects its image as an example of the German economic miracle. It was not a medieval city and developed only during the seventeenth century as a minor principality, from which it has grown into the modern banking, financial and commercial centre of North-Rhine Westphalia. As a financial centre it has a remarkable expertise amongst its *prominenz* or establishment, and it is also the administrative capital of North-Rhine Westphalia. An enormous amount of rebuilding has taken place since 1945 to create one of the most modern cities in Europe. The 'Königsallee', an expensive shopping street set in park-like boulevard surroundings, exemplifies the city's wealth. There are also impressive high-rise offices and headquarter buildings of the major Ruhr companies, Krupp Hoesch and Thyssen, as well as those of international companies such as IBM and the

The Königsallee: an elegant retail street in Düsseldorf

Chase Manhattan Bank. Not only does the city act as the financial capital of the Ruhr but it also has its own industries, principally engineering, and the huge chemical complex at Leverkusen is just to the south.

Cologne is an ancient Roman settlement which flourished as a medieval trade centre of the Hanseatic League, based upon its position where the river route from Flanders into the Rhinelands crossed the fertile loess embayment and the Hellweg. The railway development of the nineteenth century, however, gave the city its modern importance. It is still both an important railway junction and an inland port. As a commercial and business centre it is a rival to Düsseldorf, but in addition it has a very varied industrial base, ranging from iron and steel, oil and petrochemical production, to engineering and car manufacture. It also has a wide range of consumer goods including leather, cosmetics, clothing and chocolate, which are an unusual feature in the region and which originated in the traditions of medieval crafts of the old city.

Farther south again is the city of Bonn, capital of Germany until the end of the twentieth century. It is situated at the point where the Rhine emerges from its gorge, and is a relatively small city of medieval origins. Its bishopric, university and medieval prosperity were based largely upon its function as the historic seat of the Principality of Cologne. Although the Federal capital since 1949, it has remained relatively small with light industries, and its population is now 293 000. When the capital moves to Berlin, 26 government institutions and agencies will be moved to Bonn from elsewhere in Germany to counter-balance the loss of jobs, and state investment will develop the city as a centre for telecommunications and other technology research projects. Bonn will become a federal city and Germany's second capital.

NORTH–RHINE WESTPHALIA: THE ADVANTAGES OF CENTRALITY

The 'Land' of North-Rhine Westphalia is the most populous part of Germany with a total population of over 17 million within which is the Rhine–Ruhr Conurbation with over 10 million people. One in eight of the population of the EU (12) lives within 200 km of the Land capital (Düsseldorf), and around 140 million consumers are within 500 km. The Ruhr Planning Region has over 6 million people, whilst the Düsseldorf and Cologne city regions have 2.5 and 2.2 million people respectively. There is a distinction to be made between the growth of the long-established cities and outer suburban and commuter areas, and the structural problems which have caused a slackening of growth and even decline of population in the central coalfield areas. The central core of the Ruhr coalfield, the Emscher valley, has in fact lost some 300 000 people from towns like Gelsenkirchen, Bottrop and Bochum, but these have been involved in a sub-regional movement to the cities of Düsseldorf and Cologne, and to the new towns and suburbs on the edge of the coalfield. Any loss of population in the centre has therefore been compensated within the region.

The Ruhr coalfield has had several major advantages in its structural and economic reconstruction.

(a) It is part of the Land of North-Rhine Westphalia, the single most populous and industrious region in Germany, and it has benefited by its association with the Land government in Düsseldorf. North-Rhine Westphalia now has 50 universities and vocational training centres (more than four times as many as in 1970), all part of the changing image of this heavy industry region, and these provide vital support for the region's industrial diversification.

(b) The influence of the KVR can be seen in the changing quality of the environment. Although much remains to be done, the green areas, nature parks, reclaimed spoil-heaps and new urban motorways are a witness to its effect since it was set up in 1920. Of the total area of the Ruhr Planning Region, only 24 per cent is urbanised; 53 per cent is open land and farmland; over 20 per cent is woodland and leisure areas. There is plenty of room available for gradual, planned and comprehensive redevelopment within the whole area (fig. 11.2). One of the more recent developments has been the setting-up of the Emscher Park project in 1988. This is a ten-year project involving an area which covers 800 km^2 from Duisburg in the west to Bergkamen in the east, with the River Emscher running through it, and which includes seventeen towns and cities and a population of more than 2 million. The object of the project is the economic, social and ecological regeneration of the area, and it includes a scheme to transform the inner harbour at Duisburg, the development of a number of high-grade industrial and commercial sites like the industrial estate at Castrop-Rauxel, the renewal of existing workers' housing areas and the creation of an Emscher country park with large expanses of green space, for recreation, linking the unused land between the urban areas.

(c) The nature of the coalfield is of great significance. It has few of the problems of thin seams and low productivity associated with many of the other EU coalfields, and has traditionally been the most productive in Western Europe. There has been a steady reduction in the number of coal-mines, rather than the massive reductions which have been seen elsewhere. Modern investment places the Ruhr coalfield in a strong position for any up-turn in demand.

(d) The regional distinctiveness of the Ruhr owes much to the intensive interdependence of its industry and transport system. The steel and chemicals complex has been strengthened by new steel-using industries, by petrochemicals and oil-refining, and by the light-engineering and consumer-products industry. In particular, the car industry is now represented by over 20 000 workers in three factories of General Motors. Television and electronics factories have also migrated into the old central steel-making area of Bochum and Essen. The Ruhr is also a leading area for environmental-technology companies, with more than 150 000 people now working in environment-related industries. Some of the companies involved are those connected with the original industrial base – e.g. the subsidiary, Thyssen Engineering, makes equipment for desulphurisation and the removal of nitrogen in power plants and waste incinerators. Thus, not only are new industries replacing old enterprises, but the traditional industries are themselves diversifying. The business community has linked up with the Land government to transform the image of the area and revive its self-confidence. The 'rust belt' image that has been associated with the Ruhr has been very much a partial one and economic adjustment has proceeded rapidly.

(e) The Rhine waterway has remained central to Germany's economy and has also become the growth-axis of the EU (Chapter 10), underlining the position of centrality which the Ruhr possesses. The German autobahn network makes possible rapid transport to other parts of the Euro-core.

(f) Finally, the Ruhr lies on the historic lateral axis of commerce and city development, the Hellweg (fig. 11.1), and is associated with great cities like Cologne, Dortmund and Düsseldorf. The long-established structures of these cities, with their commercial wealth, financial services and shopping facilities, enables them to adapt to change and their growing industries are able to absorb the excess population from the Ruhr coal-mining areas. In addition, the large consumer market of over 17 million people is a major factor in the ability of the North-Rhine Westphalia region to adapt its employment structure. The tertiary sector has grown rapidly (57 per cent) and has now overtaken the secondary sector (41 per cent). This is a remarkable commentary upon the changing economic patterns in this erstwhile dominantly heavy industrial area.

(g) North-Rhine Westphalia is a core region on a European scale, referred to by Parker as the 'super-core', and effectively at the crossroads of Europe.

12

THE MIDDLE RHINELANDS: THREE CITY REGIONS

Varied resources

The Middle Rhine valley of Germany stretches from Wiesbaden and Frankfurt-on-Main in the north to Karlsruhe in the south, and includes the right-bank tributary valley of the Neckar, in which is the city of Stuttgart (fig. 12.1). The French city of Strasbourg also lies within the physical region. Thus defined, it is a most important economic area lying within the EU core. It has been a traditional zone of urbanisation from Roman times, and throughout the Middle Ages towns like Worms, Mainz, Speyer and Heidelberg were associated with bishoprics or universities, and later there were royal residences and planned cities such as Karlsruhe. There is an abundance of resources, and four principal factors may be identified as contributing at various stages to its development.

A rich and diverse farming region

This is a most productive agricultural area, a fact reflected in the densely populated countryside, with large and numerous villages. Particularly along the foothills, on the loess lands and on the sheltered terraces there is a wide variety of agriculture. The Rhine–Main plain to the north of Frankfurt, the Wetterau, is extremely fertile and is 70-per-cent arable, whilst to the west of Frankfurt is the Rheingau with its orchards and vineyards. The Kraichgau between the Rhine and Neckar is a loess–loam undulating lowland with arable lands, orchards and vineyards. By contrast the alluvial plains along the rivers are heavy clays liable to flooding, with damp water meadows. The advantages of the region are not only the wide variety of landscape and

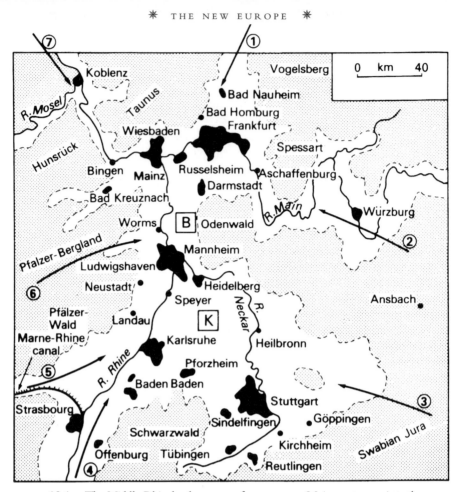

FIGURE 12.1 *The Middle Rhinelands – zone of convergence. Major routeways into the middle Rhinelands: 1. The Hessian corridor 2. Main valley from Nuremberg 3. Foreland route from Augsburg and Munich 4. Upper Rhine route from Basle 5. Saverne gap from Lorraine. 6. Route from the Saarland 7. Rhine route from Rotterdam and the Ruhr. K: Kraichgau B: Bergstrasse*

terrain, but also the occurrence of loess, which is easily cultivated and has a relatively high fertility, together with a greater amount of sunshine and hotter summers, than in the more northerly parts of Germany. In particular, the cultivation of the vine depends to a great extent upon south-facing slopes, and these are found at the point where the Rhine makes its westward turn to enter the gorge. As a result, the south-facing slopes of the Taunus ridge overlooking the Rhine have an almost continuous covering of vineyards for some 32 km from Wiesbaden to the gorge, giving one of the most famous wine-producing areas in Germany: the Rheingau. Here originate the most famous names in German wines, such as Johannisberg and Rudesheim.

Farther south, another intensive area of cultivation is the Bergstrasse, the loess–loam foothills of the Odenwald between Darmstadt and Heidelberg.

This area on the eastern side of the Rift valley cultivates vines, tobacco and fruit, and almost opposite on the western side are the Worms–Nierstein–Oppenheim vineyards on the Haupterrasse, backed by the Pfalzer Bergland.

The Kraichgau between the Rhine and Neckar is limestone covered with loess and is one of the most intensively farmed areas in south Germany. Cereals are more in evidence because of the gently undulating or even nature of the land above level-bedded limestones. In addition there are fodder crops, sugar beet, fruit, hops and the vine. The landscape is completely cleared and farming is very intensive, with large prosperous villages and a high rural density of population. It is upon this prosperous countryside that the initial wealth of the Middle Rhinelands is based.

Convergence of routes

The convergence of routes is a second advantage. Since medieval times the Rhine valley corridor has become an area of convergence as a link between the North Sea and Alpine passes, and between France and Austria. The position of the Rhine–Main valley, surrounded by the Hercynian mountain blocks yet with major gaps from north, south, east and west, has created the greatest junction in middle Europe. The traditional trade routes of the Middle Ages have been superseded by the railways and autobahns. Figure 12.1 illustrates the passageways, the Hessian Corridor, the Main valley from Würzburg, routes from Munich via Stuttgart, the Upper Rhine route from Basle and the Alps, the Belfort gap from Lyons and the Rhône, the Saverne gap from Paris, Lorraine and the Saar, and the Rhine waterway route from the Ruhr and Benelux countries. The importance of the corridor has been increased immeasurably by the development of the EU, as the whole effect of the convergence of routes has to be looked upon on a European scale rather than as hitherto on a German scale. The Rhine valley is now the central axis of the EU rather than being a frontier zone, a change which has been stressed in chapter 10.

Flourishing cities

The concentration of human resources is the most significant reason for the importance of the Middle Rhinelands. Rather than depending upon mineral resources, it has developed around the numerous medieval cities and bishoprics, and has flourished because of the cultural and economic activity associated with a continual inflow of trade, expertise and new ideas. The earliest development of towns was during the Roman period, when the Rhine was the frontier of civilisation, and later the Medieval bishoprics, such as Worms, Speyer and Mainz, developed on the west bank of the river. Heidelberg is the chief east-bank medieval and university town which has developed at the junction of plain and foothills along the Bergstrasse. Baroque towns are usually associated with the numerous principalities and minor states which existed up to the nineteenth century. Karlsruhe is the best example of a planned city, founded in 1715 by the Margrave of Baden, and has a well-preserved radial pattern of roads leading to the Royal palace. Darmstadt was the seat of the Elector of Hesse, whilst Mannheim was originally founded as a capital city by the Elector of the Palatinate, and its rectilinear pattern of streets reflects the original planned town. The trade, culture and economic activity of this river region have been developed over a thousand years, and they have depended to a great extent upon the traffic carried by the River Rhine, although the effects of this have been seen to a much greater extent during the present century.

The Rhine

The River Rhine dominates the inland waterway system of Western Europe (fig. 5.2). Long-distance commerce between Basle and the Netherlands has been considerable since the Middle Ages. It declined later largely because of the considerable sums of money required by the strategically positioned toll-enforcing castles along the line of the river, but there was a revival in trade during the nineteenth century. The river was first freed from tolls during the French Revolutionary wars, and in 1868 was made an international navigation channel. Navigation was vastly improved during the nineteenth century by the deepening, bedrock-blasting and straightening of the channel. The next step was to improve the tributaries as the converging arteries of the river. The Rhine–Marne canal was built from Paris via Strasbourg, the Main itself was improved up to Frankfurt, and with the advent of Ruhr coal and industrial products the trade south into the Middle Rhine region rapidly increased in volume. The growth of industry and cities has been directly affected by the Rhine acting as a factor of convergence. This is an industrial region far from the coast and the river has played a particularly relevant part in bringing the advantages of low-cost water transport. The advent of the EU has done much to emphasise the centrality of the region. Since 1960 enormous strides have been made. The new Rhine–Main–Danube canal (opened in 1992) links Regensburg with Bamberg and enables ships to pass from the North Sea to the Black Sea. The Neckar is navigable (1350 tonnes) as far as Stuttgart. On the west bank the Rhine–Marne canal is supplemented by a link southwards to the Rhône via Belfort. The Rhine itself is navigable up to Basle for 2500-tonne barges. The major river ports are Mannheim, Ludwigshaven, Karlsruhe and Mainz (fig. 12.2). Other smaller ports are Wiesbaden and Speyer (fig. 12.1).

On the River Main the major port is Frankfurt, but several other ports such as Würzburg and Bamberg have increased their level of traffic now that the Rhine–Main–Danube canal through to Regensburg is integrated with the Rhine waterway system. Most inland ports in the region have a four-to-five-days' transit time to Rotterdam and the coast. Thus, some comparison may be made from the following progression: the limit for ocean-going craft is Cologne; barges of 7000 tonnes reach Duisburg, 5000

River	Major inland ports	Traffic volume (million tonnes)
Rhine	Mannheim	9.3
	Ludswigshaven	9.4
	Karlsruhe	6.7
	Mainz	4.1
	Wiesbaden	1.1
Main	Frankfurt	7.8
	Offenbach	1.2
	Aschaffenburg	1.0
	Würzburg	1.6
	Bamberg	1.2
Neckar	Heilbronn	5.7
	Stuttgart	3.2
For comparison (*Lower Rhine*)	Duisburg Ruhrort	20.5
	Duisburg Works	20.7

FIGURE 12.2 *Middle Rhine inland ports – traffic volume 1980s average*

tonnes Mannheim, and 2500 tonnes Basle. If the total river traffic flows in the Middle Rhine region (fig. 12.2) are added together, they are roughly comparable to the trade of Duisburg. Although such figures highlight the importance of Duisburg to the Ruhr, the Middle Rhine region nevertheless is a very substantial focus of water transport.

The development of the Rhine–Rhône canal (plans were revived again in 1994) will be one of the more significant aspects of Europe integration. It will benefit the Rhine corridor, giving new impetus to cities like Lyons, but most significantly will enhance the nodality of the Rhine routeway by linking the North Sea and the Rhineland urban-industrial axis with the Mediterranean Sea.

THREE CITY REGIONS

There are three city regions of special note: Greater Frankfurt; Ludwigshaven–Mannheim; and Stuttgart. Each of these illustrates different characteristics and deserves separate consideration.

The Rhine–Main Complex: Frankfurt-on-Main

The area lies in a triangular zone bounded by Frankfurt-on-Main, Wiesbaden–Mainz and Darmstadt (fig. 12.3). Throughout history there have been continuing factors which have created a focal area of transport routes and economic activity. Mainz was a Roman town at the confluence of the Rhine and Main, but was overtaken by Frankfurt (Franks' ford) during the Frankish colonisation. Frankfurt developed faster due to its establishment as a 'Konigshof' and its more central position on the plain for the routeways which developed during the medieval commercial period. From the tenth century onwards the Rhine–Main valley was centrally placed in the Holy Roman Empire and became a focus for exchange between the Netherlands and Italy. Frankfurt was also a 'Reichstad', a free city in the Empire with considerable industry and commerce. Mainz became an important archbishopric and was fortified, and both towns benefited from the great

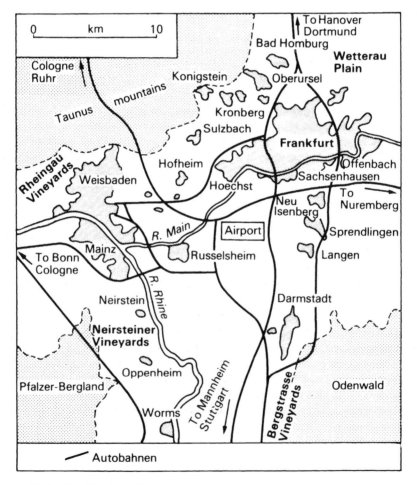

FIGURE 12.3   *The Frankfurt Cross*

medieval fairs. Wiesbaden lies on the north bank of the Rhine at the point where the Taunus mountains come close to the Rhine. It was a fortified town and seat of the Counts of Nassau, but became famous during the eighteenth century when its hot salt springs were popularised and it developed into a health resort and spa. The third apex of the triangle, Darmstadt, originated as the seat of the Elector of Hesse, and its planned origins are reflected in its rectilinear street plan.

The nineteenth and twentieth centuries have underlined the importance of the region in terms of access. Frankfurt is a focal point in the German railway network and it has developed industry on a large scale with engineering, electrical, chemical and consumer goods. The increase in Rhine traffic began during the nineteenth century, with the development of port facilities at Osthafen above the old city on the north bank of the Main. Today the German autobahn system focuses on the Frankfurt Cross, and the outlines of the city region can be discerned in the triangular network of motorways which covers the whole area (fig. 12.3). At peak periods, over 100 000 vehicles use the motorways around Frankfurt. In addition, the airport is one of the busiest in Europe, with over 30 million passengers per year, emphasising the city's role as an international communications focus.

The most important present-day function of Frankfurt, however, is finance and commerce. It is the banking centre of Germany, with the head offices of the Deutsche Bundesbank and no less than 148 German and 114 foreign banks. Its stock exchange is the largest on the continent, and 11 major fairs are held there each year.

Today the city has spread outwards and suburban growth has reached such proportions that to the north the formerly small spa towns which grew up at the foot of the Taunus massif – Bad Homburg, Königstein and Oberursel – have become dormitory suburbs. New townships such as Nordweststadt lie 6.4 km to the north. Along the River Main, west towards Weisbaden, are the chemical complexes of Hoechst, the Opel car plant at Russelsheim and a number of other towns like Hofheim, so that the 17 km between Frankfurt and Wiesbaden are suburban in nature. To the south, Offenbach and Sachsenhausen now form part of the city. The residential town of Neu-Isenberg farther south is associated with the airport, motorway junction area and state forest, all of which occupy a broad belt of land just south of the Main. To the east along the Main is the jewellery-making town of Hanau. The zone thus described is closely linked in an economic sense, and rapid transport has ensured that all parts of the area are inside one hour's journey from Frankfurt. Commuting has developed on a large scale with complex movements of workers into the factories and offices of the city, which is ranked with Düsseldorf as a business centre. The whole city region has 2.3 million people and is one of the most important growth areas in the EU.

Mannheim–Ludwigshaven

The twin cities of Mannheim and Ludwigshaven are the most important inland ports in the area, dependent upon the Rhine for imports of raw material and major heavy chemical centres. They are perhaps more akin to the heavy industrial centres of the Ruhr than the other cities in the Middle Rhine. This is certainly true, but there are also very ancient settlements in the area. Landau and Neustadt are examples of settlement along the Weinstrasse, the foothill zone on the west bank corresponding to the Bergstrasse on the east. Worms, with its famous Liebfraumilch wines, Speyer and its textile industry, and Heidelberg all lie within 12 km of the two main cities. Mannheim itself was founded as a princely residence at the confluence of the Rhine and Neckar rivers, by the Elector of the Palatinate in 1720, and became a great theatrical and musical centre.

Mannheim's modern growth dates from the increase in Rhine traffic when it became the head of navigation for 5000-tonne barges in 1885. The advantages of river ports as input and processing points dependent upon low-cost waterborne raw materials are shown clearly here. Mannheim is a major distribution and trans-shipment point, a large railway junction, and one of the largest inland ports in Europe (fig. 12.2). Heavy chemicals, petrochemicals, dyestuffs, synthetic fibres, pharmaceuticals and grain milling are important. The twin inland ports of Ludwigshaven developed on the west bank, the combined urban complex having 1.8 million people.

The German autobahn system between Frankfurt and Kassel

Stuttgart and the Neckar valley

The city of Stuttgart in the Land of Baden-Württemberg shows many of the features already mentioned. It is a city region based largely upon human resources and the convergence of routeways (fig. 12.4), and at least part of its prosperity derives from the Rivers Rhine and Neckar. Its site is an accident of history, and was chosen for a palace and fortified town from which the Dukes of Württemberg were to rule their principality from 960 AD onwards. The city was built in the baroque style and has many elegant buildings. Its general situation must be one of the most beautiful in Europe for it stands in a saucer-shaped valley on the south side of the River Neckar with wooded and vine-clad hills around acting as natural boundaries. To the south-west lies the Black Forest, and to the south-east, the Swabian Jura.

This would appear to be hardly the situation for a major industrial city, but even in the medieval period it became a focal point for Alpine routes from the south and routes from the Rhine via Heidelberg and the Neckar

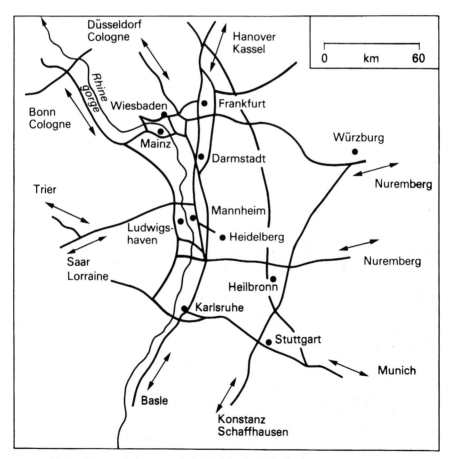

FIGURE 12.4   *The autobahn network in the Middle Rhinelands*

valley. In addition, the east–west routes from the Danube valley and Munich passed across the Neckar valley and Stuttgart. This pattern, like that of Frankfurt, was re-emphasised during the nineteenth century when the railway system made the city into a focal point of south Germany, and the Neckar became navigable for barges of up to 1350 tonnes.

The industrial wealth of the city traditionally was based on textiles from local wool, but the present-day industrial pattern shows dependence upon the production of high-value goods, the assembly components using skilled labour and the minimum of raw materials. Stuttgart is so far from raw materials that even with Rhine–Neckar transport, costs are relatively high, and skilled labour provides the one real resource. The city is the centre of a densely populated rural hinterland which provides a pool of labour, but in addition, there are many foreign immigrant workers. The machine tools, automobile components, electrical engineering, electronics, and precision and optical instruments are supplemented by chemicals and pharmaceuticals, electrical domestic equipment, textiles, footwear and food-processing. Stuttgart is a major centre of the German car industry, with motor vehicles built by Daimler-Benz (and its subsidiary Mercedes-Benz), Porsche and the Audi part of the Volkswagen group. The IBM computer company reflects the science-based and sophisticated nature of the manufacturing. Many industrial townships lie to the north-east of the city in the Neckar valley itself: Unterturkheim, Cannstadt, Feuerbach and Zuffenhausen. Some idea of the great significance of industry can be gauged from the fact that Stuttgart's industrial output is fourth among German cities, and it produces one-third of the gross domestic product of the Land of Baden-Württemberg.

Stuttgart has considerable industrial, regional, political and cultural significance as the capital of Baden-Württemberg, and within the city region are some 2.9 million people. Industrial satellite towns, based upon local supplies of labour, extend to a large distance up the valleys surrounding the city, north to Ludwigsburg and Heilbronn, south to Tubingen and Reutlingen, east to Goppingen and west to Pforzheim. Within this Stuttgart region there is a very dense movement of traffic, and the city is therefore a good example in southern Germany of a *landeshaupstadt*, or regional service centre. It is a highly specialised city with an extensive tributary rural area in the Neckar valley. Finally, it has a natural physical zone of influence, lying between the Odenwald to the north, the Black Forest to the south-west, and the Swabian Jura to the south-east. Like Frankfurt, Stuttgart has developed and prospered because of its position at the hub of a communications network and its nodality in human terms. It is the perfect example of a city which has prospered because it was there.

Baden-Württemberg

The population of Baden-Württemberg has grown from 6.4 million inhabitants in 1950 to almost 10 million, so that it is now the third largest

Land in terms of population. It has been the wealthiest Land for most of the period since its creation in 1952 (in the nineteenth century the area was extremely poor and its industry based on agriculture). It has the lowest rate of unemployment, the highest exports, the most universities and technical schools, and the greatest expenditure on research and development. This success has attracted migrants into the Land, with a net in-migration of 358 000 in the period 1980–90. In Stuttgart, 23 per cent of the population are non-German, many drawn to the urban area by the prospect of employment in the motor-vehicle industry.

However, unemployment has risen in recent years and exports have dropped, as the very factors which contributed to the Land's post-war success are now affected by recession. The regional economy is heavily dependent on manufacturing (particularly motor vehicles) and on other forms of mechanical and electrical engineering such as machine-tool building. The recession in the European car industry in the early 1990s has meant that even Daimler-Benz has reduced its workforce by 60 000 in the period 1992–94, with Mercedes cars now being assembled in cheaper countries such as Mexico, South Korea and the Philippines. Machine-tool manufacturers such as Deckel and Maho have also merged to survive the recession, with a consequent reduction in the workforce.

Nevertheless, unemployment is still lower than elsewhere in Germany, and the regional economy is still very strong, supported by an excellent educational and research infrastructure with 36 science parks. Baden-Württemberg has the highest ratio of scientists per head of population in the EU, and still produces more innovations than any other Land in Germany. The Land has been called a 'model little country', and together with Rhône–Alpes, Lombardy and Catalonia is one of the 'Four Motors of Europe' (a European cooperation group).

SUMMARY

There is a north–south division along the Rhinelands, although perhaps not as dramatic as in other parts of the EU. There is a contrast between the Ruhr, with its heavy industry re-adjusting to twentieth-century conditions, and these city regions of the Middle Rhinelands. Centres like Frankfurt and Stuttgart are much favoured because communications, markets and labour supply have replaced raw materials as the dominant factors in industrial location. The Frankfurt–Mannheim–Stuttgart corridor has both pleasant environmental conditions and a high level of accessibility and is quoted by Hugh Clout as being of one of the new 'industrial boulevards' of Western Europe.

13

BELGIUM: A STUDY IN REGIONAL CONTRASTS

LOCAL VARIATIONS

Discussion of the European growth axis tends to obscure examination of local variations within it. Belgium is such an example. Although Belgium lies almost totally upon the central belt of economic activity, there are, nevertheless, four geographical themes within the country (fig. 13.1) which illustrate major contrasts.

1 the Brussels–Antwerp growth axis;
2 the coalfield belt from Mons to Liège which has similar problems to its western extension, the Nord coalfield of France;
3 the highland area of the Ardennes which is an area of out-migration, although there is an interesting variation from the norm;
4 the language and cultural division between Fleming and Walloon complicates the economic differences within the country. Changes in recent years have swung the balance of ascendancy from Wallonia to Flanders, creating considerable intergroup tensions.

The Brussels–Antwerp growth axis

This is the most densely populated part of Belgium, and although the port and capital city are some 40 km apart, they are beginning to show all the signs of conurban linkage as Antwerp rapidly becomes similar to Rotterdam as a major input point. Brussels has grown enormously since becoming the effective administrative centre of the EU. The port and city are connected by the Willebroek canal, railways and the E10 motorway, and show signs of creating a future conurbation on the southern side of the Rhine delta,

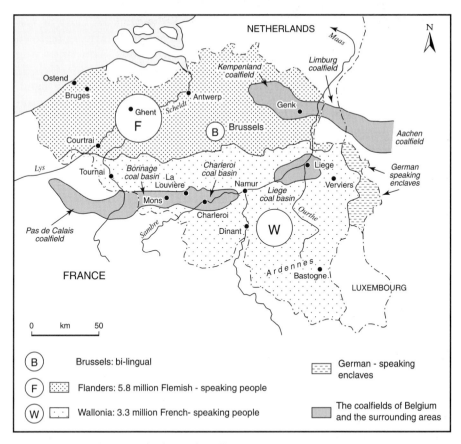

FIGURE 13.1   *Belgium – Flanders and Wallonia*

similar to the Randstad on the north. Indeed, if Ghent is included, a triangular growth area can be seen to be emerging (fig. 13.2).

Antwerp

The port and city are some 80 km from the sea, but have a modern deep-water channel through the Western Scheldt estuary, which is the southern arm of the Rhine delta. The Dutch delta plan has benefited Antwerp in terms of waterway improvements and has also given better transport links with Rotterdam.

Antwerp is a very good example of a medieval city with the original sixteenth-century fortifications marked by boulevards which now enclose the present city-centre. The old city was the principal port in the whole region up to the sixteenth century, but by the Treaty of Westphalia, 1648, the Scheldt was completely closed to sea-traffic, thus ensuring the rise and dominance of Amsterdam to the north. As a result, Antwerp and many other Belgian ports declined, and it was not until the early nineteenth century, with Belgian independence (1830) and increasing industrial traffic into the

Rhine–Scheldt delta, that Antwerp began to prosper again. Growth was then rapid and in the late nineteenth century the earlier walls were replaced by the *enceinte*, an elaborate defensive complex with forts. This larger ring now contains the city centre, inner areas and railway termini.

Since the Second World War, development has been particularly rapid. Residential districts on the east bank in particular fan out along the main roads east towards Turnhout and south towards Mechelin. Road tunnels under the Scheldt have led to modern developments on the west bank. Industrial growth has followed the development of the port, and large areas of land along the river are available for industrial development. To the north is a large and comprehensive dockland with oil refineries, car assembly plants, and the processing of imported foodstuffs – mainly tropical products. To the south of the city along the Scheldt are shipyards at Hoboken and a variety of heavy industry along the River Rupel and Willebroek canal towards Boom. These include heavy ceramics, cement, chemicals, textiles and brickmaking. There are also precision industries, such as photographic processing, diamond cutting, radio and electronics, which have grown with the increasing sophistication of the city's industrial capacity.

Antwerp has emerged as an international port, second in European rank, with a hinterland largely complementing that of Rotterdam. This has a radius of up to 400 km extending through Belgium into north-east France and to Aachen, and including a small part of the southern Netherlands. The modern importance of the city is based upon communications. There are no raw materials, but there are canal links to Brussels, Charleroi, Liège and the Meuse valley, and the Kempenland. Motorway links are becoming increasingly important, in particular the Antwerp–Brussels route, and the Antwerp–Liège–Aachen route, which follows the line of the Albert canal. The whole agglomeration has a population of almost 1 million people and is one of the fastest-growing areas in Belgium.

Brussels

The early extent of the city is indicated by the almost complete polygon of boulevards which marks the old walled city, and which now contains the administrative, commercial and retail sectors of the central area as well as the oldest parts of the city, which are a considerable attraction for tourists.

Industrial locations are highly zoned, lying along the Senne valley to the north-east and the south-west. Along the Willebroek canal to the north, reaching towards Mechelin, are heavier processing industries, timber, chemicals, heavy metals and food processing, whilst to the south along the Charleroi canal lie textile works, engineering and cable works and the Clabecq steelworks. In addition, however, the city's light and specialised industries are immensely varied and widespread, including clothing, jewellery and cosmetics (Brussels is a fashion centre), and pharmaceuticals, electrical goods, printing and miscellaneous consumer industries.

The agglomeration now stretches along the Senne valley, and towards the south it has extended around and beyond the Forest of Soignies, so this now forms an enclave of green belt surrounded by suburbs and commuter villages. Expansion eastwards to Louvain and south to Wavre has created an intensely suburbanised zone. Brussels is a bilingual island (French and Flemish) just within the Flemish-speaking part of Belgium. Near Wavre, the city's expansion has crossed into the French-speaking (Walloon) section of the country. Brussels has gained its dynamism from being a regional and political centre for much of East Flanders, although latterly there has been an increasing movement from all parts of Belgium, the attraction of the city contrasting with the declining areas of the south. Then there is its function as national capital of Belgium, now supplemented by its growth as administrative centre of the EU. There is major expansion of the tertiary sector, and most of Belgium's insurance, commerce and finance companies are in Brussels. The Berlaymont Building, which houses the EU Commission, is the nucleus around which much activity occurs. The factor of cumulative causality is reflected in the need for multi-national industrial, professional and commercial companies to have their head offices at this

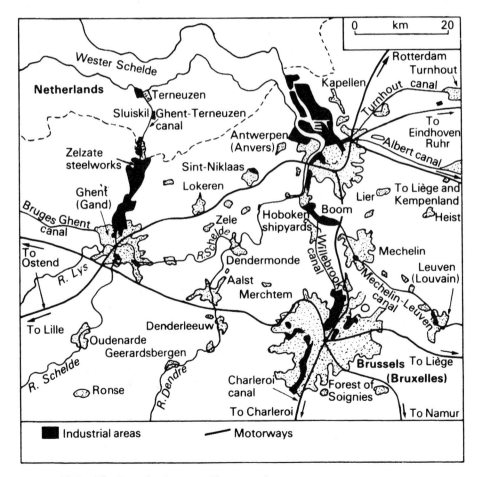

FIGURE 13.2   *The Brussels–Antwerp–Ghent growth area*

Brussels, with the Grand Place in the foreground

central point. Since 1983 a building boom, often stimulated by British capital, has exerted tremendous pressure upon land in the centre of Brussels as well as in the suburbs. Brussels has a population of nearly 1.9 million people and with Antwerp to the north constitutes a very definite growth axis.

Ghent

If Ghent is considered, with its 50 000-tonne-capacity ship canal to Terneuzen on the Scheldt estuary, and other canal links to Bruges, plus the Ostend–Ghent–Brussels motorway, then there is a third urban-industrial nucleus. Ghent has 485 000 people, and has cotton and synthetic-fibres industries. Along the Terneuzen canal, in an industrial area reaching almost to the Scheldt estuary, are shipbuilding yards, chemical plants, oil refineries, paper works and the integrated Zelzate iron and steel complex.

The Belgian coalfields with particular reference to the Borinage and Liège

Figure 13.1 illustrates the relationships between the smaller coalfields of north-west Europe, an almost continuous band stretching from Douai to

Aachen. Whilst these were much less important than the major British coalfields and the German Ruhr, they were nevertheless a major factor in the nineteenth century as national sources of energy during the Industrial Revolution. The problems of each area today vary in intensity according to the extent of exploitation, the nature of the coal seams and the degree of exhaustion, but all have come under considerable pressure because of the alternative sources of energy and the need for low-cost fuel. In the Kempenland and Sambre–Meuse valley coal-mining has now disappeared (fig. 13.3). Early exploitation meant that the best seams became exhausted and with difficult mining conditions and relatively small-scale mines, these were high-cost coalfields. Decline has been so rapid that there have been massive problems of readjustment in the industrial towns which stretch for nearly 140 km across Belgium. Government money was made available to ease the problems, but most of it was spent on redundancy and pension schemes. However, most of the miners have found work at places like the Ford plant in Genk or in the port of Antwerp. There are four regions: the Borinage, centred upon Mons; the Central basin around La Louvière; the Charleroi basin; and the eastern or Liège coalfield. Some measure of the decline may be seen in the fact that in 1953 there were still 136 pits and 120 000 men employed in coal-mining in Wallonia (compare fig. 13.3 and fig. 2.3).

Liège and the eastern basin

Although the basis of expansion in Liège and the eastern basin was coal, the district has always been based upon more than extractive industry and this is the reason for its greater economic resilience during the last 20 years. The city was an ancient bishopric and city-state and as such has traditionally been a major service centre for the eastern regions of Belgium. It covers the Meuse valley and its confluence zone with the Ourthe, Amblève and Vesdre, the Verviers textile area and Ardennes foothills to the south, the fertile Hesbaye to the north-west and the Pays D'Herve to the east of the Meuse. It is the cultural capital of Wallonia and third city of Belgium, with a conurbation population of 601 000.

In the Liège basin, the same problems of productivity arise as in the rest of the Sambre–Meuse valley, and coal-mining has now ceased. The worst problem is the legacy of the 'old industrial landscape' with masses of spoilheaps on the Hesbaye plateau above the deeply trenched Meuse valley, where most of the settlement lies. However, the Industrial Revolution has left Liège with much more than a mining economy. John Cockerill, an Englishman, was responsible for the first blast furnace in 1832, locomotive manufacture in 1835 and a large part of the metal-working tradition of the city. He was the first in Belgium to use the Bessemer process in 1863 (*The Times*, 31 May 1972). His company has now become Belgium's major steel-manufacturing concern. Cockerill has the bulk of its steel-making capacity at Seraing and Jemeppe upstream from Liège, and at Chertal downstream of the city. It also has factories at Charleroi and is now known as Cockerill-Sambre. Other important metal manufacturing industries are

	Kempenland		Sambre-Meuse	
	Production (million tonnes)	Number of pits	Production (million tonnes)	Number of pits
1961	9.6	7	11.9	47
1970	7.1	5	4.3	15
1981	5.8	5	0.3	1
1986	5.6	5	nil	nil
1993	nil	nil	nil	nil

FIGURE 13.3   *Coal production by the Kempenland and Sambre-Meuse coalfields*

zinc smelting, tubes, cables and small-arms, aircraft engineering and heavy electrical machinery. 'Geographical inertia' is characteristic of the whole area, with the metal-based industries originally dependent upon local charcoal and water power from the streams running down to the incised Meuse valley, and subsequently upon coking coal and local iron ores. Other important industries are chemicals, glassware and tyre manufacture.

Verviers and Eupen, along the Vesdre valley to the east, form an associated industrial area manufacturing woollen textiles, originating on local wool from the Ardennes and water power from reservoirs along the valley.

Despite the obsolescence of the industrial environment, unplanned piecemeal development crowded in the river valley, and relentless decline in industrial employment, Liège has already largely adapted to the decline in coal-mining and steel-making, and has bright prospects for the future. The reason is its location on the major link routes between the Rhine delta, Germany and France. Raw materials are now imported via the Albert Canal, particularly coking coal from the Ruhr. The River Meuse provides a very useful means of transport for heavy goods. More important are the motorway links (fig. 5.6). The motorways from Ostend, Brussels and Antwerp lead to Aachen, Cologne and Frankfurt. The 'Autoroute De Wallonie' (E41) links Liège with the Sambre–Meuse towns and the Lille–Paris motorway. There are major development plans along two axes. Heavy industry is zoned along the river, with a nuclear power station at Tihange, up-river from Liège, an oil refinery on the Albert canal, and petrochemical works and fertiliser plants, which will join the predominantly steel and heavy-engineering works of the river valley. New light-industry estates are zoned near the motorways on the plateau on the outskirts of the city. Computers, electronic components, clothing, fibreglass and ceramics are produced at greenfield sites such as Hauts Sarts, the industrial estate north-east of Liège. There are three other smaller industrial estates lying adjacent to the Brussels motorway (E5).

Charleroi

With its surrounding satellite towns, Charleroi is an agglomeration of some 429 000 people and its industrial structure has much in common with Liège. Although coal production has disappeared there is a steel industry, chemical works and, more recently, a plastics industry. This was also the centre of the Belgian glass industry, based upon local sands. Like Liège, Charleroi has a sufficiently broad and diversified manufacturing base to avoid the worst effects of the decline of coal. Engineering, vehicle and aircraft components, electronic calculators, printing and food processing are represented on new industrial estates near the city.

Mons and the Borinage: La Louvière and the Central Basin

	Miners	Number of Pits
1948–50	30 000	28
1956	24 000	9
1965	8000	5
1974	1500	1
1977	nil	nil

FIGURE 13.4   *Changes in the Borinage coalfield*

The Borinage stretches from the Belgian border to the city of Mons, provincial capital of Hainault and the area to the east including La Louvière is characterised by the same problems. These areas have experienced considerable economic decline and harsh adjustments have been necessary because of their over-dependence upon a single activity, coal-mining. Here there was little industrial development of any sort, and in 1953 coal-mining accounted for 56 per cent of employment. The seams of coal were almost exhausted, mines were very deep and in one particular colliery, Rieu De Coeur, galleries were specially refrigerated over 1.5 km below ground. As a small-scale producer (the Borinage produced 5.9 million tonnes in 1927, the peak year) it was a very high-cost coalfield. Not only was there heavy competition from oil and natural gas, but increased cross-frontier competition and tariff-free conditions which arrived with the EEC meant that by 1958 Ruhr coal, even after being transported to Charleroi, was considerably cheaper. With the reduction in Atlantic freight rates, American coal could be sold at Charleroi for substantially less than Borinage coal. Productivity was low, production was small-scale and inefficient from many small pits, and Borinage coal could not be made competitive. The Conseil National Des Charbonnages worked out a reorganisation and contraction plan (fig. 13.4). Coal-mining has seen a dramatic decline and is now completely extinguished (fig. 13.5). The ECSC aided the region in two ways. Loans were given, often in association with the Belgian Government,

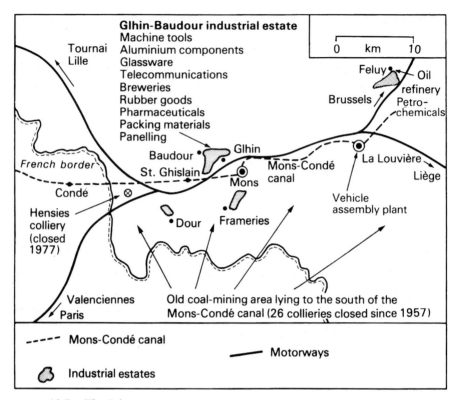

FIGURE 13.5   *The Belgian Borinage – old and new industry*

to lay out new industrial estates and encourage investment in new plant. The ECSC also shared with the Belgian authorities the cost of retraining workers for new skilled jobs. Belgian Government legislation has given the area development status, and modern growth industries have been attracted to the area.

The changes in the region are threefold:

(a) The Borinage became a region of out-migration, mainly to Antwerp and Brussels, and the employment force actually declined by nearly 50 per cent. There has also been marked demographic stagnation and an ageing population.

(b) Secondly, however, considerable industrial diversification schemes began to take effect (fig. 13.5). There are six industrial estates with consumer and light industries – pharmaceuticals, electronics and telecommunications factories. Since 1960 over 50 factories with 8000 new jobs have been created. There is a vehicle assembly plant at La Louvière and an oil refinery and petrochemical plant at Feluy to the north. With increased employment in services, the industrial structure now approaches the West European norm.

La Louvière, Belgium. The interchange between E41 Wallonia motorway and the E10 towards Paris

(c) With the introduction of fast electrified rail services between Mons and other parts of Belgium, many of the area's inhabitants now commute to work in Charleroi, Liège, Brussels, and to Valenciennes and other French towns.

The Borinage has adapted well, although the hardship was considerable during the 1960s. From being a monofunctional coal-mining area, it now has a solid industrial base. Many of the environmental problems still remain, as the landscape of the Industrial Revolution cannot be obliterated overnight. Its position and population are its main future resources: 5 million people, a large consumer market, live within 50 km of the provincial capital, Mons. The area lies at the junction of two motorways, Brussels–Paris and the Wallonia motorway (E41) (Liège–Mons–Paris) (fig. 13.5). The raw materials may have vanished, but the infrastructure is vastly improved and Borinage lies along a major growth axis.

The Ardennes Massif

The Ardennes is a heavily forested upland (fig. 13.6), lying at about 350 m but reaching 600 m in the Haut Fagnes near the German Ordnam Datum border. With rainfall reaching a maximum of 140 mm, it is a zone of marginal

FIGURE 13.6   *The Belgian Ardennes*

agriculture and experiences persistent out–migration. Most settlements are small and confined to the valleys of the Semois. Ourthe, Amblève and Vesdre, tributaries of the Meuse. Farms are small and mainly in pasture, with some cereals (oats, rye or barley), and potatoes and fodder crops. In the sheltered areas such as the Semois valley, tobacco is grown and dried on local farms. Farms are being abandoned and the whole area is the least densely populated in Belgium with a population of under 200 000. Forestry is an important occupation and timber is a major resource of the Ardennes, in areas such as Beauraing and Gedinne south of Dinant. There are isolated areas of economic activity such as limestone quarrying near Marche.

The drift of population is a continuing feature of the life of the area, but it is now alleviated by two factors. One is the outstanding scenic beauty of the Ardennes which has led to a considerable tourist industry, and the second, interrelated, is the proximity of the region to densely populated lowlands of Belgium, Holland and Germany. Its wealth potential increasingly lies in its landscape. With the attractions of woods and forests, numerous chateaux, and beautiful valleys like the Semois and Viroin, many towns have developed a tourist function. Dinant, La Roche, Bouillon, Houffalize and Spa (the original mineral springs have given their name to all towns of this type) all have a tourist function, and are supplemented by others with a market role such as Bastogne, Marche-en-Famenne and St Vith.

Depopulation is also being partially reversed by the 'weekend cottage'. The second home is a popular idea in Europe, and the Ardennes are ringed with the dense urban populations of the Meuse valley, Brussels, northern France and the Rhinelands. Barvaux in the Ourthe valley particularly, and the Dinant and Marche areas of the Condroz have large areas of sub-rural development which, if allowed to spread unchecked, will rapidly spoil the landscape they are designed to enjoy. In addition, the whole northern section of the Ardennes has fallen within commuting range of Liège and even Brussels, and towns such as Spa, Theux, Aywaille and Remouchamps, in the Amblève and Lower Ourthe valleys, are becoming dormitories.

Accessibility was always limited, with one major north–south routeway (N4) and railway line which ran from Namur through Marche, Bastogne and Arlon into Luxembourg. However, the isolation has now been removed with two motorways completed from Brussels and Liège which run south towards Luxembourg. These are of considerable importance for the economic revitalisation of the Ardennes.

The regional and cultural dichotomy of Belgium: Flanders and Wallonia

Considerable economic differences between northern Belgium (the Brussels–Antwerp–Ghent region) and southern areas like the coalfields of the Meuse valley and the Ardennes uplands have been outlined above. Belgium is a bilingual and bi-cultural state, and the boundaries between the Flemings and Walloons approximately correspond to the economic lines of demarcation between growth areas in the north and areas of decline in the south (fig. 13.1). The history of the two cultural groups adds another dimension to the dichotomy. Flanders was, in medieval times, an economic core area. The great ports of Bruges and Antwerp were part of the Hanseatic League. Trading links with Italy and the Flemish cloth trade were all part of one of the most successful commercial areas in Europe at that time.

Since the nineteenth century, however, economic power, based upon the Sambre–Meuse coalfield and its steel, engineering and chemical industries was concentrated in the south. The French-speaking south, covering the provinces of Luxembourg, Liège, Namur, Hainault and south Brabant, is known as Wallonia. French language and culture was dominant during the nineteenth century, and Belgian administration, culture and teaching was in

French. The French-speaking Walloons were an élite both culturally and in terms of prosperity. Liège in particular was the nerve centre of Walloon economic power.

The Flemish provinces lie to the north, covering West and East Flanders, Antwerp, Limbourg and North Brabant. During the nineteenth century the Flemings were effectively second-class citizens. They lived in an agricultural area with a stagnant peasant economy. Their language was a dialect of Dutch, and spoken by only about 15 million people in the world. Thus it was at a disadvantage in relation to French as a major language. After Belgium became one country in 1830, the 'Flemish Movement' set out to achieve parity for their language in their own country, and this, although a slow process, was achieved by the 1960s, when for all legal, educational and administrative purposes, Flemish and French became equal in national status. Belgium was divided into two parts by a language line, with Flemish spoken north of it and French to the south. Brussels, as already mentioned, is a bilingual island just north of the dividing line.

During the last 40 years major demographic changes have added to this complete reversal of ascendancy of the two groups. The population of Flanders has been rising by over 7 per cent each decade, whilst that of Wallonia increased by only 2.6 per cent, and although the growth of both populations has slowed, the growth rate in Flanders was still 2.4 per cent compared to 1.2 per cent in Wallonia in the period 1981–91. The density of population in Flanders is now more than double that of Wallonia. This has reinforced the Flemish majority position; they are now almost 64 per cent of the total population, and the Walloons are very conscious of their diminishing relative importance within the state. Secondly, the reversal of economic fortune from Wallonia to Flanders has reinforced the picture of 'two nations'. Sluggish growth, unemployment, declining industries, obsolescent factories, declining infrastructure, an ageing population, and a 'black country' image, is typical of the depressed Sambre–Meuse valley. By contrast, Flanders now has a larger share of the country's wealth. The integrated steel mill at Zelzate, the development of Antwerp as a port and large-scale industrial area, and the linking of Ghent to the sea are examples of the dynamism of port locations, and the Rhine delta in particular. The position of Brussels with its service infrastructure in the EU is an additional factor in the growth of the Brussels–Antwerp axis. Some 81 per cent of American investment has gone into Flanders and the Greater Brussels area, only 19 per cent into Wallonia.

SUMMARY

This picture of regional contrasts within Belgium attempts to show that not all regions within the European growth axis share equally in prosperity. Southern Belgium is one such region, but its process of adjustment is assisted greatly by its accessibility and its proximity to the European core.

14

RANDSTAD HOLLAND: THE RING CITY

THE CONCENTRATION OF POPULATION

One of the most urbanised and wealthy regions in the EU is the western part of the Netherlands, covering the provinces of North and South Holland, Zeeland and Utrecht. The concentration of population may be seen by comparing the total population of the Netherlands – 15.4 million people in 1992 – with the population of 7.2 million in the four provinces (fig. 14.2). Nearly half the country's total population is concentrated into 20 per cent of the country's area.

Specifically, the ring city is formed by two major urban regions, the cities of Amsterdam, Utrecht and Haarlem in the northern arc, and Rotterdam and The Hague in the south (fig. 14.1). Together with a number of smaller units interposed between, such as the historic cities of Leiden and Delft, the new industrial centres of Zaandam and Ijmuiden, seaside resorts such as Scheveningen, Katwijk and Zandvoort, and other towns, the whole begins to take on the shape of a broken ring, or horseshoe.

The reasons for this major concentration of population lie mainly in the central position of these cities in relation to north-west Europe. The delta region of the Rhine and Maas, opening out to the North Sea, has traditionally been important for trade, commercial and industrial activity since the medieval period when Amsterdam was one of the foremost ports of the Hanseatic League. This was underlined during the colonial period when Amsterdam became the world centre of the diamond trade. The cities now have a role as the outlet for the Rhine basin, the major industrial, transport, and population axis of the EU. The Randstad cities are literally at the centre of European integration (figs. 10.1, 10.2).

This concentration of population, even in an extremely prosperous city region, causes problems and creates the need for very careful planning.

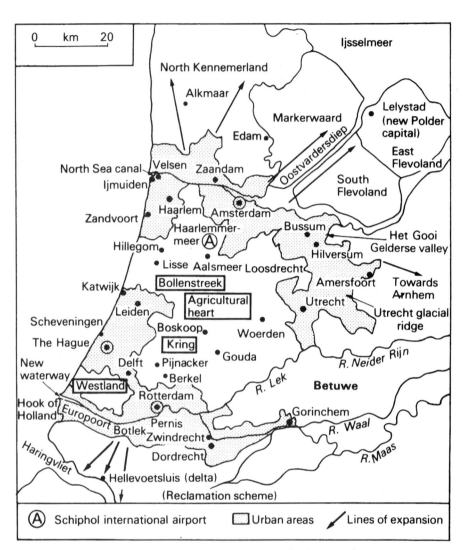

FIGURE 14.1 *Randstad Holland – cities, greenheart and development plan*
(A = Schiphol International Airport)

There are four convenient themes by which to look at the geography of this dynamic region.

1 The unusual pattern of urbanisation in this polycentric city region, based upon distinct settlements originally sited at dry points above the unreclaimed marshlands of the Rhine delta.
2 The Port of Rotterdam and its industrial development with the attendant pollution problems.
3 The needs of agriculture in this very fertile part of the Netherlands which produces 40 per cent of the country's total food.
4 Severe competition for land and regional planning.

City	Population total of agglomeration (thousands)	Functions of principal city
Amsterdam	1080	Financial and commercial centre. The main service and retail centre, entirely metropolitan in character.
Rotterdam	1060	Industrial, transhipment, storage terminals, import and export.
The Hague, including Delft	693	Administrative capital. Centre of Government and international agencies.
Utrecht	540	Historic university town, ecclesiastical centre, now provincial capital and regional service centre and communications centre.
Haarlem	219	Residential and regional centre. Engineering industry.
Leyden	363	Historic university town and regional centre for mid-western Randstad.
Dordrecht	210	Industrial town and a satellite for Rotterdam.
Hilversum	102	Residential and commuter town for Amsterdam.
Total large municipalities	4267	
Randstad (Total)	6169	(includes 70 municipalities)
Total for North and South Holland, Zeeland and Utrecht	7211	
Total population for the Netherlands	15 423	

FIGURE 14.2 *The Randstad hierarchy – a summary, 1992*

THE URBAN STRUCTURE OF THE RANDSTAD

The Randstad cities, which form a distinctive horseshoe, are in danger of coalescing except perhaps at the south-east, where an open section exists between Dordrecht and Utrecht. The Randstad's unique character derives from its 'rim' structure around the green centre, but also from its functional and hierarchical development. Unlike other European cities such as Paris or London, the multitude of functions normally carried out within the 'central business district' of a capital city is distributed here between several cities. There is a hierarchy of centres of different sizes, some 70 municipalities in all (fig. 14.2), which can be conveniently grouped as follows:

Amsterdam

This historic city is the cultural, financial and commercial capital of the Netherlands and is the most highly metropolitan in character of all the Randstad cities, with a population of over 1 million. The city has a wide range of banking, finance, commerce and luxury-shopping facilities. As a tourist centre it has museums, art galleries and luxury hotels. The industries

Canal-side housing towards the Herengracht in the historic centre of Amsterdam, showing seventeenth century merchant houses

Amstelveen, new suburban residential complex on the southern side of Amsterdam

within the city are those of printing, fashion clothing and diamond-cutting. The distinctive city centre, with its semi-circular structure bounded by quiet tree-lined canals, is a major tourist attraction.

The expansion of the city has created several sub-zones on the periphery. To the south is the international airport at Schiphol and the new residential areas of Amstelveen and Sloetermeer, whilst its commuter zones lie farther east around Bussum and Hilversum, in the undulating wooded hills of the Het Gooi.

On the north side of Amsterdam is the important industrial region around the North Sea canal. The canal was opened in 1876 to provide better communications from Amsterdam to the sea. There are two industrial complexes associated with it, Ijmuiden–Velsen and Zaandam. At Velsen is the integrated iron and steelworks of Hoogovens, with blast furnaces, rolling mills and tin-plating mills. The complex is based upon cheap imports of raw materials, coke from the USA and iron ore from Sweden and North Africa. Nearer Amsterdam is Zaandam, where the North Sea canal reaches the city. Once important for shipping, it is now concerned mainly with processing of imported raw materials and foodstuffs of colonial origin and also local dairy and vegetable products.

Haarlem

An historic city which was associated with the Dutch war of independence against Spain in the sixteenth century. Haarlem is now mainly a residential and commuter area for Amsterdam and is the regional centre for South Kennemerland.

Utrecht

Utrecht is the one city of the Randstad which is a considerable distance from the sea, and has become an inland communications centre. It is a railway focus at the eastern end of the conurbation and has now become a motorway junction. It is, however, one of the oldest cities of Holland and also an ecclesiastical and university town, and a provincial capital. Suburban development is taking place eastwards towards Amersfoort.

The Hague agglomeration

The two historic cities of Delft, famous for pottery, and Leiden, with its university, are very nearly joined by ribbon development to The Hague. Zoetermeer to the east, and Wassenaar and Scheveningen to the north are residential outliers for The Hague agglomeration. The Hague itself is the seat of government of the Netherlands and has most of the administrative and public bodies, and many international agencies such as the International Court of Justice. Otherwise it is very much an attractive residential city, and has been called 'the largest village in Europe'.

Rotterdam

Of all the centres so far described, Rotterdam has experienced the most tremendous growth in size and international importance. As the raw materials input point and trans-shipment centre, it is a most dynamic industrial growth area, and the largest port in the world. It will be dealt with in detail in the next section.

ROTTERDAM: EUROPE'S LEADING PORT

Although the picture already indicates the considerable number of industries associated with the Randstad, there are two marked concentrations. One, already mentioned, is the belt along the North Sea canal from Ijmuiden and the Velsen Steelworks to Zaandam. By far the more important is the 30-km stretch of water from the Hook of Holland to the city of Rotterdam itself along the New Waterway and thence along the distributaries of the Maas and Waal as far as Dordrecht (fig. 14.3). In 1962 Rotterdam moved ahead of New York in terms of cargo tonnage handled and in the decades since it has

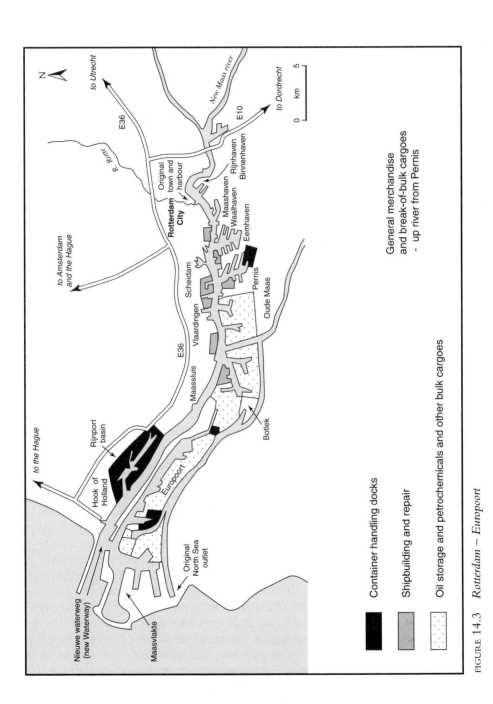

FIGURE 14.3 *Rotterdam – Europoort*

become the pre-eminent world port. Figure 14.4 illustrates the comparisons with other leading European ports. As late as the Second World War it was a port of only moderate importance and in 1945 was in ruins as a result of bombing. It has a long history but its growth to prominence can be seen in three stages, in each case initiated by a major change in transport factors.

The early port, a dam on the River Rotte, itself a right-bank tributary of the tidal Maas, was a medieval fishing village with a very long and tortuous channel to the sea. Growth was slow and unspectacular, although by the end of the eighteenth century Rotterdam had grown to 50 000, making it the second largest city of Holland. It was a prosperous pre-industrial port, with the 'Oudehaven' tucked easily into the centre of the city.

The ultimate dominance of Rotterdam over both Amsterdam and Antwerp was ensured by the cutting of the New Waterway. This is wide and lock-free, and cuts straight through the sandspit of the Hook of Holland to a point on the coastline where deeper water allows larger ships to enter the harbour. It became operational in 1872 and gave a new lease of life to the port at a critical time. The arrival of the steamship needing deeper channels coincided with the development of the vast hinterland of the port and the growing lines of waterway communication along the Rhine axis. At the same time as the Rhine and its tributaries became Europe's commercial artery, navigable as far as Switzerland, there was also rapid development of the Ruhr coalfield, Lorraine, the Saar, Limburg and the Sambre–Meuse valley. Rotterdam became the input and output point for industrial Europe, and to this major locational advantage was added the technical superiority of a modern deep-water channel. The docks of this period lie on the south bank opposite the old medieval harbour Rijnhaven, Binnenhaven, Spoorweghaven (railway harbour), Waalhaven and Maashaven. These are small by modern standards, and date from the nineteenth century. They indicate the approximate extent of the port before 1945.

The really significant change came after 1946 when new opportunities presented themselves. Rotterdam's access to the Ruhr, and its position as the outlet for the Rhinelands, the most populous part of Europe, matched its adjacency to the English Channel, the busiest stretch of water in the world. Even more important was the development of the EEC and its geographical axis along the Rhinelands. The whole Rhine delta assumed a new economic importance, and Rotterdam was one of the most central points on this axis. However, the single most significant change was the shipping revolution which developed from the great increase in size of ships during the 1960s and the increasing specialisation of cargo transport, with a distinction being made between bulk cargoes and break-bulk or trans-shipment cargoes.

The rapid decline of coal during the post-war period and its replacement primarily by oil was the great opportunity for ports like Rotterdam to become the reception, storage and refining points for West European oil. Imports of crude oil rocketed from 2.3 million tonnes in 1938 to 61 million tonnes in 1967, reaching 130 million tonnes in 1981 before dropping back to 97 million tonnes in 1991 as a result of reductions in oil-refining capacity in the EU, indicating that Rotterdam's growth has been due in large part to oil imports. The pipeline system to the Rhinelands (fig. 2.7) is an important supplement to the port facility which has helped to create a tremendous number of processing industries, such as oil refineries, petrochemical works, chemical plants and plastics fabricators. The port was well placed for the further boost to the bulk trade when the Suez Canal closed in 1967 and the era of the supertanker began. Rotterdam's deep-dredged channels enabled it to become pre-eminent as a terminal port for raw materials, including crude oil, mineral ores, scrap iron, timber and fertilisers, grain and coal, often requiring further processing. To accommodate the huge bulk-carriers, the deeper water areas from Pernis downstream have been developed since the 1950s, and by 1966 bulk carriers of over 200 000 tonnes dwt (deadweight tonnage) could enter the port. The Pernis area is a complex of storage facilities, oil refineries and petrochemical works, followed by Botlek (fig. 14.3), and Europoort which came into use during the 1960s with a capacity for 300 000-tonne oil tankers and 125 000-tonne grain carriers. The final phase was the reclamation of 2500 ha of land at Maasvlakte, an ambitious scheme to provide even more land for industry and port facilities (although the plan to build a large iron and steel works at Maasvlakte was

Europoort, Rotterdam, looking seawards towards the new development on flat estuarine land at Maasvlakte

abandoned). The post-war development of bulk shipping can be seen as a succession of newer, larger dock basins and industrial complexes, each one downriver from the original Rotterdam city docks and nearer to the sea, with over 30 km of waterfront in all.

However, the upper harbour is important and adds the other element: the break-of-bulk, trans-shipment, or 'gateway' function (fig. 14.3). The development of containerised cargo-handling has revolutionised the loading and unloading of the higher-value processed or manufactured goods which are packaged in smaller units. The 'gateway' port function is necessary principally to handle, transfer, and despatch to a variety of destinations. Traditionally this was a cumbersome inefficient operation, consuming time and labour. With the container, the high-value component or complete product is moved through the port as quickly as possible by efficient cargo-handling equipment. Larger ships have meant greater economies, provided that 'turn-round time' has been cut. For example, on the Atlantic run 'dead time' in port has been cut from 70 to 20 per cent, with consequent saving on costs. On the dockside large areas of flat stacking space are needed for stacking and marshalling and also an efficient system of inland transportation. During the 1960s Rotterdam re-equipped itself for containerisation with the Europoort container dock so that it has become the foremost container port in Europe and even takes goods destined for the UK, formerly handled by London. The upper harbour has largely been adapted for containers. This is the small group of basins on the south bank of Rotterdam city, Rijnhaven, Binnenhaven, Spoorweghaven and Maashaven (fig. 14.3) where the clutter of merchandise is replaced by huge cranes with 50-tonnes capacity, standardised boxes, and large storage zones. Waalhaven and Eemhaven are larger docks, the first one modernised, and the second built during the 1960s purely for container traffic. An extension downstream on the north bank is Rijnpoort. All the docks above Pernis are concerned with break-bulk cargoes. The successful operation of the 'gateway' function requires excellent communications to all parts of Europe. The River Rhine and its tributary systems of canals and navigable rivers are Rotterdam's principal advantage. In addition, the system of railways and autoroutes allows fast transit to all parts of the EU. The upper harbours are not only cargo-handling. Waalhaven and Schiedam are also the major shipbuilding sections of the port and its main liner terminals. There are also many other industries: glass-making, car assembly, brewing and distilling, and food processing (chocolate and margarine) in the dock areas.

Without any doubt, Rotterdam's growth and prosperity is based firmly upon its bulk-handling facilities, and in particular upon oil (fig. 14.4). One of the main problems is pollution. The Rhine is heavily polluted here by sewage, industrial and power-station effluents from up-river and from Germany (60 000 tonnes of chemicals per day is the estimate). A more serious matter is air pollution at Botlek, Pernis and Europoort, where the oil refineries and chemical and petrochemical plants foul the air with hydrocarbons and sulphur dioxide. It is the downstream residential areas which suffer most – Vlaardingen, Maassluis, Rozenburg and the Hook of

A Port	Cargo tonnage (million tonnes) 1992	B Year	Cargo tonnage (million tonnes)
Rotterdam	292	1938	42
Antwerp	104	1946	8
Marseille	90	1955	66
Hamburg	65	1966	130
Le Havre	53	1973	233
Genoa	42	1976	279
Dunkirk	40	1986	399
		1992	292

C Commodity	Per cent trade (by volume)	
Oil	58	⎫
Mineral ores	12	⎬
Coal	4	Bulk cargoes (total) 84
Cereals	4	⎬
Other bulk cargoes	6	⎭
General cargo (break of bulk)	16	

FIGURE 14.4   *Rotterdam* **(A)** *comparative trade figures* **(B)** *growth of trade* **(C)** *principal trading commodities*

Holland. The original plans for heavy industry at Maasvlakte had to be modified because of the success of local action groups, and the land reclamation was much slower than originally anticipated. Finally, there are constant worries about housing and recreation, which relates to the ever-present problem in the whole Randstad: competition for land. In Rotterdam, industrial considerations have often completely outweighed any others. The symptom of this is the outward movement of Dutch people from the port and industrial area of the Rhinemouth since 1960.

   In conclusion, it is relevant to consider the future of Rotterdam. Will improvements in pipelines allow Marseille and Genoa to reduce Rotterdam's oil hinterland? Rotterdam's bulk oil imports may not be a means of continual growth, as was assumed during the 1960s. The port and city will probably remain the major throughput point of the EU because of its superb junction position between the North Sea and the Rhineland axis. Principal future growth will probably be based upon its high-value break-of-bulk container trade.

THE AGRICULTURAL HEART

Western Holland is also a key agricultural area and formed the original core of the extensive schemes of land reclamation which began in the thirteenth century. The culmination of Dutch enterprise in this direction came in 1852 with the draining of the Haarlemmermeer of 18 000 ha. The future of the open centre of the Randstad (the Greenheart), traditionally one of the most productive Dutch farming areas, causes considerable concern. The essence of the continuing planning problem is how to ensure continued urban development without giving up the open land inside the Randstad.

Most of the Greenheart (fig. 14.1) is polder land below sea level. The principal characteristics of these polders are rich silts and clays, a reclaimed landscape of rectangular fields, and an intensive and varied agriculture. There are many lakes which are used for recreation, sailing and fishing, and have areas for picnics and camping. Water drainage is essential through a system of ditches and dykes, and the former importance of windmills is shown by their continued existence alongside the more modern pumps.

The intensive horticulture with which the Dutch have traditionally been concerned stems from the need to produce high-value foods on a relatively restricted land area, and also from the demand which built up during the nineteenth century for large quantities of food by both the Randstad population and the nearby industrial countries of Belgium, the UK and Germany. Much of the Netherlands' total crop of market-garden products is grown here. There are considerable areas of specialisation, perhaps the best known of which is the small area between Leiden and Haarlem, the Bollenstreek (Lisse, Hillegom and Keukenhof), famous for flowers and bulb production. Aalsmeer near Schiphol airport is concerned with cut flowers (roses and indoor plants) and Boskoop to the south of Leiden is a specialist area for ornamental conifers and shrubs. Two major zones of vegetables occur: Westland lies between the triangle of the cities of The Hague, Rotterdam and The Hook, and contains the major concentration of glasshouses (1400 ha in all). The predominance of glasshouses gives the area an urbanised appearance but it grows a large proportion of Dutch tomatoes, cucumber, lettuce, leeks, carrots and spinach, etc. The Kring district north-west of Rotterdam (Berkel and Pijnacker) specialises in salad crops. In addition to vegetables, there are extensive areas under fruit, both soft and orchard, largely around Utrecht and to the south of the Neider Rijn. Melons and grapes are cultivated under glass.

Whilst horticulture has been traditionally the most significant form of

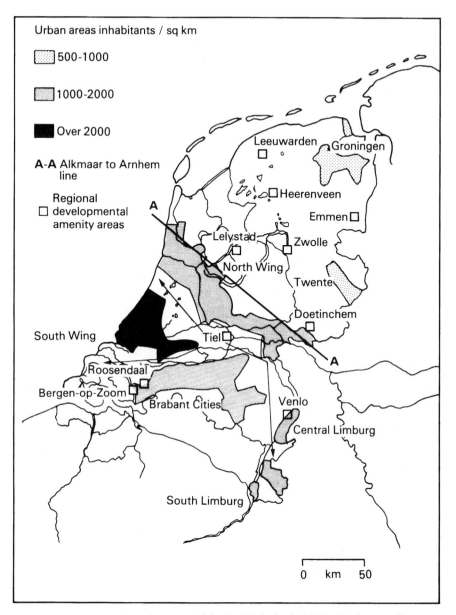

Urban areas inhabitants / sq km

500-1000

1000-2000

Over 2000

A-A Alkmaar to Arnhem line

Regional developmental amenity areas

Leeuwarden
Groningen
Heerenveen
Emmen
A
Lelystad
Zwolle
North Wing
Twente
Doetinchem
South Wing
Tiel
A
Roosendaal
Bergen-op-Zoom
Brabant Cities
Venlo
Central Limburg
South Limburg

0   km   50

FIGURE 14.5   *Projected population model for the Netherlands 2000 AD (source –* Report on Physical Planning for the Netherlands, 1966*)*

farming, arable production, dairy farming and recreational use also make major demands upon the limited space of the Randstad. High yields are characteristic with potatoes, sugar beet and wheat being the principal crops. Much arable production is geared to the supply of food-grains for cattle, particularly around the Haarlemmermeer near Amsterdam. This area has light sea-clay which is ideal for retention of nutrients, there is less wind erosion, and with effective drainage it can be ploughed easily and the water table can be controlled. Dairy farming is also important throughout most of the inner Randstad. The southern region of the Betuwe between the Lek and Waal, the Gouda cheese region, and the Loosdrecht between Amsterdam and Utrecht are primarily grassland areas containing one-fifth of Holland's total cattle, and large numbers of pigs and poultry.

Competition for land

It must not be supposed that the Randstad open heart will inevitably remain agricultural, as there are tremendous pressures upon land. Recreation is one of these. The relatively short dune coastline extending through Scheveningen to Zandvoort has a great width, often extending inland for 5 km, but is in great demand from the Randstad cities for recreational purposes, and is also accessible from German cities in the Rhinelands. The Utrecht ridge of glacial sands, stretching from Hilversum between Utrecht and Amersfoort, are low hills and wooded heaths and provide parkland and scenic amenity areas. Some measure of land pressure can be gauged, however, from the fact that residential development from the city of Utrecht has spread onto the open land on the eastern side of the ridge.

Most critical of the pressures is the demand for land for housing and industry. The heavy industry and port installations of Rotterdam have been expanding at such a rate that the Municipal Port Authority of Rotterdam has published a plan for further development: Havenplan 2010. This concludes that if there is high economic growth and Rotterdam maintains its competitive position, then it will need a second Maasvlakte as well as further development by 2010. The ancient cities and their municipal areas are rigidly defined and the outer suburban areas and the agricultural heart are experiencing strong growth pressures. The population of the Randstad cities had risen to 6.2 million by 1992. They are already crowded and short of land for all purposes.

REGIONAL PLANNING

Some form of regional planning was a necessity from 1945 onwards. The historic cities were preserved as nucleii with buffer zones between them, and the agricultural heart in the centre was preserved. The only growth allowed in this central area was limited within existing historic towns such as Gouda or Woerden. The present morphology of the Randstad therefore is dominated by the horseshoe shape of urbanisation with an effective 'green belt' inside. The 1948 report *The Development of the Western Netherlands* contained the then revolutionary proposal that in order to maintain the 'Greenheart', future growth be guided radically outwards along the main transport routes. There were four main avenues of development (fig. 14.1).

To the north of Ijmuiden and Haarlem was the peninsula of North Kennemerland, where growth could continue as far as Alkmaar, the old cheese-marketing town. On the east, the Utrecht ridge had to be preserved as open land but beyond it were a number of very suitable nucleii from Amersfoort to Arnhem, Nijmegen and along the Rhine and Waal rivers almost to the German frontier. There was considerable potential for light industry here and this was a very important future area for development. To the north-east of Amsterdam lies the polder of South Flevoland and the city of Lelystad. This is a new area which, although originally retained mainly for agriculture, is now providing open space directly adjacent to Amsterdam, the present plan being that the Amsterdam–Lelystad strip will be urbanised. Along this strip runs the main highway from Amsterdam to Groningen, via Lelystad, and also the Oostvaardersdiep, the extension of the North Sea canal from Ijmuiden and Amsterdam. The final avenue lay to the south of Rotterdam and The Hague into the delta of the Rhine and Maas. The whole area is dyked against the sea (the delta scheme) and the formerly disastrous floods, and the Haringvliet has great potential as an alternative waterway. New towns at Hellevoetsluis on the Haringvliet along with the extension of new roads south towards Middelburg have ended the isolation of the delta. These various radial schemes were positioned to relieve the points of maximum congestion: Amsterdam–Haarlem north and north-east; Utrecht eastwards; Rotterdam and The Hague southwards.

The 'spreading policy' or de-concentration of 1951/52, designed to disperse population to the under-developed eastern provinces of Groningen, Friesland, Drenthe, Overijssel and Gelderland (AA line fig. 14.5) and to the old industrial area of Limburg in the south, was a natural corollary of the guided radial development of the Randstad cities.

The First and Second Reports on Physical Planning (1960 and 1966) were designed to cope with large-scale growth pressures within the polycentric Randstad. The four avenues of radial development, combined with buffer zones between the major cities and restriction of development in the Greenheart, have already been mentioned. The 1966 Second Report also contained a remarkable population projection, Netherlands 2000 (fig. 14.5), which assumed continuous economic and population growth and the need to control vigorously the growth of the Randstad cities. To that end, the Randstad came under an investment levy with 40 per cent tax on all development projects, clearly designed to slow down its growth.

However, from 1973–76, in the Third Report on Physical Planning, attitudes changed. There was a major reappraisal of policies, which had been overtaken by events. The economic recession, a rapid decline in the birth rate, and a reduction in immigration, suggested that there was no longer such a pressing need for population dispersal from the Randstad cities. Indeed, with environmental pressure for conservation of historic buildings, and the need for renovation of inner-city areas such as the Jordaan in Amsterdam, it was realised that the physical, social and economic fabric of the major cities was now under pressure. From 1976 to the 1984 Structure Plan, the following policies were followed:

(a) the preservation of the Greenheart and the maintenance of buffer zones between the cities was continued, albeit with less rigidity;

(b) continuing radial decentralisation plans in the city region;

(c) the removal in 1983 of the 40-per-cent investment levy in the Randstad;

(d) the revitalisation and urban renewal of 12 inner-city areas, including the Jordaan in Amsterdam; continued suburban development on peripheral housing estates such as Biljemeer to the south of Amsterdam.

The Fourth Report on Physical Planning in 1989 marked a radical departure from the earlier national plans. This sees Randstad as the essential motor of the Dutch economy in competition with south-east England, Central Belgium and Rhine–Ruhr (a reflection of the Single European Market). The planning authorities therefore need to promote the region to potential investors and to encourage not discourage growth. This means that the peripheral regions of the Netherlands are no longer able to depend on subsidies from the government for development relocated from the Dutch core. However, the plan sees this as an advantage for peripheral regions as they are free to generate their own development around groupings of major urban nodes such as Groningen/Assen/Drachten, Arnhem/Nijmegen and Maastricht/Heerlen. Alongside this plan are proposals to improve the accessibility of Randstad through limiting the growth of car use and improving infrastructure by means of more sustainable modes of transport (rail and inland waterways) which are less sensitive to congestion. Developments include the expansion of Schiphol airport and the port of Rotterdam, five new cross-river road links, a high-speed rail link between Amsterdam and Paris and a rail freight link between Rotterdam and Germany (the Betuwe line).

The Randstad cities form a unique physical, morphological, functional and economic unit in the Rhine delta. Their significance is reflected in the very detailed urban and regional structure plans which have been adopted and modified by the Dutch government since 1945.

15

DENMARK: DAIRY SPECIALIST AND GATEWAY TO NORTHERN EUROPE

RURAL–URBAN CHANGE

Denmark is renowned for its dairy production based essentially upon the successful export of butter, bacon and eggs, and fresh, frozen and canned foods associated with livestock – cattle, pigs and poultry. The total population of 5.2 million people has traditionally been rural, living in small market centres, coastal ports and agricultural villages. One of the remarkable characteristics of modern Denmark, however, is the enormous growth, industrialisation and increasing importance of Copenhagen, now a city of 1.3 million people, 25 per cent of the country's total population. The purpose of this chapter will be to examine Denmark with this contrast in mind.

LANDSCAPES AND LAND–USE

The extremely complicated glacial history of Denmark has produced two areas of landscape, one in West Jutland and the other in East Jutland and the islands (fig. 15.1).

West Jutland

The outwash plain and older morainic landscape of the Saale/Riss glaciation which covers the western part of Jutland form low sandy hills rising from the

North Sea sand dunes and coastal marshes. They were for long covered in heath interspersed with birch and oak – picturesque but wasteland and agriculturally unproductive. Soils are podsolised, known locally as 'blegsand' (bleached, sterile, ash-coloured sand) often with hard pan and accumulations of sour humus or peat. The reclamation of this area from the late nineteenth century onwards is one of the success stories of Danish energy and of comparable importance to similar Dutch areas. The growth in population in Europe, coupled with rising standards of nutrition, caused a rise in the demand for dairy produce; this led to an increasing need for more agricultural land which, in turn, began the systematic reclamation of the western heathlands. The clearance of woodland and burning of the heath was followed by deep ploughing to break up the hard pan, regular draining and heavy application of fertilisers. The landscape of heather moor is now

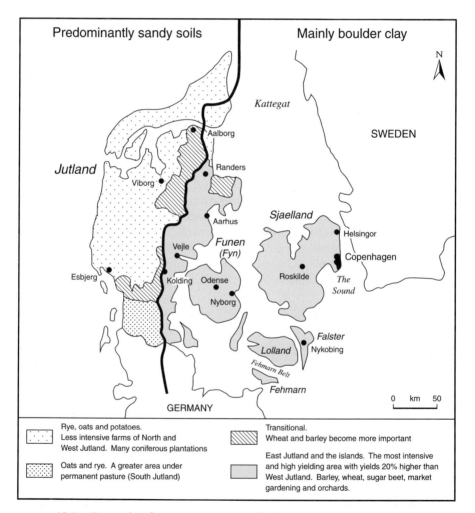

FIGURE 15.1   *Denmark – farming economy generalised*

replaced to a very large extent by coniferous plantations, fields of pasture and crops, and some of the most modern farms in Denmark. These modern farms and the straight roads which lead to them are often dispersed throughout the countryside and are outside the old villages, a pattern indicative of late reclamation and secondary settlement. So successful has been the reclamation of the heathlands that today improved farmland covers over 70 per cent of the country. This 'inner colonisation' of West Jutland has made it possible for both industrialisation and towns to spread with small loss to farmland.

East Jutland and the islands

A younger moraine landscape exists in East Jutland and the islands of the Danish Archipelago, that is the area east of the main stationary line marking the limit of the later Weichsel/Wurm glaciation. Here there is much more boulder clay, giving rise to a brown forest soil, which even here is a highly improved soil due to the rational application of manure over the centuries, continued soil ventilation by cultivation, and the practice of crop rotation. Thus there is now a farmscape which bears little relationship to the original temperate forest, marsh and heath because of human interference.

The development of intensive arable-livestock farming

Denmark's role as a high-quality dairy-food producer is illustrated by its artificial farmscape, principally created by the organisation and the vigour of the farmer, government, and the whole population. The creation of this system is a result of the economic changes which were associated with the period post-1880. Danish farmers could not compete with large imports of low-cost wheat from the new world grasslands. The system of large manorial and crown farms and peasant subsistence farms existing side by side began to change dramatically. After a deliberate land policy to encourage the break-up of the large estates, and the establishment of family smallholdings,

Type of land use	Percentage of total	
Arable	61	Total land in
Permanent pasture	5	agricultural
Fruit/other crops	1	use 67 per cent
Woodland	11	
Heathland ⎫		
Urban ⎭	22	

FIGURE 15.2   *Denmark – land-use, 1993*

the typical Danish farm now has an area of between 10 and 30 ha. There is, however, considerable variation across the country, and in the sandy poorer soils of West Jutland, the individual farm tends to be much larger.

Alongside these changes in tenure to a tenant-farmer system, Denmark also turned to intensive dairy farming as the best way of utilising its small area, and utilising the real advantage in position, that of proximity to the two greatest industrial nations in Europe, Germany and the UK, who required large quantities of food. It is upon the cultivation of fodder crops that Denmark relies for efficiency, since it must be stressed that nature has not really endowed the country with excellent conditions for dairy farming. The climate is not particularly suitable for grass growing, with a rather inadequate precipitation of below 635 mm, and spring comes later than in most dairy countries, giving a shorter growing season. Throughout the winter livestock must be stall-fed on fodder crops, some of which must be imported. The intensive use of land through arable farming and fodder crops is therefore essential in order to gain the maximum foodstuffs from a limited area (fig. 15.2). Grain crops, wheat, rye, barley and oats usually occupy 63 per cent of total agricultural land; 15 per cent is under rotation grass; 15 per cent is under pulses and root crops including beet, mangolds, kohlrabi and potatoes; and only 7 per cent is under permanent grass. This is most unusual amongst dairy-farming economies, which are usually predominantly pastureland. Denmark is probably the most intensive dairy-farming country in the world. There are variations: West Jutland still has a greater acreage under rye; East Jutland and the islands have higher yields (fig. 15.1); around Copenhagen peas, beans, carrots and market-garden and salad crops are

The Danish dairy-farming landscape with modern farm buildings, Friesian cattle and rotation grassland

298

important; and the islands contain 75 per cent of the area of fruit and market garden crops. The main theme is animal husbandry, with 85 per cent of crops used as stockfeed. The highest yields come from root crops, which are at home in the Danish soils and climate with its long autumns, and roots and grass provide rough coarse feed. Cereals are invaluable because they supply the carbohydrate for concentrated feedstuffs. Proteins are supplied mainly by oil seeds which have to be imported.

Danish cattle are principally of two national breeds. Black and white milch cows are found mostly in West Jutland because of their hardiness and ability to thrive in areas of poor grass. The Danish Red breed is widespread throughout the country. Jerseys and Shorthorns are increasing in popularity. Yields of milk are very high and the vast bulk (61 per cent) goes for butter-making. Cheese-making consumes 13 per cent, and the rest goes for cream, condensed milk and milk-powder, with the intensive nature of the operation apparent as the skimmed milk is returned to the farms for pig-feed. The number of pigs has increased considerably to 10.4 million, the main variety being the Landrace. Skimmed milk from the dairies is added to grain, potatoes and sugar-beet toppings to feed these animals which produce the high-quality ham and bacon for which Denmark is famous. The third element in the economy is a battery-rearing operation associated with smaller farms of less than 10 ha: eggs and poultry meat account for 12 per cent of the total value of farm produce.

The most important single characteristic of Danish farming is its dynamic efficiency. The cooperative movement is carried to its ultimate limits in the loan of machinery, the dissemination of research, and the organised processing and marketing of produce in creameries and factories. Government aid, the systematic construction of Esbjerg as a port for trade with the UK, agricultural schools, and price guarantees are matched by very high inspection standards. The significance of dairy products is shown by the fact that farm produce provides about 29 per cent of Denmark's exports by value. Agriculture is very dependent upon export markets for its continued prosperity, and Denmark's dilemma in the 1960s was that its two greatest markets, the UK and West Germany, were within different tariff groupings,

| | Percentage of total exports | | | |
Export	1981	1986	1990	1993
Food and beverages	30.9	27.9	26.2	26.5
Minerals and fuel	3.2	3.0	3.4	3.5
Crude materials	7.3	6.4	4.7	4.6
Machinery and transport	24.9	24.6	26.4	25.6
Other manufactures	33.7	38.1	39.3	39.8

FIGURE 15.3 *Denmark – principal exports*

EFTA and the EEC. The accession of the UK with Denmark to the EEC meant that these two major markets were assured. Denmark's principal contribution to the EU is as a very significant supplier of dairy foods. However, this picture is changing as the balance between agriculture and industry/services is altering quite dramatically (fig. 15.3).

INDUSTRIAL AND URBAN CHANGES

The traditional picture of rural Denmark has now changed considerably, with rapid industrialisation and urbanisation. There has been a marked change in the employment structure of the country. The number of workers in industry and the services has risen whilst those in agriculture have fallen dramatically. Industrial production is now much more significant than agriculture in terms of exports (figs. 15.3 and 15.4).

Denmark has a major proportion of its total population concentrated within the capital city. In 1992 Greater Copenhagen had a population of 1.3 million out of 5.2 million, approximately 25 per cent. The development of the city may be considered under four headings: site and origins; the establishment of the 'Freeport' in 1894; modern residential expansion and the city as a tourist attraction; development as a communications centre linking northern and western Europe.

Copenhagen and the Baltic Sea

The old city of Copenhagen (fig. 15.5) was built as a safe anchorage and deep-water port on the narrow strait between Zeeland (Sjaelland) and the small island of Amager, and it developed an early commercial importance as one of the major trading ports of the Hanseatic League in the thirteenth century. Its traditional role was as entry port into the Baltic Sea via the Ore Sund, the sound between Denmark and Sweden. The part of Sweden directly opposite Copenhagen was Danish territory (the province of Scania) until 1660, and thus the city was originally in a much more central position to Denmark as a whole.

| Employment sector | Percentage of employed population | | | | | |
	1950	1970	1977	1981	1986	1993
Agriculture	25	11.5	9.8	8.5	6.2	5.1
Manufacturing	28	32.5	31.5	27.1	27.0	26.5
Services	47	56.0	58.7	64.4	66.8	68.4

FIGURE 15.4 *Denmark – employment*

The Kiel canal and the 'Freeport'

A change of critical importance came with the opening of the Kiel canal in 1894. This provided the city with serious competition by giving a more direct entry into the Baltic, and therefore threatened its role and prosperity as entry point to the Baltic. One answer to this problem was the development of the 'Frijhaven', Copenhagen Freeport, which was built at the northern end of the existing city harbour where it joins the Ore Sund. This has now become one of the largest entrepôt ports of Europe, with over 50 per cent of total Danish imports including petroleum, coal, metal ores, timber, fertilisers and oil seeds (agricultural and industrial raw materials). Perhaps more significant was the resulting industrial expansion: over 45 per cent of Denmark's industrial workers are now employed in Copenhagen. Shipbuilding and repairing, marine engineering, oil storage for bunkering, and the generation of electricity are large-scale activities. There are also grain mills, milk- and meat-processing factories – with cattle-cake as a by-product – vegetable canning, tobacco processing, and brewing (particularly Tuborg and Carlsberg lagers) and fertiliser (phosphates), all of which have a clear association with agriculture. The industrial base, however, is very varied, with engineering, electricals and electronics, automobile assembly, printing, textiles, shoes, rubber, soap, paint and pharmaceuticals. Special mention must be made of furniture, stainless steel and glassware, high-quality Danish consumer goods specialities.

The expansion of the city

The expansion of the city since the eighteenth century has dramatically changed the balance of its structure and morphology. Amager Island was the initial area of expansion with Christianshavn and Sundbyern to the south of the old city. In the present century, however, the west and north have figured largely in an exceptional rate of growth, with the main area of suburban expansion in the districts of Fredericksberg and Gentofte. These are added to Copenhagen itself to give a total population of 1.3 million. The inner city is surrounded by the old canal and a ring of gardens of which the Tivoli is the most famous. A thriving tourist industry is based upon the attraction of the old city, the Christiansborg and Rosenberg palaces and the specialised traditional industries such as the Royal Danish porcelain factory, and silverware and other fine craftwork.

Copenhagen as a communications centre

A large part of the increased importance of the city since 1960 is its developing function as a communications centre. Ferry services across the Sound via Helsingor to Halsingborg, Malmö and Halmstad in Sweden, and

Bridge over the Little Belt linking the Danish island of Funen with Jutland

to Travemunde (Lubeck) illustrate the position of the city as a bridge between continental Europe and Scandinavia. The international airport at Kastrup on Amager island is just 9.5 km south of the city centre and in addition to European flights, there is the Polar route to Canada and Tokyo. Three major projects could increase the nodality of the city as a European–Scandinavian land-bridge (fig. 15.5): (1) a fixed rail and road link under the Great Belt (now under construction) to link Zeeland with Funen and Jutland and thence to Germany; (2) a 17 km road and rail bridge and tunnel across the Sound to Malmö (the 'Oresund link') via the Danish island of Saltholm; (3) a third bridge over the Fehmarn belt via Falster and Lolland across to Puttgarde on the German island of Fehmarn and thence to Kiel and Lubeck. These fixed links would be a critical step forward for the city, and would help continue its present growth. The single most significant of the three is the Oresund link which could eventually result in the fusion of Malmö and Copenhagen to create a conurbation, the first in Scandinavia. An agreement over the link was made between the governments of Sweden and Denmark in 1991, with a planned opening in 1997, but since then the link has become an emotive issue (particularly in Sweden), with fears that it could alter the Baltic Sea's ecological balance. Environmentalists argue that the link would restrict the flow of relatively clean salt water into the polluted

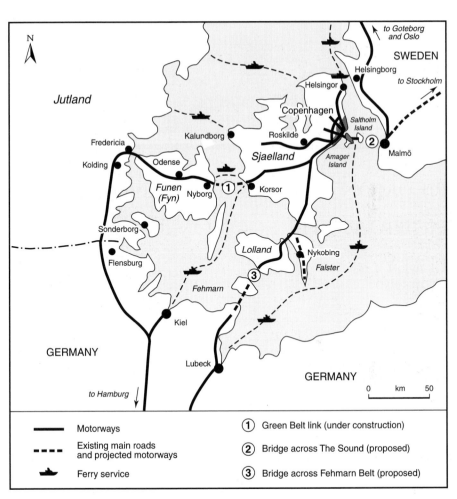

FIGURE 15.5   *Copenhagen and the Danish islands – developing transport links*

Baltic Sea. In 1994, however, the Swedish government gave formal approval for the link to go ahead, and it is now expected to be completed in the year 2000.

16

PIEDMONT, LOMBARDY AND LIGURIA: THE ECONOMIC CORE OF ITALY

The wealthy north

The administrative regions of Piedmont, Lombardy and Liguria form the extreme north-western corner of Italy, and represent a small proportion (some 20 per cent) of the total area of the country, yet they occupy a dominant place in the Italian economy. Piedmont originated as the Duchy of Savoy and from the sixteenth century its main city, Turin, has exercised an important influence over the formation and subsequent industrialisation of Italy. Lombardy is centred around the ancient Duchy and city of Milan, although it covers much of the central part of the Po basin. Liguria is a narrow coastal strip with the port of Genoa as its major focal point. Structurally the three regions are dissimilar. The Ligurian coast forms part of the Maritime Alps and Apennines and is a narrow coastal strip with fast-flowing streams and steep valleys making communications very difficult. The apparent uniformity of the Po basin masks a landscape which is rich in contrasts (fig. 16.1). It varies from the sub-alpine hilly margins, with long tributary valleys such as the Dora Baltea and Dora Riparia, to the upper and lower plains divided by the line of fontanili springs and broken by the occasional low hills of moraine, such as the Serra D'Ivrea north of Turin, and the deeply incised hill country of Monferrato and Le Langhe, south of Turin. Climatically there are also considerable contrasts. Liguria is sheltered from the north by the mountains and enjoys a dry summer and a mildness of climate more truly Mediterranean and reminiscent of southern Italy. On the other hand, the plain of Lombardy has cold winters of continental origin, hot summers (24 °C) with a tendency to thunderstorms, and a

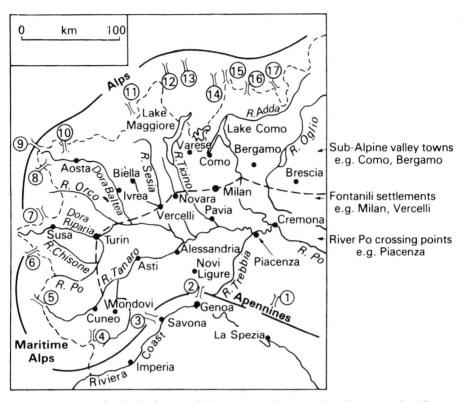

FIGURE 16.1 *Lombardy, Piedmont and Liguria   1. Cisa pass   2. Giovi pass   3. Altare pass   4. Tenda pass   5. Maddalena pass   6. Mt Genevre pass   7. Mt Cenis pass 8. Little St Bernard pass.   9. Mt Blanc tunnel   10. Grand St Bernard pass 11. Simplon pass   12. St Gotthard pass   13. Luckmanier pass   14. San Bernardino pass   15. Splugen pass   16. Maloja pass   17. Bernina pass*

well-distributed rainfall. This stimulating climate can be related to the traditional energy of the people of northern Italy.

Overriding all these differences, however, is a common feature. This is the domination of the Italian economy by the three cities of Genoa, Milan and Turin. During the Middle Ages the significant factors were the rich endowment of a well-watered plain and a climate beneficial to large-scale agriculture. The control of water supplies both for irrigation and energy has been an essential feature throughout. Equally as important has been proximity to the passes into France, Switzerland and northern Europe, and maritime access via Genoa. This has encouraged enterprise, new ideas, commerce and industry, best illustrated by the extraordinary vitality of city life throughout the region's history. This proximity to north-western Europe is now physically reinforced by road tunnels, such as the Mont Blanc, and by the growing network of autostrada (fig. 16.2). The EU has brought a fundamental change in attitudes and in economic integration, which has benefited Italy as a whole enormously. This populous triangle, rich in farmland, industry and city life, is closest to the West European growth axis, and has developed a dominating position as the economic core of Italy.

AGRICULTURE

The extensive plain drained by the Upper Po and its tributary network, the encircling mountains and their foothills, and south-facing Ligurian coast, exhibit a wide variety of farm landscapes (fig. 16.3). The whole area is one of the EU's major warm-temperate food-producing zones. The principal divisions are outlined in the following pages.

The Piedmont plain

The Piedmontese plain of fine fluvio-glacial deposits and alluvium is centred on Turin, but describes a wide arc from the Cuneo basin in the south, and is continued eastwards along the valley of the Po to the basin of Alessandria. Non-irrigated cereals are the dominant type, with wheat, maize, potatoes, beans and fodder as the main field crops; the fields are often lined with tree crops of apples, pears, plums or vines. The numerous tributaries of the Po give the area a well-watered look, and the river terraces are broken by steep bluffs commonly in woodland, whilst the flood plains are often irrigated. The plain of Alessandria, in particular, specialises in market gardening, with sugar beet at Marengo, and is the chief granary of Piedmont. The farms are substantial holdings, often over 50 ha, with large, prosperous-looking farmhouses, grain silos and outbuildings.

Monferrato hill country

To the south of Turin lie the foothills of the Apennines, the Monferrato and Le Langhe hill country. The northward-flowing River Tanaro follows an attractively varied landscape of cuestas, vales and rolling hills, with many hill-top villages and market towns such as Mondovi and Ceva, which lie on the route to the coast at Savona. The speciality of the area is viticulture, particularly around Asti and Alba. Here there are nearly 150 000 ha of specialised vineyards which produce the famous sparkling Moscato D'Asti, and Torinese Vermouth. There is also a large production of red wines, notably Barbera, Dolcetto and Barbaresco. In other parts there is a patchwork of cereals, pasture and cattle raising, with some fruit and market gardening, but farms are small, generally 2 to 3 ha, and this part of Piedmont suffers from the drift of population to the cities. As the higher slopes of the Apennines are reached, there are hazelnuts, truffles and chestnuts in valleys such as the upper Tanaro.

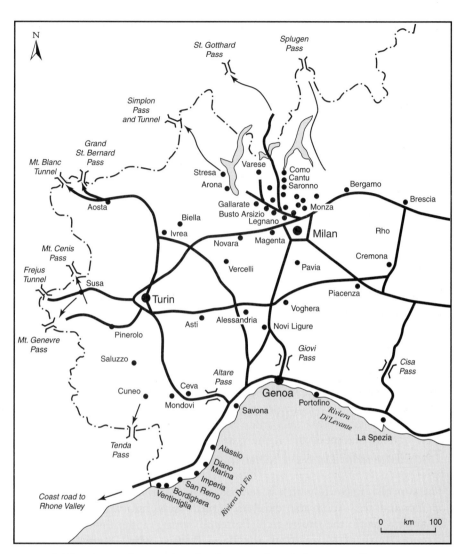

FIGURE 16.2   *Autostrada network and major routes through the western Alps*

The Alpine hill country

To the north and west of Turin the plain merges into the Alpine hill country. At the exits to the Val Di Susa and the Val D'Aosta there are extensive moraines which form irregular hills. The Serra D'Ivrea is one example, its surface covered with heathland and chestnut woods. The Val D'Aosta, which carries the beautiful Dora Baltea river has the classic Alpine succession of pasture and tiny fields of hay, rye and potatoes on the flats, orchards on the lower slopes, followed by terraced vineyards supported on trestles to counteract the effects of damp from the high rainfall (1000 mm). Above this are bare slopes and the high pastures used for the spring migration of farm animals. There are also abandoned terraces and farmhouses, indicative of the retreat to lower slopes and more beneficial soil. In the western Italian Alps as a whole only 6 per cent of the land is classed as cultivated. In the upper Po valley to the south-west of Turin are the sheltered valleys of the Saluzzese with orchards, vines, palms and magnolias, and a four-year rotation of cereals with hay and root crops.

The 'Rice Bowl'

Probably the most distinctive farming type is the 'Rice Bowl' of Vercelli and Novara. Half-a-million hectares of heavy clay soils are irrigated in vast monotonous fields which are carefully terraced and bordered with screens of Lombardy poplar and willow. The farms are large, usually over 50 ha, and isolated, mostly built around a courtyard and containing grain stores, machinery, sheds and accommodation for seasonal workers. Up to 80 per cent of the land is under rice. The ploughing, cultivation and harvesting of the rice is done by machine, but the planting is done by hand, with seasonal labour. Yields are high, averaging 12 tonnes per ha. There is heavy use of fertilisers, and although monoculture has traditionally been the pattern, there is now a growing diversification towards rotation fodder and milk production. Fontanili springs were used as early as the thirteenth century, but the real intensification of farming came with the construction of the Cavour canal in 1863. The Vercellese is an excellent example of large-scale, heavily capitalised farming, with irrigation as the basis for intensive rice production.

The Alta and Bassa Pianura around Milan

The part of Lombardy which is centred upon Milan lies mainly between the Ticino and the Adda and exhibits a more straightforward division than Piedmont, with the water-rich Fontanili spring zone dividing the Alta Pianura, north of Milan, from the Bassa Pianura which stretches south to Piacenza on the River Po. The excellent supplies of water and their control and exploitation are the key to Lombardy's historic agricultural productivity. About 60 per cent of the farmland is irrigated, and of this 40 per cent comes from the Fontanili which has been used since the eleventh century. The rest comes from the extensive canal system which utilises the waters of the Ticino, Adda, Lambro, Sesia and Oglio rivers, by crossing the interfluves in an east–west network stretching from Turin to Brescia. The most important of these are the Cavour and Villoresi canals.

Along the line of the Fontanili, the high water table encourages dairy farming. The cattle are reared on water meadows (Marcite) which are irrigated continuously ensuring a large number of fodder cuttings (ten are usual). The cattle are stall-fed in the 'cassini', which is a special variety of the 'Corte', the large Italian courtyard farm. The production of milk is geared to cheese-making, in particular Parmesan and Gorgonzola, and butter.

South of Fontanili, on the lower plain, irrigation, though still important, is more intermittent, and fodder crops are grown in conjunction with wheat and maize. There is often a seven-year rotation, with four years of cereals, followed by three years of meadow, indicating the continuing importance of dairy farming. The main hazard on the low plains is of flooding, creating the necessity for high levées.

The intensive livestock economy thus described is not typical of Italy, nor is the capitalised farm operated with wage labourers generally typical of the Mediterranean area. The medium-sized and large farm holdings with their prosperous 'Corte' are a particular feature of the Lombardy and Piedmont plains. The urban life of the cities of Milan and Turin has been sustained since the Middle Ages and has been a major impetus to the efficient production of food, the utilisation of new techniques and the specialisation associated with commercial agriculture. The administration of these provinces was more enlightened than most, and the break-up of the large medieval estates into viable farm holdings was carried out in the nineteenth century.

The Ligurian coastal fringe

Liguria forms the maritime facade for the interior plains of Lombardy and Piedmont. It also forms a considerable barrier, with over 65 per cent of its

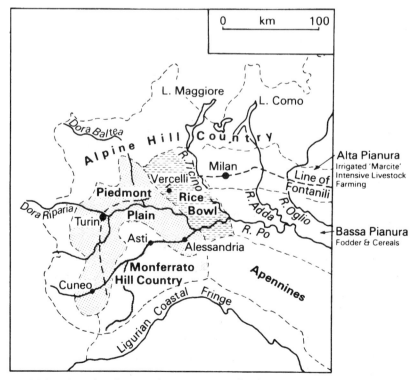

FIGURE 16.3   *Agricultural regions (source – DS Walker)*

land area classed as mountainous and the rest hilly, with only limited alluvial flats. Agriculturally, Liguria is therefore a difficult region, with only 11 per cent of the land cultivated. Tree crops dominate, with olives and vines.

There are three sections to the province: the Riviera Centrale, containing the port of Genoa; the Riviera di Levante, stretching eastwards to La Spezia; and the Riviera di Ponente, which stretches from Genoa westwards to the French frontier; and it is this last section which has the most interesting and specialised agriculture. The Riviera Di Ponente is often called the 'Riviera of Flowers' or Riviera Dei Fiori. It faces south-east, and is sheltered from the north by the Apennines. It has drier, milder conditions than the rest of Liguria, and its sheltered bays have many sub-tropical plants, exotic palms, cypresses and bougainvilleas. There is a string of popular holiday resorts from Ventmiglia (on the French frontier) to Alassio, and the hillsides are heavily terraced with stone walls and covered with glasshouses for the cultivation of garden flowers. Flori-culture is of key importance along this coast, and Ventimiglia has a famous traditional flower market. San Remo in particular is well-known for the cultivation of roses and carnations. Citrus fruits, early vegetables, and orchards of apples and plums are found on flatter alluvial fans of irrigable land, as at Albenga and Diano Marina. Vines, figs, and olives alternate on the lower slopes with chestnut woods, and there is considerable woodland on the upper slopes, petering out into poor pasture.

THE ITALIAN INDUSTRIAL TRIANGLE

Although there are other heavily industrialised zones in northern Italy, notably at Marghera near Venice, nevertheless the major industrial concentration in Italy lies within Lombardy, Piedmont and Liguria. Here lies the core of Italy's wealth production. Lombardy has little more than one-seventh of Italy's population, but provides one-fifth of the national product, and 40 per cent of industrial exports. It has a quarter of the industrial workers, and provides over 35 per cent of the taxes paid by industrial companies. Its industry is broadly based upon a vast number of small and medium-sized concerns. Around Milan there are over 100 000 industrial concerns, and the largest factory in the city employs 18 000 workers, a small figure when compared with the 70 400 workers of the main Fiat factory in Turin. Piedmont provides 9 per cent of the country's national product, and one-seventh of the industrial output, but, unlike Lombardy, its wealth is built around a few large enterprises. Fiat of Turin employs 118 000 workers, and thousands more are indirectly dependent upon it for a livelihood. Turin is an excellent example of a company city, and certainly its life revolves around the car industry. Liguria's wealth is based first upon the port of Genoa and its subsidiary port, Savona, and the modern steel mills, shipbuilding yards and engineering industries which lie on the coast. The other source of wealth lies in the old established tourist trade along the

Riviera Dei Fiori. Many well-known resorts line the coast for 150 km eastwards from the French Riviera around the Gulf of Genoa.

Milan

Milan originated as Roman Mediolanum, and became a famous ecclesiastical centre during the latter part of the Roman Empire. During the revival of city life in the eleventh century it again prospered and was a medieval industrial, commercial and banking centre of great importance. The city typifies the extraordinary tenacity of the cities of the northern Italian plains, as they survived the centuries of stagnation, warfare and misrule, and from the nineteenth century onwards industrial development came steadily, with the concentrated economic advantages which Lombardy could now exploit. These were the accrued agricultural commercial wealth, the enterprising spirit of the population, and hydro-electric power from the Alps. Perhaps most important was the development of modern communications so that the city could assume its natural position as the chief focus of road and rail routes within the plain and across the Alps, and to the Ligurian and Venetian coasts. Food processing (pasta, confectionery, etc.) is concentrated in the Greater Milan area. In particular, cheese making, with the famous Gorgonzola, Parmesan, Bel Paese and Stracchino cheeses, is found in Milan and the cities to the south – Lodi, Pavia and Piacenza.

However, the industries which are basic to the prosperity of the area are engineering of all kinds, textiles, and chemicals. The textile industry is located mainly in the upper plain to the north of Milan, and is associated with the growth of a major agglomeration of industrial towns (fig. 16.2), stretching north to the Alpine valleys, which were the original source of power. The cotton industry is represented strongly to the north-west of Busto Arsizio, Legnano, Varese and Gallarate, and to the north-east at Monza and Bergamo. Silk is manufactured in Como, and woollens in Bergamo province, whilst the newer synthetic fibres are present in Milan itself.

The chemical industry is concentrated in Milan and Novara, with many factories of the Enichem group. There are several petrochemical plants, and an important feature is the existence of substantial natural-gas deposits in the lower plain. The headquarters of ENI, the state oil and gas agency, is at Milan. Fertilisers, artificial rubber and Pirelli tyres are all important, whilst there is a major pharmaceuticals industry in Milan, based largely upon the high level of demand in the northern cities.

It is in the engineering field, however, that the real industrial vitality of Milan is based. Prior to the post-1945 movement to the integrated coastal steelworks, Italy's steel industry was dominated by Lombardy, and there were steelworks based on scrap at Sesto San Giovanni, Bergamo and Brescia. Output is now relatively small, but it has maintained its presence through investment and the large local market of steel-using industries. Foundry and steel-making equipment, presses, lathes and engines, and heavy electrical generating equipment are located at Milan. The vehicle industry is represented by Innocenti and Alfa Romeo (subsidiaries of Fiat). The light-engineering section includes machine tools, calculators, precision instrument, textile machinery, motor scooters, motor cycles and sewing machines.

The footwear industry is centred at Vigevano to the south-west of Milan, but Milan itself and Varese are other centres. Paper and furniture manufacture is also represented strongly in the satellite towns of the upper plain from Vercelli to Como.

The great variety of industry in Lombardy, particularly in Greater Milan, is a reflection of its mature industrial structure. Milan itself is a city of almost capital rank. It is the financial capital of Italy with major commercial, insurance and banking operations of greater significance than those of Rome. It has the country's most significant trade fair, it is a great publishing centre, and its cultural activities are metropolitan in character.

Turin

Turin is the chief city of Piedmont, and stands at the confluence of the Dora Riparia and Po rivers, but the modern significance of its position is the control of the passes emerging from the western end of the Alps. It rose to importance only in the sixteenth century when chosen as the capital city of the House of Savoy, under whose guidance it became the chief force in the unification of Italy in the mid-nineteenth century. During the twentieth century, with the development of roads, railways and modern autostrada, the importance of its position has again been underlined (fig. 16.2). It controls the important routes south to the Ligurian coast and Riviera, westwards via the Mont Genêvre and Mont Cenis passes, and northwards through the Dora Baltea river valley to the Grand St Bernard Pass into Switzerland and the Mont Blanc road tunnel into France.

Turin is, however, the second industrial centre of Italy. The rulers of Savoy were instrumental in giving Piedmont a measure of industrialisation which was exceptional for Italy. The Turin arsenal was followed in 1900 by the car companies of Fiat and Lancia, and by Olivetti typewriters. The utilisation of the hydro-electric power of the Alpine valleys and the development of strategic industries under Mussolini in the 1930s firmly established Turin as a leading industrial city. The engineering industry, particularly car manufacturing, has boomed since 1950, and the population of Turin has reached 1.1 million, with the absorption into the city of nearly half-a-million Italians from the south. Car production is dominated by the large integrated Fiat factory at Mirafiori: Fiat in Turin employs 118 000 workers across the city. It also produces a vast range of electrical and engineering products such as marine and aero engines, electric motors, railway stock, tractors and domestic appliances. It is even concerned with the construction of Alpine tunnels and nuclear engineering. Turin (and Ivrea to the north with the Olivetti company) are examples of 'company towns'.

The autostrada via the Grand St Bernard Pass linking Aosta, Italy, with the Rhône valley and Switzerland

Ancillary industries, such as sheet steel, machine tools, rubber and ball-bearings, complete the picture of car assembly.

Although Turin does not have a constellation of subsidiary industrial towns like Milan, nevertheless there are a number of important rank. To the south are Alessandria and Cuneo, both route centres, Novi Ligure (steel), and Asti, a famous wine-processing town. To the west is the Dora Riparia valley to the Mont Cenis pass, with light industries at Susa and Bussoleno. To the north-east lies the woollen textile town of Biella.

Perhaps the most interesting area of development is the Dora Baltea valley. Along it runs the autostrada to the Mont Blanc tunnel and Grand St. Bernard Pass, the most important routes through the western Alps (fig. 16.2). Hydro-electric power is well developed, and aluminium works at Borgofranco and rayon at Chatillon are based upon this. At Aosta itself there is a small steelworks, based upon local supplies of magnetite. Another source of wealth is the rapidly developing tourist industry, of both winter and summer resorts. Courmayeur and St Vincent in the Val D'Aosta now have a greatly increased accessibility. Before the construction of the modern roads and tunnels in the 1960s, the Val D'Aosta was isolated from France and Switzerland for seven months of the year. This change typifies northern Italy's new close relationship with north-west Europe.

Genoa

Genoa was a flourishing port in the Middle Ages, when it rivalled Venice in the Levantine trade, but its importance shrank from the sixteenth century onwards with the growth of Atlantic shipping. Cavour, the Piedmontese statesman, saw its potential as an outlet for the whole of northern Italy and the Alpine regions. Under his guidance the port facilities were considerably improved and a railway link from Turin established. At the same time the Suez canal had a major regenerative effect upon Mediterranean shipping.

Although the port has a major disadvantage due to its mountainous coastline and consequent lack of space for development, there is, however, a major transport advantage. The mountains are at their lowest and narrowest point behind Genoa, and this funnels traffic from the interior into the Giovi pass (fig. 16.2), which is traversed by two railways and the autostrada. There is also the higher Bochetta road pass close by, and the Turchino railway route. The trans-Alpine passes are important not only in allowing Genoa

The coastal autostrada along the intensively cultivated Ligurian Riviera near Savona

easy access to Piedmont and Lombardy, but also in facilitating the extension of its hinterland to Switzerland and beyond. Genoa is thus the natural outlet for Turin and Milan, and is an important corner of the Italian industrial triangle.

Genoa is now second in importance only to Marseilles on the EU southern flank (chapter 5, fig. 5.8). There are 27 km of quays and industrial suburbs, Sampierdarena, Cornigliano, Sestri, Pegli and Voltri, extending to the west of the city. Genoa deals mainly with imports and these constitute 90 per cent by tonnage of its total trade. Oil accounts for about two-thirds of the total tonnage, coal, mineral ores, grain, tropical foods, chemicals and textile fibres also being important. It is thus a major input point for raw materials, and associated with the oil terminals are the pipelines which carry oil from Genoa to Milan, Aigle in Switzerland and Ingolstadt in southern Germany.

Heavy industry has developed along the coast, particularly shipyards at Sestri and Voltri. At Cornigliano a coastal integrated steelworks has developed since 1945, and this is entirely dependent upon imports of scrap iron, West African iron ore and coal. There is also oil refining, metal smelting, machine tools and marine, electrical and railway equipment. Food processing based upon imports is also an important activity, with vegetable canning, grain-milling, soap manufacture, sugar refining, paper and pottery.

The other two Ligurian ports illustrate the importance of hinterlands. La Spezia naval base to the east has an excellent harbour, but is handicapped by difficult passes through the Apennines. Savona, by contrast, on the western side, has developed a special relationship with Turin, to which it has easy access via the Altare Pass. These links have increased rapidly since 1972 with the development of the autostrada from Turin, a spectacular example of modern engineering which joins the coastal autostrada at Savona.

TOURISM ALONG THE ITALIAN RIVIERA

The Riviera Di Levante, eastwards of Genoa, has a rugged coast of great beauty, with famous resorts like Portofino, Rapallo and Santa Margarita. The section of the coast west of Genoa has already been described as the Riviera Dei Fiori for its associations with fruit and flowers. It too has a beautiful rugged coastline and many seaside resorts including Ventimiglia, San Remo, Diano Marina and Alassio, which nestle in sheltered bays backed by wooded hills. The whole riviera coast has begun to experience considerable competition from newer tourist areas around the Mediterranean sea. It suffers from overcrowding due partly to its longstanding popularity, and partly to the difficulty of access by the inadequate roads. The completion of the autostrada along the coast from Avignon to Genoa and La Spezia, with interior links to Milan and Turin has largely removed this disadvantage (fig. 16.2). The revitalising effects of fast road transport are important to the whole region, but perhaps most of all to this beautiful Ligurian coast.

17

THE MEZZOGIORNO: ITALY'S
PROBLEM REGION

THE POOR SOUTH

The contrasts between northern and southern Italy are dramatic. The well-watered environment of the Plain of Lombardy, with its great traditions of urban life, commercial agriculture, bustling industry and busy transport networks, has no counterpart in the South. Italy is a land of two nations. South of Rome there is a clearly identifiable atmosphere of desiccation, impoverishment, lack of activity and an indefinable impression that this part of Europe is very different. To be more specific, Italians refer to the area as 'Il Mezzogiorno', the land of the noon-day sun. The Mezzogiorno comprises seven of Italy's 19 administrative regions (fig. 17.1) and contains over 21 million people or 37 per cent of the population. It still produces only about 26 per cent of the country's gross domestic product (fig. 17.2). Its population of 21 million people is more than twice that of Greece, which has much the same total area, indicating a major level of over-population. Emigration from the Mezzogiorno has been persistently high. Since 1900 over 8 million Italians have emigrated from the South, often to the northern cities, but in very large numbers to North America and other parts of the New World. Real perception of the problem began after the Second World War as illustrated by the following data. In the 1950s more than half the houses in the South were without drinking water, and 40 per cent without sanitary facilities. Most significant of all, because it underlines the basic problem, was the picture of agricultural employment. In 1950 the South had 57 per cent of its population employed in agriculture and only 20 per cent in industry, demonstrating its basically under-developed structure. The problems could be summarised as: a low level of economic activity; income levels less than half those of northern Italy; poor living conditions; an overwhelming dependence upon agriculture

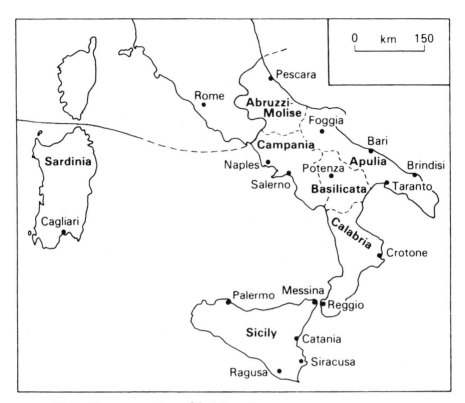

FIGURE 17.1 *The seven provinces of the Mezzogiorno*

with resulting rural overpopulation. Persistent out-migration has been one traditional answer to the situation, but it has not been enough. The population has continued to increase steadily and has remained stubbornly too high for the resources of the land to sustain. In the immediate post-1945 period the imbalance between Italy's South and North emerged as one of Europe's most intractable problems.

The disadvantages of the Mezzogiorno: physical, historical and economic

Water shortage

The small amount of rainfall and its seasonal occurrence are a major problem. Many parts of the South have only 500 mm of rainfall per annum, and in addition the summer drought, high rate of evaporation and considerable unreliability of rainfall create desiccated conditions for up to five months during the summer. Yet it is precisely during the summer period that the high sub-tropical temperatures would permit the growth of crops not easily cultivable anywhere else in the EU. Unless irrigation water

Gran Sasso mountains, Abruzzi-Molise. Droving sheep near Aquila

is available – and this is not easy because most rivers dry up in summer – intensive summer cropping is impossible, and the common answer to the drought is a wasteful fallow. There is generally under-utilisation of the land with extensive farming and heavy reliance upon wheat, olives and livestock grazing. Even grazing is limited owing to the absence of good year-round pasture, and the numbers of sheep and cattle are low compared to those in the North. The whole agricultural environment of the South is harsh, inferior, and marked by low productivity.

A mountainous landscape

Southern Italy is dominated by the Apennine mountains, and it has been estimated that over 40 per cent of the land area is mountainous and too steep for any form of cultivation. Another 45 per cent is classified as hill country which is prone to considerable soil exhaustion. Most of the southern Apennines are formed of limestone, much of which is dolomite. This hard dolomitic limestone gives a landscape of sharp peaks and bare slopes with the smallest vestiges of garigue or scrub vegetation. The highest peak, Corno Grande in the Abruzzi, rises to 2915 m. In other areas such as Apulia, the limestone gives bare karstic conditions. By contrast much of Calabria is granitic with the Pollino massif reaching 2275 m. Extensive plains are limited, and lowlands are confined to Foggia, the Naples–Salerno plain, and the 'heel' around Taranto. There is a basic poverty in the Mezzogiorno with its high proportion of uncultivable land, rugged and eroded slopes, dried-up riverbeds and desiccated landscape.

The legacy of the past

The history of the area has had a dramatic effect upon this landscape. During the period of the Greek and Roman civilisations, the South was a major granary with widespread cultivation of vines, cereals and olives. Mediterranean pines and other woodland covered the hillslopes. With the collapse of Roman power from the fifth century onwards, there was a prolonged period of political chaos and insecurity, with a succession of invasions from the North and piracy from the sea. Settlement moved inland and tended to concentrate in closely knit villages, often of great size, clustered on hilltops, where they could be more easily defended. The plains were abandoned and the foothills and mountain slopes became over-grazed and deforested, with ensuing soil erosion, extensive gullying on the hillsides, and lowland flooding leading to swamps and malarial infestation. From the eleventh century onwards the whole area, as the Kingdom of Naples, came under the corrupt rule of the Spanish House of Bourbon. Feudal serfdom with large absentee landlord estates called *latifundia* persisted into the middle of the twentieth century. These are generally large estates on the plains which practise monoculture based upon wheat alternated with fallow. This is extensive farming and under-utilises the resources of both the land and the

Villalago, near Aquila, Abruzzi-Molise. A hill-top village in the rugged Gran Sasso mountains, surrounded by abandoned terraces

people. Most of the South's sheep and cattle are grazed on the latifundia and transhumance is practised with livestock being taken to the nearby mountain slopes. The blight which they have brought to the South is seen in the under-employment of the farm labourers. Many peasants would have five or six weeks working time on their own plots of land, and then would look for work on the latifundia, some distance away. The peasants would wait, early in the mornings, in the piazzas of the towns and villages for the farm overseer to hire them for the day. Generally they would average only one hundred days' work per year, illustrating the low economic level at which the South existed well into the mid-twentieth century.

Too many people on the land

Pressure of population led to an increasing sub-division and fragmentation of land holdings. As late as 1950 over 70 per cent of holdings in the South were of less than 3 ha. These are the other side of the picture, known as *minifundia*. They usually existed on the poorer hilly mountainous land which experienced considerable sub-division amongst tenants and share-croppers. In 1950, 45 per cent of all agricultural workers in the South owned no land at all; 28 per cent were share-croppers who surrendered up to 60 per cent of their crop to the landowner as rent; only 27 per cent owned their own land. Fragmentation of farm holdings was the norm, with peasant farmers cultivating anything up to ten widely scattered plots of land. Such a system of tiny holdings, particularly with a proportion being share-cropped, was inadequate to support a family. Crop specialisation was almost impossible because of the need to maintain the family's food supply, and the pattern of farming was subsistence with very little entering commercial channels. Methods of cultivation were antiquated and labour intensive; insecurity of tenure was damaging to morale, and not conducive to mechanisation and capitalisation. Economic feudalism was the most distinguishing feature of the Mezzogiorno.

Isolation and a lack of raw materials

The essential bases for industrial development were lacking, as there was no coal or other raw materials of any significance, and the development of hydro-electric power, so important in the North, was retarded in the South by the fact that throughout the South industry was mainly small-scale and artisan in character. Perhaps most important of all was the isolation of the South from the main stream of European development during the nineteenth century, whilst the rest of Europe was industrialising rapidly. The great length of peninsular Italy (1000 km) and its physical nature was an inhibiting factor in communications. The backwardness associated with the corrupt rule of the Bourbon kings of Naples until 1861 meant that there was hardly any infrastructure of roads and railways. In 1861, the Mezzogiorno had only 99 km of railway, whilst in Italy as a whole there were 1798 km. All this contrasted markedly with the north of Italy (Chapter 16) whose

Region	Gross Domestic Product Lire ($\times 10^9$)			Gross Domestic Product as a % of EUR 12
	1960	1981	1992	1992
Italy	19 286	261 638	1 448 514	17.3
Lombardy	4147	54 040	288 986	3.5
Apulia	823	12 744	75 279	0.9
Basilicata	111	2035	9880	0.1
Calabria	374	5337	31 546	0.4
Abruzzi-Molise	370	5626	35 025	0.4
Campania	1225	16 735	99 709	1.2

FIGURE 17.2   *A comparison of gross domestic product (source – Eurostat)*

most important foundation for industrial wealth lay in its relatively easy access across the Alpine mountain passes into the core area of Europe. Furthermore, after the unification of Italy in 1861, the contrasts between North and South increased. The economic disadvantages of the South, remoteness from markets, higher fuel costs, and a feudal system of agriculture, were compounded by the illiteracy and unskilled nature of the population. In the newly unified Italy, the North held all the basic advantages, and as it rapidly became industrialised from the 1870s onwards, the gap between the two Italys steadily widened.

The Cassa per il Mezzogiorno

There have been piecemeal attempts to develop the economy and improve the environment of the South. Various projects to reclaim marshland and eradicate malaria, and to improve river channels and combat soil erosion were made during the nineteenth century. During the inter-war period, the Fascist government introduced a programme to drain and irrigate the land and improve agriculture. In the period immediately after 1945, land hunger and large-scale unemployment caused considerable unrest, and the problems of the South became really acute and were brought to the attention of the government and public opinion. The new democratic government of Italy realised that from political necessity alone, a major effort was needed to develop southern Italy. Furthermore, statistics were more readily available, which allowed assessments to be made and remedies to be suggested. A long-term strategy was favoured and a supra-regional body was proposed with direct powers and massive investment backing which could see the south as a whole and which would be able to plan a coordinated and vigorous development policy.

In March 1950 the Cassa per il Mezzogiorno (fund for the South) was

Province	NCI	Own resources Agriculture	Industry	Infrastructure and services	Total	Percentage share of total EIB loans
Campania	58	–	147	148	353	8.8
Abruzzi-Molise	–	12	10	–	22	0.5
Sud (Apulia, Basilicata, Calabria)	1	–	36	116	153	3.5
Sicily	15	–	23	38	76	1.4
Sardinia	–	–	29	–	29	0.7
Multi-regional projects	240	–	360	102	702	10.9
Total Mezzogiorno	314	12	605	404	1335	25.8

FIGURE 17.3   *EIB loans to the Mezzogiorno (million ECUs)*

	Expenditure (%) 1950 (proposals)	1950–65	1966–69	Estimated overall expenditure (%) 1950–80
Agriculture	77.0	56.1	24.7	12.7
Infrastructure	20.5	22.4	19.6	20.2
Industry	–	6.9	36.0	49.9
Tourism and special projects	2.5	14.6	19.7	10.6

FIGURE 17.4   *The Cassa per il Mezzogiorno (source – Allen and McLennan)*

established by the Italian Parliament as an executive body with powers to carry out initially a ten-year basic development plan. It was to operate in the seven regions of the South and also a small part of Latium near Rome. Considerable power was given to the Cassa. In addition to the power to initiate development projects, it also had coordinating power for development in every sector of the South's economy. The investment of government money was supplemented by private investment, both Italian and external, and by loans from the World Bank. Since the development of the EEC, the European Investment Bank has made a majority of its loans to the South (fig. 17.3). The Agricultural Guidance fund has been very important, and the Social and Regional funds have made significant contributions.

Agricultural improvement

Agriculture initially accounted for the major efforts of the Cassa, and the original planned investment earmarked 77 per cent of investment for agriculture (fig. 17.4). Industry was not included at all in the original plan. There were two principal methods of agricultural change: land reform; and the modernisation of farming techniques. Special agencies 'Ente Di Riforma' were set up to administer eight areas of land reform (fig. 17.5). These areas were set up by government decree and were not directly under the jurisdiction of the Cassa, and not all of them were in the Mezzogiorno as previously defined. Nevertheless they performed a valuable function, thereby providing landless peasants with holdings by expropriating large and inefficiently run latifundia. The large estates which were expropriated were those which generally had been badly managed and which had received

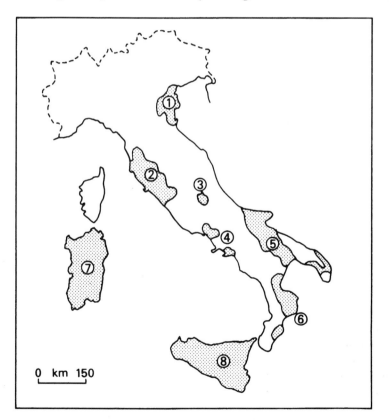

FIGURE 17.5   *Land reform agencies (source – Mountjoy)*   1. *Delta Padano*
2. *Tuscany–Lazio*   3. *Fucino*   4. *Volturno*   5. *Apulia–Basilicata*   6. *Sila*
7. *Sardinia*   8. *Sicily*

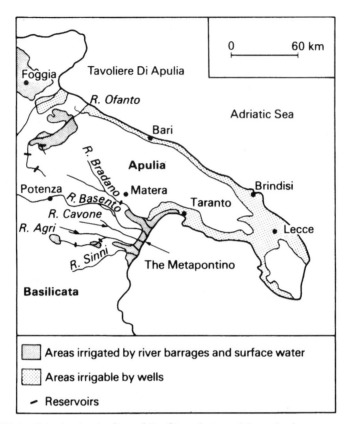

FIGURE 17.6   *Irrigation in Apulia and Basilicata (source –* Mountjoy*)*

virtually no investment. Particularly well-run farms were termed 'model farms' and exempted from expropriation. The whole object was to carry out close settlement, to provide for new villages and to increase productivity with irrigation and land-improvement schemes, so that intensive cash-crop farming on small holdings would replace extensive wheat cultivation. Viable family holdings (*poderi*) were created; in irrigated areas the minimum size was 5 ha, whilst on hillsides it could be up to 50 ha. The typical pattern of change may be seen in the work of the Ente di Riforma Apulia-Basilicata, covering the 'heel' of Italy. An area of 200 000 ha was expropriated from 1500 landowners and assigned to 31 000 families. The change to this much closer pattern of settlement involved the construction of roads, power and water supply, land reclamation, new farmhouses and villages. A complete new infrastructure was developed, with 15 000 farmhouses, 50 service centres and villages, 1700 km of roads, and 7500 wells. A large programme of irrigation transformed the lowland areas of the Metapontino, the Bari–Brindisi coastal strip (Salentine peninsula) and the Tavoliere Di Apulia (fig. 17.6). The 'wheat and olive' landscape has changed to one of citrus fruits, vegetable and industrial crops, and livestock numbers have increased dramatically. The Metapontino illustrates the transformation of the landscape. Formerly a malarial coastal plain, it was drained and reclaimed, and the mosquito eradicated. The five rivers irrigate the entire coastal strip and are instrumental in the cultivation of vines, citrus and other fruit trees. Some 750 000 pine trees act as windbreaks. Oranges, peaches, apricots, pears, salad vegetables, sugar beet, tobacco and tomatoes are the principal high-yielding crops.

The transformation of large areas has been impressive. The largest and least efficient latifundia have disappeared, and much of the day labour system with them. There has been a notable increase in intensive farming in fruit and vegetable crops. It must be remembered that land reform has only affected a small proportion of the cultivated land in the South, but it was a significant movement in the right direction.

Infrastructure

The Cassa per il Mezzogiorno was the instrument of financial assistance for many modernisation and improvement schemes in the areas of land reform. As well as irrigation schemes and new farmhouses, it financed crop and stock improvements and began the task of consolidating fragmented holdings into viable units. A significant contribution to the rural infrastructure was the establishment of packing, processing and refrigeration units. In addition, because the most permanent weakness of the South was its need to overcome the relatively long distances from the markets of Western Europe, the Cassa was very active in developing transport, distribution and marketing facilities for agricultural products. Aqueducts, reservoirs and the draining of marshes also contributed to the improvement of village life. Schools, hospitals and training centres were directly associated with the social infrastructure. The Cassa installed main water supplies for millions of people, and aided local authorities to build the systems for distributing the water to villages. The construction of hydro-electric power stations, telephone systems, new and improved roads, and the railway system from Campania into the toe of Italy at Reggio Calabria, made large areas of the South more accessible and improved living conditions immensely.

Industry

During the early period, up until 1957, the main work of the Cassa was to inject new vitality into agriculture, village life, and the rural environment, hoping that this would stimulate demand, and provide conditions favourable to the growth of industry. However, by 1957 it was realised that there would have to be more definite intervention in the industrial sector to provide new employment and to ease the burden on the agricultural sector. The passing of the Industrial Areas Law in 1957 empowered the Cassa to support the establishment of industrial zones in the South, and figure 17.4 illustrates the shift of resources into the industrial sector after 1965. There were various encouragements to industrialists. The Cassa itself provided capital for new projects and for the modernisation of existing concerns, up to as much as 85 per cent of the cost. There was also fiscal exemption, rail-freight concessions and exemption from customs duties on imported raw materials. The European Investment Bank (EIB) was of great importance here and helped to establish a large number of factories of various kinds (fig. 17.3). The largest single contribution came from the government-controlled companies such as ENI and IRI; they were required by law to place 40 per cent of their investment in the south. The state sector accounted for about 35 per cent of the growth in manufacturing employment initially. Much of the growth was in heavy industry, mainly in iron and steel, shipbuilding, heavy engineering, cement, oil-refining, and petrochemicals, because of the nature of the state-controlled companies. Major projects of international significance included the Taranto and Bagnoli steelworks, and the Montedison petrochemical complexes at Brindisi and Siracusa-Augusta in Sicily. The continuing problem was that these were mainly capital-intensive heavy industries and they did not provide very large employment possibilities, nor did they necessarily stimulate the development of lighter consumer-goods industries, which are essential to balanced growth. Such prestige projects as the Taranto steelworks have been called 'cathedrals in the desert'. Another problem was the dissipation of investment aid over the whole of the Mezzogiorno, which was often spread too thinly to have a significant effect.

Growth poles

The development of a limited number of centres which were individually capable of faster growth was adopted during the latter half of the 1960s. The idea was based upon the economies of scale which accrue when investment infrastructure, industrial linkages, and trained labour supply are concentrated into a smaller cohesive area. Altogether, 48 nuclei of industrial development were designated, and subsequent experience showed that five major areas were of greatest significance. These became 'growth poles' (fig. 17.7) into which most investment was channelled. Three of the most important of these are the Naples–Salerno pole, the Bari–Brindisi–Taranto triangle, and the Siracusa–Augusta pole. Their current development is briefly summarised below:

1 **The port of Naples** has declined considerably in relation to Italy's other ports and now occupies fifth position after Genoa, Trieste, Taranto, Venice and Livorno. Nevertheless its shipbuilding and repairing industry has been supplemented by the Bagnoli steel plant (although this was halved in size by the closure of the hot-rolling mill in the early 1990s as part of the Italian government's response to the EU steel-restructuring programme), cotton textiles, Alfa-Romeo (Fiat) cars, Pirelli cables, Olivetti office machinery, and Enichem petrochemical works. The Italian aircraft industry is based upon the Alenia Corporation (formed by the merger of the two leading manufacturers Aeritalia and Selenia). There appears to be the basis of a fairly diversified industrial structure in the Naples area.

2 **Siracusa–Augusta.** The development here is based largely upon petrochemicals, for two reasons. There is a small oilfield at Ragusa, and considerable sulphur and potash deposits in eastern Sicily. More important are the deep water facilities between Augusta and Siracusa which have led to the development of major port installations, which are able to accommodate 250 000-tonne tankers. This is one of the largest oil-refinery, chemical and petrochemical complexes in Western Europe. Cement and the refining of non-ferrous metals are other activities.

3 **Bari–Brindisi–Taranto.** The integrated iron and steel works at Taranto, built in 1960, dominates this area. It is one of the largest steelworks in Europe with a capacity of 10 million tonnes per annum. Its coastal site and the facility for low-cost imports have been instrumental in its success, and it has been accompanied by a large industrial estate with engineering and machine-tool factories, oil refinery, cement works, agricultural machinery and consumer-goods industries. At Brindisi is the Enichem petrochemical factory, producing plastics and ethylene. The European Commission has drawn up a detailed development plan for this pole of regional development, which it considers to be of major importance to the EU.

Tourism

The recognition by the Cassa that tourism could play a major part in economic development meant the increasing allocation of funds for hotel building and modernisation and other tourist amenities. The South has much to offer the tourist: beautiful empty beaches; dramatic mountainous scenery; historic cities and architecture of every type and period. It is all the more attractive by comparison with the overcrowded northern Italian resorts. Hitherto there was one major drawback: inaccessibility. The Cassa assisted in the improvement of construction of hotels and constructed local roads for sightseeing. It is surprising that the Mezzogiorno has still not attracted the tourist on a large scale. There is an immense tourist potential.

Autostrada

The construction of autostrada has now diminished travelling time quite dramatically. The Autostrada Del Sol, running from Bologna through Rome and Naples to Reggio Calabria, is the most well-known, but there are also autostrada down both west and east coasts, with cross-Apennine links from Naples to Bari and from Rome to Pescara (fig. 17.7). The remoteness of the South is now less critical both for the tourist and the industrialist, and the autostrada may well prove, in the long run, to be the most important single factor in its development.

The Mezzogiorno in the 1990s

The problem has proved deep rooted and complex: the Cassa has been in existence for over 40 years, during which time it has made massive investments. In 1984 there was a financial crisis and its role was reduced, with its powers transferred to the regional governments. A more specific set of proposals were developed, designed to foster small-scale industry, tourism, irrigated agricultural development and the rationalisation of progress in mountain areas. The region has now become dependent on EU assistance. It is difficult to see whether the economy has reached the 'take-off point' or whether the 'multiplier effect' is operating and capable of sustaining long-term growth. Yet there is no doubt that there are the beginnings of substantial industrialisation, and the employment structure has shown quite dramatic change, as seen in fig. 17.8. The infrastructure is much sounder, and agriculture has lost over 2 million workers.

During the life of the Cassa, new factories, employing a total of nearly 400 000 workers, were constructed. Most were in four districts: Latina, south of Rome; Naples–Salerno; the Bari–Brindisi–Taranto triangle; and Catania–Siracuse in Sicily. The key problem has been the concentration upon large, capital-intensive units based upon steel, metallurgy and

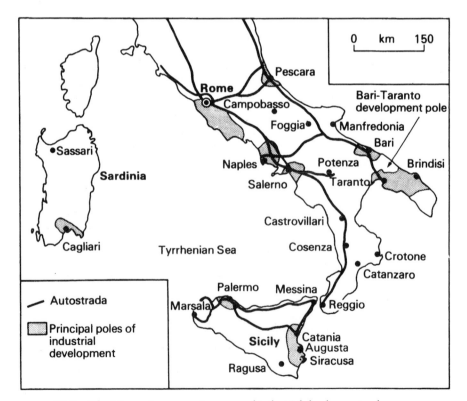

FIGURE 17.7   *The Mezzogiorno – motorways and industrial development poles*

	Agriculture	Industry	Services
1950	57	20	23
1981	24	28	48
1986	19	29	52
1990	17	24	59

FIGURE 17.8   *The percentage employment structure in the Mezzogiorno (1950–90)*

chemicals. There have been relatively few jobs in traditional, labour-intensive industries, which are necessary for sustained improvement in employment.

Agricultural productivity has improved considerably in the land-reform areas with a much greater emphasis on intensive crops and increased numbers of livestock. However, this has to be taken in context, noting that land reform has so far affected only a small proportion of the cultivated land in the South. The largest remaining problem is that of rehabilitating the eroded mountain slopes and bringing the hill farmers into a modern farming system.

The gap between the South and North of Italy remains, because, in spite of considerable advances in per capita income in the South, the North experienced such boom conditions in the decade up to 1975 that the gap has closed only partially, as fig. 17.9 shows. The per capita income in Calabria is still below half that of Lombardy. Improvements have been very uneven and within the South itself major differences are now emerging. The Adriatic regions of Abruzzo and Apulia have performed rather better than the west-coast regions, Campania and Calabria. Sardinia has progressed more than Sicily. The three regions where economic, social and political development have stagnated are Sicily, Campania and Calabria, and these are regions most in the grip of the Mafia or Mafia-like organisations like the Neapolitan Camorra. Nevertheless, the Italian South has a higher standard of living than most of the regions in Greece.

	Per capita income index				
	1950	**1970**	**1981**	**1985**	**1992**
Italy (average)	100	100	100	100	100
Lombardy	146	125	132	129	134
Liguria	151	130	126	126	121
Apulia	59	79	71	73	77
Basilicata	51	62	64	66	67
Campania	56	80	67	70	73
Calabria	42	61	56	64	63

FIGURE 17.9   *Changes in per capita income index (source – Eurostat)*

Between 1950 and 1990 population loss was over 4 million people for the Mezzogiorno (fig. 17.10). This has been of major significance in siphoning off the excess rural population. Most of the emigration has been inter-regional, to the northern cities, but emigration to other EU countries, notably Germany, has also occurred. Since 1975, in the changed economic climate, there has been a reduced rate of intake by the northern parts of the EU, and a return of migrants to their homeland. Migration from the Mezzogiorno appears to have been much reduced and even reversed – in Sicily, for instance (fig. 17.10). An increasing number of immigrants, mainly from Economically Less Developed Countries (ELDCs), are now moving into those regions and employment sectors which were abandoned by Italian migrants who left for the North in the 1950s and 1960s. Many are employed in seasonal jobs in agriculture and fishing. In the Sicilian port of Mazara del Vallo, Tunisians make up half the town's population. Other immigrants, particularly Moroccans and Senegalese, work as street traders in tourist resorts.

Global factors have had a major limitation effect. The recession of 1974 damaged the partial success of southern industrialisation, as peripheral regions were badly affected by the fall in demand and by the transfer of production by multi-national companies to developing-world countries. In the agricultural sector citrus fruits and horticultural crops have suffered fierce competition in the European market from Spain and other Mediterranean countries.

Tourism is now the principal avenue through which fuller prosperity could come. The motorway system has reduced the isolation of the South, and as yet, tourism has not touched the Mezzogiorno on any scale outside a few traditional areas such as Sorrento, Capri and Amalfi.

Important questions remain unresolved. Unemployment is still high and is particularly serious in rural areas. In Calabria and Sicily the unemployment

| | Net migration (in thousands per annum) | | | | | |
	1966	1970	1975	1980	1985	1990
Campania	−26.4	−34.9	−14.5	−	+1.7	+1.2
Abruzzi/Molise	−15.0	−6.5	−2.3	−	+7.4	+4.8
Apulia	−27.5	−26.4	−6.7	−5.5	+0.3	−0.2
Basilicata	−8.6	−10.7	−3.7	−3.2	−0.2	−0.9
Calabria	−23.3	−26.1	−10.4	−6.2	+4.6	−1.4
Sicily	−33.5	−36.8	−11.5	−6.0	+16.1	+6.4
Sardinia	−6.5	−8.9	−1.6	−1.6	+4.5	+2.1
Total Mezzogiorno	−140.8	−150.3	−50.7	−22.5	+34.4	+12.0

FIGURE 17.10 *Net migration from the Mezzogiorno (source – Eurostat)*

rate is more than double the national average and almost six times that of Lombardy, the country's most industrialised region. Rural poverty is very marked, and the lack of rural development contrasts strongly with the established growth centres. Agriculture dominated the initial stages of the Cassa's work, but only limited areas have been affected. Large state enterprises have moved into the area, but there is a lack of generative smaller-scale private industry and coordinated planning. A strong urban tradition does not exist here, as it does in northern Italy. The essential differences between North and South remain, with the Mezzogiorno remaining dependent upon the North. The Cassa achieved a qualified 'economic miracle', and has, it is to be hoped, created the infrastructure which will allow 'take-off' into sustained growth.

GREECE AND IRELAND: THE PERIPHERY

Greece and Ireland are two peripheral countries of the EU both with aspects of semi-developed countries and with a markedly lower GDP than the EU average. Their geographical characteristics illustrate the complexity of development problems, as in some ways they are similar, but in others they are unique (fig. 18.1).

Their environments are quite different, with Ireland having a maritime climate with its western mountains and plateaux open to excessive exposure

1993	Greece	Ireland
Area km^2	132 000	70 300
Population (millions)	10.4	3.6
Population density (EUR 12: 148) per km^2	78.7	50.8
GDP per capita index (EUR 12 = 100)	36	64
Percentage workforce in:		
agriculture	21.0	14.0
industry	24.0	28.0
services	55.0	58.0
Car production	nil	nil
Number of passenger cars per 100 inhabitants (EUR 12 = 40)	17	24
Energy consumption per head (EUR 12 = 3438 toe)	2020	2855

toe = tonnes of oil equivalent

FIGURE 18.1 *Greece and Ireland – an economic profile (source:* Eurostat)

from Atlantic wind and rain. Greece, by contrast, has a desiccated Mediterranean climate giving rise to aridity particularly in the mountain chain. Both climates are adverse in terms of the agricultural response. Inaccessibility affects both countries adversely. They are remote from the European core, with air or sea journeys necessary for physical contact. In Greece's case it is possible to travel overland through former Yugoslavia, a difficult journey through similar mountainous country. Marginality to the core is therefore a shared characteristic.

The economic characteristics of this marginality may be expressed in a variety of ways. These include persistent and prolonged emigration; an excess of population in agricultural occupations; a rural subsistence economy with accompanying poverty and an imbalanced economic structure with low levels of industrialisation; and excessive concentration of population and economic activity in the primate city and its region. Dublin and Athens are both cases in point.

In addition, peripherality is often affected by global factors where interdependent relationships with other countries have had adverse effects. These may be classed as political dependency, cultural disintegration and economic exploitation. Over a long historical period, both countries have been affected by these external factors. Ireland only became independent of the UK in 1926 and Greece was a dependency of the Ottoman Empire until 1830. In Ireland the Gaelic language has largely been replaced by English, although Greece has maintained its language and distinctive alphabet intact, probably because of the strength of its ancient classical culture. However, both countries have a dependence upon agriculture and the export of primary products. This is indicative of their general lack of energy resources and their failure to industrialise when other parts of Western Europe were so doing.

IRELAND

Emigration

The problem of emigration has been central to the economic geography of Ireland. Up to 1840 the population of the island as a whole (including Northern Ireland) had expanded to approximately 8 million. The countryside was relatively prosperous and had sustained the large-scale cultivation of the potato, which was the staple food of the rural population. The failure of successive harvests due to potato blight during the 1840s, and the resulting famine and starvation led to large-scale emigration, many of the emigrants going to the New World. The country never recovered, and the whole basis of life was undermined, resulting in a halving of the population in the century up to 1940. Ireland's population in 1993 was 3.6 million, with the lowest density in the EU. However, with the advent of three new

Member States in 1995, both Sweden and Finland now have lower densities than Ireland. It has been estimated that people of Irish descent living in America, the UK and elsewhere total something like 16 million, five times the number remaining in Ireland itself.

The question of the great emigration needs a little more analysis in depth. The potato famines lasted for a very short period, but they triggered off a century of decline at the same period when most of Western Europe was growing substantially in population. The answer is probably to be found in the difficult nature of the rural environment, the subsistence character of the farming, and the low income levels and depressed spending capacity of the population. This must then be placed in the comparative context of the rest of Europe and the New World. The decline of the population began before the start of the nineteenth century, with the commencement of the Industrial Revolution in Europe. In Ireland there was no industrial base to absorb the movement off the land because there were almost none of the resources to sustain the initial industrial growth which in countries like the UK was fuelled by coal and iron ore. The attraction of employment, high wages and rising standards of living lay abroad, and there was little alternative for the Irish but to emigrate. The potato famines gave a large impetus to this movement, but the underlying cause of Ireland's depopulation lay in its lack of industrial resources at the critical period of the Industrial Revolution. The fact that Ireland was politically part of the UK at this time was also a contributing factor. The close links and ease of access produced a positive inducement to emigrate to more advantageous environments outside Ireland.

Planning regions	1990 Population (1000s)	1990 Population (percentage)	1981–90 Population change (percentage)
East	1330	37.9	+3.2
South-east	382	10.9	+1.7
South-west	534	15.3	+2.1
North-east	198	5.7	+2.6
Mid-west	308	8.8	0.0
Midlands	259	7.3	+1.2
West	286	8.2	0.0
North-west and Donegal	207	5.9	−0.4
Total	3 503 000	100	+1.8

FIGURE 18.2   *Ireland – planning regions (source – Eurostat)*

Ireland today

Dublin, the capital and primate city, with its port, Dun Laoghaire, has 1 024 000 people, over a quarter of the total national population. Cork (410 000), Galway (180 000), Limerick (162 000) and Waterford (92 000) are the only other regional centres of any size and importance. Agriculture accounts for 13 per cent of the workforce. Ireland is thus characterised by an underdeveloped urban hierarchy and an enlarged agricultural sector.

In the west these characteristics are even more extreme. Substantial amounts of land are uninhabited mountains or ill-drained boglands. Settlement is dispersed and villages are rare, the main unit of rural settlement being the single farm. Towns are generally very small, but have the range of social and economic functions normally associated with a town. In many Western counties the proportion of the population engaged in agriculture rises to 40 per cent. Poor soils, small and fragmented farms, and lack of capitalisation and cooperative organisation characterise a subsistence-oriented rural economy. Ireland's population is relatively young, with 26 per cent under 15 years old and 63 per cent between the ages of 15 and 64. Nearly 50 per cent of the population is under 25 years of age. Total population decline has now been arrested in Ireland overall and population growth is the highest in the EU (due primarily to the high birth rate) although during the early 1990s the Irish birth rate has dropped considerably. Nevertheless many parts of the west are still threatened with decline as selective out-migration of young people adversely affects the birth rate and causes stagnation in many rural communities. The farm population is relatively old, with many of the farmers over 50 years of age, representing a major obstacle to change.

The north-western regions

The north-west of Ireland is agriculturally poor, and very sparsely populated. Donegal has granite mountains rising to 650 m, is glaciated and is often bare of soil, with the lower lands containing waterlogged areas with extensive blanket peat bogs. Only about 40 per cent of the total area is improved farmland and even good pasture land is scarce. On the coast are rocky headlands and deep inlets. Rainfall is heavy (up to 1500 mm per year) and the land is bleak and windswept with severe exposure to Atlantic gales. Tree growth is impossible in many areas. Subsistence farming is the norm with cottages usually situated on the sheltered lee of the mountains. Potatoes, hay and occasionally oats are the only crops possible. Sheep are more numerous than cattle and their wool serves as the basis for the manufacture of homespun cloth, knitwear and Donegal Tweeds. The only town of any size is Donegal (1725 people) which acts as county town and market centre, and exemplifies the restricted development of most Irish towns.

The mountains of Mayo and Connemara are scenically beautiful, but are also regions of difficulty, rising to 800 m. There is a combination of bare ice-scoured rocks and peat bogs, and the mountains are practically uninhabited. Where there is settlement, it is characterised by isolated farms and cottages, with low standards of living. These north-western coastlands lie on the remotest fringes of Europe and illustrate both the worst extremes of the Atlantic mountain environment and some of the most marginal economic conditions in the whole of the EU.

The South and East

The southern and eastern regions, including particularly the Limerick–Shannon lowland, the south coast from Cork to Wexford, and the East Central Plain centred upon Dublin, have a kinder physical environment and a greater accessibility to the UK and the rest of Europe. About 90 per cent of the East Central Plain is improved farmland. The generally humid atmosphere encourages a thick growth of grass on limy glacial drift soils. Dairy farming and market gardening take place around Dublin to supply the large urban market, but beef cattle are also of great importance. Live cattle, both store and fatstock, are exported. To the south-west the region merges into the dairy farming zone of Limerick and the Golden Vale. The southern coastlands around Waterford and Wexford have the sunniest climate in Ireland and the proportions of arable land are relatively high, rising to one-third of the total farmland on the Wexford plain. The Wexford plain is known as 'The Garden of Ireland' with fertile soils, based on weathered sands, clays and marls supporting crops of oats, barley, potatoes, wheat and sugar beet. Cork, with its outport Cobh, is a port of call for transatlantic liners. It has good rail links with Dublin, has an excellent ria harbour, and is the second largest city. It has a substantial manufacturing base with a small steelworks, vehicle assembly, agricultural machinery, rubber, clothing and footwear, and food processing of various types.

The growth of Dublin in particular has been a feature of the last 40 years. Although a small city by European standards, Dublin and its outport Dun Laoghaire have increased their share of the country's total population to 29 per cent. It is nearly three times as populous as the next largest city, Cork. It accounts for half the national industrial output, and employs over two-fifths of the total industrial workforce of Ireland. Its industries include engineering, clothing, footwear, meat canning and bacon processing, brewing, distilling, biscuit and jam making, tobacco, and fertilisers. Dun Laoghaire is the country's principal passenger port and Dublin city dominates Ireland's economy to an increasing extent, giving rise to a major imbalance between the western underdeveloped region on the one hand, and the richer south and east on the other (fig. 18.2).

The western underdeveloped region

Although the whole of Ireland qualifies for aid under the EU Regional Policy (Ireland currently receives more per capita than any other EU state, with European support funding now accounting for 6 per cent of GNP), the western part of the country is markedly poorer, more marginal and more isolated than the east. Dependence upon subsistence agriculture is such that purchasing power is often minimal. Average income per head is a useful indication of the differences. In the west and Donegal, the average income per head is only three-fifths of that in Dublin. Ireland had a per capita income of only 64 per cent of that of the UK in 1991. These are highly significant figures when placed into the context of the EU as a whole.

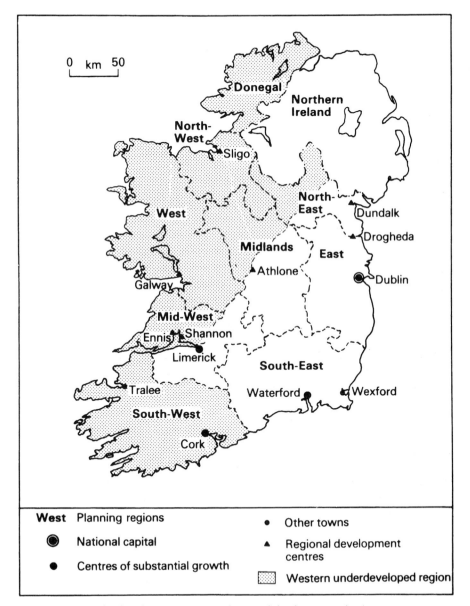

FIGURE 18.3   *Ireland — planning regions and regional development poles (source —* Buchanan)

In 1949 the Irish Development Authority (IDA) was established with two important principles: (1) the encouragement of industrial investment (particularly for export-oriented industries) by means of incentives; (2) the ending of restrictions on foreign ownership of Irish companies. Foreign capital investment rose dramatically but the problem was that much of this investment continued to go into the south-east and Dublin area.

The Underdeveloped Areas Act 1952 designated the 'Western Under-developed Region' (fig. 18.3). It comprised 12 out of the 26 counties of the Republic, and included one-third of the total population. Industries established within the region were eligible for a higher rate of aid than in the rest of the country. Aid fell into four groups: capital grants of up to two-thirds; long-term loans at favourable interest rates; tax relief of 20 per cent on buildings; and grants towards the training of workers. The launching of the 'Small Industries Act' of 1969 was another attempt to assist the modernisation and enlargement of many existing local craft industries scattered throughout the small towns in the west: the Irish linen industry was an example.

In 1968 Professor Colin Buchanan recommended to the Irish government the strengthening of the urban hierarchy by means of the designation of regional development centres (fig. 18.3). The IDA was reorganised and given wide-ranging power, and progress was made to attract investment into the three large regional centres of Cork, Waterford and Limerick, which had an existing industrial base. Perhaps more significant were projects established in areas such as Donegal. Two examples of textile factories were Snia Viscosa and Courtaulds. The lower wage levels and the reserve of under-employed female labour were two significant factors. Most industry was associated either with the agricultural processing section (such as milk-processing and fertilisers) or else classed as 'footloose', covering a wide range of light industries and consumer products ranging from bathroom scales at Sligo to ballbearings at Tralee.

In 1979 Udaras, the Gaeltacht Authority, was set up and given certain responsibilities for Gaeltacht areas (parts of Ireland where the Irish language is still spoken). Although its primary function was to encourage the preservation and extension of the use of the Irish language in these areas, it also had responsibility for the Gaeltacht's industrial development, providing financial assistance to firms.

Over Ireland as a whole, the assistance offered by the IDA tended to create growth at the edges of the large urban centres and in new centres – e.g. in Cork in the late 1970s and early 1980s, the IDA encouraged development in the harbour area outside the city, but at the same time nearly 50 per cent of firms within the city closed. To avoid this city-centre blight, the IDA policy was altered in the mid-1980s, with higher financial incentives extended to Dublin in 1983 and Cork in 1985. The latter saw the establishment of an enterprise centre with the construction of small industrial units for high-technology industry. After 1986, Urban Renewal Areas were also created in the five largest cities – e.g. the Custom House Docks area in the centre of Dublin.

Shannon airport, with the adjoining industrial zone

In 1988 FAS was established as the Irish Training and Employment Authority to assist people seeking employment, to create jobs within communities and to improve skill levels in Irish business. Then, in 1993, the Industrial Development Act replaced the IDA with Forfas, which is the policy, advisory and coordination board for industrial development and science and technology in Ireland (except for the Shannon Free Airport Industrial Zone). This board has two sub-agencies: Forbairt for the promotion of indigenous industry, and the Industrial Development Agency (Ireland) for encouraging inward investment from overseas. However, the Act of 1993 did not repeal the earlier industrial development legislation, and the investment incentives remain largely unchanged.

The IDA is now cooperating with the Northern Ireland IDB (Industrial Development Board) as the belief is that this will reinforce the image of Ireland as an island that is a single destination for US investors.

The Mid-west regional plan

The Mid-west comprises the counties of Clare, Limerick and part of Tipperary, 308 000 people in all. The regional plan focuses upon the growth pole of Limerick–Ennis–Shannon, with Shannon Development as the Regional Development Agency for the Shannon Region. The development of the Shannon Industrial Estate (now known as the Shannon Free Airport Industrial Zone) by the IDA in the 1960s provided the basis for the country's third largest industrial concentration after Dublin and Cork. The Airport Act of 1947 established Shannon as the first customs-free airport in the world. The Shannon Free Airport Development Company Ltd

(SFADCo) promotes the use of the airport – for freight handling and warehousing – and the industrial zone, and operates the financial and fiscal incentives of Forbairt and The Irish Development Agency (Ireland). Factories can be rented or purchased, and now over 400 people are employed by 30 companies. This industrial zone produces 30 per cent of Ireland's manufactured export goods. There is a wide variety of light and specialised products, predominantly high value in relation to weight and readily adaptable to air transport. The most important single type is electrical and electronic equipment. The Shannon Free Airport Industrial Zone has provided a singularly successful growth point in the west and population growth is now substantial around Limerick and Ennis.

The continuing problem

The work of the IDA has to be analysed in a complex global context. Although it had successfully created 82 000 new jobs by 1994 – concentrating on four main sectors: pharmaceuticals and healthcare, electronics, software and financial services – many of these jobs are with foreign companies (Ireland is now the leading destination for US investment in the EU for the computer software sector), and foreign investment accounts for 75 per cent of manufacturing exports, 55 per cent of manufacturing output and 45 per cent of employment in manufacturing. The Irish economy also shed nearly 60 000 jobs owing to international recession and the inability of Irish industry to withstand European competition. Levels of unemployment (at 16 per cent) are the second highest in the EU after Spain. Nevertheless, although Ireland is still one of the poorer members of the EU, its relative prosperity is improving. Average income has risen from 60 per cent of the EU average in 1986 to 74 per cent in 1994.

The problem of emigration, which has been very substantial during most of the twentieth century, has not really been solved either. Emigration was increased by the attractions of the British economy as it recovered from the Second World War. It was not until the 1971–81 period that the total Irish population began to increase and there was a substantial economic boom during that period. Although the total population continues to increase because of substantial natural increase so that the rate of increase in employment necessary to provide jobs for young people entering the labour market in Ireland is 15 times greater than in the rest of the EU, nevertheless the selective drain of labour to external attractions continues. Ireland is the only EU country with a negative net migration, and continues to suffer because of its peripheral position *vis à vis* the rest of the EU (since the opening of the Channel Tunnel, Ireland is the only EU nation without a land link to the rest of the Member States).

GREECE

Greece lies at the southern end of the Balkan Peninsula and in 1993 had 10.4 million inhabitants. Since 1987 it has been divided into 13 administrative regions for socio-economic planning purposes: Greater Athens, Northern Aegean and Southern Aegean, Crete, Epirus, Central Greece, Western Greece, Ionian Islands, Central Macedonia, Eastern Macedonia and Thrace, Western Macedonia, Thessaly and the Peloponnese (fig. 18.4). In area the country is almost the same size as England and Wales, and there are over 1400 Greek islands accounting for 20 per cent of the total area of the country. Greece is the only EU country not to share a border with another Member State. Greece had an association agreement with the EEC from 1962. From 1967 to 1974 the monarchy was replaced by a military dictatorship. During this period relations with the EEC were suspended and not resumed until 1975 when Greece, having restored a

FIGURE 18.4 *Greece – Administrative Regions*

Pendeli monastery near Athens, with the rugged Pendeli mountains, where marble is quarried, in the background

democratic government, applied to join as a full member and acceded to membership in January 1981.

The rural environment

Greece has traditionally been pictured as a poor, semi-developed country. At the end of the Second World War nearly two-thirds of the workforce were still engaged in primary activity. Even today 30 per cent of the population live in villages of less than 2000 people. About 21 per cent of the population are employed in agriculture (a larger proportion than in any other Member State compared with the EU average of 6 per cent), contributing 14 per cent to the gross domestic product. Farm holdings are small and fragmented, the average size being 4 ha. Seven out of ten farms are less than 5 ha, and only two in a thousand are 50 ha. Farms of over 20 ha make up only 3 per cent of the total. The principal agricultural products are cereals, citrus fruits and vegetables, raisins, wine, tobacco, olive oil and cotton, and the area under sunflowers has increased considerably in recent years.

The environment is extremely difficult, being mountainous with a desiccated semi-arid Mediterranean climate. Mount Olympus, at 3200 m, is the highest mountain. There are three physical regions, the rugged Pindus Mountain chain which covers some 80 per cent of the country and several small areas of lowlands principally around Athens, Thessaloniki and in Thessaly. Finally, there are the Greek Islands in the Aegean Sea, a complex group which includes Crete, Rhodes and the Cyclades archipelago (fig. 18.5). Greece has the fourth largest fishing fleet in the EU, both by number of vessels and by tonnage, but the second lowest fishing catch.

Economic development

Part of the problem of Greece lay in its history. Having been one of the pillars of Western civilisation in classical times with a great empire and the home of great philosophers and architects, Greece fell into a long decline and for several centuries was ruled as part of the Ottoman Empire in the Balkans. It emerged in the early twentieth century as a semi-developed country with an economy dependent upon agricultural exports.

Prior to 1960 national development was concerned with recovery from damage inflicted in the Second World War Nazi occupation (Greece was the only Balkan state not to become a Soviet satellite), but during the 1960s great changes began to take place. These may be examined in four key sectors: urbanisation; population industrialisation; migration; and tourism.

Urbanisation and urban problems

Urbanisation and the primate city strikes the visitor to Greece most clearly and substantially. The overwhelming importance of Greater Athens is very marked. The city, including the Port of Piraeus, has grown dramatically so that, with nearly 3.1 million people, it contains 30 per cent of the national population total. Thessaloniki, with almost a million people, and Patras,

Kalymnos island in the Dodecanese group in the Aegean Sea

Volos, Iraklion and Larisa (each with populations over 100 000) are the next largest cities.

The rapid growth of Athens (41 per cent of the national total of company head offices are now located here) has sadly damaged its historic character, and the summer heat poses a particular problem where large quantities of water and electrical energy are needed to supply the growing urban population. Conditions in the summer in cities such as Athens are less than pleasant. Smog (*nefos*) due to air pollution by industry and traffic, noise, high land and housing costs, and an increase in unemployment (it is the highest of any region in Greece) and crime led to a reduction in population growth in the Athens region between 1981 and 1991. The cutting of investment in public-transport services to reduce government expenditure means that Greece now has the worst public-transport system in the EU, with a subsequent increase in the use of private cars leading to congestion and pollution, enormous losses of working time and inefficient use of energy. According to the OECD, the number of people using public transport in the Athens area has fallen from about 1 million in the early 1960s to 850 000 in the early 1970s and to little more than 500 000 in the 1990s despite a population increase of 60 per cent over the same period. The number of private cars increased by 7 per cent a year during the 1980s. An air-pollution-abatement plan has now been implemented for the Greater Athens area to reduce the sulphur and lead content of fuels and close the city's oil-fired power station and gas-production plant. Cars can only be used in Athens on alternate days, traffic-free areas have been created in the centre and the metro is being modernised. Nevertheless, pollution levels frequently exceed the safety limits, and further measures will need to be taken.

Urbanisation in Greece, and Athens in particular, has been influenced less by industrialisation than by political causes. The civil war, immediately following the Second World War, between the monarchy and the Communists produced major population movements to the cities for protection, and few have returned to the land since. The growth of the city has therefore been singularly affected by the rural 'push' factor for other than economic reasons.

Industrialisation

Industrialisation has in a sense followed urbanisation in Greece. Manufacturing traditionally suffered from a lack of raw materials, shortage of capital and limited markets, and cottage industry has remained important for sectors such as shoe and clothing manufacture. The economy developed fast up to the early 1980s, with Greece recording the highest GDP growth after Japan in the OECD, and new heavy industries were established such as aluminium, chemicals, metallurgy and shipbuilding. Textiles, paper making and food processing also became important. Electricity generation has been a major factor in stimulating Greek manufacturing since the mid 1960s. Greece is highly dependent upon imported oil for over 59 per cent of its

FIGURE 18.5   *Greece – main features*

total primary energy requirements, but new hydro-electric power projects have also been of major importance. Most economic activity is concentrated in the Athens Piraeus lowlands which has one-third of the country's population and over 59 per cent of the total industrial employment. The Athens conurbation provides a large workforce and a ready market, and is the country's most important transport focus. There is a steelworks at Piraeus producing 1 million tonnes a year, based on imports of coal and scrap.

One of the most important features of the Greek economy is its merchant fleet, a feature of the trading capacity for which Greece is famous. The merchant fleet, mainly based at Piraeus, is 26 per cent of the EU total and a major prop to the economy. Oil tankers form a substantial part of this merchant fleet. Cruise liners are also important and Greece is the world's fifth greatest ocean passenger-carrying country.

The decentralisation of manufacturing to the provinces has only been partially successful because of high transport costs. However, mining activity is increasingly important in the north-east of the country with lignites, asbestos, nickel, bauxite and manganese being particularly important. In addition, oil and natural gas in the Aegean Sea has been extracted since the early 1980s from the Prinos field west of Thassos and South Kavala. Exploration is taking place in other areas including the Ionian Sea and Epirus.

Migration

Migration, both internal and external, has formed an important part of the economic changes in the country. During the late 1960s external migration reached a rate of 160 000 per year with many going to the boom economies of West Germany, Australia and the USA. However, since 1974 there has been a net return of people, and their skills and capital.

Internal migration is of the greatest geographical importance. Migration between rural areas is significant, motivated often by a desire amongst people in mountainous areas to settle on the plains. Attractive reception areas for rural migrants include the plains of Macedonia, the Soufi plain and the lower Thiamis valley opposite Corfu. However, most internal migration is destined for Greater Athens and Thessaloniki. The reasons for migration are complex, but include both the fundamental problems of farming and social phenomena. Inadequacies in Greek agriculture include small fragmented farms, obsolete techniques and a shortage of capital. Strict rules forbid marriage between blood relations, hence marriage partners often have to be sought outside the home community. Many rural migrants are women who have no particular attachment to their family farms. Marriage is also one of the major reasons why so many women migrate to Athens.

The Parthenon on the Acropolis, surrounded by the modern city of Athens

Tourism

The fourth key factor in the Greek economy is tourism, originally based upon the classical sites such as Delphi and the Acropolis. Numbers of tourists to the country have risen strongly since the 1950s, from 33 000 in 1950 to over 1 million in 1965, nearly 6 million in 1982 and 9.9 million in 1993. Greece has now over 9 per cent of the air package holiday market in Europe. Over 90 per cent of these tourists are from Europe, of whom most are attracted by the hot sunshine, cheap food and wine. The availability of the package holiday, charter flights and the development of airstrips in all but the most inaccessible islands have been of major revitalising importance to the Aegean islands, including Rhodes and Crete. In the Southern Aegean region just under two-thirds of the working population is employed in the services sector, with most of it in tourism, whereas in the 1960s the region was predominantly agricultural. However, the average European tourist spent less than $250 in Greece in 1993 compared with about $350 in 1983, as Greece is now seen (and sold) as a destination for the lower-spending segment of the tourist market. In addition, most holiday-makers come in the summer season and efforts are being made to make the low season, from November to February, more attractive. Only one-tenth of visitors arrive during this period. In an attempt to reduce the pressure on Greece's three main resorts (Corfu, Crete and Rhodes), the government is developing tourism in other less well-known areas (particularly northern Greece) and promoting attractions, such as cultural events like the Epidavros festival, to encourage higher-spending tourists.

Regional disparities and development problems

Significant spatial disparities exist in Greece between industrialised and agricultural regions, between contrasting physical areas and between the mainland and the islands. Environment is clearly important but probably the most important single reason for regional disparities is the distance from consumer markets. Accessibility problems are at the root of the backwardness of areas such as Epirus and the mountains and islands, by comparison with Greater Athens or the Thessaly and Macedonian plains. Agricultural contrasts are the most obvious sign of difference in prosperity. In the plains of Thessaly and Macedonia there is a relatively prosperous look to the countryside with average farm sizes larger and mechanisation and irrigation more widespread. These two regions have over half the total irrigated land and produce much of the country's tobacco, wheat and cotton. By contrast the olive and vine are the leading crops on fragmented farms in much of the mountainous hinterland and the Peloponnese, and on islands such as Cephalonia. Out-migration is the usual reaction from these regions of difficulty although this has been reversing since 1971.

Epirus is the region which has suffered most from emigration, and in 1991 its population was approximately the same as in 1951. This has created a significant change in the region's age structure. While the population grew by only 2.6 per cent between 1951 and 1991, the number of young people under 25 fell by 30 per cent. In contrast the population over 65 increased by 180 per cent. Epirus has a serious population problem which affects the labour supply and the quality of the workforce. The level of training is well below the national average as the population is widely scattered (67 per cent live in rural areas) and the mountainous terrain, adverse weather conditions and poor road network combine to prevent children from many mountain villages pursuing their studies. The main economic activity is agriculture, particularly the rearing of sheep and goats. Disposable income is below the national average, and Epirus has one of the lowest levels of per capita GDP in Greece.

Greece's economic development has been accompanied by a growing trade deficit caused by the country's dependence upon imported oil and capital goods. The trade balance is heavily in deficit and only partially covered by earnings from shipping and tourism. The economy is structurally weak with low levels of industrialisation and an over-developed tertiary sector and over-populated rural areas with high levels of unemployment and small fragmented farm holdings.

In 1983 a five-year development plan aimed at modernising industry and promoting more work on the land was established. It asked for exemption from EEC competition and industrial subsidy rules, and for the allocation of special funds to assist industrial, commercial and regional development. Greek regional development benefited from the 1.7 billion ECU investment loans approved by the EEC in 1985 as part of the Integrated Mediterranean Programmes (IMPs) which initially operated up to 1990. The funding was earmarked for regional and social schemes, agricultural modernisation, forestry, rural diversification and tourism, and training and for helping Greece prepare to cope with the increased competition, in particular from Spanish and Portuguese membership of the EU.

Despite this assistance, Greece's economy has been in severe difficulty since 1989, with rising unemployment (9 per cent) and high inflation (12 per cent). The country is the Member State furthest away from meeting the Maastricht economic convergence criteria determining a State's readiness for economic and monetary union at the end of the 1990s. Particular problems have arisen in relation to the break-up of former Yugoslavia, with a trade embargo against the Former Yugoslav Republic of Macedonia (FYROM) affecting earnings at the northern port of Thessaloniki. 'FYROM' is a UN title, but Greece sees the use of the word 'Macedonia' in this name as a threat, fearing that the new state will lay claim to the northern Greek region of Macedonia. There has also been a freezing of investments in Albania caused by disagreements over the status of the ethnic Greek minority in southern Albania.

Annual transfers from the EU made up at least 2 per cent of Greece's GDP between 1989 and 1994, and Greece is hoping that economic growth will be encouraged by further EU funds being allocated between 1994 and 1999 (these are more than double those received under the previous five-year programme and will make up 5 per cent of GDP). By the end of the 1990s more than $20 billion of EU money will be spent on projects such as new roads (like the Via Egnatia, a 660-km motorway traversing the country from west to east to allow the free movement of freight between the Middle East and Europe), the metro in Athens and a new airport for the capital.

There is evidence that EU assistance to the more dynamic regions of Crete, the Southern Aegean and the Ionian Islands, with improvements to infrastructures and agriculture, has managed to sustain high activity rates and low unemployment in these regions despite the long recession affecting the rest of the country. With further support, Greece hopes to play a major role in the developing Balkan and East European markets and become, once again, an economic and trade centre at the crossroads of Europe, the Middle East and Africa.

19

THE PARIS REGION: A PROBLEM OF DEFINITION

WHAT IS THE PARIS REGION?

The Paris region poses an important problem, that of definition. What is the Paris region? Is it the city of Paris, the Paris agglomeration with 8.7 million people (fig. 19.5), the Ile de France Planning Region which includes four *départements* and extends up to 96 km away from the city, or the Paris Basin Planning Unit (fig. 19.1)? Alternatively, there is the traditional view of the Paris Basin in which the convergence of the Seine and its tributaries is the centre of a key agricultural lowland extending from the Loire to Normandy and from the Champagne scarplands to Picardie (fig. 19.2). This problem of definition may be examined by means of two themes which stress the economic value of the area in different ways: the scale and variety of agricultural production on the fertile 'pays' of the Paris Basin; the power of the city in attracting population and resources, and the planning problems which this has involved.

AGRICULTURAL PRODUCTION IN THE PAYS OF THE PARIS BASIN

The land-use diversity of the Paris Basin depends essentially upon geological characteristics and their effect upon landscape (fig. 19.2). The four major elements are:

1 The Tertiary Basin of the Ile de France: the central area of limestones, clays and sandstones overlain by superficial deposits of limon and alluvium and divided into separate 'pays' by the tributaries of the Seine.

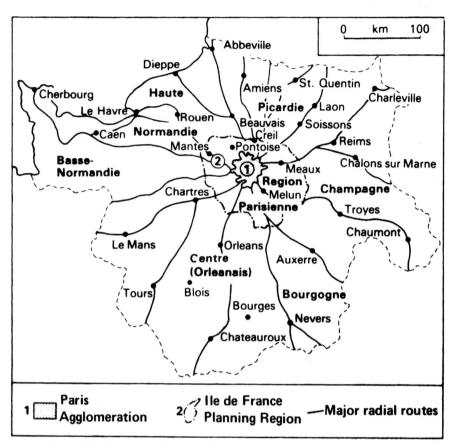

FIGURE 19.1 *The Paris Basin Planning Unit*

2 The scarplands of Champagne and Bourgogne to the east and south-east.
3 The chalk plateau of Artois and Picardie to the north.
4 Haute Normandie. The chalk plateau and lowlands of the Lower Seine.

The Ile de France Tertiary Basin

One of the most distinctive 'pays' is the **limestone plateau of Beauce**, which has a thick covering of porous limon and a lower water table than most other parts of northern France and, most importantly, is almost entirely flat. The outstanding feature is the almost complete utilisation of the land for agriculture; in many areas cereals occupy 80 to 90 per cent of the land. Beauce is the foremost wheat-growing area of France, with barley and maize as other significant crops. Maize in particular has grown in popularity because of the ease of mechanised harvesting techniques. The uniform relief has helped efficiency and mechanisation, and farms are large with consolidated holdings and large expanses of fields in a prairie-type landscape.

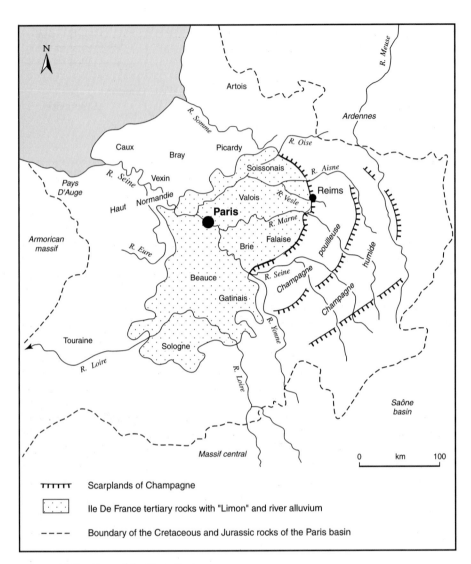

FIGURE 19.2   *Pays of the Paris Basin*

Settlement is concentrated in large villages, and there is nucleation around wet points because of the relative lack of surface water.

A significant contrast is provided by **le Pays de Brie** which lies between the Rivers Seine and Marne, south-east of Paris. Here the limestone contains bands of clay overlying impervious marls, there is abundant surface water, and the water table is much higher than in Beauce. In former times, Brie was forested and marshy, and even now there is abundant woodland and a more varied land-use. Agriculture has a more mixed character, cereals comprising often one-third, and permanent pasture another third of the agricultural land. Fodder crops are important, with rotation pasture and sugar beet cultivated as cash crops and fodder, as cattle and sheep provide much of the income. Brie cheese and butter are two significant products. The smaller average size of farm and greater dispersal of settlement is more typical of dairy-farming country. Hamlets and isolated farms are common. The contrasts between these two 'pays' of the Ile de France are almost absolute.

The Champagne scarplands

To the east and south-east of Brie lie the succession of chalk scarps and clay vales which are formed by the south-east-facing escarpments of the Falaise, the 'Champagne Pouilleuse' and the 'Champagne Humide'. The variety of landscape is compounded by the river gaps of the Seine, Yonne, Aube, Marne, Vesle and Aisne which cut large embayments through the scarps.

The Tertiary scarp, known as the Falaise de L'Ile de France, stretches from the Oise to the Seine but is best known in the region of Reims and Epernay for the vineyards of the Champagne wine district. There is a conjunction of physical factors. The chalk scarp has a generous covering of loam which promotes both drainage and aeration; the marginal climatic conditions are modified by the south-east-facing scarp slope which gives maximum insulation and which provides frost drainage; chalk bedrock reflects light onto the plants and allows warmth to penetrate the soil. The prosperity of viticulture in these marginal climatic conditions, however, is largely due to human factors. The medieval trade fairs, the commercial acumen of the Bishops of Reims and Châlons-sur-Marne, expertise in blending, and specialisation in sparkling wines, has given the wines of Champagne an international reputation. There is also considerable capital needed to sustain the blending processes, manufacturing, storage, and maturing. This was provided originally by the Benedictine Abbey of Hautvilliers, and now by the 'Maisons de Champagne', an association of manufacturing firms, including Pommery, Heidsieck, Clicquot, Bollinger, in and around Reims and Epernay. The marginal nature of the area climatically, resulting in many poor years, favours the large producer who can carry large stocks. This tends to maintain the system whereby 80 per cent of champagne is produced by the four large companies. The actual farm-holdings are, however, small. There are over 16 000 smallholding vine growers, and about 90 per cent have farms of 2 ha and below. The 'Maisons de Champagne' buy most of their grapes from these small tenant farmers.

La Champagne Pouilleuse (dry Champagne) succeeds the Tertiary scarp, and is a landscape of thin chalk without limon, with consequently little surface vegetation. It carries a poor-quality grassland with outcrops of chalk and was traditionally devoted to sheep rearing, with some cereals and large areas of fallow. The area had a history of depopulation, a low population density, and a general air of sterility, with long distances between villages. It was an almost empty land. In the last 50 years this area, under new attitudes and values, has become a valuable agricultural resource, as it provided a large under-used reserve of land for food production. Large-scale *remembrement* and a uniform open landscape has created large farms ideal for mechanised grain farming, and extensive use of fertilisers gives very profitable farming. There is a mixed farming system, with cereals, sugar beet, potatoes, fodder and root crops, and lucerne. Cattle are kept, giving dairy products for the Paris market. The landscape, still with a deserted appearance, now looks more like a prairie scene, with infrequent villages and arable fields stretching into the distance. The N44 road between Châlons-sur-Marne and Reims gives a typical view of this landscape.

The dry chalk country, terminated by a second scarpline, is followed by the Champagne Humide. This is Lower Cretaceous sand and clay, akin to the sub-scarp Wealden and Gault country of Southern England, and comparable in landscape and economy. Woodland and pasture, interspersed with orchards, produce a dairy-farming economy, of which the most typical is found in the Marne valley from Vitry-le-Francois to Chaumont. A 'bocage' landscape, well-watered and with many villages and hamlets and isolated farms, is the norm.

The chalk plateau of Artois and Picardie

North of the River Oise, the chalk plain of Picardie, with its thick cover of limon, rises gradually across the Somme valley to the outer rim of the chalk plateau in Artois. Arable farming with cereals, sugar beet, potatoes and fodder crops is the rule. Farms of over 50 ha, highly mechanised, and rationalised by *remembrement*, and open fields stretching to the horizon, underline the picture of large-scale agriculture. There is considerable variation, with several 'pays': the Bas Boulonnais near Boulogne has Jurassic clays providing good pasture for cattle and horse rearing; between Arras and Cambrai is an intensive rotation system with the highest crop yields of anywhere in Northern France; the Somme valley, often marshy, is devoted to pasture, with market gardening around Amiens.

Haute Normandie

This comprises the western side of the chalk rim of the Paris Basin, the undulating limon-covered plateau being the dominant feature, with cereal farming on medium-to-large, efficient farms, especially in the pays de Caux. Further east, in Vexin, there are greater concentrations of sugar beet, barley for brewing, and other industrial crops. Near Caen is the pays d'Auge, which is bocage country, with dairy products, including the famous Livarot and Camembert cheeses. The clays and marls in the anticline of Bray and in the valley of the Eure produce dairy farming and orchards. Cider apples and Calvados are specialities.

Description of these 'pays' is intended to illustrate the traditional picture of the Paris Basin as the 'Granary of Europe', with its vast tracts of fertile sediments overlain by limon. It is the most advanced agricultural province in France, favoured by the physical environment and also by proximity to the

Regional centre	Population 1990	Regional centre	Population 1990
Rouen	380 000	Cherbourg	92 000
Le Havre	254 000	Bourges	93 000
Tours	272 000	St Quentin	62 000
Orleans	243 000	Charleville	59 000
Reims	206 000	Chartres	42 000
Le Mans	189 000	Châlons-sur-Marne	52 000
Caen	189 000	Châteauroux	53 000
Amiens	156 000	Nevers	44 000
Troyes	123 000	Beauvais	56 000

FIGURE 19.3   *Population of regional centres in the Paris Basin*

industrial and urban populations of Paris and Northern France. This has stimulated food production. Movement off the land towards the cities has also stimulated a greater level of mechanisation, making the area one of the most efficient farming regions in France. Thus the Paris Basin has a much lower density of population and larger farms than other parts of France, providing a marked contrast to the French peasants of the 'Midi' on their smaller and fragmented farm-holdings. There is a concentration of croplands, particularly cereals, in what is known as the 'intensive grain core' extending from Beauce to Artois. At the same time the widely differing 'pays' landscapes have provided a great range of farm products. The Paris Basin has both scale and variety.

THE GROWTH OF THE PARIS AGGLOMERATION

Figure 19.1 illustrates the position of Paris as the centre of French communications, and the relatively small size of cities in close proximity to Paris (fig. 19.3). Paris has always been very much the undisputed capital city of France, the administrative, industrial and cultural centre of the country. The kings of France had traditionally centralised power in Paris, and this was underlined by Napoleon, who destroyed the power of the great historic provinces such as Lorraine and Burgundy by creating the smaller *départements*, and by focussing the system of 'routes nationales' upon Paris. There is a strong historic tradition of central government.

The economic consequences are shown by the employment characteristics. The Ile de France had 10.7 million people in 1990 (nearly 20 per cent of the French population) and employed 20 per cent of the French

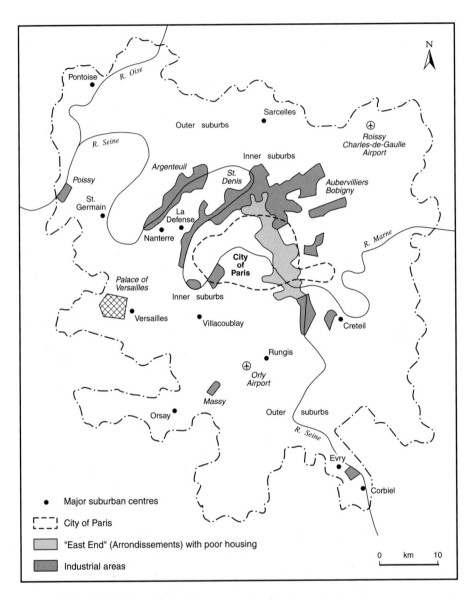

FIGURE 19.4 *The Paris agglomeration*

workforce – 4.5 million workers. Its predominance in specialised functions and skilled labour is even more significant: it has over 65 per cent of French research workers; 48 per cent of the total qualified engineers; and 40 per cent of all professional and managerial grades. It produced 30 per cent of the output of the aircraft industry, 40 per cent of French cars, and about 50 per cent of all precision, electronic, radio and television products. The service sector is even more significant, the city having a virtual monopoly on banking, insurance and company head offices. The large consumer market, pool of skilled labour, and commercial and financial institutions have given

Paris technologically advanced industries with a high growth potential and income levels well above the national average. This economic strength is matched by an equivalent concentration of educational provision, and artistic and cultural activity, which gives the city a power and relative importance in French life which is unequalled anywhere else in Europe.

At the last census (1990) there were 8.7 million people in the Paris agglomeration, but the component parts of the city and its region need to be examined in more detail.

The Paris agglomeration consists of the city and its suburbs. The administrative, cultural, financial, tourist, retail and commercial centre, together with railway termini, and mixed industrial and traditional residential districts such as Montmartre, is surrounded by the framework of the 1798 city wall, along which are famous gates such as the Porte d'Italie and the Porte d'Orléans. Along the approximate line of the city wall runs the Boulevard Periphérique, the inner ring road. In the inner suburbs lie most of the industrial zones (fig. 19.4) including St. Denis and Aubervilliers-Bobigny in the north, and the banks of the Seine around Argenteuil, which together constitute the northern arc of nineteenth-century industrialisation.

The two major inner-city problems are congestion and overcrowding. The transport system has to cope with 3 million daily commuters, of which 35 per cent travel by private car, for whom the main problem is parking.

The Basilica of Sacré Coeur, Montmartre, Paris, one of the major tourist attractions of this historic city

This seems strange when considering the wide boulevards of Haussmann (1853–70) but these have to cope with dense traffic flows, and kerbside parking is therefore highly restricted. Some 15 per cent of the commuters travel short distances by foot, and about 50 per cent rely upon public transport. The Metro, the underground system, is not as extensive as that of London, and only goes as far as the inner surburban ring, at which point commuters travelling to the suburbs have to transfer to the municipal bus service or Réseau Express Régional (RER) high-speed suburban rail service. Housing in inner Paris is badly overcrowded. The eleventh arrondissement is one of the worst examples, with a substantial proportion of its houses without basic facilities and in a very decayed condition. The problem is worst in the east-end arc of the city, from Montmartre in the north through Temple, Le Marais, Popincourt and Bastille to the Gare De Lyons. Industrial decline in the older inner-city areas has created considerable economic and social problems. The problem is one of redevelopment of the inner areas, maintaining adequate residential employment and recreation facilities, and adequate road systems.

The outer suburbs (*banlieu*) constitute the lower-density residential zone, but they also include high-density 'Grands Ensembles' such as Sarcelles (fig. 19.5), decentralised industry in the new estates such as Poissy, Massy and Creteil, and the development of public service areas such as the Rungis Food Market, Orly airport and Roissy Charles-de-Gaulle airport. Expansion along the major radial routeways and rapid population growth has incorporated many previously independent settlements such as Versailles, Pontoise, St Germain and Evry-Corbeil, which are now outer suburbs of the city.

THE ILE DE FRANCE PLANNING REGION

The Ile de France Planning Region (fig. 19.6) includes a number of *départements* adjacent to Paris which are closely linked to the economic life of the city. There are still separate but fast-expanding, medium-sized towns surrounded by agricultural land and large areas of woodland, forest, and protected areas, particularly the Forest of Fontainebleau to the south, Rambouillet on the south-west and Chantilly to the north. The area acts as an open lung for the city, a safety valve, where expansion will be directed along carefully planned lines. Figure 19.5 shows the remarkable growth of these *départements*, Seine et Marne, Yvelines, Essonne and Val d'Oise. Towns in this commuter zone such as Mantes, Creil, Lagny, Etampes, Meaux and Melun are amongst the fastest-growing places in France.

Zone	Population total (1000)				Percentage annual change		
	1968	1975	1982	1990	1968–75	1975–82	1982–90
Paris city (1)	2591	2290	2162	2154	−1.69	−0.8	−0.1
Inner departments (2)	3823	4129	4119	3988	+0.4	−0.3	−0.4
Paris agglomeration	8197	8424	8707	8662	+0.4	+0.5	−0.1
Seine et Marne	604	706	819	1074	+2.4	+2.3	+3.9
Val d'Oise	693	848	925	1047	+3.2	+1.3	+1.7
Yvelines	853	978	1074	1305	+2.1	+1.4	+2.7
Essonne	674	928	993	1083	+5.4	+1.0	+1.1
Outer Suburban ring (3)	2824	3460	3811	4509	+3.2	+1.5	+2.3
Ile de France total (1) (2) (3)	9238	9879	10 092	10 651	+1.0	+0.3	+0.7

FIGURE 19.5   *Population change in the Paris Region (Ile de France) 1968–90*

THE PARIS BASIN PLANNING UNIT

This is based principally upon the historic provinces of Champagne, Picardie, Normandy and Orléans (fig. 19.1). From the nineteenth century onwards the effect of Paris has been felt in an adverse way in the small farming communities and villages of these provinces. The drainage of labour and resources to the capital from what has been termed by J. F. Gravier as 'le désert Francais', has continued to the present day. The urban centres in the Paris Basin such as Reims and Orléans are medium-sized cities and towns which act as natural centres for the agricultural 'pays', but they are considerably smaller than would normally be expected. They have existed

View of the Place Charles-de-Gaulle and the Arc de Triomphe, Paris

under the shadow of Paris for a very long period. There is, therefore, a lack of equilibrium within the Paris Basin Planning Unit between the city of Paris and the major regional centres.

POPULATION CHANGE 1968–90

The Paris region illustrates the complex nature of population movement during the last 50 years. Until 1968 the rapid growth of the city was an integral part of the remarkable demographic and economic growth of France and, indeed, the rest of Western Europe. Urbanisation was the dominant force and by 1961 when the Paris planning strategy was begun, the city was acting as a magnet and was growing at an alarming rate.

Since 1968, however, Paris, and France as a whole, appears to be conforming to the process of counter-urbanisation, involving decentralisation from cities to suburbs and higher growth rates lower down the urban hierarchy. The net population loss in the city of Paris since 1968 (fig. 19.5) and in the agglomeration since 1982, is matched by dynamic growth in the four *départements* in the outer suburban ring. Population change is paralleled by the decentralisation of employment from the core to the outer suburbs and adjacent rural areas. However, the 1990 census indicates only a very minor loss of population in the central city between 1982 and 1990, which may be related to the completion of a number of major redevelopment projects.

PLANNING FOR PARIS AND ITS REGION

The long-term strategy for planning was begun by the PADOG proposals in 1960, followed by the Schéma Directeur in 1965. This has been an extremely flexible plan which has been adapted to take into account changing economic and demographic conditions in the city region. Revised versions were introduced in 1969 and 1975. The key feature of the Schéma was the recognition of Paris as a metropolitan world city and that limitation of its growth would be counter-productive. It therefore set out to regulate rather than contain growth, and accepted that the population of the Paris region could grow to 14 million by 2000 AD. This estimate was subsequently revised downwards in the light of the 1973 recession and the slowing-down of population growth. The principal aims were the reinvigoration of the central areas of the city, the improvement of the transport infrastructure, the creation of new service centres in the suburbs, planned growth in the lower Seine valley, and balanced development in the Paris Basin as a whole with the strengthening of regional centres such as Orléans and Reims. Key aspects of the plan were as follows.

360

(a) The 'La Defense' redevelopment scheme to create a new inner suburban node with commercial, cultural, administrative and public buildings, adjacent to the University of Nanterre. Its purpose was to establish a growth centre to the west of the existing central area of Paris. There were similar projects in Villacoublay, Rungis and Creteil to the south, and St Denis and Bobigny to the north (fig. 19.4). The strategy was to reinvigorate the inner suburban zones. Urban renewal also took place in the historic city centre, in Les Halles and in Montparnasse where public buildings often replaced housing.

(b) In addition to the expanded Metro system, a new fast suburban railway 'The Réseau Express Regional' has been built linking a major east–west line with two north–south lines (connecting Orly with Roissy Charles-de-Gaulle Airport). Three ring motorways, the Boulevard Periphérique, the Rocade De Banlieu (A86) at 15 km (still being completed), and the Autoroute Interurbaine de Seine et Oise at 20 km, link with the radiating motorways out of the city.

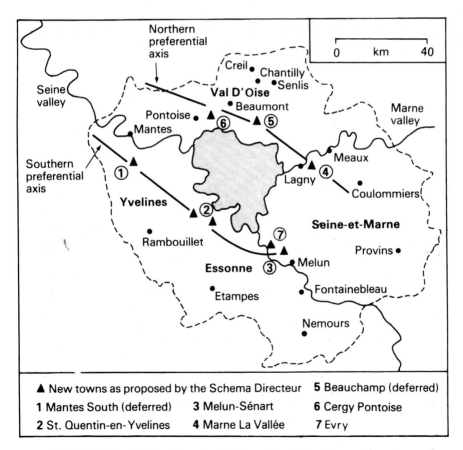

▲ **New towns as proposed by the Schema Directeur**   **5 Beauchamp (deferred)**

1 Mantes South (deferred)   **3 Melun-Sénart**   **6 Cergy Pontoise**

2 St. Quentin-en-Yvelines   **4 Marne La Vallée**   **7 Evry**

FIGURE 19.6   *The Ile de France Planning Region, with outlying towns and new towns along the preferential axes*

(c) Growth axes parallel to the River Seine were designed to preserve the open land alongside the river and to provide for up to eight new towns at a distance of up to 35 km from the city centre. These were later reduced to five (fig. 19.6) as population growth slowed after 1968. Marne La Vallée, St Quentin-en-Yvelines, Cergy-Pontoise, Melun-Sénart and Evry have been the principal foci of population growth in the region, with high levels of natural increase and in-migration levels of 5 per cent per annum. Marne–La-Vallée was also chosen as the site for EuroDisney in 1987, and its opening in 1992 was an opportunity to encourage more development to the east of Paris rather than on the favoured western side.

(d) The 'Couronne' is a ring of historic towns and cities at up to 200 km distance from Paris (fig. 19.7). These cities, such as Amiens, Chartres and Reims, lie on the major radial routeways and at key points in the agricultural 'pays'. Four areas were designated as 'support zones' (*zones d'appui*), major new revitalised centres, with other regional centres expanded where necessary (fig. 19.3).

(e) The most important single area with growth possibilities was the Lower Seine (Rouen–Le Havre) axis. This is a major line of movement via

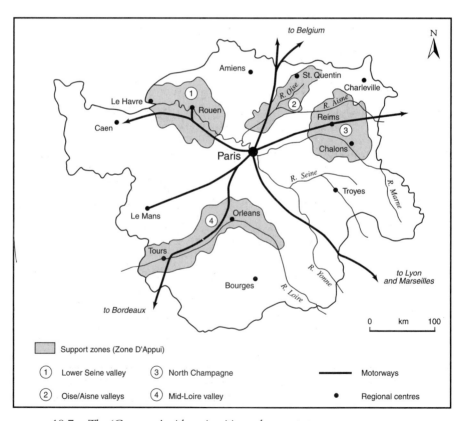

FIGURE 19.7 *The 'Couronne' with major cities and support zones*

railways, waterways, pipelines and motorways. There are deep–water–access and port facilities at Le Havre including oil refineries and terminals, and the area also includes the two largest existing urban centres outside Paris itself: Le Havre (254 000), the second port of France, and Rouen (380 000). This axis has been developed as a strategic growth corridor from Paris to the coast.

The growth strategy (d) and (e) for the outer areas was revised and reduced after 1975. The Ile de France Planning Region has tended to stabilise with a population of 10.7 million, in line with the general economic and demographic slowdown in France during the 1980s. Population shortfall gave to Paris the opportunity to redress imbalances between east and west and to make minor adjustments as the city moved towards a polycentric form. As a result the 'zones d'appui' have had a lower priority as reception areas for decentralisation from the city of Paris. Environmental concerns also began to be recognised with the new green proposals such as the new park at Belleville and a larger one surrounding La Villette.

The shortfall in population has not invalidated the Schéma Directeur plan as any future population increase will need the provisions of the plan, but in 1990 the Livre Blanc for the Ile de France region (L'Ile de France 2000) was

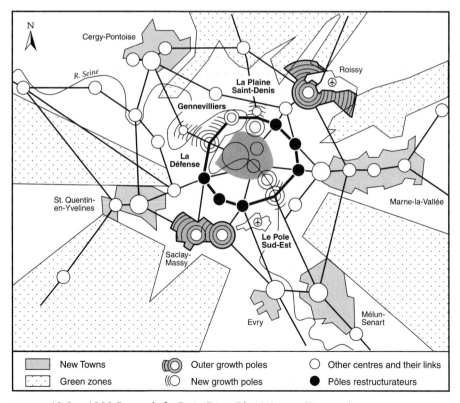

FIGURE 19.8   *1990 Proposals for Paris (Livre Blanc) (source:* Eurostat*)*

published, again revising the earlier plans but also building upon what had already been achieved. These policy guidelines for the period up to 2015 limit the region's population to 12 million by that date with a planned 5 per cent reduction in the number of government offices in the region as well as a reduction from 52 per cent to 48 per cent in publicly funded research-and-development laboratories. The guidelines also emphasise the need for open spaces in the region, an efficient transport network and a number of urban growth poles. The latter involve the extension of developments already in progress and two new growth poles: an international pole at Roissy in the north-east and a technopole in the Saclay–Palaiseau area of the south-west outer suburbs (fig. 19.8). There are three developments extending existing sectors: the westward sector of La Défense/Gennevilliers/Montesson; the south-east sector extending from the edge of Bercy-Tolbiac through Ivry, Vitry and Charenton to Maison Altfort; and the northern sector extending from the Gare du Nord and Gare de l'Est through La Villette to the Plain St Denis.

The guidelines maintain the viability of towns between 30 and 50 km from the city of Paris but also propose two new urban foci in the outer suburbs. At Roissy a new international growth pole will continue to develop based on the airport and the convergence of the TGV and RER routes (the national exhibition centre is already located here because of the high degree of accessibility). The other growth pole (the Saclay–Palaiseau technopole) will provide a counter-balance based on higher-education establishments and the excellent TGV connections to the south-west.

The agricultural and forest land on the periphery of the city is to be protected as a series of green wedges to provide recreational opportunities and access to rural areas for Parisians. Transport networks will continue to be upgraded with new RER links between the busiest stations and between the major mainline stations in northern Paris, a fourth RER line to run south-east to north-west and the completion of an improved motorway network.

The Livre Blanc is part of a national strategy to balance growth between Paris and the other French regions and to improve the quality of life, but it is also designed to enable Paris to compete successfully with other EU capitals. Paris could become the leading cultural centre of Europe and possibly the capital of a Single European Market – i.e. Paris Euro-City.

SPAIN AND PORTUGAL

Introduction

For much of this century Spain and Portugal have been on the margins of West European life, but since 1960 both countries have undergone marked economic, social and political change. Spain, in particular, achieved a very rapid economic growth rate during the 1960s whereas Portugal lagged well behind, partly because of its smaller size and fewer resources, but in particular because of the African colonial struggles which slowed progress considerably. They now stand at an intermediate level of development between the industrialised north-west Europe and the emergent nations of the developing world (fig. 20.1).

There has also been major political change from the mid-1970s when both countries emerged from the dictatorships of Franco and Salazar and entered the ranks of the West European democracies. They have simultaneously, however, had to face major change, in particular the global economic recession. Both joined the EEC in 1986.

Spain

Spain, with 39 million people, is by far the largest economy, next to Italy, in the Mediterranean region. It is a country of great potential and with significant resources, but one in which industrialisation started late.

Spain is a country of generally adverse physical character, particularly the interior Meseta plateau, rugged mountain ranges and the semi-arid south. Alpine fold mountains include the Sierra Nevada, Cantabrians and Pyrenees. The Pyrenees reach 3470 m (fig. 20.2). The Cantabrian mountains isolate the northern coasts of Spain from the semi-arid interior basin of Old Castile. The rugged landscape has given rise to great difficulties of communication,

	Spain	Portugal
Area (km²)	505 000	92 000
Population (millions)	39.1	9.9
Population density per km² (Eur 12 = 148)	78	107
Gross Domestic Product index per capita (Eur 12 = 100)	71	38
Percentage of workforce in agriculture	10.0	12.0
Percentage of workforce in industry	31.0	33.0
Percentage of workforce in services	59.0	56.0
Car production (1000)	1505	nil
Number of passenger cars per 100 inhabitants (Eur 12 = 40)	32	31
Coal production (million tonnes)	18.1	0.2
Steel production (million tonnes)	13.0	0.8
Energy consumption per head (Eur 12 = 3438 toe)	2349	1681

toe = tonnes of oil equivalent

FIGURE 20.1   *Spain and Portugal – an economic profile, 1993 (source: Eurostat)*

and major cultural differences between Castile, Catalonia, Andalusia, and in particular, the Basque region. Reference to the historic divisions between the 'Eight Spains' illustrates the cultural diversity. Historical and economic problems have a striking resemblance to Italy's Mezzogiorno.

The semi-developed nature of Spain is also illustrated by the contrasts between agriculture and industry. Agriculture involves 10 per cent of the workforce and is characterised by an absentee landlord system with large feudal-style estates, fragmented farms, many of which are below 2 ha in size, and low productivity which is generally 50 per cent below the EU average. On the other hand, Spain is also the tenth largest industrial country in the world. On the north coast are coal reserves and Spain produces 18 million tonnes of coal per year. Bilbao extracts iron ore from open-cast mines and is the centre of a declining steel-producing area. The Sierra Morena region is a producer of copper, lead, silver, zinc, manganese and mercury. Major rivers such as the Guadalquivir, Tagus and Guadiana are being harnessed for hydro-electric power. As well as irrigation control, and increased agricultural productivity, this is significant for industrial development. There are major industries of textiles, steel, shipbuilding, engineering, and car assembly. Nearly half of the economy is based on tourism, and this last fact indicates the great imbalances in an otherwise potentially large and rich economy.

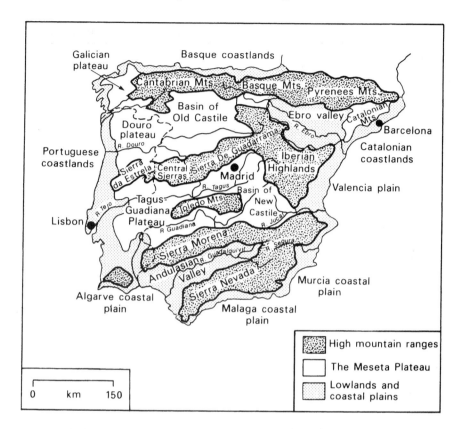

FIGURE 20.2   *Spain and Portugal – physical features*

Spain, although semi-developed, is thus experiencing substantial transformation from an agricultural into an industrial country. The change has been relatively rapid during the last two decades, for several reasons. These include the opening-up of the country to Western influence from American air bases and the enormous influx of capital from the tourist trade since the 1960s which has given Spain finance for development projects. After General Franco's death and the return of constitutional monarchy, Spain became a member of the EU in 1986.

PORTUGAL

Portugal has a long Atlantic coastline, with a narrow rugged hinterland rising eastwards towards the Spanish Meseta. Many of the Spanish mountain ridges such as Sierra da Estrela (1990 m) continue into Portugal (fig. 20.2). However, the relief is generally lower than in Spain with river basins including the Douro, Mondego and Tejo (Tagus). The lowland fringes of

Portugal face westwards towards the Atlantic Ocean and the physical division from the Spanish plateau helps to explain the traditional political separation and different outlook of the two countries.

Portugal has a different climate from most of the Iberian peninsula and is dominated by maritime influences from the Atlantic Ocean. Most of the country has an equable, warm, temperate climate with considerable rainfall, mild winters and hot summers. Natural vegetation reflects the abundance of rainfall. Portugal originally had a forest cover of evergreen oak; Mediterranean pines, cork oak and sweet chestnut, and almost one-third of the country is still wooded. Agriculture follows traditional lines, with small subsistence farms cultivating wheat, barley, maize and rearing cattle. Tree crops are widespread, including peaches, apples and olives. The special vineyards of the Douro valley are most important as is the Tejo valley around Lisbon, which produces 40 per cent of Portuguese wines. The Algarve in the extreme south has semi-arid Mediterranean-type conditions.

Portugal was one of the first European colonial powers, but since the seventeenth century has suffered a long decline for several reasons. It is almost totally lacking in mineral resources, and hydro-electric power has been retarded by irregular river regimes, although there are now major HEP schemes on the Tejo and Douro rivers. Industrialisation is limited. The African colonial empire proved a costly drain on scarce resources during the long guerrilla war in the 1960s and 1970s, after which the last two major colonies, Angola and Mozambique, became independent. There was a long period of dictatorship under which economic development was neglected,

Terraced vineyards of the Douro valley near Oporto

after which Portugal emerged with a democratic government in 1976. Portuguese industry is composed largely of small businesses, and productivity is low. The single most significant source of income has been the revenue from the tourist industry in Lisbon–Estoril, and in the Algarve.

TOURISM

Tourism is another very significant element in socio-economic change. Over 55 million people visited Spain and nearly 9 million Portugal in 1992. Spain became important during the 1960s for tourism with the development of the cheap holiday package and charter flights to airports such as Perpignan, Barcelona, Malaga and Palma. In addition the low cost of living and cheap accommodation during the early years were a major consideration. However, most important of all for north European tourists was the hot sunshine. Seventy per cent of the visitors are from Germany, the UK, Scandinavia and the Benelux countries. The tourism involved is largely coastal, for few tourists visit the interior on any scale, although this is now increasing as the historic attractions of interior cities such as Seville and Cordoba become more well-known and accessible.

High-rise development at Benidorm on the Costa Blanca

The physical advantages of much of the Spanish Mediterranean coastline include backing mountains giving a sheltered aspect, attractive scenery and sheltered beaches, warm sea with up to 10 hours of sunshine daily, rainless summers and extremely mild winters. The first area developed historically was the Costa Brava, the so-called rugged coast, which is closest to the French frontier, easily accessible by road and the initial area of interest during the late 1950s and early 1960s. It has a very attractive rocky coast with resorts such as San Feliu and Tossa de Mar. Further south is the Costa Dorada, around Alicante is the Costa Blanca, and in the south, around Malaga and facing North Africa, is the Costa del Sol (fig. 20.3). The Balearic Islands of Majorca, Minorca and Ibiza and the Canary Islands have also benefited on a large scale from air package tours, receiving 60 per cent of all visitors to Spain. Palma de Mallorca Airport alone handled nearly 12 million passengers in 1992, reaching fourteenth in the rankings of EU airports (fig. 5.7 (b)).

The physical effects of tourist development have transformed small fishing villages into a continuous ribbon of developments, with high-rise hotels and apartment blocks stretching along large sections of coastline. The rapid development has involved severe planning problems of water supply, building safety, congestion and so on. Marbella, Estepona, Benidorm and Torremolinos are some of the more well-known resorts. Of most dramatic economic importance has been the significance to the Spanish economy, where the income from tourism has been absolutely crucial. It was tourism that broke the vicious circle of Spanish underdevelopment and this has been the main financing force behind Spanish and Portuguese development. Tourism employs nearly 11 per cent of Spain's working population and accounts for some 10 per cent of GDP.

Although tourism has transformed many of the coastal economies, nevertheless it has also had negative effects. There has been a lack of physical planning resulting in high-rise development, anarchic coastal sprawl and considerable congestion and pollution. However, most important of all, tourism has been predominantly a coastal phenomenon and the economic over-heating of the coasts is characterised by seasonality in employment. Not even the seasonal income from tourism is as high as might be expected because of the control of the large tour operators who dominate the marketing of Spain and Portugal in northern Europe and who strongly influence prices and conditions. As a result even tourism along the 'Costas' illustrates a type of dependency status.

The Spanish were made more aware of these problems at the end of the 1980s when the number of visitors arriving in 1989–90 fell from 54 million to 52 million, with a consequent fall in income. A number of factors created this drop: high prices due to the strong peseta, adverse publicity (e.g. 'lager louts', terrorism and water pollution) and the Gulf crisis. Despite slow economic growth in Europe the number of visitors has grown again, but Spain realises the need to provide quality rather than quantity and has been investing in the upgrading of resorts as well as tempting high-spending market segments with 'green tourism' in areas like the northern Cantabrian coast – or inland for culture and heritage.

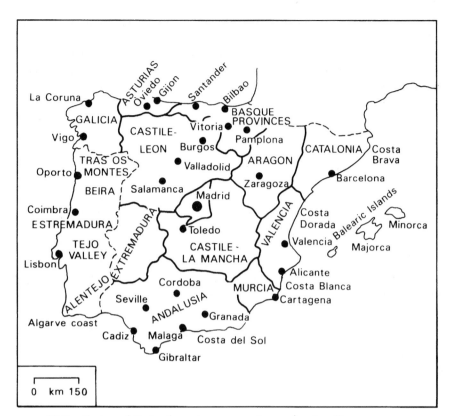

FIGURE 20.3   *Spain and Portugal – autonomous regions and major cities*

Catalonia is now attempting to attract visitors to the whole region and not just to the coast with walking and golfing holidays and winter ski-ing in the Pyrenees. The hosting of the 1992 Olympics enabled Barcelona to alter its image and almost completely revamp its infrastructure. One of the infrastructure projects, the beach project, was particularly important as the railway lines between the city and the sea were removed giving the city a beach frontage and opening it up to the sea. The Olympics placed Barcelona on the world stage as the Single European Market came into being, enabling Barcelona to become a business tourism centre rivalling Madrid and considerably boosting the self-confidence of the Catalan region.

POPULATION MIGRATION

The transformation from a predominantly rural-agrarian society into a modern urban-industrial society has gone much further in Spain than in Portugal. The principal element of geographical importance is rural-to-urban migration – the flight from the land to the city.

Barcelona – Olympic stadium and sportshall

In Portugal, the coastal areas around Lisbon, and to a lesser extent Oporto and the northern coasts, contrast with a thinly populated interior. In Spain the pattern is more complex with a pattern of densely populated coastal areas dominated by the Basque region, Catalonia and the Mediterranean coastal strip, plus the large population centre of Madrid and a hierarchy of other smaller cities such as Zaragoza, Valladolid and Burgos in the interior. The period from 1960 to 1975 saw large-scale migration from the impoverished interior provinces into the core areas of rapidly expanding economic opportunities. The socio-economic picture thus created was one of wide income differences between the well-to-do urban dwellers and the shanty towns on the edge of the city. On the other hand, rural exodus led to the decay of small towns and villages and a lack of infrastructure in the countryside. This pattern of uneven social and economic development showed widening differences between the core industrialised regions and backward agricultural regions: an industrialised and advanced Spain co-existing with a rural backward one. The present pattern of population density shows a marked contrast between the core areas in the north and east which contain the major cities, industries and services, and a peripheral south and west which is sparsely populated. Urban primacy is most marked, with the city regions of Madrid and Barcelona accounting for 25 per cent of Spain's total population.

Region	Area (1000 km²)	Population change, 1981–90
Galicia	29.4	+3.7%
Asturias	10.6	−0.1%
Cantabria	5.3	+4.2%
Basque Country	7.3	+0.9%
Navarra	10.4	+3.7%
Rioja	5.0	+4.7%
Aragon	47.7	+0.4%
Madrid	8.0	+7.3%
Castile and Leon	94.2	+1.1%
Castile-La-Mancha	79.2	+2.8%
Estremadura	41.6	+3.5%
Andalusia	87.3	+10.2%
Murcia	11.3	+11.2%
Valencia	23.3	+7.0%
Catalonia	31.9	+3.5%
The Balearic Islands	5.0	+17.1%
The Canary Islands	7.2	+16.2%

FIGURE 20.4   *Spain – population change 1981–90 (source: Eurostat)*

Since 1975 the pattern of migration has become more complex, whilst the pace has been reduced. The economic recession and the problems of integration into the EU economy have seriously affected economic growth in Spain and Portugal. Rates of depopulation of the interior have slackened (fig. 20.4). Madrid and other major cities, and the tourist coastal areas, continue to grow, but a new feature has emerged. The northern provinces of Asturias and the Basque region (Vizcaya and Guipuzcoa) have been affected by economic recession, the decline of coal-mining, steel and shipbuilding, high unemployment, and political problems – namely the terrorist tactics of ETA. Economic growth and population change in Spain is beginning to show similar patterns to other EU countries further north. The fertility rate of childbearing Spanish women has dropped to 1.2 children – the lowest in the EU along with Italy.

However, regions like Aragon still exhibit rural depopulation, with people moving to other regions (particularly Catalonia) and to the main urban centres in the region like Zaragoza and its hinterland where half of the region's population and two-thirds of its employment are concentrated. The central strip around Zaragoza and the River Ebro have exerted such a pull that the provinces of Huesca and Teruel have population densities of only ten inhabitants per km^2 – which is amongst the lowest in Spain. As out-migration involves mainly young people, the population has gradually aged with a consequent decline in the birth rate and therefore a very small population growth in the period 1981–90.

On the other hand the region of Madrid has experienced a rate of population growth well below that in previous decades as the rate of in-migration has declined and the birth rate fallen. An increasing number of the region's inhabitants are working in neighbouring regions (particularly Castile-La-Mancha) where businesses are setting up due to lower land prices.

The Balearic Islands used to be a region of out-migration, but between 1960 and 1980 the population increased by 49 per cent. This large demographic increase was essentially due to the arrival of migrants in the younger age groups, which led to an increase in the birth rate. In the 1980s the birth rate fell and the number of immigrants declined, although the proportion of the population aged 65 and over increased with 4 per cent of this sector being immigrants, reflecting an increase in retirement developments.

Regional imbalance

Both countries have some of the most severe regional problems in Western Europe. Vast areas of Iberia have little or no interaction. There are marked concentrations of wealth in the national capitals, in commercial cities like Barcelona, industrial cities like Valencia, the Basque region in northern Spain, and the tourist coastlands. These areas are bourgeois Spain, middle-class areas with an advanced economy of an industrial/service type. By contrast large tracts of underdeveloped regions include much of the north-west of Spain, Galicia, large parts of the central Plateaux, Estremadura, Castile and the Southern plain of Andalusia. In Portugal, apart from the coastal areas around Lisbon and Oporto, much of the interior is very considerably under-developed. In many of the rural areas of Spain and Portugal, the essence of the problem is not so much the harshness of the natural environment, the lack of resources and the climate, as much as the human and institutional factors. In Andalusia there are *latifundi*, the large estates of absentee landlords based upon feudal landownership patterns, with low productivity, sporadic employment, poor living conditions, lack of infrastructure, low levels of educational ability and little vertical social mobility.

Spain: growth regions

Madrid lies almost in the geometrical centre of Spain, and became the national capital in 1561 (fig. 20.6). Its importance was underlined permanently as it became the focus of the national road and rail systems. Madrid is a political, administrative and cultural capital. It has benefited from large-scale rural-urban migration providing it with a large workforce. Modern industrial development includes vehicles, electrical equipment, chemicals, food processing and consumer goods. Textile industries, fashion and leather goods are also significant employers, as is the construction industry. Madrid is the second most important industrial area in Spain (after Catalonia), with industry increasingly specialised in high-demand sectors (aircraft, electronics, pharmaceuticals, precision instruments and electrical engineering).

The service sector contributes more than 70 per cent of gross value-added and shows great dynamism due to the internationalisation of the economy after entry into the EU in 1986. Within the services sector, the distributive trades, hotels and catering, transport, banking and insurance are prominent (10 per cent of bank offices are located in the Madrid region). The major ministries are in Madrid as it is the national capital, and 70 per cent of the multinational companies operating in Spain are located there. The Madrid region is a prime decision-making and logistical centre favoured by a highly advantageous geo-strategic situation. As a result, it accounts for 29 per cent of Spanish exports and 46 per cent of direct investment from abroad.

During the recession of the 1980s the Madrid region saw the loss of 65 000 jobs, particularly in the industrial areas of the south and east of the metropolitan area. This area has experienced social problems as a result. The city also suffers substantial infrastructure problems, although there has been investment in ring roads, the metro system and high-speed rail links.

The northern coastlands include the Basque region of Navarre and Bilbao with iron ore, coal and a manufacturing industry. The Basque provinces are the most densely populated in Spain and have a distinct language and culture. Bilbao and the surrounding towns have a declining steel industry with shipbuilding, agricultural machinery and diesel engines. To the west are the ports of Santander and Gijon and the coal-mining centre of Oviedo.

Between 1982 and 1989, 20 000 heavy-industry jobs were lost in the province of Vizcaya and many plants, like the Euskalduna shipyard in Bilbao, were shut down. However, since 1985 economic growth has probably been faster in the Basque region than in any other region of Spain. Heavy industry (like the state-owned AHV steelworks just outside Bilbao) has been modernised and restructured but new companies have also been established in the areas of high technology, research and precision engineering in locations such as the Basque Technology Park 12 km from Bilbao's city centre at Zamudio. This site, only 3 km from the city airport, has attracted 37 companies since it was started in 1986, and it includes ITP, a jet-engine factory, 45 per cent owned by Rolls Royce, which is working on the

European Fighter Aircraft and components for the Airbus 330 and Boeing 777.

The recession of the early 1990s has required further restructuring, but the Basques are hoping that infrastructure developments such as the 'Basque Y' (a high-speed rail link that will connect the region's three provincial capitals of Vitoria, Bilbao and San Sebastian with France and eventually the south of Spain), urban renewal and the building of a new port in Bilbao will enable the region to prosper.

Catalonia's main advantage is its strategic location in the western Mediterranean with good communications with the rest of the Iberian peninsula. It is the centre of a region that extends across the French–Spanish border encompassing the cities of Montpellier and Toulouse and containing some 16 million inhabitants. The region can be divided into economically successful areas – the Llobregat valley, the Ripoll-Vic complex and the Barcelona metropolitan area – and economically depressed areas in the interior (including the mountain areas) which are sparsely populated, have an older population and a shortage of infrastructure and social amenities. The region's per capita GDP is one of the highest in Spain (fig. 20.6) although it is below the EU average. Barcelona is the ancient cultural capital of Catalonia, and is a financial, industrial and commercial metropolis. Much of Spain's hydro-electric power has been developed in the Catalan mountains behind the city. It is an important port with a well-established textile industry. Other industries include railway rolling stock, electrical equipment, diesel engines, vehicles, shipbuilding and food processing. Of particular importance is the SEAT car factory which is part of the Volkswagen multi-national group and also the region's leading exporter. However, the most spectacular foreign investment has been made by the Japanese, with nearly 100 Japanese companies locating in and around Barcelona. They have been attracted by the highly skilled workforce and Catalonia's location in relation to the larger EU market.

The Catalans have been keen to promote European and international links – hence their success in staging the 1992 Olympics. The C-6 cooperation network links Barcelona with Valencia, Zaragoza, Palma de Mallorca, Montpellier and Toulouse and is designed to promote tourism and economic development on a regional basis. Barcelona was also a founding city of the Eurocities movement which now includes more than 40 cities and covers more than 20 cooperative projects. It is at the western end of the new axis of European development stretching from Lombardy in Italy through the south of France to Catalonia – i.e., the 'second banana' (fig. 20.5) rivalling the 'blue banana' which consists of the wealthiest and most densely populated part of Europe. Catalonia is also one of the 'Four Motors of Europe' – a European cooperation group which consists of the dynamic regions of Rhône-Alpes, Lombardy, Baden-Württemberg and Catalonia.

Valencia forms a southern extension to Catalonia's dynamic development. At Valencia, the regional capital, is a modern integrated coastal steelworks, and a variety of industries including textiles, chemicals, shipbuilding, pottery

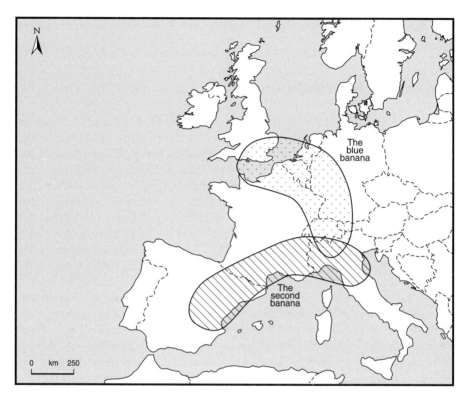

FIGURE 20.5   *The 'blue banana' and 'second banana' (source:* Drake)

and glass-making. The service sector now accounts for more than half the working population in the region, with manufacturing employing 30 per cent and agriculture 9 per cent. The Valencia region is Spain's principal tourist area for Spanish visitors and the third largest for foreign visitors, with resorts such as Benidorm.

The Murcia coastlands are one of the richest agricultural areas in Spain. Irrigated terraced coastal lowlands called *huertas* cultivate cereals, tobacco, oranges, tomatoes, artichokes, cauliflowers and rice. On the terraced slopes away from the coast are vineyards and olive groves.

Tourism in the Balearic Islands has led to rapid growth in the service sector and in construction, with the result that the islands are the only Spanish region with a per capita GDP which exceeds the EU average (fig. 20.6). Services now employ two-thirds of the working population, with half of these in the tourist trade. Tourist demand is mainly from the UK and Germany and the hotel trade on the islands offers the same number of beds as the whole of Greece. The shortage of water may become one of the islands' greatest problems. The limited rainfall and high porosity of the soil prohibit anything in the nature of a regular watercourse and the seasonal torrents are normally dry. This has led to greater efforts to extract underground water, but this has enabled sea water to infiltrate the aquifers.

The situation is most worrying on Majorca and Ibiza where water resources are limited.

Spain: underdeveloped regions

Galicia, on the north-west Atlantic coast, has good ports such as Coruna and Vigo and a pleasant wooded landscape with pasture. There are mixed farms with cattle, pigs, maize and orchards, but holdings are small and incomes are low. There is tunny, anchovy and sardine fishing. However, Galicia is one of the remotest parts of Spain, with one of the lowest per capita GDPs in the country. It has a large rural population, a lack of industry, and unemployment, and there is a steady drift of population away from the region. Almost 30 per cent of employment is still in the primary sector – one of the highest regional figures in the EU. The fishing industry accounts for 200 000 jobs and is the single most important industrial sector. The depletion of fish stocks and the extension of exclusion zones has had a serious impact on the industry, with exclusion from the tuna grounds off the coast of Namibia after independence in 1990 followed by a dispute with Canada in the waters off Newfoundland in the mid-1990s. Poor communications with the rest of Spain limit the opportunities for fishing communities to diversify into other activities. Spain's new network of motorway-standard state highways (autovias) do not connect with Galicia's limited toll motorways. However, there are plans to extend the network, including a coastal motorway connecting with the Portuguese motorway running north from Lisbon, although this is opposed by ecological groups because of its potential impact on wildlife.

The interior of Spain is dominated by a semi-arid tableland, the Meseta, which has an average height of 500 m. It is crossed and flanked by high mountain ranges. The basins of Old and New Castile are separated by the Sierra de Guadarrama. The basin of Old Castile has a steppe landscape, with vast estates (latifundi) belonging to the aristocracy and the church. Wheat and barley are grown in open fields with wasteful fallow and low yields. To the south of Madrid lies the basin of New Castile, part of which is known as La Mancha, or 'the desert'. With less than 500 mm of rainfall per year it has dry-farming, large estates and primitive farming methods. The Tagus–Guadiana plateau lies to the south-west with rugged sierras and interior basins. It is known as the Estremadura and large areas are given over to pastoral farming, with Merino sheep and goats.

In the extreme south is Andalusia (the Guadalquivir valley). It has Mediterranean winter rainfall and dry dusty summers. Since the medieval period this has been a region of rural mis-management and absentee landlords. Farming is extensive with a poor peasantry, backward methods, extensive fallow, little mechanisation and low yields. Cultivation is based upon the classic Mediterranean combination of wheat, vines and olives, but it is also important for Seville oranges and tobacco, and the town of Jerez is the chief centre for the bottling of sherry. There are historic cities like

Seville, Granada, Cordoba and Cadiz. Andalusia has great potential for intensive agriculture based upon irrigation projects. The marshes at the mouth of the Guadalquivir have been reclaimed and cotton, rice and other cash crops are cultivated.

The fruit and vegetable industry of Andalusia began to increase significantly in the early 1970s. Almeria's mild winter climate enables the region to produce out-of-season vegetables and fruit for the EU's northern markets. The Andalucians have overtaken both the Italians and the French in providing this fresh winter produce, and the amount of land under cultivation has increased by 10 per cent. Smallholders have become very wealthy (the majority of holdings are 0.74 ha in size) and the area has been termed 'an agricultural Klondike' or 'the plastic miracle' (a reference to the 116 000 ha now covered in plastic sheeting). However, there are serious problems facing the future of this intensive farming area. Water is in increasingly short supply as groundwater has become contaminated by salt water through over-extraction. There is little land left for expansion, and much of it has become exhausted with a build-up of soil diseases. In addition, production costs are rising as the plastic is expensive to erect and maintain, and labour is also becoming very expensive.

Disparities in the region have increased over the last 25 years as a result of the growth in the manufacturing industry and the service sector (particularly tourism) which has led to a concentration of population in the urban and coastal areas accompanied by the depopulation of inland areas. The provinces of Granada and Jaen have a per capita GDP nearly 40 per cent lower than in Huelva and Cadiz where much of the industrial activity of the region is concentrated – including petrochemicals and shipbuilding – and the provinces of Malaga and Almeria have boosted their GDPs with tourism.

Andalusia is designated an Objective One region for EU assistance (fig. 10.7), and the regional government has claimed that it will become the 'California of Europe'. In 1992 Seville was the location for 'Expo '92' (an international exhibition of cultural and technological achievement and a commemoration of the 500th anniversary of Columbus' voyage to North America). It was used by the Spanish, along with the 1992 Olympics, to attract investment. Approximately £7 billion was spent on projects like the new airport terminal and a high-speed rail link to Madrid. Expo '92 was built on the island of Cartuja in the Guadalquivir river adjacent to the centre of Seville. The Cartuja '93 project has kept open the Expo site as a cultural and high-technology learning centre. Malaga has also completed a 200-ha technology park (IDEA) on the outskirts of the city, and both developments are being used to stimulate economic growth in Andalusia. It is possible that Andalusia will become an extension of the high-technology Mediterranean sun-belt that already extends from Lombardy to Catalonia (the 'second banana' – fig. 20.5). It is certainly the case that the whole Mediterranean coastline (from the Costa Del Sol to the Costa Brava) has become one of the most important tourist areas in Western Europe.

Portugal: coastal and interior regions

The basic problem is again the structure of the rural sector. In 1994 12 per cent of Portugal's workforce remained in agriculture although this is a significant drop from 22 per cent in 1986. Productivity is still low and there is considerable rural unemployment. The worst-affected area is the interior. Much of it is mountainous with a sparse population. The Spanish frontier hinders communications and trade, and increases the remoteness of Portugal from the rest of Western Europe. Tras os Montes in the north, the Sierra da Estrela in the centre and the Alentejo in the south are Portugal's most under-developed areas. Villages are few, towns are small, and agriculture is largely restricted to pastoral farming with rough grazing for sheep and goats, some cultivated stretches of wheat and vines, and cork oak woodlands. Rural depopulation is a problem, and there is considerable emigration towards Lisbon. The Alentejo has the lowest population density in Portugal. Average earnings are about 10 per cent lower than for the rest of Portugal and population has declined since the 1950s (between 1980 and 1990 there was a net out-migration of 28 200 people). Renewal of the population is prevented by very low fertility and marriage rates.

Economic life is centred on two coastal cities, Lisbon and Oporto

The narrow alleyways of the historic centre of Lisbon

(fig. 20.3). Lisbon lies at the mouth of the Tejo river and is the national capital and the commercial centre of the country. It is a major Atlantic passenger port and a NATO base, and has shipbuilding and oil-refining industries. Lisbon is an important entrepôt port and exports cork, wine, sardines and petroleum products. Oporto on the Douro river in the north is Portugal's second city. It is the centre of the port wine trade, and has exported wine to England since the sixteenth century. There are a variety of industries including sardine canning, textiles, pottery, tobacco and electrical engineering.

Other important coastal lowland areas are the densely populated Minho valley in the North region with its provincial capital of Braga, and the ancient university of Coimbra in the Mondego valley in the Centre region. The Oporto conurbation is Portugal's second city and capital of the North region − Portugal's most populous region, with one-third of the population, and one of Europe's youngest regions. On the south coast, the Algarve, with a scenic coast, sandy beaches and hot dry summers, has experienced rapid growth since the 1960s as an international tourist resort. The construction of tourist accommodation over large areas − with much of it high-density − has led to unregulated urban expansion. Employment is seasonal with a 20 per cent drop in employment in the winter months. In 1992, 9 million tourists visited Portugal compared with 2.7 million in 1980, but the amount of money each tourist spends has fallen. This has encouraged the Portuguese to

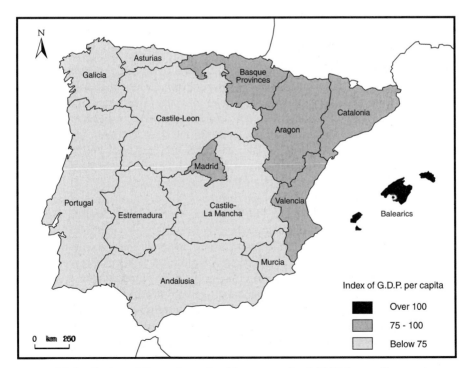

FIGURE 20.6   *Spain and Portugal − regional incomes per head 1992 (source:* Eurostat*)*

develop for higher-spending tourist market segments such as business tourism, cultural tourism and golf and other sporting holidays. However, 60 per cent of the Algarve's area is upland with a low density of population and poorly developed agriculture. There is large-scale daily commuting from the upland to the employment areas on the coast.

INTEGRATION INTO THE EUROPEAN UNION

There are two key elements in the political and economic transformation of Spain and Portugal. One of these is the new international division of labour – the challenge to the industrial supremacy of north-west Europe which is now being made by the newly industrialising countries (NICs) of the developing world. This has had graver effects upon newly industrialised Mediterranean countries, such as Spain, than on other countries in the European core. One reason for this is that the industrialisation which took place during the economic miracle of the 1960s and early 1970s in Spain was characterised by small family firms with low capitalisation and low-level technology, and inadequate distribution networks specialising in low-cost goods often for local customers. On the other hand the giant state enterprises created under the dictatorship of Franco are the older smoke-stack industries of steel, shipbuilding, oil-refining, petrochemicals and heavy engineering which were characteristic of the national-status industries of the 1960s. These now face European and world-wide intense competition.

The second step in the political transition of Spain and Portugal has been their accession to the EEC in January 1986. The overriding attraction of the EU for Spain and Portugal is the harmonisation of living standards based upon the EU principle of convergence, and the alleviation of regional poverty. Per capita incomes in Spain and Portugal are respectively a little more than 75 per cent and 66 per cent of the EU average. Spanish and Portuguese membership of the EU has widened regional disparities and substantially increased demands upon EU funds. The hopes of many regions are focussed upon funds such as the ERDF and the European Social Fund.

There are bright prospects for agriculture in some regions including some of the poorest regions in Iberia. The provinces of Huelva, Malaga, Seville, Granada, Almeria and the Portuguese Algarve are now capitalising upon their high sunshine and temperature rates and are specialising in the intensive cultivation of a wide variety of fruits, vegetables and flowers. However, the outlook is particularly grim for many farming regions in the interior and the north of the peninsula with traditional mixed farming, agriculture and livestock. Spain's dairy farms have been affected by competition from northern Europe, but Portuguese agriculture has been least able to stand up to EU competition and has required considerable assistance to restructure. The demands upon the EU's farming and regional aid budgets have been substantial. Spain alone has brought into the EU an area of farmland, mountainous and marginal, equivalent to a third of the EU's existing farm land.

In the industrial sector similar heavy demands upon the EU's regional funds have been made as labour costs have risen, and with the adoption of the Common External Tariff, industries have been open to imports from developing-world countries with which the EU has preferential access agreements. The impact of the competition has been particularly severe in Spain, and some regions specialising in traditional manufacturing, such as steel, shipbuilding, textiles, clothing and footwear, have found it hard to compete except by moving up-market. The Spanish textile industry, in particular, is concentrated in Catalonia and has been traditionally accustomed to high tariff protection. Major reductions in steel-making capacity and the accompanying loss of jobs is still occurring in Bilbao and other parts of the Basque provinces.

Spain's entry to the EU was the start of a five-year period of rapid economic growth. GDP growth averaged 4.5 per cent per annum during the period 1986–90, substantially above the EU average for the same period. The growth peaked in 1987, and since then has slowed – particularly since 1990. At the end of 1992, the economy went into recession although it has since begun to recover. Inflation is now about 5 per cent, but unemployment has been a serious problem for 20 years and is now affecting 23 per cent of those eligible to work (the highest proportion in the EU, and twice the average).

Portugal's GDP per capita has grown from 51 per cent of the EU average in 1985 to 66 per cent. By the end of 1995 the economy is expected to have expanded at an average rate of 3.2 per cent a year (compared with 2.3 per cent for the EU as a whole). Portugal has therefore been catching up with the other EU Member States over a period that represents the strongest era of growth in Portugal's modern history. The recession of the early 1990s did affect Portugal but not as severely as for many other countries, and although unemployment has risen, it is low at 6.8 per cent. The inflation rate of 4.5 per cent in 1994 was the lowest for twenty-five years.

Portugal is also investing in science parks like the Taguspark in Lisbon, and there are plans for an Expo '98 to coincide with the 500th anniversary of Vasco da Gama's voyage to India. The economies of Portugal and Spain are now interacting with each other, encouraged by EU cash transfers which can be multiplied by the joint presentation of cross-border infrastructure projects. Portugal may not meet the Maastricht convergence criteria but it is not keen to see a two-track Europe and is attempting to achieve nominal convergence. Spain's prospects of meeting the Maastricht convergence criteria in 1999 are also doubtful.

21

AUSTRIA, FINLAND AND SWEDEN

On 1 January 1995, Austria, Finland and Sweden joined the EU, bringing the number of Member States to 15. Their decision to leave the European Free Trade Association (EFTA) and join the EU had both economic and political motivations. The potential economic strength of the Single Market was very attractive and this element was strengthened by the strong trade links between EFTA and the EU (they had been formally linked together as the European Economic Area free trade area since January 1994). The political motivation stemmed from the realisation that the EU was a force to be reckoned with, and the new Member States wanted to have a direct influence in its evolution.

The accession of the new Member States has strengthened the economy

	Austria	Finland	Sweden
Area km^2	83 900	337 100	450 000
Population (millions)	8.0	5.1	8.8
Population density per km^2	95.5	15.1	19.4
GDP per capita index (EUR 15 = 100)	115	93	106
Percentage workforce in:			
agriculture	7.0	9.0	4.0
industry	35.0	27.0	25.0
services	58.0	64.0	71.0
Car production (000s)	41	nil	279
Number of passenger cars per 100 inhabitants	42	38	42
Energy consumption per head (toe)	3415	5703	5482

toe = tonnes of oil equivalent

FIGURE 21.1   *Austria, Finland and Sweden: an economic profile, 1993 (source:* Eurostat)

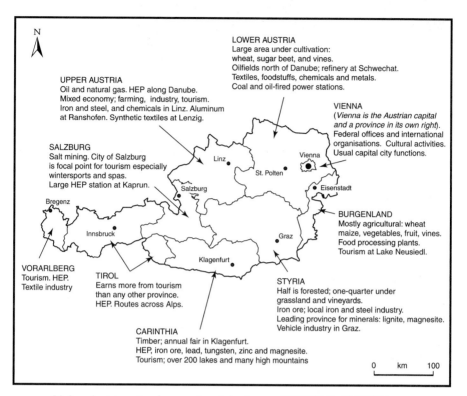

FIGURE 21.2   *Austria regional economic activity (source:* GEOFILE, *E Wallis)*

of the EU, raising its total GDP by almost 7 per cent. Austria, Finland and Sweden are relatively wealthy countries (fig. 21.1) and are net contributors to the EU budget. Two of the new Members are large countries and so the area of the EU has expanded by more than one-third. The EU also now has a border with the former Soviet Union.

AUSTRIA

The Republic of Austria (population 8 million in January 1995) is a landlocked country of just under 84 000 km² surrounded by seven other European states. It consists of nine federal states (fig. 21.2) – Voralberg, Tirol, Salzburg, Carinthia, Styria, Upper and Lower Austria, Burgenland and Vienna – called *Bundeslander* which are further subdivided into 98 Districts or *Bezirke*. More than 40 per cent of the surface area is covered by forests, and only Vienna and its environs form a large urban area accounting for 20 per cent of the total population.

Austria has the ninth largest economy in Europe, comparable to that of Belgium, but in terms of per capita GDP it is one of the wealthiest countries in Europe, with a per capita GDP equivalent to that of Luxembourg or

Germany. Trade with the EU has steadily grown in recent years (68 per cent of Austria's total external trade was with the EU in 1994), and full membership of the EU for Austria will be of considerable benefit both to Austria and to other EU members.

The path to EU membership

Austria became a member of the European Free Trade Association (EFTA) in 1958, and during the 1960s the idea of EU membership was first considered by Austria. A Treaty of Association was signed in 1972, and in 1987 a formal application for full EU membership was made. From January 1993 Austria was a member of the European Economic Area (EEA) – the EU/EFTA free trade area.

Formal negotiations on EU membership opened on 1 February 1993. A key stumbling block was a 1991 agreement negotiated with the EU limiting trans-Alpine road traffic (such traffic is expected to increase with expanded East European trade). In March 1994 negotiations over EU membership were completed, and it was agreed that the transit agreement should last until 2004, although negotiations on lifting the limits are to be held earlier if the improved railway infrastructure under construction reduces exhaust

View of Seefeld, Tyrol

pollution by 60 per cent. A further benefit to Austria was the agreement that Burgenland would qualify for regional assistance.

On 12 June 1994 the Austrian people decided in a referendum to join the EU from 1 January 1995. The 'yes' vote was unexpectedly high (66 per cent in a high turnout of 81 per cent), and represented a defeat for the right-wing Freedom Party (FPO) of Jorg Haider who at one point had gained nearly 20 per cent of the vote with his anti-immigration stance. Even in Tirol, where the Alpine transit issue was critical, over 56 per cent voted 'yes'.

A long history – the 'crossroads' of Europe?

Austria has long been a melting pot for various ethnic groups primarily due to its central geographical position within Europe. One of its most recent pressing problems has been the influx of refugees from Central and East Europe since the collapse of Communism (immigrants and refugees – both legal and illegal – now account for about 9 per cent of the Austrian population). Indeed, this problem has become so severe that it has prompted the rise of right-wing political groups, associated terrorist activity and a condemnation by Amnesty International of the mistreatment of foreigners.

The Republic was declared in 1918 after the Austro-Hungarian Empire disintegrated. This break-up involved Hungary becoming independent, part of Lower Austria becoming former Czechoslovakia, half of Tirol being given to Italy, and portions of Styria and Carinthia being allocated to former Yugoslavia. The country was so reduced in size and so impoverished that its survival seemed impossible. Seventy per cent of the country that remained was, and is, mountainous and there is a lack of certain natural resources. Under the Austro-Hungarian Empire grain came from what had now become Hungary, wine and fruit had come from south Tirol, industrial products from Bohemia (now in former Czechoslovakia), and overseas trade had been via the port of Trieste (now in Italy). In addition, a large proportion of the population was urban and was concentrated in Vienna, supported by the rest of the country. The consequence was a period of inflation, famine and widespread poverty.

Adjustments to this new situation were hampered by the intense regional loyalties of Austria's population. Each state has its own government, traditions, way of life and capital. In fact many would argue that most Austrians are generally more attached to their own state than to the country as a whole.

Austria's economic recovery was painful and slow, but by 1938 there were signs of a return to stability. At this point Germany invaded Austria and declared its annexation – the *anschluss* – creating a greater Germany, but by 1943 this had been nullified by a meeting of foreign ministers from the UK, the former Soviet Union and the USA. By the end of the war the country was occupied by the Allied forces and (like Germany) split into four zones of occupation. Full sovereignty was then granted to Austria in 1955 by the Soviets in return for a promise of 'perpetual neutrality' which still exists today, although some of the provisions were revoked in 1990.

The economy

The fact that Austria's GDP per capita is higher than the EU average underlines the view that Austria has remained 'a charmed island of prosperity and stability'. From the 1960s Austria's economic growth was steady as the country pursued an economic policy that promoted full employment and state subsidies. Only in the early 1990s has there been a marked downturn in the economy, due in part to the declining economic activity of Germany, Austria's most important trade partner (44 per cent of the overall value of Austria's external trade is with Germany). The success of the economy has to be seen largely in the light of post-war events.

State ventures

After the Second World War the Allies had done a great deal to give Austria a new start by providing capital, materials and labour for reconstruction. In 1946, under the Nationalisation Law, a large segment of Austrian industry was taken into state ownership. This covered the three biggest banks and some 70 larger industrial enterprises chiefly in the fields of iron and steel, aluminium and machinery. Later reorganisation reduced the number of nationalised enterprises to 19, but by the early 1980s state employment still accounted for one-sixth of Austria's workforce. State ownership of industry had become a way of life in post-war Austria.

In the mid-1980s privatisation became a live issue in Austrian politics. An initial wave saw the flotation of significant minority stakes in a number of enterprises such as OMV (the integrated oil and chemicals group) but a nervous Austrian establishment made sure that the state remained firmly in control. The process accelerated in the late 1980s and early 1990s but there are still significant state holdings, particularly in Vienna where there is little sign of privatisation taking off. Indeed, it may be that it will be impossible to disentangle the close links between Austrian industry, banks and government.

Eastern Europe

Despite the benefits of Allied reconstruction, ten years of occupation by foreign troops weakened the political structure of the country and the 'Iron Curtain' had shut off the eastern frontiers and hindered trade. This isolation from the East has now ended and Austria has gained immeasurably from the fall of COMECON. New developments in the former GDR, Poland, Hungary and former Czechoslovakia have helped Austria's construction industry to ride the recession. Austria is now a bridge between the East and West. In the late 1980s and early 1990s over 1000 Western companies chose Vienna as their base for expansion into Eastern Europe.

However, rising competition from low-cost producers in Eastern Europe has begun to take its toll on Austrian manufacturers, forcing the government to impose import restrictions on sensitive and important products, such as cement and fertilisers. One response to this competition has been the actual relocation of part of the production facilities of Austrian manufacturing companies to Eastern Europe itself.

Energy supplies

The availability of adequate power supplies has been one of the main factors hindering or promoting economic development in Austria. After 1918 and again after 1945 repeated shortages of hard coal imports severely hampered Austria's economy. Although Austria is still heavily dependent upon external energy sources, a significant proportion (36 per cent) of energy needs is met by domestic production. Austria is a major producer of HEP (from fast-flowing Alpine rivers or large power plants on the Danube) and of biomass but also has important, although declining, oil, gas and poor-quality lignite reserves. There are virtually no hard coal resources, the last small mine having closed 30 years ago. In 1993 hydro-power alone accounted for 40 per cent of domestic production and biomass for 32 per cent. Fossil fuels dominate energy imports with oil accounting for 44 per cent of the energy supply (90 per cent is imported), but natural-gas imports have tripled between 1973 and 1993. OPEC countries supply 60 per cent of oil imports, but Eastern Europe is a major source of energy, supplying 94 per cent of natural-gas imports (particularly from Russia) and 91 per cent of hard-coal imports (particularly steam coal from Poland). The Austrians are not enthusiastic about nuclear power. Plans to build the Zwentendorf nuclear plant on the Danube were bitterly opposed, and a referendum in 1978, the same year as the plant was completed, decided against bringing it into commission. After the Chernobyl incident arrangements were made to dismantle it. Austrian law has now outlawed nuclear-power generation.

Agriculture

In 1991 agriculture accounted for 3 per cent of Austria's GDP and employed over 7 per cent of the workforce. Farms are usually small (52 per cent are less than 10 hectares) and farmers often work on a part-time basis. However, productivity is high and Austria is almost totally self-sufficient in this sector. Many farmers are also seasonal foresters: part of a farm holding may include conifers which are felled for timber in the autumn when other farm activities decrease.

Manufacturing

This sector employs about 27 per cent of the workforce. Industrial production is dominated by the manufacture of electrical and electronic equipment (12.5 per cent of total industrial employment), the food industry, mechanical engineering, the manufacture of metal articles (aluminium production became one of the more important Austrian manufacturing industries during the 1960s and 1970s) and the manufacture of transport equipment, with timber processing based on the nation's extensive forest reserves also significant.

Tourism

On an income-per-head basis Austria's tourist industry (covering both winter and summer visitors) is the strongest in the world. It accounts for 25 per cent of Austria's total foreign-exchange earnings. Quality rather than quantity is now being stressed, with an emphasis on 'green' tourism.

Transport

Austria lies at the junction of major traffic routes within Europe and has seen a dramatic rise in the number of goods vehicles passing through. It has banned all transit traffic at night and only reluctantly amended its regulations to allow 38-tonne lorries to cross the Brenner Pass. Unlike most of Europe, Austria moves half of its freight by rail, reflecting the country's environmental awareness.

The environment

In 1991 the Austrian government spent 8 per cent of its budget (the same as for education) on the environment and pollution control. This is partly a policy of sound economics to protect its most valuable invisible export: tourism. However, the country is also perceived by its inhabitants as 'the nature reserve of Europe', and Austrians are concerned to maintain that image. They use only 3 per cent of their water resources per year, compared with 24 per cent in the UK.

EU membership has opened a new chapter in the long history of Austria, but it may be that Eastern Europe poses an even greater challenge, particularly if some of those countries on Austria's eastern borders become EU Members themselves.

FIGURE 21.4 *Scandinavia administration divisions*

FINLAND

Finland is Europe's twelfth wealthiest country on a GDP-per capita basis, and had the lowest GDP per capita in EFTA when it became an EU Member. This has not always been the case. From 1984 to 1989 Finland's economy grew more than the EU (12) average in each year of the same period, and Finland experienced an economic boom enabling Finns to enjoy a very high standard of living. Since 1989 its growth has been less, and in fact Finland's GDP has contracted since 1991. The decline into recession in 1991 marked the sharpest drop in economic growth for any OECD country at that time and was caused partly by the poor international economic climate but mainly because of the collapse of the former Soviet Union which was one of Finland's main trading partners. This has meant that Finland has now had to turn to Europe for its trade. In 1991, 50 per cent of Finland's exports and 46 per cent of imports were with the EU, and a further 20 per cent of exports and 19 per cent of imports were with EFTA. The main exports (in terms of value) are paper and paper products, metals and engineering, chemicals, and wood and wood products.

History

The first people arrived in Finland about 9000 years ago. During the first millennium BC several groups of peoples arrived, among them the ancestors of the present Finns. The nomadic Lapps, who had been scattered over the greater part of Finland, withdrew to the north.

From the twelfth century Finland became a battleground between Russia and Sweden. By 1323, after several wars between Sweden and Russia for control of Finland, peace was agreed at the Treaty of Nötegorg which divided the country into Swedish and Russian spheres of influence. By the end of the fourteenth century Finland was part of the 'Kalmar Union' which united Denmark, Sweden and Norway (fig. 21.4) under a single monarch and by the middle of the seventeenth century Finland had been fully incorporated into the Swedish Kingdom.

In the eighteenth century Sweden began to lose its role as a world power and its Russian neighbour sought to make claim to Finland. A series of Russo-Swedish wars followed, and after the Treaty of Nystad in 1721 Sweden ceded both the Baltic States and parts of south-eastern Finland to Russia. In 1808 Russian troops invaded Finland once more under Alexander I, and the Finns felt betrayed by the Swedes who did little to protect Finland from invasion.

Russian rule continued into the twentieth century, and it was only the Russian Revolution in March 1917 that enabled Finland to declare itself an independent state. After the invasion of Poland by Germany in 1939, the former Soviet Union sought to protect its borders – particularly Leningrad. The Soviet Union requested that it be allowed to establish bases in Finland, but when Finland refused the former Soviet Union launched an invasion. The Finns eventually had to surrender, and under the Treaty of Moscow in 1940 Finland surrendered land to the former Soviet Union, including a large area of south-eastern Finland (Karelia).

In 1948, a Friendship, Co-operation and Mutual Assistance Agreement (the Finno–Soviet Treaty of Friendship) was signed between the former Soviet Union and Finland. Under this, Finland agreed not to form military alliances, and this neutrality meant that Finland refused to consider any attachment with other European countries. This détente paid off as trade with the former Soviet Union rose to more than 20 per cent of Finland's total trade (including cheap oil for Finland's substantial energy needs), and the former Soviet Union returned its base at Porkkala in 1955.

Finland became a member of the Nordic Council in 1955. Nordic cooperation has led to many legislative and political similarities between Finland, Denmark, Iceland, Norway and Sweden. These include free movement across the borders of these five countries and the gradual development of a common and free labour market. The former Soviet Union did not object to Finland becoming an associate member of EFTA in 1961 while still guaranteeing rights to the former Soviet Union. In 1968 the former Soviet Union opened the reconstructed Saimaan Canal (partly on Finnish and partly on Soviet territory), but it was only after two years of consultation with the Soviets that Finland was able to apply for a free trade agreement with the EEC in 1971. This came into force in 1973, but it was balanced by a similar free trade arrangement with the former Soviet Union.

However, the continuing growth of the EEC as a major trade bloc led Finland to develop an increasingly European trade policy, and in 1986 Finland formally became a full member of EFTA. Nevertheless, it was only the ending of the Cold War and the eventual collapse of the Berlin Wall that enabled Finland to fully participate in the European Economic Area (EEA) and eventually apply for membership of the EU in March 1992. Negotiations were completed in March 1994, and in October 1994 a referendum in Finland accepted EU membership.

Agriculture

Agriculture, forestry and fishing are extremely important to the Finnish economy, although the numbers employed in agriculture have been steadily declining. One of the main difficulties for Finnish agriculture is the country's proximity to the Arctic Circle. In mid-winter there are 18 hours of darkness, with obvious limitations for the growing season so that in the north this season is reduced to 120–150 days. Most of Finland's farmland therefore lies in the south and west, where the growing season is 210–220 days in length.

Despite these problems Finland is practically self-sufficient in agriculture. In fact its egg, dairy and fodder-grain production are greater than that required, so much of it is exported. Small farmholdings dominate Finnish agriculture and the average size of farms has declined since the Second

World War as much land has been taken out of agricultural production. The average farm size is 9 ha and 53 per cent of farms have fewer than 5 ha. A controversial aspect of Finnish farming is that it is the world's main producer of farm-raised foxes, and Finnish mink furs also have a high reputation on international markets.

Although Finland has an abundance of forest resources (71 per cent of the total area is forested) and the numerous lakes and rivers make long-distance timber floating relatively easy (although truck and rail transport is rendering this practice obsolete in many areas), the forest industry faces increasing production costs.

Commercial fishing has gradually become less significant to the Finnish economy. Sea fishing is confined to the Baltic where the most important catch is herring. Fish-breeding stations have become significant. Here artificial spawning can be induced, and this can avoid the problems presented by river pollution and the impact of hydro-power stations on the migration habits of salmon and sea trout.

Energy

The only indigenous energy resources in Finland are peat, hydro-power and biofuels (in particular wood chips and other waste products from forestry). These provide approximately 20 per cent of total energy requirements (5 per cent from peat). There is therefore considerable dependency on imported fuels although these are relatively well diversified. However, Finland has succeeded in bringing the share of oil down from 65 per cent before the energy crisis of the 1970s, so that oil now satisfies 35 per cent of total energy consumption (well below the EU average). Before 1989 more than 95 per cent of Finnish oil imports came from the former Soviet Union, but less than 40 per cent of oil requirements are currently imported from this area. Nevertheless, the dependency on Russia for energy remains high as it is Finland's sole supplier for natural gas (which accounts for 8 per cent of Finland's total energy supply). This explains the proposed pipeline from Norway's Haltenbanken gas field in the North Sea across Sweden and under the Gulf of Bothnia to Finland.

Finland has constantly worried about security of supply given its geopolitical situation, and this has led to the development of a nuclear sector that accounts for 35 per cent of electricity supply. Two of the four reactors (located at Loviisa, east of Helsinki) were supplied by the former Soviet Union in the 1970s, but they have both been refitted with Western technology and back-up safety systems; they are run by Imatran Voima (IVO), the Finnish state-owned power-generating company. The other two are in western Finland at Olkiluoto. Nevertheless, in 1993, the Finnish parliament turned down a proposal to build a fifth reactor after environmental opposition. Indeed, concern about the safety of Russia's nuclear power stations close to Finland's eastern border has led to cooperation with Russia on nuclear safety on the Kola Peninsula, where there are four light water reactors, and at the Sosnovy Bor reactor in St Petersburg which is similar to the one at Chernobyl.

Manufacturing

Finland's northern location imposes certain limitations on industrial activity. Severe weather conditions make the cost of construction and heating high, and ice and snow are obstacles to transport. Industrialisation in Finland began in the 1860s but development was slow and by the early twentieth century only 10 per cent of the population was employed in manufacturing. It was not until the 1960s that manufacturing overtook farming and forestry together as an employer. In 1994, 26 per cent of the population was employed in manufacturing, with 65 per cent in service industries.

Forest products are a vital sector of the Finnish economy and include sawn timber, pulp and paper products, building materials and furniture. However, metals and engineering constitute the largest sector of the Finnish manufacturing industry despite the fact that most minerals need to be imported. The raw material for the steel industry is imported scrap, and there are works in Helsinki, Tampere and Turku. Finland is a leading producer of specialised ships such as luxury liners and icebreakers, with shipyards in Helsinki and Turku, but the collapse of the Soviet market created serious problems as a considerable proportion of production was linked to exports to the former Soviet Union. One of the main producers, Wartsila Marine, went bankrupt, but it has been taken over by the Norwegian industrial company Kvaerner which plans to diversify into the field of oil and gas exploration.

Finland's chemical industry has grown rapidly, with petrochemicals particularly important. There are textile factories at Turku, Tampere, Vaasa, Forssa and Hyvinkaa, and Helsinki has Europe's largest porcelain factory. Other industries include glassware, leather and pewter goods, beer, vodka and liqueurs. There has never been a general policy in Finland of industrial nationalisation, but in some cases the state has continued to hold a controlling interest in enterprises it has helped to establish, such as the railways, air transport (Finnair), oil refining and natural-gas distribution (Neste) and the national electrical power network (IVO). The state monopoly on alcohol (owned by Alko) is a sensitive issue in Finland, but it is having to be reviewed in the light of EU membership.

Full employment has traditionally been given high priority in Finland. Between 1964 and 1967 the annual average unemployment rate was only 1.8 per cent. This rose to 2.6 per cent between 1968 and 1973 but was still only 4.4 per cent between 1974 and 1979 and 5.1 per cent between 1980 and 1984. From the mid-1980s Finland's unemployment rate fell to 4.4 per cent and remained low by international standards. The main reason for Finland's success in containing unemployment was its investment in a large number of successful employment and training schemes aimed at placing people in jobs and matching skills to job vacancies. Approximately 1 per cent of GDP has been spent each year on 'active' employment measures in addition to the 1.5 per cent of GDP spent on unemployment benefits.

However, between 1989 and 1993 unemployment in Finland rose from 3.5 per cent to over 20 per cent, and production in manufacturing declined by 10.7 per cent in 1991 as the recession developed. The Finnish unemployment rate became higher than the EU average and affected both white and blue collar workers. Household real disposable income rose by only 0.7 per cent in 1991 and fell by 5.5 per cent in 1992. However, wage restraint, increased productivity due to the shedding of labour, and the depreciation of the Finnish currency (the Markka) have all led to improved price competitiveness for Finnish products on the international markets, which has been particularly beneficial for the forestry, metal and engineering industries. The realisation that Finland is an important gateway to the markets of the former Soviet Union and particularly to the Baltic States has also helped the recovery.

Transport

Finland is very well served by navigable waterways and has an extensive network of lakes, rivers and canals. The country's busiest port is at Skoldvik, near Helsinki. Most of the Finnish rail network is owned by the state, and the south-west is the best served area. The old rail network is a different gauge from the rest of Europe but it is being updated to make it compatible. Finland has a good network of roads and highways but the lakes in the south-east (fig. 21.4) make direct road links difficult – there are instead a number of car ferries in operation – although some bridges have improved the network's connectivity. There is approximately one car for every three people in Finland.

Population

Finland's population of almost 5.1 million is very unevenly distributed (fig. 21.6), and the average population density of 15 per km^2 is the lowest in the EU (fig. 9.3). The major urban areas are all in the southern third of the country, and some areas in the north and east have a population density of less than 1 per km^2. Increased industrialisation has led to rural depopulation, but with only 63 per cent of the population living in urban areas Finland is not as heavily urbanised as many EU Member States. A large number of cities and towns are concentrated on the coast, either on the Gulf of Finland, as for the capital Helsinki, or on the Gulf of Bothnia as for Vaasa and Oulu. The only urban area of any size in the north of Finland is Rovaniemi. Helsinki is the largest city (1 005 000) with a population about three times that of Tampere and of Turku (the country's capital until 1812).

Finland has two official languages, Finnish and Swedish. The Swedish-speaking population, found mainly in the coastal areas of the south,

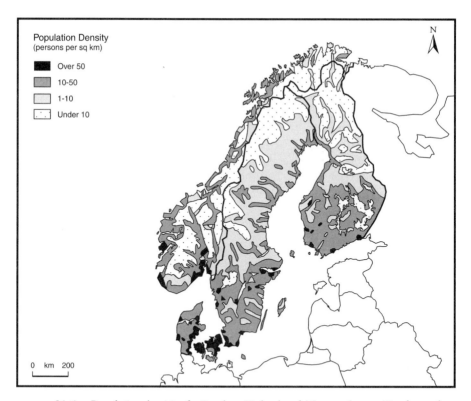

FIGURE 21.6 *Population densities for Sweden, Finland and Norway (source:* Tussler and Buckby*)*

south-west and west and in the Aoland Islands, is slowly declining and forms about 6 per cent of the total population. The remainder speak Finnish, except for the semi-nomadic Lapp-speaking minority in the extreme north (about 2000 people). In the last two decades the population has hardly grown, with a consequent ageing and an increase in the proportion of women (male life expectancy at 72.1 is the second lowest in the EU), but in the last few years there has been an increase in the total fertility rate.

Regions

Finland is made up of 12 provinces known as *Laani* (fig. 21.4). The largest provinces in terms of population are Uusimaa, Turku-Pori and Hame (all in the south-west).

SWEDEN

Covering an area of 450 000 km², Sweden is the third largest EU state after France and Spain. In the past 100 years Sweden has evolved from a largely

View from the tower of the city wall, Stockholm

agrarian country to one where only 3.4 per cent of the workforce is employed in agriculture. The manufacturing sector reached a peak around the 1960s in terms of its share of GDP and total employment, and in recent decades, Sweden, like other Western countries, has evolved rapidly into a service- and knowledge-oriented society. Swedish membership of the EU signifies the culmination of a long period of economic integration and cooperation beginning with Sweden's 1972 free trade agreement with the EEC. Sweden is likely to encourage economic cooperation with the Baltic States, Central and Eastern Europe, and Nordic countries that are not EU Members.

History

The earliest settlements in Sweden may date back to 12 000 BC when hunters migrated to Sweden across the land bridge connecting it to mainland Europe. By 2000 BC a more advanced civilisation with good continental communications based on agriculture and cattle-rearing had become established in what are now the provinces of Skane, Halland, Bohuslän and Västergötland. Trade between Sweden and the Danube Basin started around 1500 BC, and there were trade links with the Roman Empire.

At the start of the Viking age (800–1050) a number of independent tribes were settled in what is now Sweden, with the Swedes centred in Uppland and around Uppsala, and the Goths further south in the agricultural lands of Östergötland and Västergötland. The Swedish Vikings gradually took control of the whole country and controlled the eastern trade route to Byzantium and Baghdad as well as trade across the Baltic.

The Swedes resisted conversion to Christianity during the ninth and tenth centuries but the first king of Sweden was baptised in the eleventh century. However, Sweden was just a loose federation of provinces, and the twelfth and thirteenth centuries saw a series of conflicts between pagan and Christian and the many kingdoms. These conflicts involved Norway and Denmark as well, and in 1389 Margaret (Regent of Denmark and Norway) became ruler of Sweden. In 1397 the Kalmar Union saw Sweden as the dominant state in a unified Nordic bloc. Nevertheless conflict continued and the Union was dissolved in 1523.

During the sixteenth and seventeenth centuries Scandinavia and the Baltic region were vital to world trade due to their resources (particularly iron ore, grain and furs). The Swedes capitalised on this and gained control of the area, with their lands including Finland, parts of Russia and Estonia. However, competition from Russia, Brandenburg, Denmark and Poland led eventually to the Great Northern War (1700–21). This brought about the end of Sweden's status as a great world power, with the Treaty of Nystad transferring land and power to Russia.

Further wars with Russia and Prussia brought economic hardship and famine to Sweden, and at the beginning of the nineteenth century Sweden was at war with France, Denmark and Russia. A union between Sweden and Norway was agreed in 1814, and this lasted until 1905. During the First World War Sweden declared its neutrality and asserted its right to trade with any country. Trade in steel, pulp and machine parts, particularly to Germany, was boosted and the economy grew. A retaliatory trade blockade by the allies (the British Empire, France and the Russian Empire) seriously disrupted food supplies, and a more diplomatic trading policy ensued.

The Swedish economy continued to expand during the 1920s partly because two of its neighbouring competitors, Russia and Germany, had been defeated and the need for military expenditure was considerably reduced. In addition, although Sweden was affected by the Great Depression of the early 1930s, the crisis was overcome more rapidly than in most other countries. In 1939, at the start of the Second World War, Sweden again declared itself neutral, although it provided troops and equipment for Finland to resist the Soviet invasion and iron ore for Germany.

Sweden joined the United Nations immediately after the Second World War but continued its neutral position. Membership of the proposed EEC in 1957 was never seriously considered as the customs union was seen as having a supra-national authority conflicting with Sweden's sovereignty. Indeed, Sweden was the first to propose the alternative European Free Trade Area (EFTA) in 1958, and in 1959 Sweden joined the Nordic Council.

However, when the UK and Denmark, in 1960, and Norway, in 1962, applied to join the EEC, Sweden feared isolation and asked for association status. In 1972 Sweden signed a free trade agreement with the EEC, but the ending of the Cold War and the events following the fall of the Berlin Wall in 1989 negated the need for neutrality, and in 1991 Sweden formally applied for EU membership. Sweden became part of the European Economic Area (EEA) in 1994 as EFTA and the EU were linked together, and in 1995 Sweden formally became a Member of the EU.

Agriculture

Less than 10 per cent of Sweden is farmland. The best soils are found where there are young sedimentary rocks or where there are marine silts and clays or lacustrine silts. The most fertile area is the Scanian lowland in the south of Sweden with over 70 per cent of the land under cultivation, followed by the central lowland with up to 50 per cent. In the South Swedish Highlands less than 20 per cent is cultivated, and in the interior of Norrland only 0.5 per cent. This is because the growing season is shorter in the north. Sweden's farms are large by EU standards with 27 per cent between 20 and 50 ha in size. The largest arable farms are in Scania, and farm size decreases with increasing latitude. Although the agricultural workforce has declined to 3.4 per cent, large increases in productivity have kept Sweden more than 80 per cent self-sufficient in food. In 1990 a new agricultural policy was agreed reducing state subsidies, with price regulations abolished, tariffs lowered on imports and export support abolished, thus adapting agricultural production to the international market. These instruments will have to be reintroduced given the importance of price and market policy to the CAP, but full integration into the CAP has been fully accepted by Sweden from the first day of accession.

Energy

Sweden's cold climate, concentration of energy-intensive industry and high living standards mean that it has a very high per capita energy consumption. Between 1945 and 1973 the use of energy increased more rapidly than GDP, but after the first oil crisis energy consumption declined dramatically and by 1990 it was at about the same level as in 1973. Sweden lacks significant oil and coal deposits, but one of the main factors in its industrial development has been cheap hydro-power which now supplies 15 per cent of the country's energy. About 43 per cent of the energy consumed in Sweden comes from imported oil and natural gas, and 7 per cent from imported coke and coal, but this compares with 78 per cent in 1973. Sweden's 12 nuclear reactors provide over 15 per cent of total energy or almost 50 per cent of electrical energy. The rest of the energy supply comes from biofuels, peat, waste heat and other renewable energy sources (RES). After an advisory referendum in 1980 the Swedish Parliament decided that the use of nuclear power should be phased out by 2010, but the 1988 decision to close two of these reactors before 2010 was later qualified by a further parliamentary decision stressing that the new and environmentally friendly ways of producing electricity must come on stream before nuclear capacity is decommissioned. This has encouraged the implementation of an energy-conservation programme and the development of alternatives to nuclear power.

The manufacturing industry

Since the Second World War there has been a gradual shift of emphasis from traditional production of raw materials (especially timber and iron ore) towards more advanced industries with a large technology content. Such growth industries include transportation equipment, electrical and electronic equipment, and chemicals. Industries such as textiles and clothing, iron and steel, shipbuilding, wood products and pulp and paper have gone into decline, accounting for 22 per cent of industrial output in 1992 compared to 33 per cent in 1970. The more research-intensive industries, such as pharmaceuticals, electronics and telecommunications, have experienced the highest growth rates in recent decades. Sweden is among the world's biggest spenders on industrial research and development (R&D) in relation to national output (about 3 per cent of GDP) and a small number of industrial groups account for most R&D, including Asea-Brown Boveri (ABB), Ericsson, Volvo, Saab-Scania, Astra and Kabi-Pharmacia.

Engineering is the most significant sector of Swedish industry. It is concentrated in southern and central Sweden and includes several of Sweden's largest industrial companies including ABB (electrotechnology), SKF (industrial ball bearings), Electrolux (household appliances) and Atlas Copco (mining and construction equipment). An important sub-sector of engineering is the automotive industry, with 72 per cent of its products exported. The two main manufacturers are Volvo and Saab-Scania who produce motor vehicles, heavy engines and aircraft components. In 1989 Saab-Scania and General Motors signed an agreement creating a new company called Saab Automobile AB with Saab-Scania and General Motors each owning 50 per cent.

Over half of Sweden's area consists of woodland, so forest products (pulp, paper and paperboard) and wood products (timber and furniture) remain an important industry. Sweden is the world's third largest exporter of pulp and paper, with 80 per cent of exports marketed in the EU. Ten per cent of all paper production within the EU is manufactured by Swedish subsidiaries. There have been a considerable number of mergers, and Swedish forest-product firms have been acquiring companies in other parts of Western Europe. In contrast the wood-products industry mainly consists of small firms (about 500 sawmills account for 97 per cent of sawn-timber production).

Swedish foodstuff production is dominated by a relatively small number of companies. These include producer cooperatives, such as the Federation of Swedish Farmers (LRF), units of major Swedish companies like Procordia and subsidiaries of well-known foreign multi-nationals. State-owned companies dominate the production and sale of alcohol.

The chemical industry first became an important element of the Swedish economy during the Second World War, although Alfred Nobel was one of its first entrepreneurs in the mid-nineteenth century. Chemical production is largely concentrated in about 50 plants belonging to some 20 companies mainly in the far south of the country and in the Gothenburg and Stockholm areas. There are also a few factories in the north where pulp mills provide valuable by-products as well as a market for process chemicals, and where hydro-power is available locally at comparatively low cost.

More than 10 per cent of Sweden's industrial output comes from the Swedish chemical industry. Pharmaceuticals have rapidly expanded and are strongly export-oriented, with some firms selling 80–90 per cent of their output abroad. In recent years there have been quite a number of mergers and acquisitions in the Swedish chemical industry in order to rationalise production, optimise research and development, and facilitate international marketing. The basic chemical industry is owned mainly by foreign companies. The only petrochemical centre in Sweden is located in Stenungsund just north of Gothenburg and is dominated by Finnish and Norwegian interests. On the other hand Swedish-owned chemical enterprises such as Perstorp AB and Pharmacia AB have actively acquired foreign companies themselves in order to survive in the European market – e.g. the largest Swedish chemical group, Nobel Industrier AB, merged with the Dutch company Akzo NV in 1994 to form Akzo Nobel NV. The industry has had to restructure to respond to changes in the market. The drastically reduced consumption of chlorine in the pulp industry for environmental reasons (from 250 000 tonnes to nearly zero per year in 15 years) has recently led to a complete restructuring of the chlorine-alkali industry in Sweden, including the closure of three plants.

Sweden is the largest iron-ore exporter in Europe, with Germany as the main market (38 per cent) followed by Benelux (26 per cent) and Finland (11 per cent). Narvik, Lulea and Hargshamn are the main exporting ports (fig. 21.7). Steel accounts for about 5 per cent of the total value added of Swedish industry, and more than 80 per cent of the steel is exported. Almost 25 000 people (3 per cent of the total industrial workforce) are employed by the Swedish steel industry and the location of steelworks is largely a reflection of geographical inertia. Most are still found in central Sweden (fig. 21.8) where the rich iron-ore deposits were mined as early as the thirteenth century and where there was a plentiful supply of timber for charcoal and numerous waterfalls for power.

By the mid-eighteenth century Sweden had become the world's leading iron manufacturer, but the Industrial Revolution in Western Europe completely changed the market situation for Swedish iron. New metallurgical processes, using coal and coke as fuel and reducing agents,

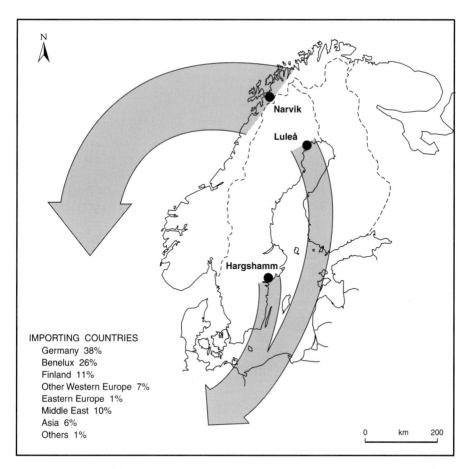

IMPORTING COUNTRIES
Germany 38%
Benelux 26%
Finland 11%
Other Western Europe 7%
Eastern Europe 1%
Middle East 10%
Asia 6%
Others 1%

FIGURE 21.7   *Swedish iron ore exports in 1991: main loading ports and importing countries* (source: the Swedish Institute)

were introduced in England and other European countries. Sweden was unable to mass-produce ordinary commercial steel by the new processes as it had no coal reserves of its own. This led to the Swedish industry shifting increasingly towards the production and export of high-grade iron and steel – a process which has continued up to the present day. Speciality steels (alloy and high-carbon steels) make up 38 per cent of Sweden's total crude steel production – a higher proportion than in other major steel-producing countries. The success of the Swedish engineering industry means that Sweden is one of the world's largest per capita steel consumers.

Economic growth was very rapid during the 1950s and 1960s, and in the period 1950–70 the annual average growth rate of manufacturing output was 4.5 per cent. After a recession in 1971–72 industrial growth picked up again until the international recession after the first oil crisis of 1973–74. While most industrialised economies recovered fairly quickly, the recession in Sweden was prolonged and manufacturing output did not return to 1975 levels until 1984. The recession led to severe structural problems in many

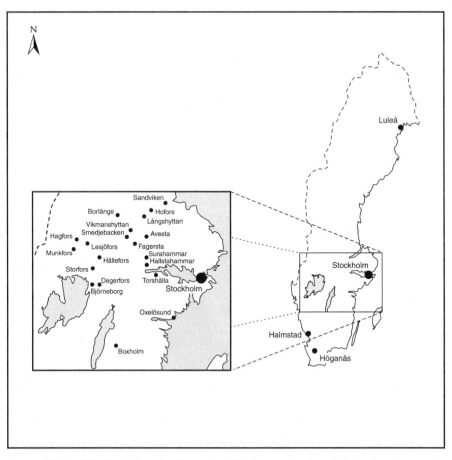

FIGURE 21.8   *The Swedish steel industry in 1994 (source:* the Swedish Institute*)*

sectors such as the iron-ore mines, the steel industry, forest products and the shipyards.

In the 1980s the Swedish manufacturing industry recovered after extensive restructuring. The annual GDP growth rate averaged 2 per cent, but the shortage of labour (Sweden had an unemployment rate of 1.5 per cent in 1989 and 1990) led to high wages and accelerating inflation as domestic demand increased. The international recession and anti-inflationary policies have led to a downturn since 1990. The policy of full employment has been changed, with unemployment affecting over 7 per cent of the workforce – a level not experienced in Sweden during the post-war period, although still rather low by EU standards. The recession has spread to all sectors of manufacturing but has been especially severe in the forest-based industries, the steel industry and the motor-vehicle industry. Manufacturing now only accounts for 25 per cent of the workforce, and the service sector has grown to become the main employer (as in other EU countries), accounting for 71.6 per cent (the second highest service-sector proportion in the EU).

Transport

A key feature is state ownership. The railways are owned and run by the state, and air services are dominated by the Scandinavian Airline System (SAS) which is mainly owned by the states of Sweden, Denmark and Norway. The state maintains bus traffic on a large scale and owns two subsidiaries that dominate the trucking industry.

Population

Sweden's population of just over 8.8 million saw a growth rate of less than 0.2 per cent in the 1980s, but this increased to 0.6 per cent in 1992 due both to a higher birth rate and to net immigration. In the period of economic growth from the end of the Second World War until the early 1970s, the natural population growth was not sufficient to meet the growing demand for labour. Immigration was encouraged (accounting for over 40 per cent of the population growth) and the female proportion of the workforce also increased rapidly so that by 1992 women accounted for 48 per cent of Sweden's workforce.

The average population density for Sweden is the second lowest in the EU at 19 per km^2, but the population is unevenly distributed (fig. 21.6). About 85 per cent of the population lives in the southern half of Sweden, but there are two minority groups of native inhabitants in the north: the Finnish-speaking people of the north-east and the Sami (Lapp) population. In the mid-nineteenth century about 90 per cent of the population lived in the countryside, but by 1994, 83 per cent lived in urban areas. Rural depopulation has occurred in the interior regions of Norrland, the

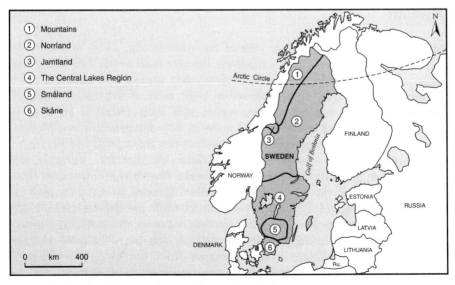

① Mountains
② Norrland
③ Jamtland
④ The Central Lakes Region
⑤ Småland
⑥ Skåne

FIGURE 21.9   *Swedish natural regions (source:* Randle)

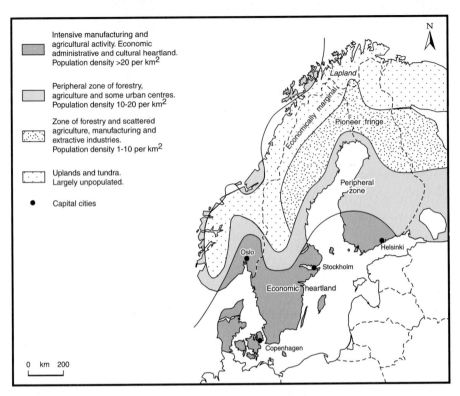

FIGURE 21.10   *Scandinavian economic zones (source:* B John*)*

north-west portion of Svealand, south-east Gotaland and the Isle of Gotland. The largest city is Stockholm with a population of 1 471 000.

Regions

Norrland, the northern 60 per cent of the country (fig. 21.9), is the region with the most problems. It is a relatively flat area with nearly 100 000 glacial lakes, and as the rocks are largely impermeable granite and gneiss, there is waterlogging and gleying and therefore large areas of marshland. Soils are thin as the rocks weather slowly, earlier soils were removed by ice and infertile moraine and outwash sand material was deposited. The climate is severe with cold and long winters (spring does not arrive until late May).

The three major resources of Norrland are forestry, minerals and hydro-power, and although Sweden's industrial economy was based on these resources, most of the recent industrial developments have taken place in other regions (fig. 21.10). However, the Swedish government encourages geographical mobility by subsidising moving expenses and granting subsidies to employers for creating jobs in Norrland which has designated regional development areas. There is also assistance from the EU under the new 'Objective Six' regional assistance status (nearly half of Sweden will be entitled to EU assistance).

22

THE INTEGRATION PROCESS

In Western Europe since 1945 there have been three distinct phases of development, all of which indicate a close relationship between geographical, economic and political factors. Immediately after 1945 there occurred the period of post-war reconstruction. This was a period of general economic recovery, and with the help of massive loans from the USA, such as Marshall Aid, the basic economic infrastructure was rebuilt. This was carried out in the presence of a general feeling, by both governments and population, that there was a need for political and social, as well as economic reconstruction. With the threat of Russian domination, there was a movement to create larger groups, more powerful and protective than the traditional nation state. In the sphere of defence, NATO was an illustration of this.

The 1950s and 1960s were a period of great prosperity. Economic growth was widespread, substantial and sustained, with many countries achieving an average yearly growth rate of over 4 per cent. Europe's raw materials, particularly oil, were cheap, and the terms of trade lay heavily in favour of industrialised countries. Agricultural production grew so that food supplies were more than adequate, leading eventually to the periodic food surpluses which have been such a feature of the contemporary scene. This widespread economic wealth and confidence was accompanied by rapid progress towards the formation of political institutions and policies which were to lead to a measure of integration in continental Western Europe. The European Economic Community Commission of the 'the Six', later to be enlarged, was formed by the fusion of three supra-national institutions, the ECSC, Euratom and the European Economic Community. The Customs Union and the removal of trade barriers were accompanied by substantial levels of convergence and harmonisation of the economies of the Member States. These include the regulation and integration of the coal and steel industries, increased intra-Community trade, the operation of the Common Agricultural Policy, the construction of the Euro-route system, regulations for fair competition, and investment aid from agencies such as the European Investment Bank.

During the 1970s the position changed dramatically. The increase in the price of oil and other commodities in 1973–74 completely altered the terms of trade, and were major causes of the inflation, loss of confidence, economic stagnation, and recession of the period from 1974–82. Growth in all the EU countries was severely curtailed, and their economies began to diverge quite seriously.

The supply and cost of energy became a major problem but the EU now has a wide range of energy sources. There are a number of choices for the future, and the 1995 Green Paper *For a European Union Energy Policy* is the first stage in formulating a policy for the next century.

Another serious problem – as mentioned above – is economic divergence at both a national and a regional level. Not only has Germany become the most economically powerful state in the EU, but on a European scale the central regions of the EU have grown at the expense of the periphery. In a sense this is the result of the free-market policies of fair competition pursued during the early years of the EU. In conditions of normal competition, the natural advantages of the Rhineland axis, with its dense population, economic resources and high levels of mobility, would have emerged in any case. The success of the EU in lowering tariff barriers and of the ECSC in restructuring the coal and steel industry of the Heavy Industrial Triangle, the effect of the CAP in favouring the efficient food producers of the Paris Basin and the Netherlands, and the concentration of motorway linkages between Belgium, the Netherlands, north-eastern France and the Rhinelands, have all enhanced these advantages. The north–south divide in the UK is related to the greater accessibility of the south-east to the European core. It may well be that the economic effect of the Channel Tunnel will accentuate the existing advantages of the South-East region. The very success of the EU has been to create a natural economic core region which is in marked contrast to some of the peripheral regions such as Iberia, Greece, the Mezzogiorno, Ireland and south-western France.

EU policy-making has gradually changed to take account of this fact. Sectoral policies such as the ECSC and the CAP have increasingly been supplemented by policies and funds which have as their aim the strengthening of the peripheral regions. The proportion of EIB funds devoted to regional development schemes is over 80 per cent of the total. The European Social Fund devotes some three-quarters of its total aid quotas to the regions, and the ERDF is specifically designed for regional development and restructuring. The imbalance between the interdependent core areas and the peripheral regions must be corrected if further progress towards economic union is to be made.

Employment change has become the most serious problem affecting the EU. The recession has highlighted the new technological revolution with the rapidly increasing use of electronics, computers and robotisation in industrial production, and a corresponding reduction in the workforce. The changing international division of labour with the cheap-labour low-cost competition from the industrialising developing world is associated with the structural decline of industries such as textiles, footwear, shipbuilding and steel. This combination of factors has led to the reappearance in the industrialised world of unemployment on a large scale. Assistance to declining industries, retraining schemes and development grants for new technology, and aid to small specialised industries are all required on a large scale to reduce unemployment. The amount of EU funds going to agriculture is still out of proportion, and the EU's budget requires urgent restructuring to deal effectively with industrial and urban unemployment. The Social Policy may be one effective vehicle for this particular purpose as it has increasingly become an industrial restructuring and retraining policy.

Geographical extent and coherence has increased, with the addition in 1973 of the northern arc countries of the UK, Ireland and Denmark, the southern arc countries of Greece in 1981, Spain and Portugal in 1986, the unification of Germany in 1990 and the addition of Sweden, Finland and Austria in 1995. Territorial enlargement has not always led to greater economic coherence. The UK has special relationships with other parts of the world, and often takes different viewpoints on many issues. The three Mediterranean countries have had major problems of integrating their economies inside the EU; they have added to agricultural surpluses, and are major recipients of aid from the EU's resources. Measured in terms of GDP per capita, West Germany was the richest country in the EU in 1989–90 after Luxembourg, whereas East Germany's in that year was only 56 per cent of the EU average (poorer than all other EU Member States except Greece and Portugal). The new Lander are therefore eligible for assistance from the EU Structural Funds. The accession of Sweden, Finland and Austria has, however, strengthened the economy of the EU by raising its total GDP by around 7 per cent. All three states are net contributors to the EU budget. The core and periphery in geographical terms has led to 'discussion' of a politically and economically integrated core with an associated, more slowly integrating periphery, a two-tier or two-speed EU. Some even talk of a 'variable geometry' Europe or an 'à la carte' Europe where countries are free to pick and choose those aspects of EU policy they want to adopt.

A major structural improvement was the change in the composition of the European Parliament. The direct elections first held in June 1979 gave the EU a new democratic base and political impetus. The parliamentarians have a more effective mandate from the population and are beginning to exercise greater control over the budget funds and economic policies, thus playing a larger part in the political development of the EU. The creation of the European Monetary System (EMS) during 1979 as a zone of monetary stability and cooperation was a major step forward in the consolidation of the EU, and an important stage in economic and monetary union.

The EU has made a significant impact in external affairs. The institutions of the EU have had a strong political element tied into their essentially economic nature since their formation. The European Coal and Steel Community had political as well as economic foundations in that one of its aims was to make any war between France and Germany unthinkable and materially impossible. In 1970 it was agreed that Member States should consult each other on foreign-policy matters using an intergovernmental approach. This early European Political Co-operation (EPC) became known as the Davignon Procedure, with foreign ministers meeting twice yearly and a Political Committee of senior foreign ministry officials meeting at least four times a year.

The targets set for European integration by the Treaty of Rome in 1958 had been only partially achieved by the mid-1980s. The EU had expanded territorially to 12 Members, which in itself brought major problems of adjustment. A whole series of internal problems included recession, regional imbalance, de-industrialisation, inflation and monetary instability, and environmental pollution. The Single Market was only partially in place and needed much development. A period of internal consolidation was necessary, to change the CAP radically, to make the regional policy more effective and to develop policies on energy, research and development, aerospace, telecommunications, transport and the environment.

The painful economic adjustments of the 1970s and 1980s were associated with a period of 'Eurosclerosis' during which few important decisions were taken and the EU was damaged by acrimonious discussions about the budget contributions of the UK and by the increasing problems of agricultural surpluses. The survival of the EU through this period seemed to focus thoughts, and to concentrate minds, upon possibilities for the future, and formed the basis for a great psychological, economic and political 'leap forward'. The European Council, at Summit meetings in 1984 and 1985, drew up the Single European Act (SEA), which came into force in July 1987. Its principal objective was the creation, by 1992, of the Single European Market (SEM).

The SEA came into force on 1 July 1987 and amended the Treaty of Rome in a number of ways. Most important of all, it extended the use of majority voting in the Council, as opposed to the old unanimity rule and veto which was very restrictive. Second, it enabled the European Parliament, through a new 'cooperation procedure' with the Council, to play a more active part in decision-making. The work of the Council, Commission and Parliament was now much more clearly coordinated.

From the late 1980s onwards, a series of fundamental changes in Europe occurred. Only a small part of this was the removal by Member States of as many barriers to trade as possible and the harmonisation of rules affecting the movement of goods, people and capital between the Member States in preparation for the Single European Market (SEM) at the end of 1992. More fundamental were the events that led to the changes in Eastern Europe from 1989, with the subsequent unification of Germany, the break-up of the former Soviet Union and conflict in former Yugoslavia. Amid this turmoil the Member States were not only completing the SEM but were also planning further developments. The Delors Report of 1989 proposed further economic and monetary integration. The logic behind this was that the economic gains derived from the Single Market could be greatly enhanced by the creation of an economic and monetary union (EMU) and, ultimately, a single currency. Two Intergovernmental Conferences (IGCs) were held – one on political union and the other on economic and monetary union – culminating in a heads-of-state and government meeting in Maastricht in December 1991.

The Treaty on European Union, the Maastricht Treaty, was signed at Maastricht in February 1992 and came into force in November 1993. It established the European Union (EU), embracing all the forms of cooperation that had been built up in the preceding institutions – foreign and security policy, justice and home affairs and economic and monetary union (the three 'pillars' of cooperation) – with an agreement that these were to be strengthened further. The Treaty was very controversial, with some fearing that it eroded sovereignty and would lead to a 'United States of Europe'. In Denmark the Treaty was narrowly rejected in a referendum in 1992 but then narrowly approved in a second referendum in 1993. All EU countries have ratified the Treaty but both Denmark and the UK have negotiated a number of opt-out clauses.

The Maastricht Treaty set the timetable for a three-stage transition to full EMU and a single currency by 1999. It was recognised that fixed exchange rates and a single monetary policy and currency could lead to serious difficulties unless the economic policies and performances of all those who adopted it were sufficiently similar. As already mentioned, the Treaty sets out clear economic tests (convergence criteria) which countries will have to pass before they can move towards fixed exchange rates, a single monetary policy and a single European currency. At the end of 1995 only Germany and Luxembourg meet these criteria in full and Germany's performance since then has led to further questions, but it may be that some countries will make the change before others. The 1999 deadline for full EMU has been called into question by the currency turbulence of 1992 and 1993 and the economic recession following that.

The SEA and the Maastricht Treaty have substantially enhanced the European Parliament's powers, although they did not go all the way to meeting the Parliament's demands for it to always have an equal say with the European Council in decisions. However, the establishment of a co-decision procedure and an assent procedure in certain areas and a cooperation procedure in others has made the Parliament into a veritable legislative body.

Cooperation in the area of justice and home affairs, with the removal of internal frontiers within the EU, is being matched by a corresponding strengthening of controls at the outer frontiers. The aim is to make it more difficult for criminals and illegal immigrants to enter the EU in the first place. Nevertheless, border checks on people at internal frontiers have been among the most difficult to remove. The Schengen Treaty, signed in 1985 by seven Member States (Belgium, the Netherlands, Luxembourg, France, Germany, Portugal and Spain) in the village of Schengen on the borders of Luxembourg, France and Germany, came into effect in July 1995, although France is temporarily continuing passport controls. Its purpose is to remove all controls at internal land, sea and airport frontiers. Italy, Greece and Austria have also signed though not yet completed preparations for implementation, and Denmark, Finland and Sweden have asked for observer status. However, the Schengen Agreement is an intergovernmental agreement concluded outside the EU framework.

European Political Co-operation (EPC) was brought into the system of European treaties by the SEA. There has always been an interaction between political and economic actions, and the SEA enabled this to be more formalised, with examples including the economic sanctions applied against Iraq following the invasion of Kuwait in 1990 and the regulations needed to impose UN sanctions against the parties in the conflict in former Yugoslavia.

The Maastricht Treaty is bringing a common foreign and security policy (CFSP) into being as a global foreign policy is a necessary adjunct to global trading and economic interests. The main decisions on CFSP will be taken by Member governments acting unanimously but there will be limited majority voting, if the Member States agree to this, on specific policies or actions. The decision to add security issues to the common foreign policy came in the run-up to the Maastricht Treaty as a result of the shift in the balance of forces following the unification of Germany and the changes in Eastern Europe. It became clear that the existing structures like the North Atlantic Treaty Organisation (NATO) and the Conference on Security and Co-operation in Europe (CSCE) could not adequately deal with new situations that might arise within Europe.

The Member States also agreed under Maastricht to work towards the framing of a common defence policy and to integrate the Western European Union (WEU), which acts as the European section of NATO, into the EU's future decision-taking procedures. However, the Treaty did not propose the establishment of an EU army, despite the setting up of a 40 000-strong peace-keeping force (Eurocorps) by Germany, France, Belgium and Spain in 1993.

THE CHALLENGE OF THE TWENTY–FIRST CENTURY

The EU has come a long way from the Treaty of Rome in 1958. With 22 per cent of world imports and nearly 20 per cent of world exports, it is the world's largest trading bloc. However, each of the 15 countries still have their own sovereignty, institutions, traditions and currencies. Language differences still remain a constraint, as does the key spatial concept of accessibility, which continues to favour core areas as against peripheral ones. Nevertheless, the economic gains of integration have included better exploitation of the economies of scale, improved technical/economic/research efficiency, a stimulated flow of innovation, new processes and products, and rationalisation based upon the enhanced law of comparative advantage.

In a global context, the super powers now no longer have the dominating superiority in all aspects of life that they all possessed, and the EU, a potential super power in its own right, has substantial relationships with many other parts of the world. As the 1990s end, political developments in

Eastern Europe, with their potential social and economic implications, look set to continue. The emergence of Europe as a world power and the current economic disparities within the EU may be significantly affected by developments in the East European countries as the millennium draws to a close. The EFTA countries have negotiated an EEA agreement, and some have become EU Member States. Other applicants await to be admitted, including a number of former East European states.

However, before the twenty-first century dawns the EU will have to resolve a number of differences between its Members. Many wish to see further progress towards deepening the EU by means of more majority voting in the Council, more powers to the European Parliament and stronger roles for the Commission and Parliament in developing a Common Foreign and Security Policy (CFSP). Others believe that the integration process has now gone far enough and that further deepening would require unacceptable transfers of sovereignty from the Member States. They want to preserve and expand the intergovernmental spheres of action and possibly even transfer some areas of competence which currently belong to the EU back to national governments. This debate is likely to dominate the 1996 Intergovernmental Conference which was set up in 1991 to review the workings of the Treaty on European Union.

Nevertheless, four decades of European integration have taken Member States away from a period in which two world wars had set citizen against citizen. The EU's institutions now have supranational elements: they have legal powers that can override those of the Member States. EU law has primacy over the law of Member States, and Member States are now 'pooling' at least a part of their sovereignty. The EU acts in the spirit of subsidiarity, a principle that was enshrined in the Maastricht Treaty. Subsidiarity limits EU action to areas where it is better placed to act than the individual Member States. The evolution of high-level policy-making will eventually involve monetary union, a European currency, common fiscal policies and a common budget. Some visionaries see this as the first stages of the process in which the fragmented pattern of nation states in Western Europe is changed into the United States of Europe. This would be a state with resources, population and economic power superior to any other in the world.

APPENDIX

KEY DATES IN EUROPEAN INTEGRATION

September 19, 1946	Winston Churchill, in Zurich, urges Franco–German reconciliation within 'a kind of United States of Europe'.
October 29, 1947	Creation of Benelux – economic union of Belgium, Luxembourg and the Netherlands.
April 18, 1951	The Treaty setting up the European Coal and Steel Community (ECSC) is signed in Paris.
February 10, 1953	ECSC common market for coal, iron ore and scrap is opened.
May 1, 1953	Opening of the ECSC common market for steel.
March 25, 1957	Signature of the Rome Treaties setting up the Common Market and Euratom.
January 1, 1959	First tariff reductions and quota enlargements in the Common Market.
July 18, 1961	The six EEC countries issue Bonn Declaration aiming at political union.
November 8, 1961	Negotiations with the UK open in Brussels.
January 14, 1962	EEC fixes the basic features of Common Agricultural Policy.
January 14, 1963	President de Gaulle declares that the UK is not ready for Community membership. UK negotiations broken off.
January 22, 1963	Franco–German Treaty of Cooperation signed in Paris.
June 1, 1964	Yaoundé Convention, with 18 African countries (ex-colonies) as associated states, comes into operation.
March 31, 1965	Commission proposes that, as from 1 July 1967, all Member States' import duties and levies be paid into EEC budget and that the powers of the European Parliament be increased.
July 1, 1965	Council fails to reach agreement, by deadline fixed, on financing common farm policy; French boycott of EEC institutions begins seven-month crisis.
January, 1966	Crisis resolved by the Luxembourg Accords.
May 11, 1966	Council agrees that on 1 July, all tariffs on trade

	between the Member States shall be removed and that the common external tariff shall come into effect, thus completing the EEC's Customs Union.
May 10–11, 1967	The UK, Ireland and Denmark submit formal applications for membership of the EEC.
July 1, 1967	Merger of executives, ECSC High Authority, and EEC and Euratom Commissions.
November 27, 1967	General de Gaulle, in a press conference, objects to UK entry.
July 1, 1968	Customs Union completed 18 months ahead of schedule; Common Agricultural Policy also complete.
July 18–19, 1968	The Six adopt basic regulations for common transport policy.
July 28, 1968	Single market introduced for dairy and beef products.
July 29, 1968	Six decide to remove last remaining restrictions on free movement of workers.
December 10, 1968	Commission Vice-President Sicco Mansholt announces 'Agriculture 1980', the Commission's radical ten-year plan to reform farming in the Six.
April 28, 1969	President de Gaulle resigns; succeeded in July by Georges Pompidou.
December 1–2, 1969	Heads of government of The Six, meeting at the Hague, agree to complete, enlarge and strengthen the EC.
December 19–22, 1969	Marathon Council session agrees on permanent arrangements for financing the common farm policy, providing the EU with its own resources from 1978 and strengthening the European Parliament's budgetary powers.
March 4, 1970	Commission submits a three-stage plan for full monetary and economic union by 1980.
June 30, 1970	Membership negotiations open in Luxembourg between The Six and the UK, Denmark, Ireland and Norway.
November 19, 1970	Foreign ministers of The Six meet for the first time in Munich to concert their views on foreign policy.
February 1, 1971	Common fisheries policy negotiations begin.
March 24, 1971	The Six take first steps to carry out the Mansholt Plan to modernise farming.
July 8, 1971	UK government white paper recommending EEC entry is issued upon successful completion of negotiations.
January 22, 1972	The Treaty of Accession is signed by the UK, Ireland, Norway and Denmark (Norway later withdraws).
March, 1972	The 'Snake' (alignment of Member States' currencies) is introduced.

October 19, 1972	First Summit meeting of heads of government in Paris. The summit meetings become part of the EC structure and are known as the 'European Council'.
January 1, 1973	The EC is formally enlarged to nine members.
December, 1973	Copenhagen Summit meeting.
January, 1974	Oil crisis. Oil price quadruples in three months.
December, 1974	Paris summit. Agreement to set up a Regional Development Fund.
March, 1975	Regional Development Fund in operation.
March, 1975	European 'unit of account' (UA) to be used in the 'Snake' to relate each national currency to the others.
May, 1975	Lomé Convention signed by the EC with 47 developing countries.
June 5, 1975	Referendum in the UK shows a two-thirds majority in favour of remaining a member of the EC.
January, 1976	The Tindemans Report on Economic and Political Union.
February, 1976	The Council of Ministers recommends that Greece be admitted to the EC over a phased period.
January, 1977	The 'new' EC Commission takes office for a four-year period, headed by Mr Roy Jenkins of the United Kingdom.
July, 1977	Spain formally applies to become a member of the EC.
April, 1978	The JET project (Nuclear Fusion) under the Euratom Treaty is established at Culham in Oxfordshire.
April, 1978	The EC and the People's Republic of China sign their first trade agreement.
July, 1978	The heads of governments at the European Council in Bremen agree to set up the EMS (European Monetary System).
October, 1978	Formal negotiations are opened for the accession of Portugal to the EC.
February, 1979	Opening of formal negotiations with Spain for accession to the EC.
March, 1979	EMS formally in operation.
June, 1979	First direct elections to the European Parliament.
October, 1979	The second ACP-EC Convention is signed at Lomé.
June, 1980	European Council and Western Economic Summit at Venice.
September, 1980	Cooperation agreement between the European Community and Brazil.
October, 1980	The Commission establishes production quotas and market regulations for the steel industry.
January 1, 1981	Greece becomes the tenth member of the European Community.
January 1, 1981	The second Lomé Convention comes into force.

March, 1981	The Council adopts the resolution on a steel-recovery policy.
June, 1981	European Investment Bank capital is doubled.
March 25, 1982	Twenty-fifth anniversary of signing of the Treaties of Rome.
April, 1982	European Community support for the UK over the Falklands conflict, and the application by Member States of sanctions and embargoes against Argentina.
July 6, 1982	The European Parliament passes a resolution giving guidelines for the reform of the Treaties and the achievement of European union.
December, 1982	The European Council reaffirms its political commitment to the negotiations for the accession of Spain and Portugal.
January, 1983	Negotiations on the establishment of a Common Fisheries Policy (CFP) successfully completed.
June, 1983	European Council at Stuttgart: declaration on European Union.
March, 1983	European Council in Brussels: outline agreement on budgetary control, financing of the Community of twelve, and reform of the CAP.
June, 1983	Second elections to the European Parliament.
March, 1985	IMPs (the Integrated Mediterranean Programmes).
June, 1985	The Commission's White Paper on the Single European Market.
July, 1985	The Commission's Green Paper on the agricultural situation in the Community.
December, 1985	The drawing-up of the Single European Act at the Luxembourg European Council – the creation of a Single European Market by the end of 1992.
January 1, 1986	The accession of Spain and Portugal to the European Community.
July, 1987	The Single European Act comes into force.
February, 1988	Summit Agreement where reform of the CAP, budget reform and the doubling of regional aid is agreed.
June, 1989	Third elections to the European Parliament.
November 9, 1989	The Berlin Wall opened.
December, 1991	Heads of state and government meet in Maastricht.
February, 1992	The Treaty on European Union (Maastricht Treaty) signed.
January 1, 1993	The Single European Market comes into force.
November, 1993	The Treaty on European Union comes into force.
January 1, 1994	The European Economic Area (EEA) Treaty takes effect.
January 1, 1995	The accession of Austria, Finland and Sweden to the EU.

GLOSSARY

1 **CNABRL** Compagnie nationale d'aménagement du Bas Rhône–Languedoc.

2 **European Currency Unit (ECU)** The monetary unit of account used in pricing agricultural commodities and in the EU budget. It is a 'basket unit', calculated according to the relative weighting of each Member State currency. Formerly known as the EUA.

3 **FASASA** Fonds d'adaptation sociale pour l'aménagement des structures agricoles.

4 **Federalism** An approach to integration by which supra-national political institutions are superimposed over national authorities although certain responsibilities still remain at a lower level of decision-making.

5 **Footloose industry** Manufacturing industry which is not based upon resource constraints such as coalfields, but which has the ability to choose a wide range of locations.

6 **Functionalism** The recognition that states have common interests and that cooperation to solve common problems will be useful (functional) to the population of the states concerned.

7 **Geographical Inertia** The tendency of older industrial regions to survive by the contraction and adaptation of old, heavy industries, and by the development of new light industry.

8 **Gross Domestic Product (GDP)** The total value of goods and services produced inside a country.

9 **Kennedy Round** A major agreement in 1967 on tariff reductions amongst the industrial nations.

10 **Marshall Aid** The aid and investment programme for the recovery of Europe provided by the United States after 1945 and named after its initiator, General Marshall.

11 **The 'Original Six' or 'EEC Six'** Belgium, the Netherlands, Luxembourg, West Germany, France and Italy.

12 **PADOG** Plan d'aménagement et d'organisation générale.

13 **Remembrement** The French policy of rationalisation and enlargement of land-holdings to create a more efficient farming system.

14 **SAFER** Société d'aménagement foncier et d'établissement rural.

15 **'Von Thunen Landscape'** An idealised series of concentric agricultural zones around a city in which the most specialised farming is nearest the city market followed by less intensive farming types.

16 **DATAR** Délégation à l'aménagement du territoire et à l'action régionale.

17 **Nation state** An independent state in which all (or most) of the

inhabitants share a general sense of national cohesion and subscribe to a general set of common values.

18 **OEEC** The Organisation for European Economic Cooperation. Set up in 1948 to administer the post-Second World War European Recovery Programme (Marshall Plan) for European economic recovery.

19 **OECD** The Organisation for Economic Cooperation and Development was founded in 1961 and took over from the OEEC. It currently consists of 25 countries and its objectives are to achieve high, sustainable economic growth, full employment and rising standards of living in member countries.

20 **'Home Energy Zone'** (Parker 1979, page 35) The area identified by G Parker that contains the majority of EU energy resources.

21 **Law of comparative economic advantage** The principle that areas tend to specialise in the production of those goods in which they have the greatest ratio of advantage over other areas.

22 **Economies of scale** The gains arising from large-scale production i.e. as the scale of production increases (and hence output) the average cost of production falls.

23 **Invisible exports** Services rendered to a foreign country, e.g. trade conducted for foreign countries by national shipping lines or interest earned by national capital invested abroad.

24 **Structural Funds** These consist of the European Regional Development Fund (ERDF), the European Social Fund (ESF), the European Agricultural Guidance and Guarantee Fund (EAGGF) and the Financial Instrument for Fisheries. They are all aimed at reducing regional disparities.

25 **Comecon** The Council for Mutual Economic Assistance. Founded in 1949 it was an international organisation to promote harmonisation of supply and demand within the Soviet bloc.

26 **European Economic area (EEA)** An agreement to extend the Single European Market to EFTA countries. It came into effect in January 1994 but Switzerland decided to have only observer status.

27 **European Free Trade Association (EFTA)** Founded in 1960 to establish free trade in industrial goods and to establish a forum for consultation on international economic problems for its Members. Its current Member countries are Iceland, Liechtenstein, Norway and Switzerland.

28 **Objective 1–6 status** The six priority objectives in applying the Structural Funds.

29 **Association status** This follows an agreement establishing a special link with a non-EU country. It extends beyond the purely trade aspect to include close economic cooperation and financial assistance.

30 **Gross domestic product (GDP)** The total value of goods and services produced inside a country.

31 **Lander** The system of states to which most government power is devolved in Germany. There are now 16 Lander.

32 **ECOSOC (or ESC)** The Economic and Social Committee is a

consultative committee which brings together different economic and social interest groups. It is made up of 222 appointees of the Member States and these are divided into three groups – employers, workers, and other interest groups e.g. farmers, craftsmen, families, ecological movements.

33 **EMS (European Monetary System)** This was established in 1978 to bring about monetary stability in the EC. It covers four main areas – the Exchange Rate Mechanism, the European Currency Unit (currently referred to as the ECU but to be called the Euro), the European Monetary Cooperation Fund and the Very Short Term Financial Facility.

34 **RECHAR** This programme, operational since 1989, draws on the Structural Funds to help coalmining regions cope with the social and economic problems of industrial decline.

35 **Combined heat and power (CHP) schemes** The use (e.g. as hot water) of otherwise wasted low-grade heat from electricity generation.

36 **THERMIE** A programme to promote energy technology development.

37 **ALTENER** The Alternative Energy Programme, set up in 1993, to explore the potential for new and renewable energies.

38 **SAVE** The Specific Action for Vigorous Energy Efficiency programme, introduced in 1991, to modify consumer behaviour with regard to energy use.

39 **RETEX** A programme to assist textile regions to help small and medium sized businesses to improve management organisation and skills.

40 **Horizontal integration** The linking together of two or more firms operating at the same stage of production and within the same industry.

41 **Vertical integration** The linking together of two or more firms in the same industry but at different stages of production.

42 **FEOGA** The French initials for the European Agricultural Guidance and Guarantee Fund that came into operation in 1962. It has a 'guidance' section that gives assistance to help reform farm structures and to develop rural areas (one of the four Structural Funds) and a larger 'gurantee' section that is responsible for the CAP's price support system.

43 **'Set-aside' policy** A number of schemes that have aimed to reduce food surpluses by taking land out of production for a period of time.

44 **STABEX** The export earning stabilisation scheme whereby the EU provides a fund to guarantee the ACP States (the African, Caribbean and Pacific states that have agreed to the Lome Conventions) against adverse fluctuations in the export earnings of certain of their products over a period of time.

45 **Generalised system of preferences** The component of EU trade policy that allows duty-free access to the EU, subject to ceilings, to a wide range of manufactured exports from a list of Economically Less Developed Countries.

46 **Most-favoured–nation (mtn) status** A designation that accords the same treatment, as regards tariffs and quotas, to another country as to the most favoured nation which is traded with.

INDEX